Endorsements

In writing this sequel to his powerful book, *God's Generals,* Roberts has done a remarkable job of stimulating our faith to believe God to do the seeming impossible by compiling explicit and authentic information about some of God's choice leaders. These men have laid a foundation on which we are able to build.

The Roaring Reformers is a well-named book about men who truly fit the title. They were average men who answered the call of God to make a difference in the lives of those in their generation. In reading this, we are faced with the question, Does God expect less of us than He did of them?

Is it really important to read about revivals of the past and those whom God used to birth them? You will think so as you read of the successes and failures—the strengths and weaknesses—of the ministers and of the acceptance and denial of the people in witnessing the supernatural demonstration of God in the meetings. Your faith will grow with your awareness that God uses whom He wills. You will discover new flames of passion for the lost and find fresh desire to be a powerful witness of Christ.

—Pastor Iverna Tompkins

Roberts Liardon, a pioneering young preacher, who has fought his own demons, sometimes slipping but always fighting back, has known all his life that someday he would capture the spirit and faith of the men of God—Wycliffe, Hus, Luther, Knox, Calvin, and Fox—who broke the back of the religious system of the dark ages, bringing us the Gospel of Jesus Christ of Nazareth in its purest form: Man is saved by grace, not of works, lest any man should boast.

A monumental work to stir men's souls.

—Dr. Oral Roberts

Roberts Liardon is an excellent student and author on church history. His book on Reformers will shed much light on the people God used and the price they paid for the liberty we freely enjoy.

—Pastor Rick Godwin

The Roaring Reformers

☆☆☆☆☆

GOD'S GENERALS

The Roaring Reformers

GOD'S GENERALS

ROBERTS LIARDON

Unless otherwise indicated, all Scripture references are from the King James Version of the Holy Bible. Scripture quotations marked (AMP) are taken from the *Amplified® Bible,* © 1954, 1958, 1962, 1964, 1965, 1987 by The Lockman Foundation. Used by permission. (www.Lockman.org)

GOD'S GENERALS II:

THE ROARING REFORMERS

hardcover edition

★★★★★

Roberts Liardon Ministries
P. O. Box 2989
Sarasota, Florida 34230
www.robertsliardon.com

ISBN-13: 978-0-88368-945-5 ISBN-10: 0-88368-945-6
Printed in the United States of America

Whitaker House
1030 Hunt Valley Circle
New Kensington, PA 15068
www.whitakerhouse.com

Library of Congress Cataloging-in-Publication Data

Liardon, Roberts.
God's generals II : the roaring reformers / Roberts Liardon.
p. cm.
ISBN 0-88368-945-6
1. Reformation—Biography. I. Title: God's generals 2. II. Title: Roaring reformers. III. Title.
BR315.L48 2003
270.6'092'2—dc21
2003005031

11 12 13 14 15 16 17 12 ᴡʜ 32 31 30 29 28 27 26 25

Dedication

I want to dedicate this book to four groups of people who have shown me unconditional love and support and who have given of themselves to fulfill the heavenly vision.

To the Operation 500 missionaries and the Spirit Life Bible College students and graduates: Thank you for leaving what the world could offer you to follow God's heart. Remember, the men in this book were severely persecuted and sometimes murdered for discovering the simple truths you will carry to the nations.

To the Embassy Christian Center family: Not only have you loved and held to the local territory, but also you have become a hub of international ministry activity. Thank you for being such an overwhelming support to the thousands of people who, over the years, have come to be blessed by God in this place.

To the Embassy Ministerial Association churches and ministers: Thank you for loving the truth and for not bowing to the territorial spirits that have tried to keep people and communities bound. May the stories of the lives in this book reaffirm that you are on track in your work for the kingdom.

To my partners and friends worldwide: I believe I have the most faithful, tried-and-true partners and friends in the world of international ministry. Thank you for your incredible faithfulness to my family and me. For every word of encouragement, prayer, e-mail, card, letter, and donation I am eternally grateful.

Friends, I am grateful for each of you.

Acknowledgments

I want to personally acknowledge the Roberts Liardon Ministries staff and volunteers who have kept the vision alive and have seen this project through a winding road into completion.

Especially, I want to acknowledge my mother, Carol, for her incredible strength of character and love. Where would we be without you? Priscilla, my sister and a woman of God, I acknowledge you for your strong faith and ability to stand when others wouldn't. And Grandma, "Grams," Gladolyene Moore, all of this, even this book, came from your prayers. You three are the grittiest women alive.

Contents

INTRODUCTION

When I was almost twelve years old, the Lord appeared to me in a vision and told me to study the lives of great preachers so I could learn the reasons for their successes and failures. In that quest, I learned the importance of history. History is a blueprint of our past. With all of its mistakes and triumphs, it tells a story that is always repeated somewhere else in time, some place in every generation, but many times under a different disguise or a different method.

I've appropriately entitled my second book in the God's Generals series, *The Roaring Reformers.* I believe it is vital that we understand the past history of the Reformation and the character of those who brought it to pass. Every generation needs a reformation, because when we forget our history or our reason for living, then our reliance upon the Holy Spirit can grow dormant, and the heavens close and become brazen.

This second book is more detailed than the first because the volume of study was more expansive. It includes methods of thinking and doctrines that might seem foreign to us. That's mainly because we are living in and enjoying what these great men had to pioneer. We live in the benefits of what these men gave their lives for. Today, we can hear in one service what took them years and years to understand!

I also wrote this book because I want you to understand the process of the Reformation and the spirit behind it. Reformation brings a complete upheaval to a dark situation and, through great physical and spiritual strength, creates an atmosphere of freedom and relationship between God and His people. As you read, you will see how each of these men built upon the work of his predecessor to accomplish reformation in his generation.

Although the actual period of the Reformation is historically recognized in the sixteenth century, the workings of it began generations before—and that's why I've included John Wycliffe and Jon Hus as primary figures. Each of the six men I've chosen was different in personality and method—but their goals were the same. They each had an assignment from heaven. They each gave their lives in hopes of seeing it come to pass, and some died as martyrs. And each of them (except Fox) had the hypocrisy and blasphemy of the medieval Catholic Church to conquer.

Chapters 1–5 have the same religious setting. Let me briefly summarize the situation. Before the fourteenth century, if one was deemed a Christian, then that person belonged to the Catholic Church. You were either Catholic or a pagan. As early as the fourteenth century, the Catholic Church had become delirious with power, and the abuses began to show up in extreme hypocrisy and blasphemy. It had set itself up as the absolute voice and judgment of God throughout the known world. It controlled secular governments and royalty, unseating whomever it wished at any time it wished, especially if there was a threat to its own prosperity and power. Even though some kings had an inherited throne, they were charged a "rent" by the pope to keep their crown—they had to pay or suffer the consequences.

To keep this dictatorship, the Catholic Church made sure that the Bible was translated into Latin only. The common people couldn't read or understand Latin, so they were victims of whatever the Church taught them. The common person was forbidden to own a Bible because it was believed that only the priests could have that honor. But the clergy seldom—if ever—read the Bible, and many priests had no idea what it said. They made up stories and fables, all clouded with a sense of mysticism. The unknown kept them in a position of prestige among the people. It was made clear that the common person could never know God—much less please Him—so the people were left to serve under whatever whimsical bondage the religious hierarchy created. They invented purgatory and the infallibility of the pope. They created indulgences and sold them as a means to pay off the excessive debt that one pope had incurred. The people were taught that if they spent enough money for an indulgence, then the clergy could grant them entrance into heaven. If a child died before its parents could pay for the baptism, legend said the child was doomed to roam the earth as a firefly or some other bug or beast.

Since religious politics was the dominant spirit behind it all, the Catholic clergy sought after riches and prominence more than the welfare of the people. The Catholic Church and clergy were draped in wealth while the common man suffered. Every doctrine they created, every system of worship they instituted, all had the lust for money behind it. They made whatever laws they felt necessary to insure more money, more land, and more power for themselves. In the fifteenth century, the papacy itself was shrouded with murder and the "sudden deaths" of those who tried to gain power. Immorality was rampant as priests had numerous mistresses as well as homosexual or adulterous affairs.

Since the priests didn't know the Bible, they didn't have any revelation of its contents. The blood of Jesus wasn't enough for them, so they invented the reconciling power of dead saints like Anne (mother of Mary), Joseph, Mary, and countless others. By the sixteenth century, if anyone challenged this system, the person was put on trial amid a torrent of lies, and either excommunicated or killed.

In the midst of these dark times, men such as John Wycliffe, Jon Hus, Martin Luther, John Knox, and John Calvin arose. By the seventeenth century, the Reformation was in full swing. George Fox challenged the cold, religious lethargy and civil discrimination in another way; he stayed in the Catholic Church and sparked life back into the Church through the ministry of the Holy Spirit. Each of these six men rose to meet the voice of God within them. Through unflinching spirit and determination, they stood for the truth and became reformers for God. Each of them slowly began to penetrate the darkness around them with the truth of Jesus Christ and the surety of His Word.

Now it's our turn. History is still being made and the eyes of heaven are upon us. Take your place. Take the stand for your generation and for your nations as we continue to turn the world to the light and truth found in Jesus Christ. Refuse to allow any fear or any torment to cloud your vision for God. Refuse to cower or allow evil to silence His voice through you. May reformation come again in our generation—and may it come through you.

★★★★★

CHAPTER ONE

John Wycliffe

c. 1330–1384

"The Bible Translator"

"The Bible Translator"

I profess and claim to be by the grace of God a sound [that is, a true and orthodox] Christian and while there is breath in my body I will speak forth and defend the law of it. I am ready to defend my convictions even unto death. [1]

I like to refer to John Wycliffe as a Reformer before the Reformation. Historically, his life doesn't fall within the years of the actual Reformation period. But his life and his theology are almost identical to what the other Reformers stood and fought for.

Wycliffe was a forerunner of the great revolution that was about to hit the known religious world. Yet interestingly, none of the other Reformers, except John Hus, gave Wycliffe credit for the highly controversial road that he paved. I believe this was largely due to the fact that the printing press was not invented until after Wycliffe's death, and many of his writings were burned by the Roman Catholic Church. Still, I see him as one who amply seeded the earth with the truths of Reformation; those after him watered and harvested the fruits Wycliffe had sown.

Wycliffe was a figure of stability—a man who strongly associated with the rich and powerful—yet he unflinchingly fought for the common people and identified with their right to know God in a personal and intimate way. During Wycliffe's day, the concept of a common person knowing God intimately was unheard of and extremely controversial. It is no wonder that he is called "the Morning

Star of the Reformation"—he changed the barometer of spiritual ignorance and, from his efforts, a new horizon for the church dawned.

He was also called the "most learned man of his generation in England," [2] yet little is known about him except that he led a very simple life marked by tireless study, lecturing, and writing. I believe his life embodies God's principle that where one sows, another waters, and yet another reaps the harvest. (See John 4:37). As you read about Wycliffe's life, don't ever underestimate the role you might have in sowing a seed, or a good deed, into the lives of others. Your actions today, when done by the faith and inspiration of God, can powerfully affect the future. Many of us will never know the powerful results of the seeds we've planted in the lives of others until we get to heaven.

Wycliffe's Early Years

John Wycliffe was born in Yorkshire, England, around 1330. Little is known of his childhood and young adult years until 1360 when he entered Balliol College in Oxford, England. The life of Wycliffe comes alive for us as he reaches the age of thirty and begins his life as a great Reformer before the actual Reformation.

Wycliffe fought for the common people and identified with their right to know God in a personal and intimate way.

Before those years I can only speculate that young Wycliffe was raised by a modest land-owning family in a secluded area and was taught in school by a village priest. In those days, the Catholic regime controlled the government as well as Church affairs. Priests were assigned to every village to oversee the affairs of life from the Church to the common market, from the schools to civil affairs.

It's important to note that John of Gaunt (the second son of King Edward III) was the feudal overlord of Wycliffe's boyhood home. This simply means that Gaunt owned the land, and those who lived there and worked the land were given protection and favors from Gaunt.

The fact that Gaunt was the natural protector of this area's citizens became an important point later in Wycliffe's life.

Wycliffe entered the priesthood, but his ordination date is not recorded. He probably left for Oxford somewhere around 1346, at the age of sixteen, the common age for entering a university at the time.

Tragic Times Drive Him to the Word

The plague sunk its deadly claws into England in 1349. By the time the Black Death had finished with the nation in 1353, England had lost nearly half of its population. As a result of the chaos, Wycliffe's university education was somewhat sporadic for a while, and his desperation grew as he watched many of his friends and associates die.

While some turned to the answers of men, Wycliffe turned to the Bible, where he discovered an unshakable foundation.

While some in the ministry turned to the answers of men, Wycliffe turned to the Bible for comfort and answers to battle the despondency and fear that he felt. During this time of turmoil, Wycliffe's dependence on the written Word of God built a foundation inside him that proved unshakable—no man could overturn what Wycliffe knew to be true from the Scriptures. It didn't matter how high up on the political or religious ladder one was—to Wycliffe, God had the final say in every matter.

It's important to remember that, at the time, there were no English Bibles; all Bibles were written in Latin, and only the skilled and highly educated men of the Roman Catholic Church could read it. The common people were left to the often mystic and pagan views of the village priests—many of whom had never read the Bible themselves!

Riches and wealth ruled the thinking of the priests, and, as a result, their doctrine was also based upon how much money someone had. Money was charged for every service of the Church—from the baptism of babies to the forgiveness of sins.

"Indulgences" were created by the Church. These provided a way for a person to pay for the remission of his sins. The common thief or murderer believed he could do whatever he wanted and then redeem himself by buying his way into heaven. If parents were too poor to have their baby baptized before it died, then the family was told that their infant couldn't enter into heaven and would probably be doomed to live on the earth as an animal or an insect! As bizarre as it may sound, teachings like this abounded during Wycliffe's time—but God was grooming a man who dared to stand against the status quo and bring about a divine change!

Oxford's Brightest Scholar

Wycliffe loved the writings of Augustine (c. 354–c. 430), the patron of the early Catholic Church. He used Augustine's individualism as a platform for his own, pursuing further research and study, particularly the study of the Bible. Renowned for his intellectual capacity, Wycliffe was able to enter Balliol College and become the regent master, or the dean, during the years of 1360–1361.

Students in Wycliffe's day didn't have the option of campus housing, so they had to find residence elsewhere, making life very difficult for the majority of them. There were a number of houses where monks and friars were sent to live while receiving university training; but the clerics (ministers) were many, and the list was long—favor had to be strong on a minister for him to be placed in one of these houses.

Wycliffe writing.
North Wind Picture Archives

Wycliffe, undoubtedly recognized as a prized scholar, was offered Oxford's finest living accommodations in the village of Fillingham, Lincolnshire, where he held the position of rector, head of the parish. His time there was taken up with the government of the Catholic Church, and Wycliffe developed into a fine diplomatic spokesman. His administrative abilities surfaced, and when these coupled with his intellectual discipline, Wycliffe soon found himself on the threshold of receiving the highest honors in the Church. In this way, Wycliffe's entire life was soon wrapped up in the school.

Of the five-fold gifts mentioned in Ephesians 4:11 (apostle, prophet, pastor, teacher, evangelist), Wycliffe was gifted as a teacher—so, besides his work in the priesthood, he was extremely fulfilled in his position as an instructor in the university. At this time, the Catholic Church was very pleased to have someone like Wycliffe growing into such a position of prominence.

By 1369, Wycliffe had obtained his bachelor of divinity. By 1371, Wycliffe was recognized as the age's leading theologian and philosopher at Oxford, a school that was second to none in all of Europe. By now, Oxford had surpassed the famed university in Paris and was the greatest educational facility in the entire known world. In 1372, Wycliffe received his cherished doctorate, celebrating sixteen years of intensive study and research. [3]

Opening His Eyes to the Corruption

In 1374, Wycliffe's notoriety and individualism began to surface. Until then, though renowned for his intellectual and theological skills, he had been an obscure priest serving over various parishes. But the winds of change had been blowing over Europe, and they were constantly heated by a debate between the Church and the government. The various governments throughout Europe wanted total control over the civil and social affairs of their countries, and they were fighting the papacy for that control. England was no different.

In this particular year, Wycliffe (agreeing with ancient theologians) began to speak out against the Church's possession of total political and social control. He believed that there was a legitimate need for a secular power to govern the affairs of each nation.

Through vast research, including the study of concepts of Augustine and the principles of Scripture, Wycliffe came to the conclusion that the Church should limit itself to its own jurisdiction. He believed that the Church's primary responsibility was for spiritual affairs, not political ones. It was here that Wycliffe developed his controversial concept called "dominion by grace."

Wycliffe's disgust at the quest for riches that ruled the Catholic Church was steadily growing. In his "dominion by grace" concept, Wycliffe said that all things belonged to God, and men only had a right to them if they were living free from sin and transgression. He believed the Catholic Church was deeply in transgression, so Wycliffe opposed the ownership of English land by the papacy. He felt the true responsibility of the Church was to meet the spiritual needs of humanity and to care for the flock, turning them to Jesus Christ. Wycliffe began to proclaim that, in owning land and living in excessive wealth at the expense of the people, the Church had become secular and of no use to anyone.

The true responsibility of the Church was to meet the spiritual needs of humanity and to care for the flock, turning them to Jesus.

The papacy was outraged at Wycliffe's stand, realizing that such a change would affect the Church's wealth, control, and land ownership. At this time, the papacy was declaring taxes upon kings and nations to be paid to the Church—and Wycliffe, one of their star theologians, stood against them in their pursuits!

Wycliffe Stands against Papal Government

England had a long history of unrest with the papacy. It's important to see some of the basic conflicts in order to fully understand Wycliffe's position.

For example, King John (c. 1215) had been excommunicated and then forced to submit unconditionally to the pope. He was also required to pay a vast sum of money for the right to continue in his legitimate inheritance as the king of England. Even after this king died, the papacy continued to demand payment from the king—taxes for his right to rule in England.

The English were opposed to the pope's taxations for many reasons—but especially because some of the monies were going to enemy armies. The English government was also outraged because the Church ruled the economic growth of their country. For example, if an Englishman died and didn't leave something to the Church in his will, then the Church took over his affairs!

For over a hundred years, this humiliation had continued, and now England was searching for ways to break from papal control. The ideal moment came when the papacy petitioned to collect its annual "rent" for the king's throne, and Wycliffe stepped to the forefront to intervene for the English government.

"There cannot be two temporal sovereigns in one country; either Edward is king or...[the pope] is king. We make our choice. We accept Edward of England and refuse...Rome," Wycliffe wrote. [4]

Wycliffe's political stand for the throne of England gained the favor of King Edward III, and the king appointed Wycliffe as rector of Lutterworth—a position that brought a comfortable living—then chose him to represent the crown in negotiations between the king and the papacy.

The negotiations never came to a satisfactory conclusion, but the incident marked Wycliffe as a potential troublemaker in the Church. He was now aligned with the anticlerical party—those who sided with the government's right for control over the nation—which, among others, won Wycliffe the favor of John of Gaunt, the king's second son.

The anticlerical party clung to Wycliffe, seeing in him the intellectual ability to attack the Catholic Church and win the cause of the English government. Wycliffe proved to be a useful ally to the government during this time of unrest, and the king's protection succeeded in keeping Wycliffe from any bodily harm that disgruntled Catholics might inflict upon him.

Exposing Deception Little by Little

By now, Wycliffe was the clerical advisor for the wealthy John of Gaunt, who, in the late fourteenth century, had become England's most powerful—and most hated—political figure. Wycliffe admired and respected him because Gaunt was a wise diplomat, always faithful to what he thought best for England. Gaunt had the ability to attract the ablest of men, and Wycliffe served as Gaunt's personal cleric for the next two years.

Wycliffe's greatest strength was his adherence to the Scriptures. From reading and studying his Bible, Wycliffe gained greater knowledge and understanding of what the Word of God was saying, and it became a personal revelation to him.

Allow me to make a simple point here. *The devil doesn't care if you own a Bible.* He's not afraid of how big it is, how often you carry it around, or where you might display it in your home. He doesn't care if you sleep with it, or chase others with it. The devil is afraid only of the Scriptures that you plant in your heart and apply, through divine revelation, to your life. He is terrorized by the life produced from the revelation of those Scriptures. The power in the Word of God alone terrorizes the devil.

Please quit displaying your Bible and start reading it! Make it a vital revelation in your life. You'll find every answer you need within its pages. Why? Because it is the only book on the earth that is alive! You can't read the Bible without life arising within you!

The revelations of the Scriptures separated the true from the false and enabled Wycliffe to see that the Church was in opposition to the Bible.

That's exactly what Wycliffe did. He didn't think that the Bible was so holy that it couldn't be touched. No—he opened it, read it, and applied the Scriptures to his life and circumstances. The revelation of those Scriptures separated the true from the false and enabled Wycliffe to see that the entire system of the Catholic Church was in opposition to the overall message of the Bible. He began to realize that many of the sacraments and doctrines of the Church were hypocritical and heretical. The religious system of the day had been formulated entirely for the quest of money, power, and control.

Wycliffe understood that he was in a position to expose and attack this system. I'm sure he pondered his approach and strategy with great deliberation. Wycliffe knew his words would carry great authority. How would he begin? How could he effectively communicate the falsehoods of the Church and bring truth to the people? The deception was so vast that to reveal it all at once would be overwhelming. So he decided to expose the heretical fallacies little by little.

In 1376, Wycliffe began writing tracts proclaiming his stand against the excessive wealth of the Church. He wrote *On Divine*

Dominion, On Civil Dominion, On the Duty of the King, and *On the Church.*

In these tracts Wycliffe stated that civil and temporal church matters should be under the king and *not* the clergy, that the church clergy had a greater calling. Because the clergy were called to serve in spiritual teaching and guidance, they should be stripped of all temporal possessions except the necessary food, lodging, and clothing. Wycliffe also wrote that no clergyman should desire to hold any civil office and that the king had the right to remove any unworthy clergyman from his position.

Revealing the political motives of the Church was the first step. Wycliffe was right on target with his plan, and the ripples could be felt miles and miles away—even to the very seat of the Vatican.

I'll Drag You Out by the Hair

William Courtenay was the popular and prestigious bishop of London—a man who, from his youth, had his eyes on the coveted office of the archbishop of Canterbury, the position that held all the ecclesiastical power in England.

The pope had been in contact with Courtenay, ordering him to intervene in the situation between the Church and the government. Eager to climb the political ladder and gain favor with the pope, Courtenay worked feverishly to undermine the current archbishop of Canterbury, Simon Sudbury, by getting the results that Rome wanted and Sudbury couldn't provide.

Because of Wycliffe's relationship with the anticlerical John of Gaunt, Courtenay's vengeance became focused upon Wycliffe. In February of 1377, Courtenay summoned Wycliffe to appear in London to answer to charges of heresy.

Wycliffe appeared at St. Paul's in London, under the escort of John of Gaunt and four friars from Oxford. Those who served Gaunt could expect his protection. To Gaunt, it was a point of honor as well as a mark of character to make their quarrels his own.

The bishops waited for Wycliffe in a chapel outside of St. Paul's. They saw his striking appearance as he approached the chapel. Wycliffe was described as " a tall thin figure, covered with a long light gown of black colour, with a girdle about his body; the head, adorned with

Wycliffe appearing before the Prelates at St. Paul's to answer the charge of heresy.
The Bridgeman Art Library, N.Y.

a full, flowing beard, exhibiting features keen and sharply cut; the eye clear and penetrating; the lips firmly closed in a token of resolution—the whole man wearing an aspect of lofty earnestness and replete with dignity and character." [5]

The air was tense and filled with energy. In order for the bishops and Wycliffe's entourage to reach St. Paul's, they had to push their way through a great crowd that had come to watch the show. The attempts to push through caused an immediate scuffle, which was so loud that Courtenay left St. Paul's and ran to the spot where Wycliffe was. By the time Wycliffe was able to pass into the court, tempers were so riled that threats were being bellowed between the parties.

Wycliffe was asked by Gaunt to take a seat and make himself comfortable. Courtenay spoke up that the accused should stand before the court. Immediately, there was an argument between Gaunt and Courtenay as to whether Wycliffe should stand or be seated. The crowd of onlookers became even angrier listening to Gaunt and Courtenay's repetitive insults. Finally, Gaunt "muttered a threat to drag the bishop from his cathedral by the hair of his head." [6]

The Londoners were proud supporters of Courtenay; and the mere presence of Gaunt had already infuriated them. When the unruly crowd heard Gaunt's threats against Courtenay, they revolted. Abusive language and angry shouts filled the air as the crowd rushed forward—Gaunt was forced to flee for his life. The entire scene was so chaotic that there was no way Courtenay could conduct a trial. Wycliffe, who remained silent the entire time, was allowed to leave untouched!

★★★★★

After the court scene, the citizens were still so outraged that mobbing and rioting continued in the streets as they searched for allies of Gaunt. Courtenay finally had to intervene so that the citizens would settle down.

In the meantime, Wycliffe was far away from the riot, quietly making his way back to Oxford. The incident never marred him. Wycliffe remained popular with the Oxford scholars, the government, his students, and the people of his parish, despite censure from the Catholic hierarchy.

The Truth Hurts

Upon hearing from Benedictine monks that the heresy trial had failed, and believing that it was unwise to attack Wycliffe in England, Pope Gregory XI took the situation in his own hands. From Rome, Gregory XI issued five scathing bulls (official documents from the pope) against Wycliffe. In May of 1377, copies of these bulls were sent to the archbishop of Canterbury, to Oxford, and to the king.

These bulls cited eighteen errors from Wycliffe's tract, *On Civil Dominion.* To the Oxford scholars, the pope rebuked their leadership, stating that, "...through negligence and sloth on your part [you have allowed] cockle to spring among the pure wheat in the field of your glorious university...and (what is worse) to grow up." [7] The pope went on to say that if they could not silence Wycliffe, the result would be the peril of their souls, the blemish of the Oxford name, and the decay of the entire orthodox faith. The pope arrogantly declared that if Oxford did not get rid of Wycliffe, the university would no longer receive the graces and support of the Catholic Church.

Despite the threats, Oxford took Wycliffe's side. A council of doctors declared that the "propositions attributed to him [Wycliffe], though ill-sounding, were not erroneous." [8] In other words, if we used today's vernacular, Oxford might have said something like, "the truth hurts."

Oxford realized the pope was embarrassed and extremely threatened by Wycliffe's accusations. I believe the Oxford scholars were proud of Wycliffe's insight and secretly wished they had the personal boldness to address the Catholic Church's hypocrisy. Although they supported him and gave him the liberty to continue teaching, Wycliffe decided to place himself under house arrest to spare the university from further action by the pope.

The bulls also ordered the government to turn Wycliffe over to Courtenay, who, in turn, was to examine Wycliffe regarding his errors. But the government never paid any attention to the bulls—King Edward III died before he received them.

I Deny the Pope Any Right

Of course, Courtenay's political and religious ambition prompted him to scurry to summon Wycliffe before a court in Lambeth to address the pope's charges. Wycliffe accepted the challenge and answered the summons.

Standing before a very large crowd of priests, bishops, and supporters, the archbishop of Canterbury and Bishop Courtenay began to address Wycliffe's "errors." Unruffled, Wycliffe answered them, and stated his position:

> I deny that the Pope has any right to political dominion: that he has any perpetual civil dominion: that he can qualify or disqualify simply by his bulls. [9]

Wycliffe arraigned before the Archbishop of Canterbury.
North Wind Picture Archives

Wycliffe's stand was incredible—and it left the court almost speechless! We must understand that, up to this point, *no one* had *ever* openly challenged the authority of the pope! As you read on through this book, you'll see that this sort of challenge became a common occurrence among the Reformers.

Can you imagine the ripples of shock that penetrated through them all? Can you feel the nervousness and tightness? How would they answer Wycliffe? This was a first! How would they justify themselves? How could they defend the hypocrisy that Wycliffe revealed? The only thing they could do was shout at Wycliffe in outrage—and so they did.

But the shouts and outrage never indicted Wycliffe—Joan of Kent, the Queen Mother, sent a message to the court at Lambeth, forbidding them to pass sentence upon Wycliffe. The Queen Mother's intervention on Wycliffe's behalf caused great fear and concern among the bishops and their supporters. Miraculously, no one sought to defrock or excommunicate Wycliffe, and again he was allowed to leave without penalty.

The Catholic Church had no idea what to do with him. Powerlessly, they ordered Wycliffe to stop preaching. Wycliffe obeyed, but his pen was not silent, nor were the groups of men that he personally mentored.

The Apostolic Men

By now, it seemed that Wycliffe's religious enemies couldn't touch him. It was clear to the Catholic Church that Wycliffe, still an ordained priest, was establishing himself as "the leader of a party." [10]

Presiding over several parishes, Wycliffe had already formed his own group of street evangelists that he called the "poor priests." This group of clergy had all been personally mentored by Wycliffe, and they were instructed to travel throughout the countryside and preach wherever people would listen. These "poor priests" lived simple lives, shunned wealth, and dressed in a humble manner. Some were ordained; some were laymen; but none were tied to a parish, allowing them the freedom to be wherever the need was greatest.

Up to this time, the ignorant village priests had simply told stories to entertain the people or, when asked a theological question, answered it with whatever sounded good at the moment. Wycliffe's preachers did just the opposite—they preached from the Bible, bringing understanding and comfort to the villagers.

Wycliffe defended their right to preach as long as these men felt they were called to do so. He called them "evangelical men" or "apostolic men." [11] These "apostolic men" went throughout England, denouncing the abuses of the Catholic Church and teaching sound biblical doctrine—not in Latin, but in the common language of the people so that they could understand.

The "poor priests" lived simple lives, shunning wealth. They preached from the Bible, bringing understanding and comfort.

Wycliffe wrote tracts for these men to distribute, and, although he didn't preach himself, Wycliffe wrote hundreds of sermons for these "apostolic men" to meditate on and preach. Unfortunately, the majority do not exist for us to enjoy today.

His Most Startling Revelation

I want to point out some historical facts concerning confusion in the Catholic Church that Wycliffe found himself blamed for. While the Church was busy sorting through the turmoil, Wycliffe was left alone to discover more truths. The Holy Spirit was indeed in charge of the situation.

In the 1370s, there was great confusion in the Catholic ranks concerning the pope and where he would reside. I'm not going to elaborate on all of the details. In short, there was a dispute over where the Vatican headquarters should be. In 1309, the headquarters were moved from Rome to France, basically because of the political influence of the king of France. He was tired of paying papal taxes and felt he could control the situation better if the papal headquarters were located in his nation. The Catholics called it "The Babylonian Captivity."

Finally, in 1376, Pope Gregory XI moved back to Rome. But two years later, the people were still divided, and they elected two popes—one for Avignon, France, and one for Rome. Both popes claimed to be infallible, and each excommunicated the other. It was called "The Great Schism," and Wycliffe was named as a primary cause. [12]

The Catholic Church believed that Wycliffe's "heresies" led to the unrest of the people because he poisoned them with his doctrines and confused their minds. For the next thirty-nine years, the papal headquarters remained divided.

Because of the attention focused on this schism, Wycliffe himself was almost ignored, despite the fact that the blame fell on his doctrines. While he was out of the spotlight, Wycliffe used his time to reveal, step-by-step, the other heresies he found in the Church. From 1378 through 1379, Wycliffe began to formulate his most startling revelation, a statement unheard of to the known world at that time. What was it? It was that *Scripture (the Bible) was the sole foundation of all doctrine.* [13]

Wycliffe's most startling revelation was that the Bible was the sole foundation of all doctrine.

In March of 1378, Wycliffe released a booklet entitled *On the Truth of Holy Scripture* that sent the Catholic hierarchy skyrocketing with anger. From this one foundation—that the Scriptures alone contain the truth for the Christian lifestyle and doctrines—Wycliffe began to skillfully dissect the various heresies and hypocrisies that had blossomed in the Catholic Church. This one booklet contained thirty-two chapters upholding the truth of the Scriptures against the lies of the papacy.

Wycliffe had crossed into a new frontier.

The Vision Was Forming

After King Edward III died, his young son, Richard II, was pronounced king. John of Gaunt became the head of England, ruling as regent, until young King Richard II was old enough to take charge of the throne in 1381.

For the next three years, Wycliffe defended the validity of the Scriptures. The government still supported him, but Wycliffe was not its major concern; instead, the task of running the country without an official king took center stage. The Church was caught up with its own self-induced troubles. Rumors of Wycliffe's heresy began to surface, but nothing came of them. Wycliffe countered that the real heretics were those who found inconsistencies and obscurities in the Scriptures and thought they needed "official" interpretation by the Church.

Wycliffe didn't believe that "official" interpretation of the Bible was necessary. He thought that the Bible could be safely placed in the hands of even the most ignorant. Unlike the Catholic hierarchy, Wycliffe preached that the true "church" was made up of *all* God's elect people—not just the leadership. Because of his belief, Wycliffe felt that everyone who trusted in the Lord had a right to know His Word. He said, "All Christians, and lay lords in particular, ought to know holy writ and to defend it," [14] and, "No man is so rude a scholar but that he may learn the words of the Gospel according to his simplicity." [15]

Wycliffe thought that the Bible could be safely placed in the hands of even the most ignorant people.

From Wycliffe's statements, it is obvious that God was forming a plan and a vision in his heart. No English person was able to read the Bible—it was all written in Latin! The difficulty of language allowed the Catholic Church to remain in control, because only scholars—the priests—could read it.

So, it's clear to me that Wycliffe had a plan to support his statements. Somehow, the Latin Bible would have to be translated into common English—but when? Others in the thirteenth and fourteenth centuries had already urged the translation of an English Bible, but no one had acted upon it. [16] Timing was the only key, and Wycliffe was not a man to rush or act hastily. He knew that God would provide the correct situation and the accurate timing for such a feat. It *had* to be done, and it would be—eventually.

☆☆☆☆☆

The Catholics were outraged by Wycliffe's teaching that the Bible was the *only* source for doctrine. They believed that the Church (i.e., priests, monks, friars, bishops, and the pope) was the sole source of all doctrine and that the Bible served only as an aid, filled with stories that served as illustrations for living a good life. But their outrage didn't faze Wycliffe.

Using the Bible as his foundation, Wycliffe began to separate the man-made ideas of the Church from the God-inspired principles of the Word.

Below is a summarized list of several Catholic heresies that Wycliffe attacked. He believed these heresies were all invented and propagated by man. Remember, Wycliffe wrote these findings while acting as a Catholic priest. He loved the ministry and the work of God, but he hated the abuses found within the Catholic Church system. Wycliffe felt these abuses were against God and against the people.

First, I'll briefly state what the Catholics believed; then, I'll provide a quotation from Wycliffe stating what he denounced.

1. He Attacked Confessionals

The Catholics instructed the people to come and confess their sins to a priest before they could be forgiven and taught that the priest, bishop, etc., was the only one who had the power to cleanse them from their sins. After confession was made, the priest would impose several acts of penance that the sinner had to perform in order to receive complete forgiveness.

Wycliffe wrote,

> It is not confession to man but to God, who is the true Priest of souls, that is the great need of sinful man. Private confession and the whole system of medieval confession was not ordered by Christ and was not used by the Apostles, for of the three thousand who were turned to Christ's Law on the Day of Pentecost, not one of them was confessed to a priest....It is God who is the forgiver.
>
> Trust wholly in Christ...beware of seeking to be justified in any other way than by His righteousness. Faith in our Lord Jesus Christ is sufficient for salvation. [17]

2. Absolution

The Catholics taught that only a priest, bishop, etc., could release a person from the guilt of sin by merely speaking it over the person. Many times, absolution was paid for with money or some other sort of possession.

Wycliffe wrote,

> There is no greater heresy for a man than to believe that he is absolved from sin if he gives money, or because a priest lays his hand on his head and says, "I absolve you;" for you must be sorrowful in your heart, else God does not absolve you. [18]

3. He Attacked Indulgences

Indulgences were created as a money-raising technique to keep the Vatican out of debt—or to pay off the already-accrued, excessive debts of the Church. The Church taught that, through indulgences, the people could buy their way out of purgatory (a holding place after death where the consequences of sinful actions could be satisfied). The people were instructed that if they bought indulgences, the pope would command the angels to carry a departed soul straight to heaven (bypassing purgatory) because their sins were paid for. So, people did whatever they wanted and acted however they pleased, thinking that if they bought an indulgence, every action would be wiped away.

Wycliffe wrote,

> It is plain to me that our prelates in granting indulgences do commonly blaspheme the wisdom of God, pretending in their avarice [greed for money] and folly that they understand what they really know not. They chatter on the subject of grace as if it were a thing to be bought and sold like an ass or an ox; by so doing they learn to make a merchandise of selling pardons, the devil having availed himself of an error in the schools to introduce after this manner heresies in morals.
>
> I confess that the indulgences of the Pope...are a manifest blasphemy, inasmuch as he claims a power to save men

> almost without limit....But I say to you for certain, though you have priests and friars to sing for you, and though you each day hear many Masses, and found chantries and colleges, and go on pilgrimages all your life, and give all your goods to pardoners; all this shall not bring your soul to heaven. [19]

Wycliffe condemned such practices in his tract O*n Indulgences* long before Luther posted his 95 theses. Wycliffe concluded the tract with these statements,

> By the means of the tail of this dragon—that is, the sects of friars, who labor in the cause of this illusion, and of other Luciferian seductions of the church. But arise, O soldiers of Christ! Be wise to fling away these things, along with the other fictions of the prince of darkness, and put ye on the Lord Jesus Christ...sever from the Church such frauds of antichrist, and teach the people that in Christ alone and in His law, and in His members, they should trust...learn above all things honestly to detect the devices of antichrist! [20]

The blood that Jesus Christ shed for us was enough—yet the medieval Catholics undermined that incredible price by adding to it and making people pay money for forgiveness. May God have mercy on those who believe this doctrine and open their eyes so that they may see the truth!

4. He Demanded the Use of Preaching

Many in the Catholic Church looked upon the ministry as an occupation where they would always be taken care of. As a result, many priests never realized the spiritual position they could have, and should have, held. So, priests were often found in worldly situations—for example, in the taverns, playing various games—and they lived careless lives. Except possibly for isolated monks, most of the priests never gave themselves to prayer and learning the Word of God. Many had never even read a Bible, so they could only tell stories and tales to keep the interest of the people. I can only imagine the gross error and deception that abounded because of it.

Wycliffe wrote,

> The highest service to which man may attain on earth is to preach the law of God. This duty falls particularly to priests, in order that they may produce children of God.... And for this cause Jesus Christ left other works, and occupied Himself mostly in preaching, and thus did the apostles, and on this account God loved them....We believe there is a better way—to avoid such that please and, instead, to trust in God and to tell surely His law and specially His Gospel. And, since these words are God's words, they should be taken as believed, and God's words will give men new life more than the other words that are for pleasure.

Wycliffe could not betray what he felt from the Scriptures to be true, even if it meant the loss of support.

> O marvelous power of the Divine Seed, which overpowers strong men in arms, softens hard hearts, and renews and changes into divine men....Obviously such miraculous power could never be worked by the word of a priest, if the Spirit of Life and the Eternal Word did not, above all things else, work with it. [21]

Wycliffe Attacks the Eucharist

Little by little, Wycliffe continued to expose the errors and deception of the Catholic Church. In 1379, Wycliffe took a position against the Church that made even his friends tremble. John of Gaunt had trouble with it and begged him to recant on this monumental position. But Wycliffe could not betray what he felt from the Scriptures to be true, even if it meant the loss of support. As a result, the English government held Wycliffe loosely, not knowing how to react to his latest revelation.

Wycliffe's most famous controversy was over the Eucharist, or the Holy Communion. Catholics believed in *transubstantiation,* which simply meant that when a priest performed a Mass, the bread and wine of communion were transformed into the actual body and blood of Jesus Christ, while keeping the appearance of mere bread and wine. They also refer to this as "The Blessed Sacrament."

Wycliffe found transubstantiation totally unscriptural. In his tract entitled *On the Eucharist,* he outlined his beliefs from two foundational points: First, transubstantiation wasn't in the Bible and, second, the belief of it was totally unknown until the twelfth century. [22] It had not become a Catholic dogma (absolute truth) until 1215 at the Fourth Lateran Council.

Wycliffe stated that the doctrinal theology of transubstantiation was simply man's invention—or misinterpretation—all for the purpose of keeping the Mass mystical and the priests superior. To him, transubstantiation dangerously exaggerated the importance of the priestly office, it exposed Christ to passive indignity, and it encouraged people to become idolatrous.

Wycliffe urged people to return to the faith and practice of early Christians and to reject man's invented doctrine.

Instead, Wycliffe believed in the *spiritual presence* of Christ and His blood and claimed that Jesus Christ was to be remembered in communion by personal faith in the price He paid. He urged people to return to the faith and practice of the early Christians.

He wrote, "The consecrated Host we priests make and bless is not the body of the Lord but an effectual sign of it. It is not to be understood that the body of Christ comes down from heaven to the Host consecrated in every church." [23]

Wycliffe went on to explain how to interpret the Word of God and used communion as an example. "Some expressions in Scripture must be understood plainly and without figure, but there are others that must be understood in a figurative sense. Just as Christ calls John the Baptist Elias, and St. Paul says that Christ was a rock....You will meet with such modes of expression constantly in Scripture and in these expressions, without a doubt, the production is made figuratively." [24]

Wycliffe wrote that the meaning of figurative speech in the Bible was hidden from those who did not know Jesus Christ.

"Therefore, let every man wisely, with much prayer and great study...read the words of God in the Holy Scriptures...Christ saith, *'I am the true vine'* [John 15:1]. Wherefore do you not worship the vine for God, as you do the bread?" [25]

He went on to state that Christ was not an earthly vine, "so neither is material bread changed from its substance to the flesh and blood of Christ." [26]

When Wycliffe protested against the superstition and idolatry he saw associated with the Mass in his tract *On Apostasy*, he was labeled a full-fledged heretic by the Catholic Church. Although no steps were made to excommunicate him, Wycliffe was now a man whom most tried to avoid.

Cutting Off His Influence

The alarm at Wycliffe's beloved Oxford finally sounded in 1380. Because of pressure from the papacy, the chancellor had begun to oppose Wycliffe's doctrines in the schools and finally decided that the time had come for action to be taken against him.

A group of twelve doctors of divinity met in a council to discuss Wycliffe's Eucharist doctrine. At the end of the discussion, a majority of seven moved that his teachings were erroneous. The chancellor was somewhat alarmed that the remaining five felt that Wycliffe had done no harm. In an attempt to silence any further support of Wycliffe, the chancellor threatened that those who taught or defended Wycliffe's doctrines would be imprisoned, suspended from all university functions, and excommunicated. [27]

Wycliffe was found disputing theology in the school when the verdict and sentence were publicly read to him. When Wycliffe heard the condemnation of his work, he was confused, yet he vowed that the opionions of these men could not weaken his beliefs. [28]

Wycliffe appealed to the king to overturn the chancellor's decision; it was ignored. John of Gaunt hurried to Oxford and attempted to persuade Wycliffe to obey the chancellor, but Wycliffe chose to disregard his pleas.

Wycliffe remained obscure until May of 1381 when he wrote *Confession,* a tract that defended his condemned opinions.

In the spring, Wycliffe withdrew from public life and finally detached himself from Oxford. It was a difficult decision for him, because the majority of his life had been wrapped up in the affairs of the university. It was unusual for a person to mention the name of Oxford without thinking of Wycliffe.

Wycliffe had now moved back to thc isolation and obscurity of Lutterworth. But it was different this time. He didn't have the luxury or the outlet of being associated with Oxford.

I'm sure that we can all relate to how Wycliffe must have felt. He had been cut off from the place where his earthly identity had been established. Oxford had been his place of temporal security, and now, Wycliffe had to find his way without that avenue.

The change proved to be the highest point of his destiny on earth.

Destiny: The Door No Man Could Shut

Wycliffe felt cut off from everything. It was during this time that he turned to the Lord for direction. He knew he had a purpose on the earth, but Wycliffe had to hear from God. I believe it was through such prayers that Wycliffe came to understand the reason for his life.

In Lutterworth, Wycliffe would begin the venture he is known for today—the translation of the Bible from Latin into English.

Suddenly inspired, Wycliffe realized that Lutterworth would not be an obscure "prison" for him but instead would be a place of divine destiny—a place where the timing of the Lord and the vision in his heart would finally meet.

Now he understood. In the obscurity and peace of Lutterworth, Wycliffe would begin the venture that he is most known for today: the translation of the Bible from Latin into common English.

✯✯✯✯✯

Several of his most loyal followers accompanied Wycliffe to Lutterworth. Among them were John Purvey and Nicholas of Hereford.

Purvey was one of Wycliffe's closest companions. He was Wycliffe's personal secretary and constant attendant until the end of Wycliffe's life. Now fifty-one years old, Wycliffe dictated much of his prolific writing to Purvey, because it was clear to Wycliffe that his anointing and vision for writing would be passed on to Purvey.

Hereford was one of Wycliffe's most educated colleagues from Oxford. A doctor of divinity, Hereford worked tirelessly along with Purvey in translating the Latin Bible into English. Unlike Purvey and Wycliffe, Hereford was known for his rowdy personality, noted as "the most violent" of the Wycliffe followers. [29]

For the next few years, the group worked night and day. Wycliffe felt that the greatest anointing he had ever experienced was upon him, giving him the strength and energy to supervise the project. It is generally accepted that Wycliffe did the translation of the New Testament himself, while Hereford and Purvey translated the Old Testament under his constant supervision.

The Five Rules for Bible Study

Why did Wycliffe take on such a tremendous feat? In the natural realm, the task was against all odds. In all of Europe, there had never been a Bible in the common language. The Latin was preserved because the language was deemed holy and mystical, reserved only for the educated. In addition, most of the common people in England were illiterate. Furthermore, the printing press would not be widely manufactured until the next century, so the supply of common English Bibles would be very limited. It was a massive endeavor, and only one who had truly heard from God would have even attempted it; without a doubt, Wycliffe had heard.

As I've stated, his unflinching conviction was that the Bible was the sole authority for all of life. Wycliffe wrote,

> Forasmuch as the Bible contains Christ, that is all that is necessary for salvation, it is necessary for all men, nor for priests alone. It alone is the supreme law that is to rule

> church, state, and Christian life, without human traditions and statutes. [30]

Wycliffe knew that the common people would never know the true basics of faith unless they knew what the Bible said. Wycliffe also realized the people would never know the Bible unless it was in their own language. He stated,

> Christ and His apostles taught the people in the language best known to them. It is certain that the truth of the Christian faith becomes more evident the more faith itself is known. Therefore, the doctrine should not only be in Latin but in the vulgar [common] tongue...believers should have the Scriptures in a language which they fully understand. [31]

Wycliffe's heart was heavy for the common people. He realized that if they obtained a Bible in their language, and if they could read it, they would need instructions on how to study it. So Wycliffe completed his task by outlining five basic rules for the translation and study of the Bible:

1. Obtain a reliable text.
2. Understand the logic of Scripture.
3. Compare the parts of Scripture with one another.
4. Maintain an attitude of humble seeking.
5. Receive the instruction of the Spirit.

So Wycliffe and his staff proceeded to translate the entire Bible from the Latin Vulgate into the Midland English dialect. Although many translations have followed since this incredible feat, we can still see the effects of some of his terminology. Some of the terms such as "mote," "beam," and "strait gate" came from Wycliffe's translation. [32]

Medieval "Hot Air"

I want to take some time to share some of the responses that the Catholic Church made concerning Wycliffe's translation. It's amazing how thoroughly religious deception can blind a person through the attitude of control.

Translating the Bible into the language of the common people was considered total heresy by the medieval Catholic Church. An early and very famous church father, Jerome, had already revised their Latin edition around 450 A.D. Jerome's revision was called the Latin Vulgate, and it was the only official and "sacred" version the Catholics recognized. To divert from the Vulgate was in the ranks of blasphemy.

Wycliffe's feat was that the Bible was made available to the people so they could know God in a personal way.

A Catholic writer in Wycliffe's time wrote,

> Christ gave His Gospel to the clergy and the learned doctors of the Church so that they might give it to the laity and to weaker persons....But this Master John Wyclif[fe] translated the Gospel from Latin into English—the Angle [Anglo] not the angel language. And Wyclif[fe], by thus translating the Bible, made it the property of the masses and common to all and more open to the laity, and even to women who were able to read....And so the pearl of the Gospel is thrown before swine....The jewel of the clergy has been turned into the sport of the laity, so that what used to be the highest gift of the clergy and the learned members of the Church has become common to the laity. [33]

I don't know about you, but if I was a church member, I wouldn't appreciate being called a "swine." However, the article perfectly illustrates the mind-set of the day: If you weren't a part of the elite Catholic clergy, your life amounted to nothing. Women were reduced to dirt. Why he wrote that the Bible was the "highest gift of the clergy" I'll never understand. They seldom—*if ever*—read it! And Scripture says nothing about the angels speaking Latin as a common language.

Years later, Arundel, the archbishop of Canterbury was even more venomous with his disturbing comment. I believe this particular archbishop was one of the most evil and wicked men of his time.

He said,

> That pestilent and most wretched John Wycliffe, of damnable memory, a child of the old devil, and himself a child or pupil of Antichrist, who, while he lived, walking in the vanity of his mind—with a few other adjectives, adverbs, and verbs, which I shall not give—crowned his wickedness by translating the Scriptures into the mother tongue. [34]

The only thing these harsh words produced was the hot air that carried them through history. The real substance—the true feat already accomplished—was that the Bible was made available to the people so they could know God in a personal way. Wycliffe's actions honored the blood that Jesus shed for us all, and for that, we can be eternally thankful. The Catholic Church attempted to keep the price that Jesus paid in a secret box. They attempted to elevate themselves to a man-made position of divinity.

God does not live in statues; He lives in the heart. He is not the Head of a clique; He is the Head of the true church.

They Still Hate Him

I've noticed that, in many theological references written or edited by Catholics, Wycliffe's name still appears in the list under the heading "Heretics." Some seem to feel that Wycliffe undermined the unity of the Catholic faith. Yes, he did this, but it was an action ordained by God. God cannot be found in religious politics; He is not found in controlling tactics or deception. God does not live in statues; He lives in the heart. He is not the Head of a clique; He is the Head of the true church.

John 3:16 clearly states that *"whosoever"* believes and trusts in Him will have everlasting life. That simply means that the opportunity for salvation is open to *anyone* who will hear.

Romans 8:14 maintains that *"as many as are led by the Spirit of God, they are the sons of God."* To know God in the Spirit comes from a personal relationship with Him. It doesn't come from a mere religion.

✯✯✯✯✯

Those Loud Lollards

The last three years of Wycliffe's life were very eventful. In 1381, the famous Peasant's Revolt erupted, in which the English common laborers arose in a struggle for civil liberty. They were tired of being overtaxed and oppressed by unfair laws. In the early summer, one hundred thousand angry peasants descended upon London, demanding to see the young King Richard II. [35]

Wycliffe's name was attached to that revolt, although everyone knew and agreed that he had nothing to do with it. He was busy translating the Bible in Lutterworth. But the Church still held that it was the Wycliffe doctrine and teaching that produced this sort of unrest.

Historians agree that, during this year, the "Lollards" became a prominent group of people. Many mistakenly place the name of the Lollards totally with Wycliffe's followers, but it was not so. That mistaken identity came as a result of Courtenay banning the teachings of Wycliffe and silencing the major Lollard leaders of Oxford that associated with him.

The name *Lollards* meant "mumblers" and, eventually, it simply classified *any* group that opposed the Catholic Church. The Church also referred to this group as heretics.[36]

Wycliffe sends the Lollard men out into the world.

☆☆☆☆☆

Some of the educated Lollards *were* Wycliffe followers—to be historically correct, they were the Wycliffites. But the uneducated, peasant Lollards didn't hold to a particular set of doctrines; they were simply political activists who hated the unfair burdens the Catholic Church imposed upon them.

The centers of Lollard activity were in the cities of Oxford and Leicester. [37] The Lollards were so popular in Leicester, the saying was that "every second man was a Lollard."

It is difficult to pinpoint the exact beliefs of these people, as they are varied according to personal circumstance. But basically, the Lollards were parishioners who refused to pay tithes, denied the authority of the Catholic Church, belittled papal authority, attacked the doctrine of transubstantiation, and regarded all of the Catholic liturgy and doctrines as arrogant necromancy, or telling the future by communicating with the dead. [38] The list goes on and on.

But in 1382, the Lollards met with their first official trouble. Wycliffe's name was involved with it, although he was far from the action. Hereford, one of Wycliffe's most loyal followers, decided to hold a Lollard meeting on the Oxford campus. He gave a rousing and rowdy sermon, calling for the loyalty and support of Wycliffe against the Catholic hierarchy. Hereford and all of Wycliffe's followers who had remained at Oxford were excommunicated as a result of this meeting.

The Earth Quaked

The year of 1382 was even more eventful than the previous.

Sudbury, the former archbishop of Canterbury had been murdered during the Peasant's Revolt. Finally, Courtenay had obtained his dream—he was inducted as the new archbishop of Canterbury. His first and primary goal as the new archbishop was to take care of Wycliffe's doctrines and followers.

Courtenay called for a council to meet at Blackfriars to officially and formally condemn Wycliffe's opinions. He invited nine other bishops and thirty-six graduates of theology to make a decision on twenty-four of Wycliffe's writings. Interestingly, Wycliffe's name was never mentioned at the council—only his writings.

The proceedings were brought to an end on May 21, 1382, after four days of discussion. Ten of the propositions were found to be heretical and the rest erroneous. Courtenay decreed that the king's officers were to arrest any of the "poor preachers" who were caught preaching throughout the countryside. He also passed sentence that all Wycliffe's teachings and tracts—anything he had written or edited—were to be immediately seized. Any student at Oxford found guilty of following the Wycliffe doctrine would be expelled without discussion.

Determined to silence the followers of Wycliffe, Courtenay left Wycliffe himself untouched. History has never discovered why. [39] Perhaps John of Gaunt made a secret deal with Courtenay, probably involving money, if Courtenay would leave Wycliffe alone. Given his hatred for Wycliffe and knowing his love for wealth and influence, this may be the only logical answer for why Courtenay never pursued Wycliffe personally. Wycliffe was never summoned, and he never intervened. He remained secluded and unmolested at Lutterworth, translating the Bible.

However, on this particular day, Courtenay's council was cut short by an uncanny and unusual earthquake. Both sides—Courtenay and Wycliffe—attributed the unusual occurrence to the judgment of God upon the other. Courtenay felt that God was on his side; Wycliffe believed God was angry at the council's conclusions. That famous council meeting is known today as "The Earthquake Council."

Undercurrents of Reformation

The year of 1382 also brought another very important event. It was the marriage of England's young King Richard II to Anne of Bohemia. The marriage united the separate countries and, at the urging of Queen Anne, opened the door for Bohemian students to become educated at Oxford.

Once at Oxford, the Bohemian students began to secretly study and agree with the writings of Wycliffe. One of the most famous Bohemian students to attend Oxford was Jerome of Prague. Jerome eventually carried back the writings of Wycliffe to Bohemia, where they fell into the hands of the famous Reformer John Hus. Although Wycliffe had been silenced in England, within a few years, his

Religious reformer John Wycliffe preaching from his bed.
Getty Images

teachings exploded in Bohemia, and the Hussite movement carried us into the Reformation.

In 1382, Wycliffe found time to write his most famous document to date, entitled *Trialogue.* The writing takes the form of a discussion between Truth, Falsehood, and Wisdom, and covers briefly all of the subjects Wycliffe had previously dealt with in length. It was his first writing to be printed, although Wycliffe never saw it. It wasn't printed until 1525; but, historically, it is credited for being the one original Wycliffe writing that linked him to the Reformers in the sixteenth century. [40]

Amid the torrent that flowed from Wycliffe's pen, he suffered the first of two strokes in 1382. This first stroke left him partially paralyzed. The pope attempted to summon Wycliffe to Rome to answer certain charges, but because of his weakened condition, Wycliffe was unable to comply.

Death of "The Parson"

The year of 1383 was somewhat uneventful for Wycliffe. Because of his profuse writings, it is doubtful that he personally pastored the church at Lutterworth. Although he was the main figure there, no doubt other pastors tended to the people on his behalf.

Wycliffe's second stroke came at the end of December in 1384 while he was listening to Mass. This stroke caused acute paralysis. Wycliffe could no longer speak. Three days later on December 31, 1384, Wycliffe died, leaving the earth to be with the Lord.

Even with the Catholic Church's hatred of him, Wycliffe was never excommunicated. His funeral was simple, and Wycliffe's body was buried in the consecrated ground of the Lutterworth church.

Purvey, his faithful associate, continued to work on the English Bible. The first version was finished before Wycliffe died, but a revision was put into motion by Purvey, who named it, appropriately, *The Wycliffe Bible.*

Wycliffe's influence spread far past the clergy. He didn't stay isolated in a ministerial "box"—Wycliffe obviously had friends in every arena of life. We know he had good friends in the government and faithful friends among the common laborers. The famous English poet Geoffrey Chaucer lived during Wycliffe's time, and the two were friends. Both wrote in the Midland English dialect, and both shared the same friendship with John of Gaunt. It is said that in Chaucer's famous *Canterbury Tales,* the part of "The Parson" was written as a tribute to John Wycliffe. It says,

> A kindly Parson took the journey too.
> He was a scholar, learned, wise, and true.
> And rich in holiness though poor in gold.
> A gentle priest; whenever he was told
> That poor folks could not meet their tithes that year,
> He paid them up himself; for priests, it's clear
> Could be content with little, in God's way.
> He lived Christ's Gospel truly every day,
> And taught his flock, and preached what
> Christ had said. [41]

Wycliffe's friends are a tribute to the way he lived his life. He never compromised his principles or his values, but it's clear that Wycliffe affected every person he came in contact with.

★★★★★

It's sad to see ministers so caught up in the church world that they can't identify with the common man, or with someone who is not in their particular field or calling. To truly be effective as believers, we must learn that our security doesn't come from those who believe like we do. Jesus came to touch the world—not a part of it, but all of it.

Live your life for God before every man, regardless of what they believe or how they act. Don't isolate yourself; instead, allow the Holy Spirit to work through you, and dare to go into every arena of life, turning others to God through your example, your witness, and your good works.

They Still Tried to Win

Although Wycliffe had many good and faithful friends who cherished his memory, his death could not satisfy the hatred and contempt that the Catholic Church still had for him.

In 1408, twenty-four years after Wycliffe's death, Arundel, the archbishop of Canterbury, summoned a group of clergy and decreed that no further translations of the Bible could be issued by way of book or tract and that no man was allowed to read such a translation, in private or public, as "composed in the time of the said John Wycliffe...under penalty of the greater excommunication." [42] If a person was caught with one of Wycliffe's translations, he would lose his land and all his personal property to the Church.

Twenty-nine years after Wycliffe's death, a papal decree in 1413 ordered his books to be burned.

In 1415, thirty-one years after his death, the general council of the Western church met in Constance and condemned Wycliffe's teachings on three hundred accounts. They condemned his memory as "one who died an obstinate heretic" and ordered his bones to be exhumed from their resting place and "cast at a distance from the sepulchre of the church." [43]

By then, a bishop by the name of Philip Repton was the head of the Lutterworth diocese. To his credit, Repton left Wycliffe's grave untouched. [44]

It wasn't until 1428, some forty-four years after Wycliffe's death, that the pope commanded that Wycliffe's bones be exhumed and burned; the new bishop of Lutterworth, Richard Fleming, carried out the task. After Wycliffe's bones were exhumed and burned, the ashes were cast into the Swift River in an attempt to be free of any trace of him. But there was no chance of that. His memory was etched in the foundations of Christian liberty.

Thomas Fuller, describing the events, engraved his words forever in history. He so beautifully wrote, "They burnt his bones to ashes and cast them into Swift, a neighboring brook running [nearby]. Thus this brook hath conveyed his ashes into the Avon, Avon into Severn, Severn into the narrow seas, they into the main ocean. And thus the ashes of Wicliffe are the emblem of his doctrine, which now is dispersed the world over." [45]

The burning of Wycliffe's books.

His Vision Exploded throughout the Earth

Wycliffe never lived to see the effects of his vision. He never lived to see if his Bible translation caught on with the people; all he had was the vision in his heart and his love for the common people.

☆☆☆☆☆

All he knew to do was to plant the seed and trust God to complete what He began—and God certainly did it.

After the printing press was invented in 1450 and began to be widely used, large volumes of the English Bible were printed at a rapid rate. The Catholic Church could no longer contain the "heresies" of the Reformers. Now the people were free to examine the Word of God and to know Him in a personal way. They were free to examine the fruits of their actions by His words—not the words of men.

The coming Reformers would translate the Bible into thirty-four languages. In a period of less than three hundred years, three-fourths of those translations were for Europeans. By 1818, Bible translation was worldwide as missionaries carried the Word to other nations and translated the Bible into their own language. By 1982, there were 574 translation projects listed by the United Bible Societies, involving members of two hundred different denominations and missions.

Wycliffe planted a seed and then trusted God to complete what He began. Today, we can examine the fruit.

In recent years, a high percentage of Bible translations has been done by believers in their native lands. For example, in the United States, Native American tribes are translating Bibles into their own languages. They have realized that they are able to establish their own churches if the Bible is in their native tongue. The concept is simple: first a Bible, then a convert, then a church!

In 1942, Bible translation became a career with the formation of Wycliffe Bible Translators. Founded by William Cameron Townsend, the organization's sole purpose is to fulfill the Great Commission (see Matthew 28:19) through Bible translation. In this organization, translators, literacy specialists, and support workers from thirty-four countries have teamed together to produce over five hundred translations, and one thousand more are in progress. They have estimated that there are still more than three thousand groups of people waiting for a Bible translation in their language. [46]

☆☆☆☆☆

Today, Bible translation is offered in four American universities, and in England, Germany, France, Brazil, Japan, and Australia. The nations of Nigeria, Ghana, Brazil, Philippines, Cameroun, Kenya, Korea, and New Guinea have started their own national Bible translating organizations.

I will add that today, since Vatican II, the Catholic Church has somewhat changed its attitude toward Bible translation and the common man having access to the Scriptures. Of the 574 projects listed by the United Bible Societies in 1982, Roman Catholics were actively involved in 133 of them. [47] However, they still have their own translation of the Bible, as well as several Old Testament books that Protestants do not accept as the inspired Word of God.

If only Wycliffe could have seen what his vision was to become. You can see why, at the beginning of this chapter, I stated that you should *never underestimate the power of planting a seed.* Don't be discouraged if God has instructed you to do something and nothing seems to be happening. Continue to be obedient—continue to plant the seed no matter how hard and cold the ground, or the work, seems to be. As the seasons of the earth always evolve, so will the fruits of your labor. Just remember that underneath the cold, hard ground of winter lies the makings of a beautiful flower or the fragrant fruit of spring! The timing is in the hands of the Lord and the obedience of your heart to do what He has asked you to do.

So, I close this chapter with the words of Jesus in John 4:34, 36–37, fitting verses for Wycliffe's life.

> *My meat is to do the will of him that sent me, and to finish his work....And he that reapeth receiveth wages, and gathereth fruit unto life eternal: that both he that soweth and he that reapeth may rejoice together. And herein is that saying true, One soweth, and another reapeth.*

★★★★★

Notes

[1] "John Wycliffe and the 600th Anniversary of Translation of the Bible into English," *Christian History Magazine* 2, no. 2, issue 3 (Worcester, Pa: Christian History Institute, 1983): 18.
[2] "Wyclif, John," *The Encyclopedia of Religion* 15, (New York, N.Y.: MacMillan Publishing Co., 1987): 488.
[3] *Christian History Magazine,* 11.
[4] "John Wycliffe," EPC of Australia. <http://www.epc.org.au/literature/bb/wycliffe.html> (5 June 2001)
[5] *Christian History Magazine,* 12.
[6] K. B. McFarlane, *John Wycliffe and the Beginnings of English Nonconformity* (London, England: English Universities Press, Ltd., 1952): 76.
[7] *Christian History Magazine*, 18.
[8] "John Wyclif," *The Catholic Encyclopedia.* <http://www.newadvent.org/cathen/15722a.htm> (25 May 2001)
[9] *Christian History Magazine*, 18.
[10] *Catholic Encyclopedia.*
[11] *Christian History Magazine*, 17.
[12] *Catholic Encyclopedia.*
[13] "H371—The Reformation before the Reformation: John Wycliffe." <http://www.theology.edu/h371.htm> (15 May 2001)
[14] McFarlane, 91.
[15] Ibid.
[16] Ibid.
[17] *Christian History Magazine*, 25.
[18] Ibid., 24.
[19] Peters, Edwards, "Heresy and Authority in Medieval Europe." <http://topaz.kenyon.edu/projects/margin/indulge.htm> (4 June 2001) [This information has moved to www2.kenyon.edu/projects/margin/indulge.htm as of August 2003.]
[20] *Christian History Magazine*, 24.
[21] Ibid., 34.
[22] Ibid.
[23] Ibid., 24.
[24] Ibid.
[25] Ibid.
[26] Ibid.

★★★★★

[27] McFarlane, 98.
[28] Ibid.
[29] Ibid., 102.
[30] *Christian History Magazine*, 26.
[31] Ibid.
[32] "History of the Christian Church." <http://www.ccel.org/s/schaff/history/6_ch05.htm> (1 June 2001)
[33] *Christian History Magazine*, 26.
[34] Ibid.
[35] "Wat Tyler's Rebellion," *The World Book Encyclopedia* 21 (Chicago, Ill.: World Book, Inc., 2003): 113.
[36] McFarlane, 100–104.
[37] "Lollards," *The Catholic Encyclopedia.* <http://www.newadvent.org/cathen/09333a.htm> (16 May 2001)
[38] "Lollard Conclusions, 1394." <http://topaz.kenyon.edu/projects/margin/conclu.htm> (1 June 2001) [This information has moved to www2.kenyon.edu/projects/margin/conclu.htm as of August 2003.]
[39] McFarlane, 115-116.
[40] Ibid., 117.
[41] "John Wycliffe, The Parson," *Word Alive.* Reprinted with permission from *Word Alive* magazine, Wycliffe Bible Translators of Canada. <http://www.wycliffe.ca/wbthist/john/parson.html> (9 June 2001).
[42] *Christian History Magazine*, 26.
[43] "History of the Christian Church." See also http://www.island-of-freedom.com/wycliffe.html.
[44] McFarlane, 120.
[45] "History of the Christian Church." See also http://www.island-of-freedom.com/wycliffe.html.
[46] "History of Wycliffe Bible Translators." <http://www.wycliffe.org/history/wbt.htm> (9 June 2001)
[47] *Christian History Magazine*, 27–29.

CHAPTER TWO

John Hus

1372–1415

"The Father of Reform"

"The Father of Reform"

I desire to be as Balaam's ass. Because the prelates sit on me, wishing to force me to go against the command of God to stop preaching, I will press the feet of their desire and will not obey them, for the angel of the Lord stands before me in the way. [1]

Narrowing his deep-hollowed eyes and pointing his long, lean fingers into the air, John Hus loudly and solemnly declared his intentions against the hierarchy of the Catholic Church.

His audience in the church building sat silent, each one filled with admiration and loyalty to their pastor. He was a hero in their eyes, a true leader who dared to speak out and rebel against hypocritical wrongs. The atmosphere was a stick of dynamite—calm and quiet, with explosive power brewing just below the surface. Each person was acutely aware that even the slightest movement could ignite a holy revolt, but Hus' resolute character kept them intact.

Hus was not a man who warred with swords. He made war with words, and a violent revolution could have started from his speech alone. This inward spiritual strength has carried his name through the halls of history.

Although his thin frame gave him the appearance of being frail, Hus was a warrior. He vowed that his life would count for one thing—reformation of the Catholic Church from within. He had no desire to pioneer a new denomination. Instead, he felt that if he could shake and expose their hypocritical doctrines from the inside, the Catholic Church would have a chance to return to the spirit and beliefs of the early church.

Hus was a revolutionary man, but little is known about him. I'm writing this chapter to change that. We have only a limited amount of books about his life that have been translated into English, but these few references are very thorough and precious.

Hus was a warrior. He vowed that his life would count for one thing—reformation of the Catholic Church from within.

With our great debt to Hus, it's amazing that we know so little about him. For the sake of perspective, allow me to list the great "generals" that Hus affected. He influenced the beliefs of Martin Luther (who said, "We are all Hussites" [2]), John Calvin (whose reformation focused on dedicating all aspects of life and culture to the lordship of Jesus Christ), and George Fox (who taught that we are led by the inner witness of the Holy Spirit). Through the Moravians (a Hussite branch), Hus' influence reached down through history to touch John Wesley. As this chapter progresses, you'll even see some of the beliefs that the modern-day Word of Faith movement incorporated—many probably don't realize that Hus was one of the first to acknowledge biblical confession and the priesthood of all believers!

Hus' story is one of heartbreaking betrayal and two-faced fraud. Reading about his love of and stand for truth, witnessing his impeccable character, and then reliving the betrayal involved in his death will bring you to tears. We still believe and fight for the same things Hus stood for. In the midst of a disillusioned generation that has erased the line between right and wrong, in the midst of a world that is dying from its bondage while thinking it is free, we still teach and preach the truth that Hus taught and wrote.

May the spirit of reform and of might engulf you as you read this chapter. May the strength of God consume your life and encourage you to stand for the truth and against the corruption and the evil of our day.

A Mother Who Prayed

Born in 1372 to poor peasant parents, Hus began his life in a village called Husinec, located on the Blanice River in the southern part of Bohemia. The house where Hus was born still stands today, but a fire destroyed most of it in 1859; only the room where he was born was saved. [3]

In a world that is dying from its bondage while thinking it is free, we need the truth that Hus taught.

Husinec, Hus' hometown.

Birthplace of John Hus.

We know little of Hus' parents. His father's name was Michael, and, outside of that, we know nothing of him. We do know that Hus was very close to his mother; she was the one who taught him to pray and trust in God. Later in his life, Hus gratefully wrote that his mother was the one who taught him to say, "Amen, may God grant it." [4] She was also the one who gave Hus the initial desire to become a priest.

The Golden Age

Hus was born in a generation that was called the "Golden Age," largely due to the great Emperor Charles IV. [5] When the Emperor came into power, he bypassed Rome as his royal residence and returned to his native land of Bohemia, where he refurbished Prague into one of the greatest cities in Central Europe. The Emperor's main goal was to establish an educational center within Prague, so he founded Prague

University (today, Charles University). Because he embellished his university with all the privileges enjoyed by the famed University of Paris and Oxford University, Prague soon surpassed the other schools and became the only university in Central Europe.

It was this setting that motivated Hus' mother to get her son the best training possible to secure his future. Because of the time in which they lived and due to her limited circumstances, she knew that the priesthood would be the best occupation for her son.

To give you some historical background, in 1378, when Hus was only five or six years old, the Great Schism between the two popes (one in Avignon, France; one in Rome) was taking place. Hus, of course, paid little attention to it, being only five or six years old. He didn't realize that, in the coming years, the effects of this papal unrest would lead to his own death.

But for now, Hus was undisturbed; he enjoyed playing and tending to the flocks of geese that his parents owned.

His Home Away from Home

The first step toward Hus' career came when he was thirteen years old. Determined that her son would be educated for the priesthood, Hus' mother took him to the commercial city of Prachatice, an hour away from his home, and enrolled Hus into the Prachatice elementary school. Elementary schools of that time were totally different from our current school systems. The earliest that one could enroll in a school was around twelve years old, and most were never afforded the luxury of attending school at all.

According to tradition, Hus' mother took a loaf of bread as a present to the schoolmaster and knelt down seven times along the way to pray for him. [6] Hus' father faded into the background from this point, and his mother became a predominate influence in steering his future.

On a personal note, I admire the sacrifices that Hus' mother must have made, because I also had a mother and a grandmother who taught me to pray and seek the Lord from my youth. I can relate to the dedication and love that Hus' mother gave to her son. The love of a mother remains the same, no matter what generation she lives in.

In Prachatice elementary school, Hus learned the educational basics of the time, most importantly, the foundation for learning Latin.

This knowledge would be an important step for the priesthood, since, as you know from the Wycliffe chapter, all Bibles were written in the Latin Vulgate.

From "Husinec" to "Hus"

In 1386, Hus left Prachatice for Prague, where he enrolled in a preparatory school. Since Prague was now a universal center of affairs, there were students from many different nations—some from as far as Finland—living in the city. Aside from the native Czechs, the area was heavily populated by Germans. Here, Hus learned German as a second language to his native Czech.

At fourteen years old, Hus was a fun-loving boy, with the mischief and antics of other boys his age. Hus told the story that, at Christmas, he and the other choir boys performed a sacrilegious play—one dressed up like a bishop, then rode a donkey into a church, and joined the others in performing a comical Mass. [7] Of course, such antics had been outlawed by the archbishop of Prague, but Hus and his friends ignored this.

In 1390, at eighteen years old, Hus was admitted into the University of Prague. This feat was exceptional, as few from his region made it to the university level. When Hus enrolled into the university, he decided to change his name. Instead of being known as John of Husinec, he shortened his name to "John Hus." [8]

Poverty, Disillusionment, and a True Relationship

Like many students who came from a poor background, Hus earned his wages by singing in a local church. Although it was a time of hunger and scraping to get by, Hus spoke of it with humor. He said, "When I was a hungry young student, I used to make a spoon out of bread to eat peas with...until I consumed the spoon as well." He also said, "When I was a student and sang vigils with others, we sang them rapidly just to get the job done quickly." And then the priests took the money for it and cheated them of their income! [9]

While struggling so hard for his own welfare, Hus began to notice how well-fed and happy the priests were. He associated the ministry with living well and being respected. Seeing how the priests always had plenty of money, Hus admitted that, at first, he sought the priesthood for ulterior reasons. He thought the ministry meant instant prosperity. He wrote, "When I was a young student, I confess to have entertained an evil desire, for I had thought to become a priest quickly in order to secure a good livelihood and dress well and to be held in esteem of man." [10]

Hus was always heard proclaiming, "Search the Scriptures!" The Word transformed his religion into a relationship with Jesus!

Had he been rich, Hus would have had no trouble reaching his goal. Money talked. With the hundreds of priests in Prague, wealth would have secured Hus a position. But since he was poor, he had to work extremely hard to prove that he could be a priest and hope for a position to be granted to him.

History never specifically mentions when Hus found a personal relationship with the Lord. I believe it was somewhere in these years as a university student. This was the time that Hus diligently searched the Scriptures and found what he believed and what he didn't. He stated that, when he was younger, he thought the ministry consisted of simply climbing the ladder to the top. It was when, as Hus recalled, "the Lord God gave me the knowledge of Scripture," [11] that he became a passionate follower of Christ. From that point on, if anyone came with a question or a problem, Hus was always heard to proclaim, "Search the Scriptures!" [12] The Word of God transformed his *religion* into a personal *relationship* with Jesus Christ!

The Character of "The Goose"

Coming from such a poor background, Hus worked extremely hard in his studies. From his teens, Hus established a characteristic that proved to be the foundation of his ministry. He said, "From the earliest time of my studies I have set up for myself the rule that whenever I discern a sounder opinion in any matter whatsoever, I gladly and humbly abandon the earlier one. For I know that those things I have learned are but the least in comparison with what I do not know." [13] Wouldn't it be great if everyone established that same rule for their lives and was as teachable as Hus? As you read, you will see that every stand Hus took was based solely on the revelation he had and the love for God that he possessed.

Because of his zeal and diligence for learning, he received his bachelor of arts degree in 1393. The man who introduced Hus and presented his degree made an interesting statement. The name *Hus* had come from Husinec, meaning, "goose town." When he shortened his name to Hus, he was nicknamed, "Goose." The introducer took liberty with his name and turned it into a joking description of Hus. He remarked that during the examination for his degree, Hus had prepared a good feast for them all—in other words, "they cooked his goose."

The introducer then made a more serious statement, remarking that, like a bird, Hus possessed wings by which "he lifts himself to higher spheres." [14] I'm sure the man had no idea of just how high Hus would go and how great his reputation would grow!

By now, Hus was taking the priesthood more seriously. He had even bought his first—and last—indulgence in 1393.

Spiritual Patriots!

During the years of 1398 to 1402, Hus lived in the King Wenceslas College, a small section of the university. There, he studied for his masters degree and became very good friends with a man named Stephen of Palec. Palec and Hus studied together night and day, conversing regularly with their favorite instructor, Stanislav of Znojmo. Obviously inspired by Stanislav, Hus stated that this instructor had "no equal under the sun." [15]

Hus was also a frequent visitor to the parsonage of a friend, the pastor of the Church of St. Michael. Many of the burning issues surrounding Wycliffe's life were discussed in this circle of men. I can just see the heated debates carried on by candlelight as the four men passionately talked about the Lord into the wee hours of the morning. I wish I could have been there among them! Unfortunately, at his death trial years later, Hus was betrayed by some of the people who were part of these very discussions.

Hus was attracted to Stanislav because of his love for the teachings of the English Reformer, John Wycliffe. Stanislav studied every turn of Wycliffe's theology—one of his theological issues would become a sore spot in Hus' life.

Stanislav followed all Wycliffe's beliefs, even accepting his teaching against transubstantiation, believing, instead, in the doctrine of remanence—the idea that the bread and wine remain as such after consecration and do not turn into the actual body and blood of Jesus. Stanislav fervently taught this doctrine, and, although Hus viewed Stanislav as his mentor, he never followed Stanislav in that belief.

Although the teachings of Wycliffe had been banned in England, they were alive and well in Prague. The marriage of Anne of Bohemia to King Richard II of England had opened the door for Bohemians to be educated at Oxford, and the teachings of Wycliffe made their transfer into the spiritually hungry city of Prague.

Not only Stanislav but the majority of the Czech masters that Hus studied under were followers of Wycliffe to some degree. The spirit that Wycliffe carried was steadily kindling the reform that was brewing in the hearts of the Czechs.

Hus was a passionate patron of the Czech reform movement. He believed that the Czech language should be the primary language of Bohemia, and that his native people should have their voice heard. His friends Palec and Stanislav were even more passionately involved in the cause. The three became so close that the other university students made jokes and rhymes about their close patriotic and spiritual friendship.

In 1396, Hus passed the rigors of his masters degree, and Stanislav awarded the honor. In the same year, Hus began teaching in the faculty of arts, where he copied some of Wycliffe's works for his own use. The Swedish army carried away one of the manuscripts in the Thirty Years' War, and today, it is on display in Stockholm. In the margins of his manuscript, Hus wrote many approving remarks that can still be read, such as, "Wyclif, Wyclif, you will unsettle many a man's mind," and "May God grant Wyclif the kingdom of heaven." [16]

A Wide Circle of Friends and Mentors

Hus was now lecturing several times a day as well as training students how to use what they had learned and put it into speeches. After teaching for two years, Hus was chosen to promote students to the grade of bachelor. Hus cherished mingling with the students and becoming their friend and mentor. He was well known for being a good and faithful friend, as he truly cared for each student's well-being. The relationships he developed in this period lasted a lifetime. Only one turned against him later on.

In 1401, Hus' old friend, Jerome of Prague, returned from Oxford University where he had been studying. Jerome brought a chest of treasures back with him—Wycliffe manuscripts! Jerome had hand-copied each of Wycliffe's works before he left England and hurried back to his native land to share them with the Czech reformers.

Hus dearly loved Jerome, although his personality was totally opposite of Hus'. Jerome was hotheaded, impetuous, and full of adventure. If someone said it couldn't be done, Jerome was the first to show you it could be.

As Hus and the others devoured the Wycliffe manuscripts, Jerome set off for Jerusalem. He returned two years later—only to leave again and travel throughout Italy, France, and Germany, each time getting into trouble over his doctrine and barely managing to escape. This rowdy preacher would stay away from Prague until 1412, when he reappeared in Hus' life.

As you can see, Hus surrounded himself with a variety of passionate men who loved God and their nation. This variety of friends and their discussions would formulate the doctrines Hus would be known for in the coming years.

The "Father" before Hus

In 1402, Hus was appointed as the pastor of Bethlehem Chapel—the church that was the center of the Czech reform movement. Although the chapel was only eleven years old when Hus took over, it had an incredible history.

The early Czech reform movement had a leader by the name of Milic. Hus was only about three years old when Milic died, but the Czech patriot had caused major reform waves throughout the nation. Condemning the Catholic hierarchy for its many abuses, Milic was not content to merely condemn the vices of his day—he put work into active reform. Finding the red-light district of Prague, he converted the prostitutes and founded a shelter for them to live in, based on a vision he had. He called the shelter, "New Jerusalem." [17] In this shelter, Milic housed over two hundred ex-prostitutes who were determined to live their lives for God. Outside the shelter, he started a church, appropriately named the Mary Magdalene Church. In its vicinity, Milic also built a house where he intended to educate an "apostolic priesthood"—young men who would carry on the work of the reform in the same spirit. [18]

Of course, the Catholic hierarchy had a fit about it all and summoned Milic to Avignon to answer outlandish charges. Milic died there while defending his cause. [19] He is called "the Father of the Czech Reformation," but he was never able to complete the reforms he had begun. [20]

His followers and supporters carried on his vision and put their money together to start Bethlehem Chapel, a continuation of Milic's Czech reform movement. The preaching in the chapel was to be totally in the Czech language so it could serve as a reform center. The Czech masters at the university were responsible to uphold the chapel. Their appointment of Hus as pastor showed his outstanding reputation among them as a promising reformer. Like Milic, the Czech masters knew that Hus had the character and the wisdom to live on the edge and that he would rightly divide the truth from error. Hus, a young Czech patriot, would fight for what was right.

When Hus accepted the pastorate of this famous church, he entered into the most important phase of his life. He had already been preaching regularly, filling in for his friends who were pastors—he would need the practice because his new post would bring a demand. In a year's time, Hus would preach over two-hundred fifty sermons at Bethlehem Chapel alone. On top of that, he lectured and mentored students at the university. [21]

Living on the Edge: Bethlehem Chapel

Bethlehem Chapel was quite a place. It held three thousand people and the Czech population thronged to the chapel for each service. In Prague alone, there were forty-four Catholic churches, twenty-seven chapels, sixteen monasteries, and seven convents—but Bethlehem Chapel was the only church that preached in the national language! [22]

Hus had a heart for the Czech people, and he did everything he knew to pastor them effectively. The chief function of the chapel was to feed the Czech people with the Word of God. Hus not only powerfully preached sermons in Czech, but he used other means of getting the true Gospel across as well, such as paintings.

At Bethlehem Chapel, Hus used everything he could to spread the Gospel, from religious paintings to preaching in the national language.

On the walls of the chapel, Hus made sure that the paintings told the true story, just as his sermons did. He realized that the common people could not read; therefore, they couldn't study what he preached to them. So Hus used visuals to help the Gospel message become firmly planted in their minds. [23]

Here's what I mean: On one wall was a painting of a pope sitting on a large horse, complete with all the papal pomp and outlandish splendor; beside it hung a painting of Christ in all his poverty, carrying a cross. The next set of paintings showed the rulers of nations donating the city of Rome, along with a palace in all its glory and power, to the pope. There was a crown on the pope's head, and a purple mantle draped over his shoulders; the opposite painting showed Christ standing before Pilate as an accused man, with a lowly crown of thorns upon His head. The third set of paintings showed the pope haughtily sitting on a throne, having his feet kissed; the opposite painting showed Jesus in a kneeling position, washing the feet of His disciples. [24]

Bethlehem Square, site of Bethlehem Chapel.

The dramatic contrast of the paintings had an enormous effect. Hus understood that the mind had a firmer grasp on things seen instead of heard; the visuals accomplished his goal. I admire Hus' creativity in capturing the hearts of the people and turning them toward the true Jesus Christ. [25]

Hus taught that the highest attainment a man was capable of was loving God absolutely.

The Emerging Reformer

Hus further put his love for the common people into action by establishing a residence for poor peasant students behind the chapel. He called the residence "Nazareth." Hus not only supervised Nazareth, but he also pastored the chapel, taught in the university, and mentored students. Hus empathized with the needs of the poor, and it won him national attention. The people identified with Hus because he came from a poor Czech background, and he proved he could relate to their needs. They knew that Hus was truly for them. He soon won their hearts unconditionally.

His fame as a preacher was soon firmly established, and Hus was recognized as the unrivaled leader of the popular Czech movement. Aside from the common people, the university masters and students also attended his services in large numbers. Hus had both a scholastic theology and a heart for the common man. This unrivaled combination would educate a generation of upcoming reformers.

John Hus.

He taught that the highest attainment man was capable of was loving God absolutely. From his pulpit and in his lectures, Hus denounced pride, luxury, fornication, and the love of money.

Hus' life was intermingled with many different people, all taking their valiant stands. His life was much like a chessboard, with pawns, knights, and several kings. Each move depended upon another. I want you to meet the primary figures that caused him the greatest trouble, and one who attempted to help him.

Two Kings and a Wanna-Be Bishop

As I mentioned at the beginning, due to the Great Schism, two popes were ruling the Western world. Neither pope recognized the authority of the other, and the controversy pitted nation against nation. Hus never involved himself with the conflict, but those who had direct influence over him did.

One was King Vaclav (Wenceslaus), the oldest son of Emperor Charles IV. Vaclav was the King of Bohemia, and he was well-known for his drunken rages and weak will. His moods would change at the snap of a finger. [26] He made numerous administrative blunders and interfered in church affairs. His first wife was mauled to death by his dogs, which he kept in the bedchamber. [27] This was the man whose influence would be in and out of Hus' life.

Vaclav's second wife, Queen Zofie, was a friend to Hus. Zofie understood Vaclav and knew how to keep his favor. She became extremely fond of Hus, attended his services at the chapel, and was a main proponent of the Czech reform. When she attended Bethlehem Chapel, her bodyguard, Jan Zizka, accompanied her. After Hus' death, he became a feared Hussite leader. [28]

The second influential figure in Hus' life was King Sigismund of Hungary, Vaclav's younger stepbrother. Sigismund didn't have a kingdom until he married a princess in Hungary. When her father died, Sigismund came in to rule.

The two brothers violently hated each other. At one time, Sigismund was kidnapped and imprisoned by Vaclav because Sigismund wanted Bohemia. He eventually bought his way into becoming the Holy Roman Emperor, and he proved to be Hus' deadliest enemy.

The last figure was the archbishop of Prague, Zbynek. When the archbishop's job became available, only Zbynek had enough money to pay the pope the large fee necessary for appointment, including the back money that was owed by the previous archbishop. When Zbynek came up with money to pay the high price, he was immediately appointed to the post. In 1402, Zybnek was only twenty-five years old, with no training in religious affairs, little education, and not enough maturity to handle the office. Though unprepared, he was a wealthy military genius with an enthusiasm and desire to do God's work.

At first, Zbynek and Hus got along extremely well. Zbynek had no idea that Wycliffe's theology was circulating throughout the university—he didn't even know what it was. He didn't understand the debates and, for a while, took little notice. He trusted Hus, and asked Hus to review all of his decisions and correct him if he was ever found in any error.

The history behind Queen Zofie and these men is important because each wove in and out of Hus' life.

In a world that is dying from its bondage while thinking it is free, we need the truth that Hus taught.

An Urgent Demand for the Spirit

John Hus in the Pulpit of Bethlehem Chapel, Prague.
(Ad. Liebscher)

Hus' ministry blossomed at Bethlehem Chapel. He was not only filled with the Word of God, but he had a cause—to bring the Czechs into a deeper relationship with God.

He realized that his Czech congregation was in an "urgent demand" for a genuine spiritual transformation. [29] Thus, Hus always dealt with moral conduct, stressing motives rather than outward actions. He taught the congregation to be renewed in the spirit of their minds and to put on the new nature. He warned that all other speaking would be in vain if the Word of God did not first speak within their hearts and teach their souls. Much like Wycliffe and Milic, Hus preached that men's lives must be reformed before their doctrine could be pure. [30]

While Hus grew in prominence, maturity, and godly character, the Catholic Church continued to operate around him, unwilling to change its putrid and diseased form of religion. The priests made up fables and lied to illiterate people in order to get money, promising them forgiveness and eternal life. The clergy reeked with fornication and adultery; priests sometimes housed several mistresses. If a particular priest was making good money for the Catholic Church, the pope overlooked sins and, many times, even promoted the hypocrite! Doctrines were invented according to the money they could raise, and mysticism was encouraged because it exalted the clergy and kept the people at bay, fearful of touching God's anointed.

Money ruled the Catholic Church. Many people bowed to the quest for riches—but not Hus.

Hus was disgusted by what he knew and what he saw. He viewed his position as a holy office and vowed to use his mouth as a trumpet for God to speak the truth. His mission was to reform the Catholic Church, and he knew it. So Hus used his pulpit and his lectures to speak out against the Church for two reasons: the hope of reforming it, and the need for raising up a new generation of clergy that wouldn't fall into sin. Hus knew the Spirit of Truth as a friend; he knew that truth would always prevail. The truth he spoke was so revolutionary, we're still writing about it almost six hundred years later!

In the following pages, I've included excerpts and summaries of the truths Hus brought to the earth. They may be common understanding for us today, but in the days of a dark Europe shielded from the Light by the misguided—and misguiding—Roman Catholic Church, these truths were revolutionary. They were also a deadly threat to the false government of medieval Roman Catholicism.

His Message to the Priests

Although Hus remained a dedicated Catholic, he preached that nothing harmed spirit life as much as the sins of the priests. Hus didn't want a radical change in the Church's teaching; instead he wanted the church to become worthy of its calling. [31] He felt that, if the ministers paid more attention to their own condition, the doctrines would be purer. Hus constantly called for a return to the model of the early church and for a complete reevaluation of what it meant to be a priest.

One of his foundational teachings concerning the priests was this: Hus believed that the true authority of a priest was linked to his character, not his office. [32]

Hus called for a return to the model of the early church and for a complete reevaluation of what it meant to be a priest.

Of course, this infuriated the Catholic regime, which believed that, as long as the priest was in good political standing with the hierarchy, morals didn't matter. Hus said that the love of money had destroyed their morals. Here is a summary of the topics that illustrated his belief.

1. *Hus hated the pomp and prestige that the pope and many of the priests surrounded themselves with.* Preaching a message on the humble entrance of Jesus into Jerusalem, Hus said, "I know not how well the pope or bishop could read...[the story], although perhaps he could. For many have been popes, archbishops, cardinals, bishops, canons, and priests who could not read books. How could he read it, since it all contradicts him?" [33]

2. *Hus denounced the pompous and elite attitudes of the cardinals who accompanied the pope.* He was amazed that the people and the clergy considered the cardinals' attitudes right and proper. Hus then added, "As I also had regarded it as right before I knew Scripture and the life of my Savior well. But now He has granted me to know that this is a veritable blasphemy of Christ and repudiation of His Word and the following of Him; as such it is truly anti-christian." [34]

3. *Hus denounced the Catholic hierarchy that promoted war.* He believed that there were two swords: One was for the nobility to protect the Christian faith and the truth; the other was a spiritual sword that was used by clergy to fight a spiritual evil. Catholics knew little if anything about spiritual war. Hus believed that the

Catholics fought wars solely for the love of money. He said, "Christ on a high cross, they on a great war-horse; Christ with a crown of thorns on his head, they with a crown covered with precious stones and pearls; Christ let his side be pierced by a spear for our sake; they want to kill their fellow-men for the sake of the refuse [rubbish] of this world." [35]

4. *Hus soundly rebuked the priests who did not pastor their churches but used them only for personal gain and prestige.* He said, "We, today's shepherds, do not know our sheep, except those which have wool more abundantly. The sheep which bring more wool and offering we regard higher and know them better; those, however, which bring less, we know less." [36] Hus believed it was the pastor's job to know his people; the responsibility was not upon the people to make the first move and acquaint the pastor with themselves.

5. *In all his sermons, Hus never failed to include the chastisement of immorality, especially adultery.* He once wrote that if the apostle Paul wrote an epistle to Prague, he would surely censure them for adultery—especially the clergy! When he preached against the sins being commited, Hus gave a summary of how things really were. He

Hus preaching the Gospel to some of his followers.
Getty Images

said, "Whoever preaches that priests should not commit adultery, rob people by avarice [greed for money] and simony [selling something spiritual],...him they immediately dub a slanderer of the holy priesthood, a destroyer of the holy Church, and a heretic who should not be allowed to preach. They drive him [to court] and condemn him. And when that devil's net does not suffice, they stop the services." [37] In other words, if they couldn't stop the preaching by intimidation, they stepped in and shut down the services!

6. *Hus sharply rebuked the priests for conducting mystical worship services where the people were more caught up in the surroundings and dress than in God.* Hus blasted the clergy for relying on their robes and elaborate services to create a mystical feel instead of teaching the truths of God's Word so that the people could have spiritual substance. He said, "[They gape] at the pictures, the vestments, chalices, and other marvelous furnishings of the churches. Their ears are filled with the sound of bells, organs, and small bells....They [priests] are clad in sumptuous robes, hoods, caps with pearl knots, silk tassels....They carry crosiers [the bishop's staff], staffs, and silver crosses....Thus a simple man wastes his whole time in church and returning home, talks about it the whole day while he says not a word about God." [38]

People should be able to tell there's something different about you. You don't need an outward sign to demonstrate God's inner work.

Even in the current-day church we need to be careful not to get caught up in a title, bishop or otherwise, a robe, or a collar. Just because you have a certain title or wear a robe doesn't make you anointed. I'm not saying you're not anointed if you have a title, robe, or collar. But these outward signs have nothing to do with the anointing. If the people won't listen to you in a suit, a dress, or even your blue jeans, what makes you think a collar and a robe will change anything? If people can't pick you out by knowing something is different about you, because of a work God has done in your life, you don't need a robe; you need to let God do that inner work.

★★★★★

I've Never Heard of Simony!

If you thought Hus' words to the priests were tough so far, this section is even tougher! You may be wondering what simony is. The term originated from the biblical stories of Simon, who offered money to the apostles for the power of the Holy Spirit, and Gehazi, who took money from Naaman for the cure of leprosy. You can read the accounts in Acts 8:17–24 and 2 Kings 5:20–27.

When Simon wanted to purchase the power of God, Peter told Simon that his money would perish with him because Simon thought he could buy the gifts of God. Peter then told Simon that his heart was not right—he was full of greed, envy, and jealousy—and he needed to pray for forgiveness.

In Hus' day, the Church was infected with the practice of simony, mainly through the sale of indulgences, absolutions, etc. We shake our heads in disgust when we think of the evil practices of his day, but even today we need to guard our hearts against this evil and deceptive spirit. Nothing has changed. Remember, there's nothing new under the sun—it only comes in different packages.

I believe in prosperity God's way. The book of Proverbs is filled with warnings for the righteous saying that if we focus on riches, or desire them more than God, it is an abomination to God. Proverbs 28:20 in the Amplified Version states, *"A faithful man shall abound with blessings, but he who makes haste to be rich [at any cost] shall not go unpunished."* If you have a question in this area, read the book of Proverbs—it's all outlined there, and you'll see the right way to live in health and prosperity.

The reason for prosperity preaching is not to feather your world. The reason for prosperity is not to pad your comfort level. Prosperity is preached because we must have money for the tools to get the job done on earth. Money finances the tools that bring salvation, deliverance, healing, and discipleship. Money is a tool to get the job done in the areas He has called you to.

Why do some not get the money they want? Some don't get the money because the will for it is not found in the will of God. It's found in their own personal desires or in their longings to build their own personal empires in their own names for their own legacies. Many will be accountable before God for it.

✯✯✯✯✯

I've included Hus' beliefs on simony because I believe it is a good jolt for us all in this generation—especially when money seems to totally rule our societies, our cultures, and yes, sometimes even our ministries and our churches.

Strong Statements on Simony

I think Hus understood what God intended money for. If it was used otherwise, he called it "trafficking in holy things" and rated it in the category with apostasy and blasphemy. [39]

1. *Hus stated that anyone in ministry for the sake of money, worldly possessions, or dominance was guilty of simony.* He said of those kind, "There is no estate in Christendom more liable to fall....Therefore, everyone who runs after and strives for that dignity on account of material gain or worldly eminence is guilty of simony." [40]

If you are in the ministry or the church for anything other than God, you will have a period of time to repent and change. But if you don't change, without a doubt, your wrong motives will eventually be revealed and your character will show itself. Even more fearful and sobering is the thought that you will have to stand before God and give an account for your motives.

2. *Hus disapproved of all clergy who took money for "extracurricular" ministerial services.* Hus believed that the clergy should be supported financially after their basic needs, but he scolded them for charging money for extra services such as ordinations. Hus believed that an ordination was a spiritual office that couldn't be bought. He even rebuked them for charging money for marriages and funerals, because Hus saw them as a spiritual duty of the pastoral office. He branded those who charged for confessions and absolutions "unscriptural," pointing out that Jesus never received money or checked the tithing records of those who came to Him for help.

Hus rebuked the notorious monks who paid to gain entrance into the order. As for their vow of poverty and their refusal to love money, Hus commented that the monks kept that vow "about as well as a prostitute does chastity." [41]

3. *Hus insisted that no one should attend a Mass conducted by a priest who was involved in simony or immorality and that the congregation should withhold tithes from him.* Many of the priests paid

a tax to the bishop in order to keep mistresses. Some priests had children from those mistresses, for whom they had to pay an additional "cradle" tax. Hus said, "I know not how the holy Church can rid itself of them unless the community follow the order which Christ and St. Paul have established." [42]

4. *Hus believed that the best way to avoid simony was to elect good men as bishops and priests, those whose hearts were after God and not consumed with money.* This would, of course, cause a radical reform within the papal system.

Realizing that he could do little except preach against this evil, Hus concluded all his sermons with the statement he ever insisted upon and, even today, is the most famous for—that is, "Truth conquers all." [43]

Hus concluded all his sermons with the statement he ever insisted upon and is most famous for—"Truth conquers all."

Hus firmly believed that to deny the truth was to betray it. He knew that truth would always prevail no matter what came against it, no matter how it was outnumbered, and no matter how much time it took. And I say, "Amen!"

His Message to Lay People

Hus had a heart for common people and looked upon their lives as a loving shepherd would his flock. The core of his rebukes to the clergy came as a result of the people being disillusioned, mislead, or hurt by the actions of the priests. Hus believed that God did not take it lightly when the clergy misled His flock.

At the same time, Hus sought to mature the people and bring them into an understanding of what the Word of God said so they could act appropriately.

Aside from his exhortations to become transformed from within, Hus instructed the people to become wise and not to lose their common sense simply because they were Christians.

1. *He taught the people to simply repent from the heart if a priest wasn't present.* He scolded the believers who had become so superstitious that they believed their forgiveness could only come from a priest. Hus explained that forgiveness comes from God alone, and the priest can only verify it if true repentance is present. Hus taught, "... the priests who think or say that they can of their own will loose or bind without the previous absolving or binding by Jesus Christ, are ragingly insane." [44]

Repentance is from the heart. Forgiveness comes from God alone. A priest can only verify if true repentance is present.

2. *He taught the people to obey the clergy based on their ethics, not on their positions.* That's still a controversial statement today! Hus believed that every person must discern the lives of those over them or else they would become like slaves, believing that the priests could never be wrong and that their commands must be obeyed as if they were God's mandates. Hus taught his people that if a priest or a superior commanded something that was not contained in Scripture, no faithful Christian was bound to perform it.

Hus thought the people had a right to know what the minister taught and to compare it with how he lived according to Scripture.

Hus instructed them to never allow a minister to rebuke them, asking, "What business is it of yours to pay attention to our lives or acts?" He believed the lives of the ministers should always be on display for the people to see. The people had a right to know what the minister taught and how he lived according to Scripture. He added, "For no superior is above correction." [45]

3. *He taught the people to be circumcised in their hearts so that the true life of God could flow from them.* Hus was not a man who put on a show. Faith in God came from the heart; it was not just an outward appearance. He wanted the people to understand that the Church

was not restricted to the popes, cardinals, bishops, and clergy, and that the congregation also had an important place in the kingdom of God.

Only a man with nothing to hide—someone very secure in his or her role and position—could teach such things in a time when the common man was reduced to almost nothing.

As we jump back into the story of Hus' life, we not only find him preaching to a people hungry for these reforming truths, but we also see a door opening into the very heart of the Roman Catholic Church through an archbishop who would show him favor.

Rank Relics

Zbynek was the young, dashing, and rich archbishop of Prague. He liked the daring personality of Hus and took him in as a friend and confidante. In 1403 and again in 1404, Zbynek hosted two synod conferences at which he asked Hus to be the featured speaker. The conferences were well-attended by the elaborately dressed and starched clergy, and, as the thin and lanky Hus took the platform, he used the opportunity to denounce their vices through his sermons. The packed room would grow chillingly cold as Hus began to elaborate on Scriptures. Sometimes the priests would be so shocked at his revolutionary boldness that they would sit with blank stares. But Zbynek was delighted with what he heard and became so enthralled with Hus that he even instituted several beliefs of the Czech reformers into the Catholic churches throughout Prague!

For the next five years, Zbynek would be an avid supporter of the Czech reform movement. Unfortunately, his love for money and power eventually changed his position. But for a period of time, Hus was one of Zbynek's favorite priests.

For example, in 1405, Zbynek received reports from Italy and parts of Bohemia of the alleged appearance of the true blood of Christ on the consecrated elements. [46] Zbynek was suspicious of such reports, so he chose Hus, Stanislav, and another unnamed member to go to these regions and investigate the claims.

The three intimidating men interrogated several Czechs who had returned from the region. Unable to keep the fraud going, the Czech men confessed the lie to Hus—the miracle had been invented by a priest who was trying to earn money to make up for the loss of a church that had burned. Hus listened intently as the Czech men explained how the priest had dipped the wafer into blood and then hysterically exclaimed that it had been miraculously transformed. For a while it had worked; people were coming from near and far, bringing lavish gifts to the priest and the church. Hus quickly pursued and apprehended the priest. Under rigorous examination and hard-hitting questions, the priest confessed that it was all a hoax.

There had also been a wide outbreak of people worshipping articles throughout central Europe, and Hus wanted to put an end to it. This is going to seem crude, but I want you to understand the times. The Catholic hierarchy in Rome said they actually had in their possession the foreskin of Jesus! In Prague, they said they had Jesus' actual blood and beard and the milk of the Virgin Mary on exhibit! [47]

Hus was a crusader against such gross error. He fervently sought to protect the hearts of people and taught against believing in and worshipping false relics such as these. He blasted the deception and the hypocrisy of the Catholic Church and the priests who encouraged this idol worship. Hus roared, "These priests deserve hanging in hell, for they are fornicators, parasites, money misers, fat swine." [48] While these priests claimed apostolic succession, they bore no resemblance to the apostles. Hus solemnly claimed that all of these relics were absolutely false.

Again, Hus was depriving the Church of the money they would have received from gullible people coming to worship these false relics.

The Living Voice of the Gospel

By now, Hus had been pastoring for four years. Caring for the people, he looked for every possible way to bless and prosper them. One of those ways was to spotlight the native Czech language. Hus took this time to perfect the Czech alphabet by translating the Latin alphabet into the Czech language. Every syllable was to be expressed by one letter instead of a combination of letters. His translation of the Czech language to a modernized form is still used today. [49]

In 1406, Hus revised and improved the Czech New Testament. He also revised portions of the Old Testament. Toward the end of his life, Hus took on the project of revising the entire Czech Bible, making it easier to read.

He valiantly fought for the right of the Czech people to read the Bible in their native language. When Hus heard of some priests forbidding the Czechs to read in their language, he rebuked them by pointing out that John wrote his gospel in Greek, Simon preached his gospel in Persian, and Bartholomew preached in Judean—"Why then do you allow the priests to forbid that the people read the law of God... in Czech?" [50]

As the Czechs came to understand the Word more and more as they read it in their native language, Hus illustrated the importance of preaching what they had learned. Living in an age when printed books were not yet available, Hus stressed the importance of becoming "the living voice of the Gospel." [51]

To Hus, public preaching was a sure sign of the true Church. He believed that the Scriptures must be proclaimed freely, without constraints or censures. Preaching was a gift inspired by God, and to stop it would be to hinder the Word of God.

John wrote in Greek. Simon preached in Persian. Bartholomew spoke Judean. Hus thought his people should hear the Gospel in their tongue—Czech.

Hus said that since preaching is divinely inspired by God, no one has the authority to stop it. Preaching is a matter of obligation, not of choice. Of course, the Catholic hierarchy was furious at such a comment, because they believed they had the power to state who could minister and who couldn't. Hus believed that if any authority attempted to stop a priest from preaching, the priest was to ignore it and continue. He stated, "Preachers count for more in the church than prelates [high-ranking bishops]." [52] He believed that all ministers had the right to proclaim the truth they believed. Wycliffe had believed the same.

Hus constantly exhorted the clergy and the young students in his audiences to "preach the gospel, not some entertainment, or fables, or plundering lies, so that the people with attentive minds will accept the Gospel and both the preacher and the hearer will be grounded by faith in the Gospel." [53]

✯✯✯✯✯

However, Hus would not live to see such freedom. In fact, many generations after him never saw it either. It wasn't until the late 1600s, when the Act of Toleration was passed (see chapter 6 on George Fox) that individual preaching of conscience was allowed in Europe without penalty.

If You Find an Error, Tell Me!

By now, in 1408, Stanislov had encountered severe persecution for his Wycliffe teachings and had grown noticeably absent from the Czech reformers. Distancing himself more and more, he eventually alienated himself from their cause and joined sides with the opposition—the extreme papists. Stanislav soon convinced Palec to join him. Now, in a strange turn of fate, both Stanislav and Palec were outspoken enemies of Hus and the rest of the Czech reformers.

Sensing a mutiny within the Czech reformers, the Catholic hierarchy made their move against the uncompromising condemnation of their immoral lifestyles and heretical practices. They held a synod meeting and formally denounced the preaching against their lifestyles in any Czech sermons. They also charged the entire Czech reformist party with Wycliffe heresy.

Zbynek wanted to look good in the eyes of the hierarchy, so he ordered that all Wycliffe's books be brought to him for examination. Hus personally delivered the books to the court and laid them down in front of Zbynek. Then Hus smiled and told Zbynek that if he found any errors to let him know.

Stanislav and Palec's change of loyalty did them little good. Stanislav's persecution of others had gotten them both into trouble, and the hierarchy wanted to see them. They had been ordered to appear before a synod court in Italy. Upon arrival, they were arrested and thrown into prison.

Hus was not yet accused of heresy but of causing divisions in the Church because he denounced the sins of the various clergy. Zbynek was backing the charges, and he and Hus wrote back and forth to the court, Hus standing by his convictions and arguing his theology.

All this arguing back and forth troubled King Vaclav. He feared that the reputation of Bohemia would suffer from it, so he ordered

Zbynek to write a confession stating that, after an examination, he found no heresy or heretics in Bohemia. Zbynek was hesitant because he had been involved with Stanislav and Palec going to prison. He began to resent King Vaclav and the Czech reformers. How would this make him look in the eyes of the pope? How would he be promoted if he looked so fickle?

By 1409, King Vaclav, favoring the Czech reformers and weary of all the controversy, overturned a law, which made the Germans furious. They pulled out of Prague by the droves. The rector position was now vacant and the Czech reformers overwhelmingly voted for Hus to fill the position.

The Church with Three Heads

In 1409, another major controversy was brewing. Two popes were still ruling (Rome and Avignon), and neither would concede to the other. When one pope died, another was immediately inducted to fill the position. Benedict XIII was the pope in Avignon; Gregory XII was the pope in Rome.

With no end to the schism in sight, some of the cardinals went to Pisa, Italy, and called for a general council. The council was to elect a pope that would be accepted in the entire Western world, and the other two would be disposed of.

The Council of Pisa was impressive. Masses of cardinals and bishops descended upon Pisa, all dressed in their finest array and decked from head to toe with elaborate jewels. Because of the large number of high-ranking clergy present, they declared themselves as the final authority. They elected a third pope, Alexander V, and instructed him to hold a second council before 1412. The Council of Pisa called for the resignation of the other two popes.

The two other popes refused to resign. Now the Church had three popes and none of them acknowledged the others!

Hus had agreed with the necessity of the Council of Pisa, hoping for an end to the pope controversy. When none of the popes resigned and all three chose to remain in rule, Hus was disgusted. He harshly rebuked the three popes saying, "Well, you apostolic vicars! See whether you have the Holy Spirit, which is the spirit of unity, peace, and grace. For then you would live as the apostles did. However, because you quarrel about dignity on account of possessions, murder people, and cause contention in Christendom, you show by your deeds that you possess an evil spirit, the spirit of discord and avarice [greed] which has been a killer or murderer from the beginning." [54]

It's interesting that Hus called them murderers. Out of the eight popes who reigned from 1378–1417, five died suddenly. The suspicious nature of their deaths implied murder. [55]

"Here a Pope, There a Pope" [56]

King Vaclav saw the election of yet another pope as his golden opportunity. He had a plan. He hoped that if he could align himself with the new pope, Alexander V, and gain his favor by taking a leading role in the schism, he might win back his right to contend for the title of the Holy Roman Emperor.

So in 1409, Vaclav shifted his allegiance from Gregory XII to Alexander V—and commanded Zbynek to do the same. Zbynek was then ordered to remove any trace of heresy in Bohemia, clearing the way for Vaclav's election as emperor.

Zbynek grew even more bitter at Vaclav for changing allegiance to Alexander V. At first, he refused to do it. The king was furious that Zbynek sought to disobey him. When Zbynek remembered the king's murderous personality, he thought better of his decision, changed his allegiance to Alexander V, and sought all-out vengeance against any heresy in Bohemia. That made Hus one of Zbynek's main targets.

Alexander V issued an order condemning Wycliffe's books and prohibiting preaching in any place except a Catholic cathedral or a monastery. This was directed at Hus because his chapel was the only place not deemed a cathedral.

It seemed that the king and Zbynek were going to make some headway with the new pope. But before Vaclav could gain the favor of the new pope and Zbynek could get into full swing against Hus, Alexander V was found dead. He had been poisoned!

Little Minds Start Fires

John XXIII was installed as the new pope in place of Alexander V. He had originally been passed over, with Alexander V winning out over him. History states that John poisoned Alexander V. [57]

☆☆☆☆☆

As you can gather, John XXIII was an evil man. When he had been the bishop in Naples, his secretary confirmed that he seduced two hundred virgins, matrons, widows, and nuns. He taxed everything, including prostitution. [58] And now, he was the new pope!

Zbynek was still enforcing Alexander's order, but Hus ignored it from the beginning. You remember what he believed about preaching; he felt the pope had no authority to tell anyone where they could preach. Hus argued that the order was invalid because the pope who issued it was dead.

Since Hus refused to stop preaching, Zbynek organized a physical attack against Bethlehem Chapel, trying to destroy it. The attack was staged while the chapel was filled to capacity and Hus was preaching. Zbynek's army stormed the doors of the chapel, but they weren't ready for the rough Czech reformers! The small army was pushed into the streets, bloody and bruised from a battle with the Czechs. Hus denounced the efforts of Zbynek from the pulpit as the scuffle was taking place. It was a miserable defeat for Zbynek.

After the attack, the fire was fueled within the Czech ranks. The people were incensed against Zbynek, rallying together with incredible unity. In a sensational service at the chapel filled with patriotic singing and comradery, Hus publicly read his response to John XXIII concerning Alexander's order. He also added that, in 1409, there had been a prophecy stating that a man would arise who would persecute the Gospel and the faith in Christ. [59] When Hus dramatically asked the overflowing crowd if they would support him in stopping this man's efforts, the shouts of agreement were thunderous.

Hus not only appealed Alexander's and Zbynek's order, but he also wrote a pamphlet defending his stand.

Zbynek was so embarrassed and outraged that he ordered all Wycliffe's books to be burned in a public ceremony. On July 16, 1410, complete with bells tolling and somber priests singing, some two hundred copies of Wycliffe's manuscripts were burned to ashes.

Hus responded with a public declaration, "I call it a poor business. Such bonfires never yet removed a single sin from the hearts of men. Fire does not consume truth. It is always the mark of a little mind that it vents its anger on inanimate objects." [60]

Hus' clear remark sent the Czech citizens to open revolt. They began mocking Zbynek, making up sarcastic remarks about him. For example,

> Bishop Zbynek, ABCD,
> Burned books
> Not knowing what was written in them. [61]

Furious and embarrassed, Zbynek retaliated—he excommunicated Hus. Then, Zbynek fled from Prague in fear of his life.

Spies in the Hood

In the Catholic Church, there are several phases of excommunication. Meant to be a punishment, it bans a member from taking part in the rites and services of the Church. In its early form, it usually allows the offender to join in some parts of the worship service, but only on a level with the unbaptized.

Sometimes excommunication was for a certain period of time. In this case, the offender is not even allowed to enter the church building.

The most serious form of excommunication resulted in the offender being completely cast out from the shelter of the church. It even affected his position in society. [62] In those cases, high-ranking superiors determined what action was taken. Many times, if the offender came anywhere near the church building, services couldn't be conducted there for three days afterward.

Hus would experience all four levels of excommunication.

Hus ignored the first excommunication and went on preaching and conducting his ministry as if nothing had happened. He received overwhelming support, even from as far away as England. English nobles wrote to King Vaclav, encouraging him to continue supporting the Czech reformers. Hus received a letter from a Wycliffe supporter in England, which said,

"Therefore you, Hus, beloved brother in Christ, although unknown to me in person, but not in faith and love;...Labor like a good soldier of Jesus Christ; preach, stand firmly in word and example, and call to the way of truth whomever you can." [63]

Hus read the letter to his congregation, now totaling over ten thousand people!

☆☆☆☆☆

Zbynek couldn't stand that Hus was getting the upper hand, so he began sending spies into the chapel, waiting for quotes from Hus that would condemn him.

But it was difficult to outsmart Hus. He recognized every spy among them, pointing out several and publicly humiliating them. Once, during the middle of his sermon, Hus stopped and yelled at a spy he recognized, "Hey, you in the hood, make a note of this, you sneak, and carry it over there," pointing where he believed Zbynek was! [64]

Never underestimate a reformer filled with the Holy Spirit!

"No-Show"

In the fall of 1410, Hus was ordered to appear in Italy to explain why he disobeyed papal orders. Zbynek took advantage of the situation and slapped Hus with another excommunication. It was the second one, cited as an "aggravated excommunication." Hus ignored the second excommunication as well. He continued to preach and go about his duties. He had far more support in Prague than Zbynek did. [65]

But Hus did write a humble letter to the pope, asking that he be permitted to preach at Bethlehem Chapel and that there be no further burning of Wycliffe's manuscripts. King Vaclav, somewhat irritated by all the negative attention on Bohemia, also wrote the pope, saying, "If anyone wishes to accuse him [Hus] of anything, let him do so in our kingdom before the University of Prague or another competent judge. For our kingdom does not see fit to expose so useful a preacher to the discrimination of his enemies and to the disturbance of the whole population." [66] Queen Zofie also wrote to the pope and to the cardinals, urging them to not press any charges against "our faithfully devoted chaplain." [67]

Receiving no reply, the king and queen both wrote a second time, informing the pope they were sending two emissaries in the place of Hus.

When Zbynek heard of the king and queen's intervention, he sent elaborate and expensive gifts to the pope and cardinals, such as horses, precious cups, and rings. Money was also sent to the pope's servants. Zbynek asked that they show their gratitude by commanding Hus to appear.

✯✯✯✯✯

The expensive gifts worked. In February of 1411, Hus was excommunicated a third time by a superior cardinal in Italy for not appearing before the pope.

It Might Be Fair to Die

Thrilled at his newfound power with the papacy, Zbynek didn't know where to stop. He attempted to take action against Vaclav by excommunicating him and all the royal court! Vaclav was outraged and threatened Zbynek.

Zbynek responded with an outrageous move—he placed the entire city of Prague under interdict! That meant that all church activities were suspended—funerals, marriages, and preaching.

Every magistrate in Bohemia sided with the king and stood valiantly against Zbynek. Through a brief struggle of power, Zbynek realized he was totally outnumbered. Again, fearing for his life, he submitted to the King and was forced into unconditional obedience.

Wanting to save the reputation of his nation, the first thing Vaclav ordered Zbynek to do was declare that all his proceedings against Hus were null and void, specifically the excommunications. Zbynek was commanded to send Pope John XXIII a certified letter, explaining his irrational actions against Hus, declaring that Hus was innocent of all heresy charges. Zbynek was even ordered to declare that he and Hus totally agreed when it came to doctrine! After that, Zbynek was to make a public declaration stating the same. [68]

Vaclav ordered Hus to write a letter of submission to the pope and the cardinals, humbly professing his faith and asking for a suspension of all the charges against him. Hus gladly complied and had the letters written in two days.

Within two weeks, Hus was back doing what he was called to do—publicly defending Wycliffe and the majority of his doctrines and attempting to reform the Catholic Church. Hus remained silent about the doctrines he didn't agree with. Hus argued that whenever truth is not defended, it is denied. For that reason, he could not remain silent about what he believed. [69]

Meanwhile, Zbynek was seething with anger and nursing a damaged ego. Vaclav's demand proved too much for him. Leaving a letter for the King, Zbynek wrote a list of his own grievances, then stated he would not change his position against Hus and would not write a letter to the pope. Zbynek wrote to the king that he was leaving for Hungary to take refuge with King Sigismund (Vaclav's stepbrother and enemy).

Sigismund was scheduled to meet Zbynek the next day on the way to Hungary, escorting him into the city. But a strange thing happened before the meeting. Zbynek was found dead—poisoned by his own cook. [70]

The Apostolic Reformer

There was no lack of candidates who desired to fill Zbynek's position. Twenty-four men applied, but Vaclav chose his own personal physician and university professor, Dr. Albik of Unicov.

Albik was the highest bidder for the job of archbishop, and he was no better prepared for it than Zbynek. At the start of his office, Albik, like Zbynek, was content not to cause a stir; he wasn't interested in making Hus an enemy.

But there were those who wanted to continue their attack against Hus. Two of them were Stanislav and Palec, now out of prison and back in Prague. Palec approached Albik and forced him to call Hus for questioning concerning his erroneous doctrines. Albik commanded Hus to appear at the archiepiscopal palace.

Written contentions were sent back and forth between Hus and the council. Finally, Hus conceded to appear.

Walking into the council, Hus found himself face-to-face with the hypocrisy he had spent most of his life preaching against. Cloaked in all their splendor, complete with jewels, pearls, and luxurious robes, the archbishop's council asked Hus if he was willing to obey the apostolic mandate.

Hus promptly responded that he heartily intended to fulfill the apostolic mandates.

The council members looked at each other in obvious pleasure, grinning and nodding their heads that they won the argument.

It was then that Hus took advantage of their terminology. In their minds, the word *apostolic* meant papacy. He stated, "Lords, understand me. I said that I heartily aspire to fulfill the apostolic mandates and to obey them in everything; but I call apostolic mandates the teaching of Christ's apostles. In as far as the mandates of the Roman pontiff are in harmony with the apostolic mandates and teaching...to that degree I am most willing to obey them. But should I find any of them opposed, those will I not obey, even if the fire to burn my body were placed before my eyes." [71]

The council was speechless. Hus let the silence fall. Not knowing what else to do, they quickly dismissed Hus from their presence, then wrote the King and explained what a troublemaker Hus was for the king, for the Church, and for the entire country of Bohemia.

Fleas, Flies, and Rowdy Rumblers

In the meantime, King Vaclav was still looking for ways to pursue his own aspirations. In 1412, Pope John XXIII declared war against the King of Naples, who had seized control of Rome. To raise funds for the war effort, the pope instituted a large-scale selling of indulgences. Vaclav was promised a cut of the money for all the indulgences sold in Bohemia. Realizing his potential profit, Vaclav campaigned for the wide distribution and sale of these indulgences. Three of the main churches in Prague became major indulgence purchase centers.

Hus was outraged at the king, the war, and the sale of indulgences, which was blatant simony. Rebuking the king and the priests who sold these indulgences, Hus wrote, "What a strange thing! They cannot rid themselves of fleas and flies, and yet want to rid others of the torments of hell." [72]

Hus' rebuke against indulgences was too much for the king. After all, it might damage his profit. From the time of the sale of these indulgences on, King Vaclav never again supported Hus. In the end, the king allied with greed for money.

In the meantime, Hus' old friend, Jerome of Prague, had returned to the city from his travels. Hearing of all the trouble that Hus had gone through, the matter of Stanislav and Palec's betrayal, and now of the indulgences, the rowdy Jerome was ready to fight.

Riots broke out all over Prague in protest to the sale of indulgences. Jerome was the principal organizer of these demonstrations. Many times, the protestors disrupted sermons, calling for the people to wake up and come out of deception. The money boxes for the indulgences were smeared with filth, and the sellers themselves were abused and heckled.

At these demonstrations, Jerome was often found declaring loudly that the indulgences were worthless. Once, a Minorite friar yelled abusive language at Jerome, and Jerome boxed his ears! [73] He reportedly drew a knife on another priest and would have killed another had he not been stopped. In another incident, Jerome threw an indulgence-preaching friar into a small boat and rowed him into the middle of a swift river. He then pitched the terrified monk into the turbulent water and gave him only a thin rope as a lifeline! [74]

Hus! I'll Burn You Myself!

Hus was openly disgusted with Pope John XXIII for the sale of indulgences and rumors of his immoral lifestyle. He said of him, "In a word, the papal institution is full of poison, Antichrist himself, the man of sin, the leader of the army of the Devil, a limb of Lucifer, the head vicar of the fiend, a simple idiot who might be a damned devil in hell, and [a] more horrible idol than a painted log." [75]

Several of the demonstrators joined with Hus in declaring the pope as the Antichrist. The protest turned bloody.

At the three principal churches where indulgences were sold, three men stood outside, protesting their sale. Immediately, the three were arrested and thrown into prison.

Hearing of the ordeal, Hus went to the prison and interceded on their behalf. He even asked that he be taken in their place, feeling that the men acted on impulse from his statements against Pope John XXIII.

The councilmen promised that no serious punishment would be inflicted on the men. After Hus left, they proceeded with the king's order—to have the young men beheaded.

The execution created a tremendous commotion. The Czech people were in total shock and dismay. The bodies of the men were carried reverently to Bethlehem Chapel, where Hus celebrated the Martyr's Mass for them.

Afterward, the crowds rioted at the town hall, wanting the blood of the councilmen. The terrified councilmen ran to the king for help. Infuriated, Vaclav shouted that even if there were a thousand rioters, they would all suffer the same fate; if there weren't enough councilmen in Prague, he would have them brought in from other areas.

With his royal revenue now in serious doubt, Vaclav's rage turned toward Hus. In a violent fit of anger, Vaclav saw Hus as the only obstacle between him and wealth. He shouted, "Hus, you are always making trouble for me. If those whose concern it is will not take care of you, I myself will burn you." [76]

Even Queen Zofie was powerless to help at this stage.

Forget You! I'll Appeal to God!

Since Hus, now deserted by his former friends and out of the king's favor, continued to defend Wycliffe and oppose the sale of indulgences, the Catholic superiors renewed his trial before the pope. They knew that because of Hus' harsh comments against the pope and his opposition of indulgences, things would now work in their favor.

During the Roman Council of 1412–1413, the documents were presented to the cardinal, who immediately declared Hus' excommunication. This was Hus' fourth excommunication. The cardinal further declared that if Hus did not appear before the council in twenty days, the entire city of Prague—or any other city where Hus chose to reside—would be under interdict.

The interdict meant that the faithful were forbidden to communicate with Hus in food, drink, greeting, conversation, buying and selling, shelter, or any other way. In any place where he might seek shelter, all church services must be stopped and remain suspended for three days after his departure. Should he die, he must not be buried; if he was buried, his body must be exhumed. [77]

Hus did not appear before the council.

Therefore, the sentence was pronounced in Prague, complete with the ringing of bells, the blowing out of candles, and the throwing of stones in the direction of Hus' dwelling. These ceremonies nearly caused another riot as the crowd loudly protested against the priests' actions. The priests quickly left to find a safe shelter.

Hus took a step wholly unknown to the Catholic laws up to this point—since any other appeal to the pope was obviously useless, Hus appealed to God and Christ, "the most just judge who knows, protects, judges, declares, and rewards without fail the just cause of every man." [78] It was his final break with the papacy. They would be sure to remind him of it in the coming days.

A Fathering Shepherd

Despite the elaborate excommunication, Hus continued to preach. When he heard of it, the pope issued an order for Bethlehem Chapel to be pulled down.

The order reached Prague in late fall. The remaining German parishioners saw it as an opportunity to attack the hated chapel. They staged their attack during a worship service, but so many were in attendance that the German group was driven away and threatened.

Unable to find a way to destroy the chapel, the priests resorted to other means. If they thought anyone was a proponent of Hus', the person would be dragged into a Catholic sanctuary and beaten. Then the person would be dragged into his residential quarters and whipped. [79]

When the interdict was imposed on Prague, Hus was faced with a painful decision. Being such a dedicated pastor, Hus felt he would be a hireling if he left the sheep during trouble: A good shepherd always stayed with his flock.

Hus was a shepherd. He was never so caught up in his cause for reform that he neglected the "sheep" under his care.

But, on the other hand, Hus realized that if he stayed, his members would be severely persecuted, maybe even to death. I can only imagine the agonizing moments that Hus must have spent, wondering what to do. He finally made the heartbreaking decision that, for the good of his members, Bethlehem Chapel, and the city of Prague, he needed to leave. When nobles in southern Bohemia offered him refuge, Hus knew God favored the exile.

Nevertheless, Hus intended to secretly visit the chapel to "strengthen the sheep" whenever the opportunity presented itself. [80]

One of Hus' outstanding characteristics was that he was never so caught up in his cause for reform that he neglected the duties of pastoral care. He was truly a spiritual father.

✯✯✯✯✯

The Country Preacher

On October 15, 1412, Hus left Prague. He remained somewhere in the vicinity, but no one knew where. We do know that from January 1413 until Easter, Hus secretly visited the city from time to time. When Hus visited, the officials soon heard he was back, but they didn't impose the interdict unless he preached. He wrote, "But when I preached once, they immediately stopped the services, for it was hard for them to hear the Word of God." [81]

We also know that he continued to preach in various places outside Prague, and I'm sure many traveled to hear him. He wrote, "I have preached in towns and marketplaces; now I preach behind hedges, in villages, castles, fields, woods. If it were possible, I would preach on the seashore, or from a ship, as my Savior did." [82]

During this time of exile, he also wrote many letters to his members, the university masters, and his friends. Instead of being depressed and mired with self-pity, Hus used these letters to encourage the faith of those who remained behind. He had not lost heart; he still believed that truth would conquer all.

Hus used his time in exile to write several manuscripts, through which he continued to sound the alarm against church abuses like simony and indulgences. Hus didn't write these things flippantly—he had a goal. Hus once said that he preached against the sins of the clergy in order to "obtain their reformation, not to defame their reputation." [83] What a great quote! And it truly portrayed the heart of Hus—no matter how harsh his words seemed.

His most important work, entitled *De Ecclesia*, "On the Church," was written in 1413. In this work, Hus repeated his beliefs on what the true church really is and on the spiritual headship of Jesus Christ. He wrote of the layperson's position in the Church and the important role of the ministers. Again, Hus cursed the abuses found in the ministers who were filled with greed and the love of money, using their positions to get what they wanted. He wrote, "Let the disciples of Antichrist blush who, living contrary to Christ, speak of themselves as the greatest and the proudest of God's holy Church. They, polluted by avarice [greed] and arrogance of the world, are called publicly the heads and body of the holy Church. According to Christ's Gospel, however, they are called the least." [84]

★★★★★

That statement, and many others like it, condemned Hus. The work that Hus is most celebrated for is the very manuscript that the Council of Constance used to condemn him.

The Invitation of Death

Sigismund was not only the King of Hungary and now Germany, but he was deemed the Holy Roman Emperor as well. Vaclav allowed his stepbrother Sigismund to be crowned emperor on the condition that he end the Hus affair in Bohemia. [85] The two brothers carried out a carefully planned plot to end the life of one of God's greatest Reformers.

Sigismund had been urging Pope John XXIII to call another council in order to end the schism between the three popes. Pope John had put the matter off as long as he could, but since he needed the support of Sigismund, he decided to act and called the council to convene in November of 1414. Sigismund designated the council to be held within his jurisdiction in Germany, setting the city of Constance as the site.

Two Czech knights had served in Sigismund's army and were returning home to Bohemia in the spring of 1414. As part of the plan, Sigismund took the opportunity to have the knights send a message to Hus. The knights were to invite Hus to be a guest at the Council of Constance later that fall in the king's name and under his safe-conduct order. The council would provide Hus with the opportunity to clear his name and the nation of Bohemia from the persistent charges of heresy that overshadowed them. Despite Sigismund's evil nature, the two knights truly believed that Hus would be safe.

When Hus was presented with the invitation, he discussed it with his friends and, at first, decided not to go. But when the pope began to place extreme pressure on King Vaclav to purge Bohemia of all Wycliffism, Hus changed his mind.

Before accepting, Hus asked for further clarification on the terms of the safe-conduct. Sigismund sent his own courtier to reply, and his answers must have satisfied Hus' questions. Hus was promised that he would be allowed to return to Bohemia.

Fully Prepared

Hus' friend Jerome was against Hus going to Constance. "Master," Jerome cautioned, "you may take it for certain that you will be condemned." [86] Hus probably realized that his legal case was definitely lost, but he still determined to go to Constance so that the entire Christian world would know his defense and his cause.

Trusting the promise of Sigismund, confident of his cause, and eager to give reasons for the faith he held, Hus planned his trip to Constance. He was ready to submit to the council and abandon whatever errors he might have embraced—provided those errors were proven by Scripture.

Before Hus left Bohemia, he carefully prepared himself for all the demands that might be made upon him. He made sure that he had written and secured all the proper presentations of his views. He anticipated his enemies, along with their accusations and witnesses, and he was careful to collect all the evidence he had to prove them wrong. Hus even secured a certificate of orthodoxy from the Prague inquisitor, Bishop Nicholas of Nezero. [87]

Hus also took time to write a sermon, which he planned to present to the council. He planned to ask them to hear him first and then to judge him based on his statement of faith.

On October 11, 1414, in the company of two knights assigned to him for protection, Hus left the castle where he had been in exile and headed for Constance.

It was the last time that he saw Bohemia.

Peace before the Storm

Hus' trip through Germany was almost a celebration. He traveled with his face uncovered; nowhere was he challenged. He was not treated as a condemned, excommunicated heretic, nor were any church services stopped on his account. He had friendly conversations with priests and officials along the way. In the common people he met, without exception, his views were accepted as totally orthodox. [88]

Hus arrived in Constance on November 3. Upon arrival, Hus and the knights lodged in the house of a widow (the house still stands today). Pope John had arrived in Constance a week earlier and had suspended the interdict to allow the city to continue with religious services even with Hus' presence. Thus, Hus was free to move about as he wished. However, he never set foot outside the widow's home until he was summoned.

While Hus was taking refuge in the widow's home, the Council of Constance officially began its session. The council's goals were to end the Great Schism by securing one pope and to put an end to heretical acts that were dividing the Church.

Sigismund and his entourage were not scheduled to arrive until December. Along with the Catholic Church's representatives, enemies of Hus had also descended upon the city. Stanislov had died, but Palec was there, presenting the pope with the first list of accusations against Hus. The accusations stated that Hus believed all of Wycliffe's articles were orthodox, which wasn't completely true.

Lodgings of Hus, Constance, on Hus Street, before being thrown in the dungeon.

Outsmarting the Smartest

Less than a month after his arrival, Hus was visited in his lodging by two bishops, the mayor of Constance, and a knight. They declared that they came by order of the pope and the cardinal and that the cardinal wished to speak with Hus.

Although one of Hus' knights sensed immediate danger, Hus calmed him and agreed to go.

When they arrived at the pope's residence, the cardinals spoke a few words to Hus and then left the room. Immediately a Franciscan theologian came in the room and, pretending to be a simple monk, he asked Hus if he believed in remanence. Hus responded that he did not. The disguised theologian would then talk about something else, stop, and again ask Hus bluntly if he believed in remanence. This happened several times, and each time, Hus told him that he did not.

The disguised theologian asked several other doctrinal questions. Hus discerned that the man was not a simple friar, but he didn't let on that he knew. Instead, he simply answered the friar's questions. The man finally left the room, obviously disappointed. After he left, the armed guard told Hus that the disguised man was actually one of the keenest theologians in all of Italy. [89]

Deep in the Dungeon

When evening came, the knights were told they could go home, but Hus had to remain. Furious at the deception, one of the knights bolted into the presence of the pope and the cardinals, confronting them and denouncing their treachery.

The pope calmly responded that he had not ordered the arrest. They spoke to the young knight, telling him to calm down and to view the situation in a mature manner. They assured him that Hus would be well taken care of. After all, they had allowed Hus to come to Constance in order to state his case. Helpless, the knight could do

Hus preaching to his jailers in prison.
Getty Images

nothing but go home. Later, in a letter to the University of Paris, the pope admitted that he did order the arrest.

News quickly spread that Hus had been arrested. When Palec heard of it, he and another man danced around the room in excitement, declaring that this time Hus would not get away from them. It is hard to believe that, at one time, Hus and Palec had shared such a close friendship.

Eight days later, Hus was taken to a dungeon in the Dominican Monastery located on an island off the shore of Lake Constance. There he was kept in a dark, wet cell next to the sewer. Hus fell extremely ill from disease rampant in the cell and almost died. Only a visit from the pope's physician and relocation to a better cell saved his life. [90] However, Hus was held in this prison for three and a half months.

Centuries later, developers turned the monastery into a luxurious hotel, the Steigenberger Insel Hotel. Frommer's travel guide calls it "the single finest place to stay along the German side of the lake." [91]

Muffled!

During Hus' imprisonment, Wycliffe's forty-five articles were taken to his cell, where the representatives, filled with rage, shoved them in his face. The council representatives demanded to know if Hus supported all forty-five articles. Looking at their grimacing faces, Hus silently prayed for the wisdom of God. At first he refused to answer specifically, giving a general answer that he did not wish to hold to any error. Unsatisfied, his judges began to yell sarcastic remarks and threatened to condemn him outright. Calming them, Hus answered that he would write what he believed about the articles and submit them to the council.

Realizing that he needed assistance, Hus requested a lawyer, but the request was flatly denied. So Hus wrote his reply, stating that he did not hold to thirty-two of Wycliffe's articles but that he believed thirteen of them, some with minor adjustments.

Understandably, Hus was very disheartened because he had come to Constance to defend his own views, not those of Wycliffe. What was going on? Why had things taken such a strange turn? He had hoped for the opportunity to defend himself before the entire council—not from a wet, dark cell. Hus decided to be aggressive. His answers must be in the form of a protest, not only for his illegal arrest, but also for not being allowed a trial.

When his friends in Prague heard the news of his arrest, they were very troubled. They all feared that Hus would be condemned without a trial.

On January 4, 1415, Hus was again interrogated about each of the forty-five articles. Hus replied with the same answers he had already written.

Later in the month, Hus received a letter from a Bohemian noble announcing that he had spoken with Sigismund and that Hus would be granted a public hearing.

Hus waited and waited. The sun rose, then it set. Not a word came to his cell. His health was nearly depleted, and he had to work at keeping his spirits high. He made jokes about being known as "the goose," stating to all that the goose wasn't cooked just yet. [92] With no plans evident for a public hearing, he was completely at the mercy of those who brought news of what was happening.

By early spring, Sigismund revoked and annulled all safe-conduct passes issued to anyone who was then in Constance. His act of treachery was now very clear.

The Vigilante, Palec

Disappointed in their first attempt on December 6, the council assigned Palec to prepare a list of errors from Hus' own writings. When Hus heard of it, he wrote to friends, "[Palec] labors directly for my condemnation. May God forgive him and strengthen me!" [93] Day after day, Hus sat alone in his cell, trying to keep his mind from fears about what Palec might be inventing against him.

Palec wrote a thesis of twenty pages, exposing the "errors" he found with Hus. When Hus received the copy, he answered each accusation in just one night! He answered the question, "Did you say the pope is the Antichrist?" over and over. Hus wrote back that if the pope's lifestyle was not pleasing to God, then, yes, he was the Antichrist. [94]

Finding Palec's theses filled with lies, Hus humbly requested that if any of his replies were found to be in error, someone would show it to him in the Scriptures and he would recant. That was all he wanted!

If someone could just show Hus in the Word of God where he was in error, he would repent! No one took the time; no one on the council cared. Even if they had, no one would have been able to attack Hus' replies using Scripture.

By the time Hus' answers were read, the council itself realized that the majority of Palec's accusations were false. Nevertheless, Palec was relentless. He wanted another chance to prove Hus' error, so Palec wrote thirteen more errors that he remembered from candlelight debate among friends—the conversations between Hus, Stanislav, and himself years ago!

If someone had shown Hus that he was in error based on the Scriptures, he was prepared to recant. But no one could.

Priesthood of the Believers: Give Them the Cup!

To heat things up further, the Czech reformers were allowing a radical thing in Bethlehem Chapel—the members were being allowed to actually partake of the Communion cup and the wafer. The Czech clergy had taken Communion off its mystical throne and were now allowing the believers to partake of it with them. This practice would eventually be the center point of a bloody war between the Hussites and the Catholics.

By early summer, the practice had created such an uproar that the council passed an order forbidding the cup to laity under severe penalty. If any priest disobeyed, he would be declared a heretic. If he still persisted, he would be punished—if need be, by the secular arm of government.

Even in his vulnerable state, Hus denounced the council's decree as madness. He believed it was condemning a practice that Christ Himself commanded. He was particularly disgusted that the customs and doctrines of the Catholic Church were being placed over the Word of God, such as allowing only the priest to drink from the Communion cup. [95]

From his prison cell, Hus wrote to the Czech reformers to ignore the papal command and to continue sharing the Communion cup with believers. In Hus' condemnation of this papal order, he openly supported the Eucharist practice—a belief that all Protestants still share.

Today when you take Communion in a church, you can thank Hus and his followers for demanding that right.

Hus' friends were still outraged that he was being held in a prison without a trial. Since Vaclav wanted nothing to do with the situation, Czech noblemen who were friends of Hus signed their names and placed their seals on numerous formal protests over the treatment of Hus. When the Council of Constance received the protests, they ordered the 452 nobles to appear before the council. Not one of them obeyed. [96]

Vultures Will Eat Their Own

While Hus was wasting away in prison and struggling to keep his mental sharpness, the councilmen were having a grand time. Constance was a small city, but due to the council, it had expanded into an armed camp since close to five thousand people attended the meeting. After the council convened each day, fifteen hundred prostitutes offered their services after hours. [97]

In this atmosphere of fraud and hypocrisy, Pope John XXIII found himself betrayed. He was shocked to learn that some of his enemies were preparing to present a record of his immoral crimes, including murder and sodomy, to the council. [98]

A committee of cardinals advised him to avoid the conflict and resign. John took their advice, read a formal resignation, and then fled, disguised as a laborer. But the council turned on him and sent a committee to find John and bring him back as a prisoner.

Fifty-four charges were presented against him, the least of which found the former Pope John XXIII a liar and a thief. Sixteen other accusations were suppressed for being too severe. On May 29, 1415, the council deposed him, and John XXIII was imprisoned for three years. [99]

The council celebrated its triumph over John XXIII with a grand parade through the city of Constance. Pope Gregory of Rome and Pope Benedict of Avignon were ordered to resign. Gregory was willing to comply on the condition that he would not be banished. The council agreed, declared him a valid pope in spirit only, and named him governor of Ancona in Italy. Benedict refused to resign. [100]

Chained in a Castle

When John XXIII fled, his jailers left the keys to Hus' cell with Sigismund. At that moment, Sigismund could have released Hus. But instead, Sigismund had Hus transferred by night, under heavy guard, to a castle in Gottlieben. There, Hus was kept in strict isolation, having his feet in bonds during the day and one of his hands chained to the castle wall at night. [101]

Since all of ex-pope John's men had fled, a new council of judges was assigned to the Hus case. Of course, the council was unjust. Each new member hated Hus as much as the first council; Hus realized he would receive no justice from them. Hus had to undergo the same questions over and over again, just as the first council had interrogated him.

Finally, the Czech and Polish nobles intervened on Hus' behalf. The nobles' appeals that only a public trial would prove if Hus was guilty or not eventually convinced the council. They promised to hear Hus at a public meeting on June 5, 1415. After five months in prison, Hus would finally be able to publicly state his case!

But when the long-desired and hard-fought-for morning of June 5 came, the council met, as usual, without Hus. They proceeded to discuss the heretical issues that Hus was accused of—all in his absence!

A servant of one of the Czech nobles happened to overhear it. He ran to tell the other nobles, who immediately informed Sigismund. Sigismund sent an order that stopped the meeting, forbidding that anything be decided in Hus' absence.

Castle Gottlieben, on the Rhine, where Hus was chained to the wall in isolation.

Only then was Hus—weak, filthy, and smelling rank from the dungeon dampness—brought into the dining hall of the monastery for a hearing. However, none of his friends were permitted inside; they had to stand outside, listening as Hus tried to defend himself against the shouts of the council.

Whenever Hus tried to explain himself, the council ordered him to answer only yes or no. When Hus remained silent, the council claimed that the silence was an admission of guilt. Finally, the council decided there was too much anger and commotion for a useful meeting, so they adjourned until the next Friday.

For the Sake of Conscience

Before the next meeting, the Czech nobles urged Hus to recant and save his life. But Hus would not hear of it. They finally told Hus to follow his conscience and, under no circumstances, to do anything that violated his conscience. Hus followed that advice. [102]

The next Friday, a weary Hus was again brought into the dining hall of the monastery. This time Sigismund was present. Over and over Hus was questioned about the sermons he had preached and asked if he believed in doctrines contrary to the Catholic Church. Over and over Hus tried to give his answers, but they always cut him off.

When Hus was questioned on his beliefs and answered that a charge wasn't true, one of the council would smirk and point out that there were twenty witnesses against him. Any word from a witness was "the truth" and any answer from Hus was "a lie."

Then they asked Hus if he once stated that he wanted to be where Wycliffe was. Hus responded, "I desire in hope that my soul were where the soul of John Wyclif is!" [103] The council laughed loudly at Hus' response—they all believed that Wycliffe was in hell.

I can't help but shake my head at these men. If history had not accurately recorded it, it would be hard to convince the world that these men were so demonized. I can only imagine the hopelessness that threatened to engulf John Hus.

Even in his weakened state, Hus refused to recant. The council stood up at various times with their fists in the air and shouted at him. Even Sigismund took part in the dispute and told Hus he should be willing to recant any and all errors, whether or not he was guilty of them. But for truth's sake, and for conscience' sake, Hus could not recant something he was not guilty of. Truth to him meant more than that. Hus was then led away and returned to his cell.

King Sigismund, the Slime

After all the others had departed, only the cardinals and Sigismund remained. The Czech nobles sensed that something was going on, so they stood outside the window and listened. The silent horror on their faces grew in distorted measures as they actually heard Sigismund urge the group of council dignitaries to burn Hus if he would not recant. One of the cardinals spoke up and asked, "What if Hus did recant?" Sigismund answered that even if Hus recanted, "Do not believe him, nor would I believe him." [104] He warned them not to allow Hus to return to Bohemia because he would continue to encourage heresies and their purpose would be defeated. He reminded the cardinals that their goal was to exterminate all known heresies and heretics, and that specifically included Hus. Sigismund even told them to burn Jerome of Prague as well.

The nobles were frozen with disbelief. Finally, they had heard the true character of Sigismund. They quickly ran to tell the others what they had heard. History writes that the words heard from that window were soon broadcast throughout Bohemia. Sigismund had become their most hated enemy, and for seventeen years after the death of Vaclav, Sigismund was unable to secure the Bohemian crown because of the people's intense hatred for him. [105]

When Hus heard the news, he was deeply hurt and emotionally wounded. He realized that Sigismund had condemned him even more quickly than his enemies. Slowly, he began to realize that he would never return to Bohemia. He knew that he had come to the end of his life; at this point, all his efforts to keep his ministry were fruitless. Strangely, of all the things he had to think about, Hus was most concerned with paying the money back that he had borrowed from a friend to make the trip to Constance. He was troubled that he wouldn't be able to pay back the debt.

I Can't Renounce What I Didn't Do!

The next day, Hus was brought before the council again and underwent more questioning. He patiently endured the testimonies of false witnesses, saying only to their accusations, "It is not true." [106]

The council ordered that Hus' writings be condemned. From this point on, Hus knew his fate was sealed. He mentioned this in his letters, writing in one, "This is my final intention in the name of Jesus Christ: that I refuse to confess as erroneous the articles which have been truthfully abstracted and, to abjure [renounce] the articles ascribed to me by false witnesses....For God knows that I have never preached those errors which they have concocted...." [107]

But the council still did not render a verdict, returning Hus to his cell again. A great many people came to Hus' cell, begging him to recant, some saying that it was honorable to submit to the Church, even if one was not guilty of the crime charged. An Englishman came and read him some of the recantations that Wycliffe's followers made. A certain doctor argued with Hus that if the council said he had one eye although he had two, he should consent to their opinion. [108]

The entire ordeal was a long, drawn-out process with many ups and downs—from the false words, the prisons, the council, the delays, down to the many questions that were asked of Hus.

Amazing Character

Hus could discern that the sentencing was near. With all the emotional instability the council was creating, Hus probably almost hoped for the sentencing to come.

Even with all that Palec had done to him, Hus wanted one more chance at reconciliation with his old friend. So Hus asked that Palec be his priest for confession.

It had to have been a very moving scene. Palec came to Hus' cell and haughtily tried to talk him into recanting. Hus looked Palec in the eyes and asked him what he would do if asked to recant something he never believed. Palec hesitated, then looked away as he whispered, "That is difficult." [109] Then Palec began to weep.

Hus then touched him on the shoulder and asked Palec to forgive him for calling Palec a deceiver. When that was settled, Hus mentioned the many lies that Palec had hurled at him, most of which Palec denied. The two men wept as they talked. [110]

How many of us would have asked our enemies to forgive us for calling them what they were? The situation again showed the impeccable character of John Hus.

The Sentence: "God, Forgive Them"

On the morning of July 6, 1415, Hus stood before the council one final time. His appearance was now very different from the man who had pastored and preached in Bethlehem Chapel. His frail body was so weakened that he could hardly stand; his emancipated hands seemed tiny as they hung down underneath the heavy iron shackles.

Thirty articles were read against him. When he tried to protest certain statements, he was told that he should be silent and that he could speak at the end. But when the end came, Hus was not allowed to speak. The cardinal told Hus they had already heard enough from him.

A bishop then stood to read the sentence. Hus was declared an obstinate disciple of Wycliffe, repeatedly disobedient to church authorities, who unlawfully appealed his case to Jesus Christ. As an incorrigible heretic, Hus was to be stripped of his priestly office and then turned over to secular authorities and burned. His writings were also to be publicly burned at the same time as Hus' sentence. When Hus quietly asked if the writings had ever been read, he was met with a cascade of angry shouts to silence him.

Condemnation of Hus. *(Brozik)*

As the shouts echoed through the halls, Hus turned to look at Sigismund for the last time. Red in the face, Sigismund turned his head and looked away. Perhaps, the innocence and purity of Hus was too much for him to look upon.

Realizing that his hour had come, Hus fell to his knees and prayed aloud, "Lord Jesus Christ, I implore Thee, forgive all my enemies for Thy great mercy's sake." [111]

Hus' entire life had been preparation for this one final moment.

At the hour of his death, Hus implored the Lord, "Forgive all my enemies for Thy great mercy's sake."

True Confessions

The seven arrogant bishops stripped Hus of his priestly office. Hus was ordered to mount a platform and put on the priestly vestments, as if he were conducting a Mass.

Then, a bishop haughtily took the cup from Hus' hands and pronounced a curse upon him. Hus loudly answered back, "But I trust in the Lord, Almighty God,...that He will not take the cup of His salvation from me. I have the firm hope that I shall today drink of it in His kingdom." [112] They took off his vestments, pronouncing another curse with each article. To each curse, Hus responded that he would suffer only for the sake of Christ. They cut off his hair in four different sections, depriving him of all ministerial rights. Finally they placed a paper crown on his head, which was painted with three red devils fighting for his soul. It was inscribed, "This is a heresiarch." [113] They backed away, put their hands out toward him, and committed Hus' soul to the devil. Hus responded that he was committing himself to Jesus Christ.

Then he was turned over to the soldiers.

"I'm Gladly Willing to Die"

A sad procession accompanied Hus to the meadow where he was to be burned; nearly the whole town followed him. As he passed the church cemetery where his books were being burned, Hus smiled.

Once at the meadow, Hus again fell to his knees to pray. He was stripped of all his clothing, except for a thin shirt, and then tied to a stake by a rope and an old rusty chain. They stacked bundles of wood mixed with straw up to his chin.

Before the fire was set, Hus was approached one last time and asked to recant. As a hush fell over the crowd, Hus lifted his voice and, speaking in German, said, [114] "God is my witness that...the principal intention of my preaching and of all my other acts or writings was solely that I might turn men from sin. And in that truth of the Gospel that I wrote, taught, and preached in accordance with the sayings and expositions of the holy doctors, I am willing gladly to die today." [115]

Murmurs and gasps rippled through the massive crowd. Then all grew quiet. The executioners were ordered to set the fire.

As the flames began to grow, Hus could be heard singing in a loud voice, "Christ, Thou Son of the living God, have mercy on me." [116] He was only able to sing it three times before the wind blew the flames into his face. Hus dropped his voice and prayed silently until the flames consumed him. While the flames on earth were still ravishing his body, Hus' spirit was already in heaven with the Lord.

Hus' execution: He was burned to death as a heretic on July 6, 1415.

✯✯✯✯✯

The executioners found Hus' heart. Piercing it with a stick, they watched as it was incinerated. The body continued to burn until nothing was left but ashes. When Hus' entire body was consumed, they loaded the ashes in a cart and threw the entire load into the Rhine River. [117]

Hus' Death Unleashes God's Warriors

The execution of Hus sent shock waves throughout Bohemia. Nearly five hundred Czech nobles gathered in Prague and protested his trial and his death. They entered into a solemn covenant, pledging to defend Hus' teachings and the Czech reformation against any and all threats.

They kept their word.

By 1419, four years after the death of Hus, this group was one to be reckoned with. They became known as the Hussites, one of the most feared groups of people in central Europe. And Jan Zizka, who attended Hus' services as Queen Zofie's bodyguard, became their renowned and feared leader!

After Hus' death, his cause lived on, through a group of Hussites, led by Jan Zizka—the queen's bodyguard who had attended Hus' church.

Unlike Hus, the Hussites refused to diplomatically settle their disputes with the Catholic Church. Hus' death only proved to them that the papal system couldn't be reasoned with, so they didn't try to compromise. They valiantly laid out their requests; if the requests were denied, they answered the Catholic Church with a bloody force.

For example, if the Catholics took one of their reformed churches, the Hussites would break the door down, reclaim it, and hold Communion—where everyone partook of the cup. If Catholic councilmen held reformers in jail and wouldn't release them, the Hussites threw the councilmen out the windows to their deaths. Extreme? Yes. But it was a revolution!

Under the fearless leadership of Zizka, their settlements were fortified and a militia was skillfully trained. Lacking conventional weapons, his men adapted their farming tools into utensils of war. Zizka called his trained militia the "Warriors of God." [118]

Sigismund, whom they called the Dragon of the Apocalypse, was their deadliest enemy. When Vaclav died, Sigismund had the rightful seat for the crown of Bohemia—but the Hussites wouldn't allow him in their country! When Sigismund declared war on Bohemia, the Hussites readily accepted.

The Hussites created a banner with the image of the chalice (Communion cup) that soon became the symbol of the entire movement. The banner read, "Truth conquers," one of Hus' famous quotes. [119] The Hussites were said to have created such fear by their fighting that an army once fled just at the sight of the Hussite banner.

The Hussites also invented the first armored war wagon, loaded with bowmen and gunmen. The armored wagons protected the shooters while they reloaded. Before the Hussites, guns had never been used in open-field battle. They were credited as having the first documented use of mobile firepower in Europe! Once the Hussites filled the war wagons with rocks and rolled them down a hill. The attacking force reacted with such panic that fourteen hundred soldiers were flattened or killed while trying to retreat! [120]

Although they were vastly outnumbered, their sheer tenacity to fight for the truth regardless of the circumstances allowed them to successfully repel six crusading armies led by Sigismund against them.

For twenty-one years, the Hussites remained a force to be feared, especially by Sigismund. Only when Sigismund came to an agreement with the Hussites was he able to secure the crown of Bohemia. He had been waiting seventeen years for the moment to be crowned—and he died after only a year of wearing it. [121]

The Truth Conquers All: Pope John II's Admission

I stated at the beginning of this chapter that the life of Hus affected most of the reformers who were to come. His doctrines are many, but the area that strikes me the most was his stand for truth.

On December 17, 1999, Pope John Paul II told an international symposium, "Today, on the eve of the Great Jubilee, I feel the need to express regret for the cruel death inflicted on Jan Hus." [122] He complimented the moral courage Hus demonstrated in the face of death and adversity and even went on to announce that Catholic scholars were now making Hus a subject of dialogue.

The pope's announcement was 584 years too late to save Hus, but the truths that Hus believed in did rise to the top. From the pope's declaration in 1999, we see that truth conquered and prevailed.

Truth does conquer all. Absolute truth—truth for all people, for all times, and for all places—will always win out. It will always rise to the top, no matter how covered over with lies or how disguised with deception it may be. It doesn't matter how long it takes; truth will always prevail. Lies and deception will fall away and truth will remain.

Times and customs will change. Guidelines change with differing circumstances. But know this: Truth is not a matter of personal taste; it's not a matter of personal likes and dislikes. Truth is not relative—truth is absolute.

Today our generation believes that everything in life is negotiable and that there aren't any rights or wrongs. They think that if someone believes something is right or if something feels right, then that must be truth. Or they'll say, "Just because it's wrong for you doesn't mean it's wrong for me." This is incorrect. There is only one true God, and His rules must be followed.

Jesus said in John 8:32 that known truth will keep our lives free. The known truth comes only from the Word of God. I challenge you to know the truth, because our generation is crying for it. Don't stop at the letter of the law. Don't be self-righteous or judgmental about it. Dig deeper and find out why God instituted that absolute truth; find out His spiritual laws and principles. There's much more written in the Word of God than we'll ever discover in our lifetime on earth.

So I close this chapter with the incredible words of an incredible man, John Hus. These words caused him to strive to the very end—and they still live on almost six hundred years after his death.

> *Therefore, faithful Christian, seek the truth, hear the truth, learn the truth, love the truth, speak the truth, adhere to the truth, defend the truth to death; for truth will make you free from sin, the devil, the death of the soul, and finally from eternal death.* [123]

★★★★★

Notes

The print of Hus on the title page is courtesy of the Billy Graham Center Museum, Wheaton, Ill.

[1] Matthew Spinka, *John Hus' Concept of the Church* (Princeton, New Jersey: Princeton University Press, 1966): 102.

[2] Timothy George, "The Reformation Connection," *Christian History Magazine* 19; no. 4, issue 68: 36.

[3] Matthew Spinka, *John Hus: A Biography* (Princeton, New Jersey: Princeton University Press, 1968): 22.

[4] Ibid.

[5] Ibid., 4.

[6] Ibid., 23–24.

[7] Ibid., 24–25.

[8] Ibid., 28–29.

[9] Ibid.

[10] Ibid.

[11] Spinka, *John Hus' Concept of the Church,* 41.

[12] Spinka, *John Hus: A Biography,* 46.

[13] Ibid., 29.

[14] Ibid., 32.

[15] Ibid., 34.

[16] Ibid., 38.

[17] George, 36.

[18] Spinka, *John Hus: A Biography,* 14.

[19] Ibid., 15.

[20] Spinka, *John Hus' Concept of the Church,* 14.

[21] Ibid., 43.

[22] Ibid., 56.

[23] Spinka, *John Hus: A Biography,* 49.

[24] Ibid., 48.

[25] Ibid., 49.

[26] Maartje M. Abbenhuis, "Foes in High Places," *Christian History Magazine* 19, no. 4, issue 68: 20.

[27] Thomas A. Fudge, "To Build a Fire," *Christian History Magazine* 19, no. 4, issue 68: 12.

[28] Abbenhuis, 21.

[29] Spinka, *John Hus' Concept of the Church,* 45.

[30] Ibid.

★★★★★

[31] Bruce L. Shelley, "A Pastor's Heart," *Christian History Magazine*, 19, no. 4, issue 68: 30.
[32] Ibid.
[33] Spinka, *John Hus' Concept of the Church*, 296–297.
[34] Ibid., 297.
[35] Ibid., 298–299.
[36] Ibid., 303.
[37] Ibid., 304–305.
[38] Ibid., 306.
[39] Ibid., 308.
[40] Ibid., 309.
[41] Ibid., 312.
[42] Ibid., 313.
[43] Ibid., 393.
[44] Ibid., 269.
[45] Ibid., 283.
[46] Spinka, *John Hus: A Biography*, 67.
[47] Ibid., 68.
[48] Fudge, 12.
[49] Spinka, *John Hus: A Biography*, 75–76.
[50] Ibid., 77–78.
[51] George, 37.
[52] Shelley, 31.
[53] Ibid.
[54] Spinka, *John Hus' Concept of the Church*, 296.
[55] Peter E. Prosser, "A Plethora of Pontiffs," *Christian History Magazine* 19, no. 4, issue 68: 23.
[56] Fudge, 12.
[57] Prosser, 24.
[58] Ibid., 24–25.
[59] Spinka, *John Hus' Concept of the Church*, 96.
[60] Fudge, 13–14.
[61] Ibid., 13.
[62] Spinka, *John Hus' Concept of the Church*, 137.
[63] Ibid., 99.
[64] Fudge, 13.
[65] Spinka, *John Hus: A Biography*, 116.
[66] Ibid.
[67] Ibid.

[68] Ibid., 126–127.
[69] Ibid., 127–128.
[70] Abbenhuis, 19.
[71] Spinka, *John Hus: A Biography,* 140.
[72] Ibid., 138.
[73] Ibid., 151.
[74] Frieda Looser, "The Wanderer," *Christian History Magazine* 19, no. 4, issue 68: 29.
[75] Fudge, 15.
[76] Ibid.
[77] Spinka, *John Hus: A Biography,* 161.
[78] Ibid., 162.
[79] Ibid., 163.
[80] Ibid., 164.
[81] Ibid., 165.
[82] Shelley, 32.
[83] Spinka, *John Hus, A Biography,* 101.
[84] Spinka, *John Hus' Concept of the Church,* 261.
[85] Abbenhuis, 21.
[86] Spinka, *John Hus' Concept of the Church,* 331.
[87] Ibid., 353.
[88] Ibid., 337.
[89] Ibid., 340.
[90] Fudge, "To Build a Fire," 15–16.
[91] Elesha Coffman, "Did You Know?" *Christian History Magazine* 19, no.4, issue 68: 2.
[92] Fudge, 15.
[93] Spinka, *John Hus' Concept of the Church,* 346.
[94] Ibid., 234.
[95] Ibid., 354.
[96] Fudge, 16.
[97] Ibid., 25.
[98] Spinka, *John Hus' Concept of the Church,* 377–378.
[99] Prosser, 25.
[100] Ibid.
[101] Spinka, *John Hus' Concept of the Church,* 356.
[102] Fudge, 16.
[103] Spinka, *John Hus' Concept of the Church,* 363.
[104] Ibid., 369.

[105] Abbenhuis, 21.
[106] Spinka, *John Hus' Concept of the Church,* 374.
[107] Ibid., 374–375.
[108] Ibid., 376.
[109] Ibid., 377.
[110] Ibid.
[111] Ibid., 381.
[112] Paul Roubiczek and Joseph Kalmer, *Warrior of God* (London: Nicholson and Watson, 1947): 241.
[113] Spinka, *John Hus' Concept of the Church,* 381.
[114] Spinka, *John Hus: A Biography,* 25.
[115] Fudge, 18.
[116] Spinka, *John Hus' Concept of the Church,* 382.
[117] Ibid.
[118] Elesha Coffman, "Rebels to be Reckoned With," *Christian History Magazine* 19, no. 4, issue 68, 40–41.
[119] Ibid., 41.
[120] Coffman, "Did You Know?" 2.
[121] Abbenhuis, 21.
[122] Elesha Coffman, "Accidental Radical," *Christian History Magazine* 19, no. 4, issue 68, 8.
[123] Spinka, *John Hus' Concept of the Church,* 320.

CHAPTER THREE

Martin Luther

1483–1546

"The Battle-Ax of Reform"

"THE BATTLE-AX OF REFORM"

I was born to war with fanatics and devils. Thus my books are very stormy and bellicose [war-like and belligerent]. **I must root out the stumps and trunks, hew away the thorns and briar, fill in the puddles. I am the rough woodsman, who must pioneer and hew a path.** [1]

These are the words of a man who would accidentally reform the world as fourteenth-century Europe knew it. I say accidentally because Martin Luther's early life as a submissive young monk showed no signs that, within him, he had the potential to lead a spiritual revolution that would blow up the age-old doctrines of the Roman Catholic Church. He was a man on a mission, but it wasn't to expose the errors of religion. His mission was simply to make peace with God. He wasn't taught what most of us know: that Jesus came to reconcile us to God and that believing in Him was what appeased God.

He knew only what had been passed down for generations through the tradition of Roman Catholicism and the myths of German paganism: God was angry and Jesus was a hard and impossible-to-please Judge who delighted in sending men, women, and children to hell. Luther lay awake quivering many nights as a boy, afraid of the goblins and demons that religion taught lived in the woods.

The Dark Ages were what they were because there was no light of truth from the Gospel penetrating the hearts of the people. It was illegal for a common man to own a Bible. The only Bibles available were in Latin, for the exclusive use of the priests, many of whom had never read them. Spiritual darkness always ends up making entire territories, nations, and, in this case, continents dark in every walk of life. And for sensitive Luther, these wrong teachings about God brought unending torment. Convinced that the only answer for pleasing God was to become a monk, he joined the priesthood. Much to the devil's dismay, Luther came into contact with the Bible. Educated in Latin as a boy, he dug through it with ease and even learned Greek to further examine the texts.

Luther was a man on a mission. His mission was not to expose the errors of religion but simply to make peace with God.

Luther's story is one that shows the power of what can happen to someone who gets into God's Word and doesn't come out. The light of revelation began to shine in Luther's dark mind, leaving no shadows where the devil could torment him.

He didn't get into trouble until he wanted to share the Good News with his mentor and other leaders. He also got in trouble for having some questions that, if it weren't for divine providence, could have gotten him burned at the stake. These ninety-five questions, known as the Ninety-Five Theses, are printed in their entirety at the end of this chapter. The revelations of most of the biblical truths we consider common today came from them.

Luther's posting of these Ninety-Five Theses on the Wittenburg Church door is one of the most famous events in church history and had such a divine impact upon the earth that we are still experiencing its repercussions today. Although many great men and women had an integral part in what became known as the Reformation, whenever it is written about or spoken of, Luther's name is at the top of the list of people who spearheaded it. Because God used him in this way, Luther often stood alone, lost friendships and family, stirred international conflict, angered leaders of nations, and created chaos for the Roman Catholic Church.

My prayer for you as you read Luther's story is that you will see that your past or circumstances have no bearing on what a touch from heaven, a revelation of God's Word, and a sense of mission and calling can do for you. There is no way Luther could ever have imagined what his road of obedience would lead to. God used him to affect the whole world, but I'm sure that, as a frightened little boy, this was the last thing on his mind.

Spare the Rod, Please

Martin was born November 10, 1483, in Eisleben, Germany, to Hans and Margaretha Luder (Martin would change his last name to Luther in college). Within six months of his birth, the family moved to Mansfeld, Germany, and his father took work in the copper mines.

Martin learned the rewards of hard work from his parents' diligence. He watched as his father endured the severest of labors, pulling his family up from one economic class to the next. Starting as a worker in the mines, the elder Luther eventually established two smelter furnaces of his own and became respected in the community. This introduced the Luther family to a whole new class of people. Soon Martin was sitting down to dinner with people of stature in the community, officials from surrounding territories, schoolmasters, and the clergy.

Not only was young Luther's mother a woman of prayer, but his father would nightly tuck him in bed and kneel to pray at his side.

Though the Luthers had graduated out of the peasant class, there was one trait characteristic of the peasant class that they didn't leave behind. Most among that class were extremely God-fearing. Not only was young Luther's mother a woman of prayer, but Luther recalled nightly being tucked away in bed, with his father kneeling to pray by his side.

For the Luthers, prayer and discipline went hand in hand. Martin didn't remember his parents ever sparing the rod, though he wrote later that he wished they had. Never questioning their good intentions, Martin was critical of his parents' beatings. His mother once drew blood while beating him with a cane for stealing a nut. On another occasion, his father's discipline was so intense that Martin needed quite a bit of time, coaxing, and numerous apologies to warm up to his father again.

By today's standards, these punishments would be deemed as child abuse, but, in that day, they were common, and the school system took up where the parents left off. A student could get up to fifteen birchings (whippings) a week! The school's main objective was to teach Latin. Latin was the language of the church, law, diplomacy, international relations, scholarship, and travel. To instill Latin, the instructors used drill exercises. Failure in the drills resulted in the rod. [2]

During the morning hours of the day, one student, an appointed spy, would listen to see if any of the other students slipped and accidentally spoke in German. If a student spoke German instead of Latin, he had to wear a donkey's mask until another student made the same mistake. At that time the mask was passed on. Demerits for making mistakes throughout the week were accumulated, and discipline was administered at the end of each week. Most of the boys didn't resent the technique. They actually rose to the challenge, and Martin so excelled through this technique of learning that he was nicknamed "The Philosopher."

Luther's childhood schooling was already preparing him to be a man of influence. God had determined his destiny.

The intense training and discipline was part of Martin's conditioning, which prepared him to be a man of influence and position. He knew power was his destiny, but he didn't know how that destiny would play out. He had watched his father rise above the odds and break his family out of the peasant class. In young Luther's mind, his father was a hero, so he thought he must be just like his father. All he would need to do was walk out the plans his father had for him—to be successful, wealthy, and marry well enough to care for his parents in their old age.

After completing his baccalaureate and masters degrees at the University of Erfurt in record time, he stayed on to study law, which was his father's ambition for him.

★★★★★

Martin seemed content with his lot in life and the expectations of his father. On July 2, 1501, when he was twenty years old, he was on his way to attaining these goals when it was all interrupted by a thunderstorm.

"Help Me, St. Anne. I Will Become a Monk!"

I love thunderstorms! I remember the massive thunderstorms that would roll in and rattle the Oklahoma plains where I was raised. They were refreshing to me. Living in southern California, I really miss the flash of lightning, the sound of rumbling thunder, and torrential rains.

But people in the Middle Ages didn't share my fondness for thunderstorms. A thunderstorm is nothing in and of itself, but to the men and women of Luther's era, it was a sign of God's judgment.

Up to this point, Luther's life was on track and in motion for his career as a lawyer. He had a good life ahead of him. His family was happy. However, all of this was about to change. He had been home for a visit to see his family when, on his walk back to school, that fateful thunderstorm rolled in.

He was coming through the forest, anticipating a clearing just ahead. No doubt, he was consumed with fear as his imagination played games with him. Luther had been taught well, so he knew that to his right and left, in front of and behind him, lurked elves, gnomes, fairies, sprites, and witches. He had seen them depicted in the popular wall hangings of the day. He believed entire geographical regions were inhabited by devils and knew of a lake that held captured demons in its waters. Legend had it that throwing a stone into the lake could awaken the demons and they would stir up storms. [3]

Demons received a lot of blame in his day; even his mother blamed evil spirits when eggs, milk, or butter were stolen. But worse than the demons stirring up the storm was the idea that God might have. It was a common thought of the day that God used storms to judge people. The most famous wood carving in the known world of Christendom portrayed Jesus and demons working in collaboration with each other to send evil men to their doom. In the picture, Jesus sat, very displeased, on the throne of judgment. Below Him, demons were dragging men and women away into the fires of hell. Luther saw pictures like this when he was just a boy, and they built impenetrable strongholds in his mind.

Walking through the woods that night was possibly the most frightening experience of Luther's life. You can imagine the scene; he was terrified and his heart must have been beating out of his chest. As he approached the clearing, he remembered the death of a friend who fell to a similar judgment when a lightning bolt struck him dead. The scene was all too familiar. He knew his hour had come. He started walking through the clearing when lightning struck so near to where he was walking that he was knocked to the ground. In a desperate plea for his life, he cried out to the only help he knew: "St. Anne help me! I will become a monk." [4]

With these two short sentences, lifted up in a desperate cry, Luther was sure he was calling on all the power available to him. He cried out to Anne because she was the merciful grandmother of Jesus, or so legend had it.

Why would someone change his life pursuit from becoming an attorney to becoming a monk with one strike of lightning? In this case, it wasn't a sense of calling as some historians have said. Everyone in Luther's day knew the best assurance for salvation from hell was to become a monk. Out of sheer terror for his life, he disappointed his family and moved into the monastery.

The Power of Saint Anne

Because few in the Roman Catholic Church had a personal relationship with Jesus, it was difficult for the pagan German culture to understand why people worshiped an invisible God. The problem dated back to A.D. 300. The answer to the problem then was the creation of statues: statues of Paul, statues of Jesus and, last but certainly not least for the Roman Catholics, statues of Mary. From that point on, it became a common practice in both the Roman Catholic and Greek Orthodox Churches to honor and pray to the dead saints. This, of course, is not permissible according to Scripture.

For the Luther family, the favorite saint was Anne. She was known as the patron saint of the mines. Hans Luther, a miner, had called upon her assistance throughout young Luther's life, and his family gave her due credit for the successes they had achieved. Added to his experiences in which she granted the family favor was the idea that she was Mary's mother.

The spirit of religion in the church had completely twisted the image of the Godhead in the minds of the people. Terrified of God and Jesus, the people would pray to Mary, the mother of Jesus. To the people, Mary was the only approachable one of the bunch. Only she could exercise influence over Jesus, the impossible-to-please judge. It was even believed that she, being a woman, wasn't past cheating both God and the devil on behalf of the person praying to her. Once petitioned by His mother, Jesus might then intervene on the wrath of God and provoke Him to mercy. [5]

But here's another twist. The people knew that, with the demands of an entire world of people being placed on Mary, she might be too busy to help them. So they were taught to call on St. Anne, Mary's mother, who would go to Mary, who would go to Jesus, who would, in turn, go to God, who might reverse the coming judgment. [6]

We don't have to find a roundabout way to approach God. We have an Advocate with the Father and can enter His presence boldly.

This was a very roundabout way to approach God. Though it may seem laborious and perhaps amusing, these were, and still are, the common, daily practices of a people who are sincere before God. Aren't you glad that we have an Advocate with the Father and that we can enter into the throne of God boldly, without shame, to obtain help in time of need? Probably the only people who knew this in Luther's day were beheaded or were burned at the stake for attempting to tell someone else.

People who challenged the principles of the Roman Catholic Church in the Middle Ages with real, scriptural truth often faced execution. Maybe you have never realized the price paid for you to have a Bible, which may be collecting dust on your coffee table. Let us all remember and turn to the Word of God with a revived respect and hunger.

The Power of Becoming a Monk

The other component of Luther's cry in the night after he had been knocked to the ground was his vow to become a monk. Again, this was not out of a sense of calling, though I think his obsession with God and the supernatural was evidence of that calling. Why become a monk, though? The answer is found in what becoming a monk would ultimately do for him. It was the one thing he hadn't done to attain the assurance of salvation. One of his autobiographers said, "To the monastery he went like others, and even more than others, in order to make his peace with God." [7]

Becoming a monk was the surest way to receive preferential treatment with God. People believed that the monk's vow was the second baptism, which restored a man to a state of innocence. Legend said that a monk had died without his frock and came to the gate of paradise only to be denied entry. Only after he returned to earth for the frock and came to heaven's gate dressed appropriately was he allowed in. [8]

I'm sure you can see why the Dark Ages were so dark. No one publicly acknowledged the truth and light of Jesus Christ. Even those who could read Latin couldn't, or wouldn't, discern the true from the false.

There were no Protestant preachers yet—Luther himself made the way for them. A person was either a Catholic or a heretic, and there was no in-between. All Luther knew to do was surrender and become a monk. And God worked with that cry and with what I believe was a sincere heart that sought after God. In the dark corner of Luther's monastery, God led and guided him to the truth. It wouldn't be long before he would come forth with a truth that would loose all of Christendom from its bondage.

Taking the Oath

In spite of his father's fury with his decision to become a monk, Martin chose the strictest monastery, the Order of the Augustinian Hermits in Erfurt, Germany. He knew what he was getting himself into when he lay before the prior, the head of the monastery, prostrate on the steps. He was committing to at least one probationary year of scant diet, rough clothing, vigils by night, labors by day, mortification of the flesh, the reproach of poverty, and the shame of begging. He agreed to it all. He was allowed into that year of initiation with a kiss on the cheek from the prior and his admonishment that a man was only saved if he endured to the end.

★★★★★

Martin could think of only one monk who had endured to the end. It was William of Anhalt. William had given up nobility to become a begging friar. Everyone in town knew him. Luther once wrote:

> With my own eyes I saw him....I was fourteen years old at Magdeburg. I saw him carrying the sack like a donkey. He had so worn himself down by fasting and vigil that he looked like a death's-head, mere bone and skin. No one could look upon him without feeling ashamed of his own life. [9]

Watching this monk from a distance, all those years ago, Luther had decided that this was the way to salvation. And for that probationary year, he was convinced he had finally arrived at a place of peace. He lived one full year without the torments and nightmares that came over him like a cold chill when he considered God and his own soul.

But, true to form, the religious spirit always comes back to say, "Not even this is enough. You must do more. You must be better." After his probation, Luther took the next step and made his life commitment to God. With that vow of commitment, the torment returned. Torturing religious spirits would come upon him, bringing bouts of oppression, depression, and hopelessness. Luther would seem fine one minute, and then, suddenly, he would be driven into despondency. Trying to stop the agony, he began to search for new ways to appease God.

If joining the monastery wasn't enough, then he thought the answer must lie in adhering to every rule and following every guideline. He bombarded heaven with works in pursuit of attaining holiness. Luther made his decision to be the most intense of all the monks. He would sleep fewer hours, fast more meals, and spend more time in confession than any of the others. In fact, he wearied his priests with his confessing. He once spent six hours confessing to a priest. All this would bring only short spurts of relief. The torment would soon return, and he would have to dream up new ways to chastise the flesh and become acceptable to God.

The Bible in the monastery was fastened to the wall by a chain, and Luther constantly returned to read it, hoping to find the peace he desperately needed. But instead, it spoke to him only of a holiness he could not attain. Finding no relief, he shut himself up in his room, repeating Latin over and over. For seven weeks he hardly slept, and for four days Luther did not eat or drink. He refused to answer the knocks at his door. When fellow monks broke the door down, they found Luther lying on the floor, apparently dead. Worn-out from fasting, lack of sleep, and despair, Luther was finally restored to consciousness when he heard the echoes of the boy's choir singing hymns down the hallway.

"I was indeed a pious monk," he recalled years later. "If ever a monk could obtain heaven by his monkish works, I should certainly have been entitled to it. If it had continued much longer, I should have carried my mortifications even to death, by means of my watchings, prayers, reading, and other labors." [10]

In his quest for holiness, Luther's works were more intense than the other monks'. He constantly returned to the Bible, searching for peace.

Celebration of First Mass Ends in Defeat and Doubt

The day came in 1507 when Luther was ordained at the age of twenty-five. He now qualified to perform his first Mass. The day of the Mass had been postponed for one month because his father wasn't able to make it until then. When Luther's father did come, he entered town grandly with twenty horsemen and made a sizable donation to the monastery.

Luther was very excited to see his father and to have his father see him in his new lot in life. As wonderful as the day should have been for Luther, it would end in torment. He was so scared during the ceremony of transubstantiation (which is the part in the Catholic Mass where the bread and the wine are believed to actually become the body and blood of Jesus) that he was trembling and nearly ready to flee the altar. But his sheer terror of the almighty God and the thought that God's tangible presence was before him in the cup kept him glued to the altar. The Mass was a very nerve-racking experience. This was the highest ceremony man could participate in, and the performance of it was exalted in all of society. By his actions, the priest was symbolically reenacting Calvary.

Insecure about his performance, he sought his father's approval following the Mass. He asked his father why he didn't approve of him becoming a priest. His father replied that Luther had not followed the commandment of honoring his father and mother, and now they would have to fend for themselves in old age.

But Luther knew the right response. He knew that one had to follow the leadings of God in spite of what others thought. He felt that, if he followed God, his parents would be taken care of. If Luther didn't follow the Lord, they would all suffer.

Eventually, his father got over his anger, but only after he lost two sons to the plague and heard rumors that Luther was dead also. When he discovered that Luther was alive, his father forgave his son and forgot all their disputes.

But before their reconciliation, his father planted strong seeds of doubt and confusion in Luther's mind. On the day of Luther's first Mass, Hans Luther made a statement that sent his son into inner turmoil.

Luther felt that he needed to justify his calling and reminded his father of what happened to him during the thunderstorm. Not paying attention to any of the priests who were listening, Luther's father blurted out, "But what if it [the storm] were only a ghost?" [11]

In other words, his father asked him how he could prove the storm wasn't from the devil intended to throw off the course of the entire Luther family. His father's question rang in Luther's ears. How could he know for sure? After all, everyone knew that even the devil could masquerade as an angel of light.

This was a direct missile into the heart of all Luther's insecurities. Now, more than ever, he would give in to his pursuit of holiness. Eventually he could be consoled only by some means of self-chastisement or mortification of the flesh. At night, Luther would cast off the scant blankets issued to each monk and shiver, all in an attempt to chatise the flesh. In fasting alone was he content. And even with all the fasting he would ask himself, "Have I fasted enough?" He preferred Lent to Easter because it involved sacrifice.

He vacillated between being proud of his works, and the number of them, and being completely burdened by doubt and despair.

Religious Spirits Will Kill You

You can never please a religious spirit. I have said this hundreds of times, and I'll say it again. In all my travels throughout the world, I've encountered all kinds of evil, deceptive spirits. But I've never seen a meaner, more vicious spirit than the spirit of religion. It disguises itself so that you think you are serving God. Its nature is wicked, spiteful, jealous, and malicious. It is a murdering spirit with a "nice" camouflage. It demands horrific works that eventually send people into sin, error, or the grave. It was one of the spirits behind the betrayal of Jesus. You'll never appease it, nor will you ever please God through it.

Today, in our society, religious spirits don't openly burn people at the stake or martyr them like the Catholic Church once did. However, some acts of terrorism have a religious spirit connected to them. A common way a religious spirit tries to murder someone is by assassinating that person's reputation with gossip. We need to recognize the strategies of a religious spirit. Too quickly we run from a minister who is gossiped about. When we hear slanderous things, we need to recognize the possibility of persecution behind them and ask, "What did this person do right to be so attacked?" Our mind-set has been lulled by that religious spirit, making us want to run from the person being slandered instead of finding the truth and joining with them to bring about divine change in the earth. Our mind-set *must* be awakened and changed!

Luther was striving to please God, but God was already appeased with the blood of His Son. It was the religious spirit that demanded works.

Luther was in the process of changing his mind-set. He was striving to appease God, but God was already appeased with the blood of His Son. In reality, it was the religious spirit that couldn't be appeased, and it was working to send Luther to his grave. All Luther really wanted was acceptance from God. His whole goal was to know how to be a friend of God's. Luther thought receiving God's forgiveness was the only way this could happen, so he repented and repented at one confessional after another. But he found no relief.

Works, Works, Works?

In Hosea 4:6, the Bible says God's people perish for lack of knowledge. Through an ignorant and mostly corrupt priesthood, the Roman Catholic leadership was inventing and establishing its own religion. When the traditions stopped accomplishing their desired end, the Church would change or add to the rules.

Guilt and fear were two of the leading emotions that the church instilled to keep people coming to church. To deal with the questions of death, hell, paradise, and purgatory (a halfway point for people who were neither good enough to get into heaven, nor bad enough to go to hell), the pope and his hierarchy created a system that worked to stabilize the Church's economy and alleviate the people's guilt.

The priests taught that there was a banking system in heaven that held in its vaults the goodness the people lacked in their personal lives. They taught the people how to transfer that goodness into their accounts so they wouldn't come up short, standing before God.

The Church taught that Jesus, Mary, and the saints behaved much better on the earth than they needed to in order to get into heaven. The extra credits of their goodness were stored in the heavenly banking system, which the pope kept track of. This credit, referred to as "pooled goodness" or "treasuries of goodness," was available to common people through assigned activities from the priests, which depended on the sins the people confessed. These activities were referred to as "works." Evidence of works was issued in a kind of receipt or proof of purchase, known in that day as an indulgence. The pope alone could determine how many years could be shaved off your sentence in purgatory, and the indulgence would be written proof of that adjustment in your account. After all, the pope was the successor of St. Peter and the sole possessor of the keys to the kingdom—or so Roman Catholicism taught. [12]

Today, if you look intently enough, you can see the works mentality among fellow believers. The people who are imprisoned by a religious spirit struggle to receive forgiveness from God as they try to pay for their own sins through good deeds. In charismatic circles, it can often be seen in over-volunteering for church activities out of a need to be accepted by the leadership. These people are looking for pats on the back and a sense of approval from men. If they can attain that, they feel that God approves of them. In the Catholic Church, this feeling of appeasement comes from attending Mass no matter what. A traditional Roman Catholic won't let anything interfere with attending Mass. But the motive isn't about fellowshipping with other believers and worshiping God, as it should be; it's about earning God's acceptance. Even today, some Catholics confess their sins to a priest and then say a certain number of "Hail Marys" or light candles at an altar. This seems harmless, but it is really rooted in the same spirit that drove the people in the Middle Ages to do good works in exchange for salvation.

The works mentality causes people to try to pay for their sins through good deeds. They are imprisoned instead of set free.

In Luther's day, however, the works required a little more energy. Because the Church was trying to create an interest in the things of God and keep attendance up, they began forgiving sins for visiting certain holy sites, specifically in Rome, and viewing certain artifacts from the past. Those artifacts, or relics, included what was said to be the silver coins that Judas received for betraying Jesus and a sampling of the milk from the Virgin Mary's breast.

When a holy site or relic was visited and viewed, the pope would issue an indulgence, which was evidence of the credit of goodness that had come to a person's account based on the relic he viewed. For instance, viewing Judas' coins could take fourteen hundred years off a person's time in purgatory. Rome was the place to go if someone wanted to really stockpile goodness into his account.

Some sites were worth more than others, and Rome was filled with all kinds of relics that were taken from Jerusalem in A.D. 70 when the Roman Empire ransacked and burned the city. Rome became the new home for Pontius Pilate's staircase, the Scala Sancta, where Jesus stood to be judged by the crowd before his crucifixion. Since Jesus had once stood on them, they had the greatest value in terms of pooling goodness. But a person couldn't just look at them; he had to walk up them saying a specified prayer for each of the twenty-eight steps. One trip up the stairs had enough power in it to release a dead relative from purgatory.

Rome was also the supposed burial ground for both Paul and Peter's bodies. Church officials cut them in halves and split them between four churches so more churches could benefit from the people's visitation. Forty popes and seventy-six thousand martyrs were buried in Rome, and visiting each site added more merits. One church claimed to have the twelve-foot beam on which Judas hanged himself.

Rome was the place to go to appease God. So in 1510, when Luther was chosen to go with another representative from their cloister in Erfurt to settle a local dispute with the pope, he couldn't wait to take advantage of being near so many relics. When he got there, he stayed with the local Augustinian order, taking part in daily routines, prayer, worship, and confessions. But with every spare moment of time left in the day, he visited the sites. And not just for the value they had in reducing a sentence to purgatory but also for his very real interest in the things of God.

To give you an idea of the importance of this to him, Michaelangelo was in Rome at this time, working on the Sistine Chapel's ceiling. This held no interest for Luther. Instead, he longed to see the painting of the Virgin Mary, thought to be painted by the apostle Luke.

Rome disillusioned him though. He found the priests there loose and flippant. They raced through Mass, performing seven to his one. He was shocked one day when he overheard a conversation between the priests who were preparing the Communion. One mumbled, "Bread art thou and bread thou wilt remain, and wine art thou and wine thou wilt remain." It was very disheartening to him to see such irreverence. But he never lost faith in the sacraments, the ceremony, or the faithful priests from home. He was able to disassociate this looseness from his beliefs and convictions. So he carried on in Rome with his good works. [13]

But even in the midst of this monumental occasion, doubt entered in, and Luther questioned the validity of the whole experience. In fact, he was on the Sancta Scala, Pilate's staircase, when some of the questioning began. He was kneeling and kissing each step while saying his prayers, but he found that he was wishing his parents were already dead; he didn't wish they were dead because he didn't want to see them again. He wished they were dead so he could release them from purgatory while he was in Rome. He realized it had all become a game—where was the true authority, and who actually had it? Luther was now questioning the validity of the whole event. How could he know if even this trip to Rome pleased God? How could he be God's friend? [14]

Where was the true authority and who had it? How could a trip to Rome please God? How could Luther be God's friend?

Encounter with a Mystic

Luther returned to Erfurt from Rome and was transferred to Wittenburg, Germany, to the Augustinian Cloister there. He was going there to teach at the university. Wittenburg was a small town compared to the city of Erfurt. But the elector of that region, Frederick the Wise, wanted to build up the university in Wittenburg to rival the best in the nation.

In Wittenburg, Luther found a mentor whose faithfulness toward him stayed to the end, a priest named Johann von Staupitz.

Luther wearied his priests in Wittenburg just as he had in Erfurt. Luther knew there could be no remission of sins without confession and repentance to a priest, a priest's forgiveness, and some act of penance to pay for the sins. But to confess all of his sins, he had to first remember them. He knew the "soul must be searched...memory ransacked...motives probed," [15] to be able to draw to light all sin. But even then, Luther knew the self-protecting nature of his own ego and the fact that he may never be able to recall some sins. Therefore, even the penitential system failed him.

When no act of goodness, site of relics, or confession would help, and Luther had exhausted all the Church's ways to salvation, he fell into complete despondency. He entered into panic, and his conscience so bothered him that he trembled over the smallest thing. He also had nightmares and later said his mental state at the time was worse than any physical ailment imaginable. [16]

Staupitz tried to ease Luther's conscience through a method Luther had never considered or thought existed. Staupitz was a mystic. Not to be mistaken with witches or New Age mysticism, the mystics were a group of monks who actually found the tangible presence of God. In A.D. 300, when the church became secularized and pagan, there were a group of people who went to the desert and lived alone in search of God. They were called hermits, and the ones who experienced God operated in great signs and wonders. The name *mystic* became the label used exclusively for the hermits, later to be called monks, who had this dramatic experience in God's presence. In His presence, they found they could be changed. They also came to terms with how evil human nature was and fell into God's presence to be absorbed by His goodness.

The Mystics found that in God's presence, they were changed. The evil nature fell away as they were absorbed by His goodness.

Staupitz knew this experience firsthand, which was unusual for the people of his time. He tried to introduce Luther to God in this way, explaining that dealing with human nature through works was like dealing with chicken pox one scab at a time. The mystics did all the works that the other monks did, except they were doing them, not to be forgiven, but to be granted just one visitation from God. They fasted, worshiped, prayed, confessed, and did penance, too. But for them, it was all to draw the presence and nature of God into their lives. They were truly seeking God.

"Love God? I Hate Him."

Staupitz would try to ease Luther by encouraging him to simply love God. Luther mocked the idea of simply loving God. His image of God and Jesus was distorted. To Luther, They were angry and righteous—and, out of Their righteousness, They were going to judge man.

Later on, he spoke of the despair he felt at the time, saying,

> Is it not against all natural reason that God out of his mere whim deserts men, hardens them, damns them, as if He delighted in sins and in such torments of the wretched for eternity, He who is said to be of such mercy and goodness? This appears iniquitous, cruel, and intolerable in God, by which very many have been offended in all ages. And who would not be? I was myself more than once driven to the very abyss of despair so that I wished I had never been created. Love God? I hated Him! [17]

At last, Luther realized the greatest of all his sins. He hated God. He hated that God would judge man. He hated that he could never attain to His standard. He hated that God would turn men over to demons to be dragged away to hell when they had tried so hard to please Him. To Luther, it seemed impossible to love God.

Road to Revelation

It seemed all hope was lost. What could be done with this tormented friar? Staupitz had an idea. He gave up his own position at the University of Wittenburg and gave it to Luther. Obviously, considering Luther's state of mind, this seemed ludicrous to Luther. As far as he was concerned, he was inept, unprepared and, most of all, unworthy. Nevertheless, he was made a doctor of theology in 1512. He was twenty-nine years old.

To teach the Bible, Luther had to study the Bible. Staupitz thought perhaps Luther could work out answers to his questions in his studies. The Bible was rather new to him. It wasn't inaccessible to him or any of the other clergy, but reading it wasn't emphasized. In fact, other materials of the day were more the theological staple in his education as a monk, friar, and priest.

Turning Luther loose with a Bible was the Catholic Church's greatest mistake. *Know this: it's the ones who read the Bible that cause the trouble for dead religion.* Why? Religion works in the realm of ignorance and in the realm of the soul. It bases its facts on thoughts, legends, and what denominations dream up instead of what the actual Scriptures state.

In 1513, Luther began studying the book of Psalms, and here he started down the road of revelation that would set him free. The twenty-second Psalm cracked the door and began to let in the light. It reads,

> *My God, My God, why have You forsaken Me? Why are You so far from helping Me, and from the words of My groaning? O My God, I cry in the daytime, but You do not hear; and in the night season, and am not silent.* (vv. 1–2 NKJV)

Luther was amazed by what he read. Jesus felt abandoned and alienated by God, too. Luther's picture of an unmerciful Jesus sitting over mankind condemning them to hell was being changed. Rather than on the throne of judgment, Luther could see Jesus on the cross. Now he could almost see God's heart. He could see a glimmer of compassion behind God putting Jesus on the cross.

But he couldn't shake the image of a righteous God judging unrighteous men when it was impossible for them to be anything else. He knew God wanted justice, but even with this growing understanding of the love of God, the thought of justice made him tremble.

Faith Alone

It wasn't until he studied the Pauline Epistles that Luther began to understand the true meaning of righteousness and the justice of God. He wrestled with Paul's letters, trying to grasp the concept. One thing about Martin Luther, he used Scripture to investigate every area of personal torment. He took his questions to Paul's letters to the Romans and Galatians. Between the years 1515 and 1517, when he was lecturing on these two books of the Bible, Luther began to see what the justice of God really meant.

When Luther read in Romans 5:1 that the righteous were justified by faith, he was furious! He couldn't comprehend it! Captured by a conviction that he must understand, he turned to the Greek to find the meaning of justice. *Justice* was defined as strict enforcement of law and a pronounced sentence, just as he had always thought. So far, it still seemed like man was doomed.

But it was the Greek definition of *justification* that set him free. Justification was different than justice. Justification spoke of a process that takes place as the sentence is suspended. Justification was a process through which man could be reclaimed to God and regenerated.

Now he could see it! God didn't seek to damn but to regenerate mankind and give men a new chance at life.

But more than anything, Luther saw that even this process of regeneration, or expectation of regeneration, wasn't what made man *acceptable* before God. It was faith. Faith was a gift, and by man's faith, he was justified. Simply *believing in* the redemptive work of Jesus made His righteousness available to you. Man, through Jesus, was right with God. Faith in Jesus' work on the cross was enough! God *was* a Friend to all of mankind!

Faith is a gift, and a man is justified by his faith. Jesus' work on the cross is enough! God is a Friend to all of mankind!

Connecting these ideas of the justice of God and the Scripture *"the just shall live by faith"* (Romans 1:17) created a new theology, but it didn't come overnight. Meditation and study over a four-year period developed the strength of this revelation.

Luther said,

> At last, meditating day and night and by the mercy of God, I...began to understand that the righteous live by a gift of God, namely by faith....Here I felt as if I were entirely born again and had entered paradise itself through gates that had been flung open. [18]

In the Toilet?

Somewhere between 1518 and 1521, Luther's final revelation came to him—and it would set off a revolution.

As I study the faithful Christian leaders and the truths they brought or the miracle power they began to operate in, I think it would be encouraging for you to know that the point of revelation or power was often on the heels of great despair. Take Luther for example, or look at some of the life stories of the healing evangelists. Many of them were on their deathbeds before they functioned in a dramatic healing ministry. I'm not saying this is how it has to be. However, it is encouraging if you are going through something to know that the devil often attacks very dramatically right before a breakthrough.

Luther wrote of the days immediately preceding his breakthrough as a time when he was depressed. To quote him exactly, he said he was "in cloaca." Literally, "in cloaca" means *in the toilet.* Though some historians took him literally, he was trying to express the status of his emotions. [19]

Historians would refer to this transformation from depression into freedom as his "evangelical breakthrough" or his "tower experience." [20] Now, the phrase "justice of God" brought a pleasantness to mind rather than a hatred.

You can almost feel the peace of God in Luther's heart as he wrote of his revelation, saying,

> If you have a true faith that Christ is your Savior, then at once you have a gracious God, for faith leads you in and opens up God's heart and will, that you should see pure grace and overflowing love. This it is to behold God in faith that you should look upon his fatherly, friendly heart, in which there is neither anger nor ungraciousness. He who sees God as angry does not see him rightly but looks only on a curtain, as if a dark cloud had been drawn across his face. [21]

Luther's new revelation of Scripture resolved all the worries about demons that had been instilled in him since childhood. All his battles stopped with the Cross. In the Cross, he saw the mercy of God. And in the Cross, he saw Christ's victory over Satan and his demons.

A hymn he wrote would tell of his convictions:

> Thus spoke the Son, "Hold thou to Me,
> From now on that wilt make it.
>
> I gave my life for thee
> And for thee I will stake it.
> For I am thine and thou art mine,
> And where I am our lives entwine,
> The Old Fiend cannot shake it." [22]

✯✯✯✯✯

Nailing His Revelation to the Church Door

When Luther began to see the revelation and truth of God's redemption, he immediately saw the error in the Catholic Church. Overwhelmed by the hypocrisy, he sought to bring the Church to the light, vowing to speak out and divert the people from the path they were following.

I previously likened indulgences to a proof of purchase or receipt of sales. To have an indulgence was to have a written document that showed attainment to a certain degree of forgiveness, depending on what was done to get it. But historically, one had to perform a certain work to get an indulgence. In times of need, however, like when money needed to be raised for the Crusades, indulgences were sold to the people outright with no required activities, such as visiting Rome. Eventually, Pope Leo X would take this abuse to a new level in his attempt to complete the grandest cathedral of all time, St. Peter's Bascilica. Leo salivated at the thought of being the pope credited with finishing it. The bills for the building were enormous, and they were sure to send the Vatican into its deepest debt yet. To assist in the payment of these bills, the pope granted the new archbishop of Brandenburg the right to sell indulgences.

Tetzel selling indulgences.

To expedite the procedure and assure optimum sales, the archbishop hired himself a priest who was gifted in the sale of indulgences. His name was John Tetzel. He would ride with great pomp to the edge of town, meet there with the town's officials, and then ride ceremoniously to the town square, drawing a crowd as he went. He would plant a large cross bearing the papal arms on it and begin preaching that, with one payment, people could release their relatives from purgatory. He would earnestly manipulate the people:

"God and St. Peter call you. Consider the salvation of your souls and dead loved ones. Are you concerned, considering the temptations, etc., whether you will make heaven? Consider your confession here and contributions as a total remission—hear your dead relatives: 'Pity us, pity us...We bore you, nourished you, brought you up, left you our fortunes, and you are so cruel and hard that now you are not willing to set us free.'" [23]

Throughout Germany, the singsongy phrase of Tetzel went forth: "As soon as the coin in the coffer rings, the soul from purgatory springs." So many coins were thrown into the coffer that new coins had to be minted on the spot. [24]

When Luther found out about this, he was extremely troubled. The pretense of the indulgence upset him. He hadn't yet come into enough truth to cause him to throw the idea of selling indulgences out completely, but he was in disagreement with this kind of abuse.

Luther nails his Ninety-Five Theses to the church door at Wittenburg.
Art Resource.

So, faithful to the Augustinian order and to its original beliefs and convictions, Luther had it stamped upon his heart that the foundation of any penance, indulgence, or confession had to be contrition. A person had to be truly sorry for what he had done. With the new papal bull (order from the pope) allowing Tetzel to sell an indulgence without penance, the people had skipped an important component in the process of reconciliation—repentance.

From this state of mind, stirred by Tetzel's manipulation and the pope's abuse of power, Luther began work on a list of concerns, questions, and challenges regarding the use of indulgences. There were ninety-five when he was finished. Not even sure of the scriptural accuracy of some of his comments, he went ahead and posted them to the door of Castle Church in Wittenburg.

This act, in and of itself, was nothing extraordinary. It was what everyone did if they wanted to gather a group of people together for debate and discussion. Luther was comfortable with not even being sure of some of the statements on the document because discussing their validity was his motivation for posting them. He knew it would all get ironed out in a roundtable discussion.

While awaiting a response, Luther went about his business, not knowing that what he had casually posted to the church door would go down in history as the greatest and most confrontational affair the Christian world had known since Jesus and the apostles.

What Was the Controversy?

The main points in Luther's theses were: (1) his objection of indulgence money going to build St. Peter's Bascilica; (2) his denial of the pope's power over purgatory; and (3) his consideration of the welfare of the sinner.

Luther attacked the idea that the pope could reduce the penalties of purgatory. He also questioned whether saints had a treasury of merits. Surely, only Jesus did. And whatever Jesus had was freely given *without* the use of the pope's keys of binding and loosing. He complained about the sale of indulgences. He believed they replaced true repentance and heartfelt acts of charity. Added to this, he felt the sale of indulgences was giving the people a false sense of security and leading them into a state of complacency.

Luther dug more deeply into the foundations of the Church when he questioned the existence of purgatory. What if purgatory was nothing more than the mere misery of life on planet earth? He wrote,

> Indulgences are most pernicious because they induce complacency and thereby imperil salvation. Those persons are damned who think that letters of indulgence make them certain of salvation. God works by contraries so that a man feels himself to be lost in the very moment when he is on the point of being saved. When God is about to justify a man,

> He damns him. Whom He would make alive He must first kill. God's favor is so communicated in the form of wrath that it seems farthest when it is at hand. Man must first cry out that there is no health in him. He must be consumed with horror. This is the pain of purgatory. I do not know where it is located, but I do know that it can be experienced in this life. I know a man who has gone through such pains that had they lasted for one tenth of an hour he would have been reduced to ashes. In this disturbance salvation begins. When a man believes himself to be utterly lost...even though he be absolved a million times by the pope, and he who does have it may not wish to be released from purgatory, for true contrition seeks penalty. Christians should be encouraged to bear the cross. He who is baptized into Christ must be as a sheep for the slaughter. The merits of Christ are vastly more potent when they bring crosses than when they bring remissions. [25]

While he went on with his studies, unbeknownst to him, the Ninety-Five Theses he had posted had been translated from Latin into German and were circulating among the common people as well as the church officials. They were doing a work in the spirit realm. As they angered Church leaders, they were opening the eyes of the people. This created the biggest threat to the enemy who ruled over the people through their ignorance.

Luther sat in his study, oblivious to the fact that, beyond his door, a back draft was building. In reality, it had been building for hundreds of years. It started with John Wycliffe and his translations of the Bible for the common man. It passed to Jon Hus, who began to pry open the darkness of the Middle Ages with some of the same revelations that Luther would bring forth. They both died without seeing the fruit of their labor, but Luther would see it. More than that, he would bring the whole world into it. Legend says that Hus, while burning on the stake for what the Church called heresy, prophesied Luther's coming. Reportedly, he called to the Church leaders from within the flames and told them that a man was coming in one hundred years whom they would not be able to kill.

Hus didn't call Luther by name, but it could have been only one man about whom he spoke. Luther came on the scene nearly one hundred years after Hus' death, and, though every attempt was made on Luther's life, the enemy would never succeed in killing him.

Some historians like to argue whether Luther nailed the theses to the church door or whether he merely distributed copies of it. They say that if copies were distributed, then the Reformation's beginning wasn't as strong. [26] That argument is ridiculous and misses the point of what was contained in the theses. An attempt to water down the impact of those Ninety-Five Theses, whether nailed to the church door or passed out, reveals ignorance. Obviously, we are all affected by the work Luther did five hundred years ago. Despite the exact manner of his declaration, the impact of the Reformation remains unchanged.

Yes, Luther *nailed* his beliefs and concerns on the church door, inviting whoever was inclined to take part in the discussion. He also mailed copies to those who didn't read them on the church door. Let me emphasize that the mailing of the theses was another bold stand for truth. In fact, the archbishop who helped Leo X instigate the sale of indulgences for profit was one of the people who received a copy. There's nothing weak about that!

Luther's Ninety-Five Theses spread across Germany within a matter of weeks, which, in itself, was remarkable. Almost everyone who read them praised Luther's boldness. Luther was a little unnerved by it all, but the people were so glad to have their first glimpse of light that a movement was set in motion. Rome was alarmed, and a case was established against Luther for further inquiry.

The case would spend the next four years in limbo, which was just enough time for Luther to turn the questions he had in his heart into established revelation in his spirit. Now, he didn't need a discussion. As he would say later in a trial over his theses, "my conscience is captive to the Word of God." [27]

As I've already stated, leaving Luther alone with the Scriptures was the Catholic Church's biggest mistake. Luther was getting stronger and stronger and questioning more and more of what the papal church commonly practiced.

It wasn't long before he declared that Scripture alone was the final authority, not the pope, because the pope and councils could make mistakes. He denied the pope's power over purgatory—then threw out the idea of purgatory altogether.

Luther was threatened with excommunication, but that didn't stop him. Finally secure in the Scriptures and his own relationship with God, he knew that even if his fellowship with the Church was broken, nothing could keep him from the love of God. Not even the thought of execution frightened him. He was ready to die for what he believed. As a result, he boldly declared that bishops who excommunicated parishioners because of money should be disobeyed. [28] Luther was beginning to realize that the new wine within him couldn't be put into old wineskins. His days as a Roman Catholic were numbered.

Scripture was the final authority—not the pope. Threatened with excommunication, Luther knew nothing could keep him from the love of God.

Road to Excommunication

Initially, Luther didn't want to leave the church; he just wanted to correct any errors. His attempt at this brought him multiple attacks from church leaders. Excommunication was reserved for heretics, and Luther wasn't yet deemed a heretic because he hadn't gone against any papal order. A papal order, or papal bull, was a document from the pope to the church defining a certain stand on a certain issue. Since no written stand or direction regarding indulgences had come forth from the pope, Luther had really done no wrong in questioning their sale.

Since Luther couldn't be excommunicated, the pope laid a trap for him in 1517. He lured Luther to Augsburg in the fall of that year for a debate. This forum for discussion was what Luther had wanted all along, so he went. He thought this debate would be the first step toward the goal of ridding the church of error. However, what he experienced there was his first showdown with the religious leaders of the day. The enemy first came against Luther through Cardinal Thomas de Vio Cajetan.

Luther bowed down before the cardinal, then he lay prostrate before him. The cardinal commanded him to get up. Luther got up to his knees, and the cardinal, again, commanded him to get up. With one word out of the cardinal's mouth Luther knew the agenda. "Recant," Cajetan ordered. It was obvious there would be no discussion. The cardinal laid it out. Luther needed to repent, recant, promise not to teach his Ninety-Five Theses, and refrain from all activity that would disturb the peace of the church.

Luther had so stirred the pot of Christendom that even the pope referred to Luther as a wild boar who had invaded the Lord's vineyard. Cardinal Cajetan was instructed to allow no debate at the meeting in Augsburg. The Church's agenda for the meeting was that Luther recant or be bound and taken to Rome. Luther was unable to strike up a discussion. However, Luther managed to say the unthinkable: It's faith that justifies, not the sacrament. Cajetan was no match for Luther, and he knew it. With no scriptural foundation to work from, Cajetan exposed his insecurity by blurting out: "This you must recant today, whether you wish to or not. Otherwise I shall, on account of this one passage, condemn everything else that you might say!" [29] Luther boldly declared that he would not, stating that a common man armed with Scripture had more authority than the pope and all his councils. Cajetan fired back that the pope had more authority than even the Scripture.

Luther was next accused of pretension because he thought he could interpret Scripture, something only the pope was allowed to

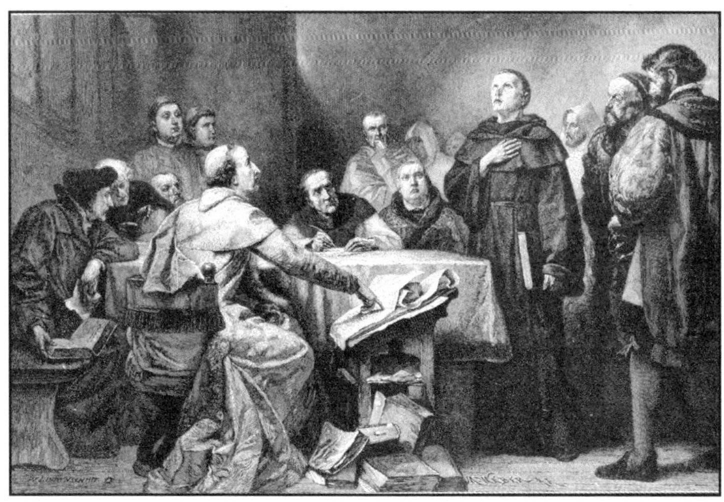

Luther before Bishop Cajetan.
North Wind Picture Archives.

do. On this point Luther questioned the very foundation of the pope's authority. Luther asked them why the church felt the pope was Peter's successor, and, furthermore, why the church thought Catholicism's foundation was on Peter since Paul said, "I have no other foundation but that of Christ." (See 1 Corinthians 3:11.) The discussion ended with Cajetan ordering Luther out of the building.

Luther left the court and wrote a friend, saying, "The cardinal may be an able Thomist, but he is no clear Christian thinker."and so he is about as fit to deal with this as an ass is to play a harp." Luther drove his point home by saying that the cardinal was as fit to deal with the situation as a donkey is to play a harp. [30]

The insult got out and soon there were woodcuts and wall hangings throughout the community depicting a donkey playing a harp with the head of, not Cajetan, but the very pope himself!

Frustrated at not being able to get an advantage over Luther, Cajetan appealed to Staupitz, Luther's spiritual father figure and mentor. He asked him to help reason with Luther to get him to recant. But even Staupitz felt unmatched against Luther's understanding of Scripture and refused. Staupitz knew the road ahead for Luther was one filled with hardship and decisions that would alienate him from his commitments to the Augustinian order. Foreseeing this, he released Luther from his Augustinian vows. Luther would later call this one of his three excommunications.

Luther waited in Augsburg to be summoned to the courts again for discussion, but nothing came. Realizing his vulnerability in staying much longer, he fled in the night by horseback, wearing only his pants and socks.

Once he was back in Wittenburg, he would be safe because of the favor of the people there. For every one person in the territory of Saxony who favored the pope, there were three who favored Luther. [31] Another advantage was that the elector of the territory, Frederick, loved Luther and actually worked to keep him safe. Frederick had gotten Luther the rite of safe passage, allowing him to escape from Augsburg and get home safely.

Frederick stood in an awkward position. After the incident in Augsburg, the pope asked Frederick to either imprison Luther and bring him to Rome or ban him from the territory. Under this ban, if

Frederick stayed faithful to Luther, he could be charged for harboring a heretic. Though Frederick slightly downplayed his relationship with Luther to the papal officials, he would not bind him and bring him to Rome. Frederick appealed to the secular officials and requested that Luther's case come to a secular hearing of impeachable judges in Germany. Frederick reminded Cajetan that Luther had never been legally charged with heresy and that there were no grounds for his capture.

A Decree from the Antichrist

With that sort of news from Frederick, Cajetan got very busy. He and other opponents of Luther began work on a papal bull that would outline the pope's official stand on indulgences. Once the order was signed by the pope, Luther would be one step closer to being charged with heresy, because his theses questioned the validity of indulgences. The bull was essentially a formal charge against Luther's Ninety-Five Theses.

The papal bull was officially titled The Bull Exsurge Domine. Luther received the bull in October 1520. He called it "the execrable bull of the Antichrist." [32] Because of the bull, Luther's books were being burned in Rome, Cologne, and other cities. Luther was given sixty days to recant.

Luther condemned those who issued the bull, saying,

> You, Leo X, and you, cardinals, and everyone else who amounts to anything at the curia: I challenge you and say to your faces, if this Bull has in truth gone forth in your name and with your knowledge, I warn you, in virtue of the power which I, like all Christians, have received through Baptism, to repent and leave off such Satanic blasphemies, and that right quickly. Unless you do this, know that I, with all who worship Christ, consider the Seat of Rome to be occupied by Satan and to be the throne of Antichrist, and that I will no longer obey nor remain united to him, the chief and deadly enemy of Christ. If you persist in your fury, I condemn you to Satan, together with this Bull and your decretals for the destruction of your flesh, in order than your spirit may be

> saved with us in the Day of the Lord. In the name of Him whom you persecute, Jesus Christ, our Lord. [33]

Luther made sure the community of Wittenberg knew he was unaffected by the charges. Facing criticism and religious spite, he was nevertheless infused with a boldness that allowed him to say,

> Be it known to all that no one does me a service by despising that outrageous, heretical, lying Bull, nor can anyone spite me by esteeming it. By God's grace I am free, and this thing shall neither console nor frighten me. I know well where my consolation and my courage abide, and who makes me safe before men as well as devils. I will do what I believe to be right. Everyone will have to stand up and answer for himself at his death and on the Last Day; then, perhaps, my faithful warning will be remembered. [34]

A Holy Bonfire

The sixty days passed, and Luther did not recant. Instead, he burned the bull along with the entire cannon law, which was the law governing the whole church from the beginning of Roman Catholic history! Some historians say that this bonfire, more than the posting of the Ninety-Five Theses, was the beginning of the Reformation. [35]

The burning was scheduled for the morning of December 10. Luther even posted an invitation. The notice read, "All adherents of the truth of the Gospel to be present at nine o'clock at the Chapel of the Holy Cross outside the walls, where the impious books of papal law and scholastic theology will be burned according to ancient and apostolic usage." [36]

People came from throughout the university, professors and students. First the volumes of the canon law were thrown into the flames. This was no small affair as the canon law was to the western world what the Talmud is to Judaism or the Koran to Islam. It was the law book of Latin Christendom, invested with religious authority. According to beliefs of the day, the canon law was the same as the commandments of God. [37]

After the canon law was consumed, Luther stepped up to the flames and threw in the bull with these words: "Because thou hast brought down the truth of God, may the Lord today bring thee down unto this fire!"[38] Luther further commented, "Since they have burned my books, I burn theirs."[39] With that, he went back to town with the other professors. The students stayed on though, full of life and energy, charged by the evening's events. Though at that time they lacked the revelation to realize what really took place there, Luther would bring them a bold definition of what the ten-minute ceremony meant and what stand they would have to make now that they knew the truth.

Spiritual Strength

The students, young and innocent, might have been like any other group of university students excited by the latest protest, carrying banners and chanting.

Though the atmosphere was full of unbridled energy, and people in such an environment can get caught up in rebellion, the burning of these documents was not an act of rebellion; it was an act of revolution. Luther had stared the spirit of religion straight in the eye and refused to flinch or back away from his stand. That is the spiritual strength of a Reformer. It is the strength of someone who knows his

Luther burning the papal bull and the entire canon law.

place in Christ, who knows what the Word says concerning truth, and who draws the line between it and deception. That kind of strength must come again to the church.

This kind of strength is not only a gift from God. This kind of strength must be developed and exercised just as one would develop and exercise faith. How do you develop this spiritual strength? By devouring the Word. And I'm not talking about your favorite "pet" Scriptures. You must devour both the "bless me" Scriptures and the "punish me" Scriptures—and stand strong upon them! Once you know the Word, you must rid your thought life of *any* thinking contrary to those Scriptures. When an adverse thought comes into your mind, don't listen to it, don't agree with it, and don't be nice about it! Yell out, "No! That's not the truth according to God!" Make your mind bow to the Word and the plan of God. Pray in strong tongues and build up your inner spirit man.

Luther took a stand. He knew what the Word said and fought for that truth. This spiritual strength comes from truly knowing the Bible.

By doing this, little by little you'll build spiritual strength inside of you. It's just like physical exercise. Physical exercise prevents your muscles from becoming loose and helps protect your body from disease. The same is true in the spirit. Spiritual exercise keeps your inner spirit man strong; it keeps your spiritual equipment working, enabling you to discern between the true and the false. Christians are often weak and flaky because they have neglected to build their spiritual strength. Their churches are weak, because their leaders are weak. They grab for every wind of doctrine, looking for something new because they have neglected to build the true strength inside that sustains, fulfills, and propels them forward.

If you'll build a lifestyle of exercising your spiritual strength, then someday you'll be able to stand strong without flinching or backing down in the face of persecution, disaster, calamity, deception, and any hypocritical or evil spirit. You'll stand just as Luther did. The principles of developing spiritual strength work for everyone who applies them and *"God is no respecter of persons"* (Acts 10:34).

Either Hell or Martyrdom!

The next day, standing to lecture before his class of about four hundred students, Luther gave an explanation for the previous day's event. The students crowded in to hear what the Reformer had to say. The fun and pranks from the evening before were sobered with this lecture.

Luther told the students they had to choose between hell and martyrdom. He warned them that they were in danger of hell if they didn't make a decision in their hearts to carry out, to the end, the struggle against the "anti-Christianity of the papal church." [40] With that comment, he pointed out that such a fight with the Church could lead to martyrdom.

The thought of martyrdom might have shook up some of the students, but it didn't frighten Luther. He now knew what he came to earth to do. He had no alternative. He must break with Roman Catholicism and take on the endless fight against the Antichrist. He was driven by a duty to God, by a divine call to bring reform. He was purely motivated in his heart to save as many people as he could from the deception of the Catholic Church.

With a resounding soberness, Luther told the students,

> The Church needs reformation. This reformation is not, however, the concern of the pope alone, nor the concern of the cardinals;...It is rather the concern of the whole [Christian] world, or much more, of God. When it will come He alone knows. Meanwhile, it is our task to expose the notorious evil conditions....
>
> I do not wish to do battle for the Gospel with force and slaughter. The world is overcome by the Word; the church has been preserved till now and will also be reformed by the Word....It is not our work that is now going on in the world, for man alone could not begin to carry such a thing. It is another who is driving the wheel, one whom the papists do not see; therefore they put the blame on us. [41]

Luther was speaking of God in his reference to "another who is driving the wheel." And though the blame fell on Luther, he was ready to begin the Reformation for God.

Liberation Writings

As fearful and sobering an act as burning the bull was, it cut Luther free into a liberty he had never known. He would report later that he was "more pleased over this deed than over any other deed of my life." [42]

This liberty sent him into a year of great productivity.

Luther was maturing, his popularity was growing, and he was becoming further established in his doctrine. More than ever, he poured himself into his pastoral duties, preaching, teaching, and writing works that began to define the state of the Church and mankind.

Luther wrote a whole series of small devotional booklets, another on the seven petitions of the Lord's Prayer, and several sermons on preparation for death, repentance, baptism, and the Lord's Supper. He put out studies in the book of Psalms, and a commentary on Galatians. [43]

Writing came easy to Luther. "I have a swift hand and a quick memory. When I write, it just flows out; I do not have to press and squeeze." He was especially inspired in his writings when stirred by an opponent. He would say of himself that writing flowed best when "a good, strong anger stirred in my blood." [44]

Many of the writings throughout the history of the church were written in response to error or direct criticism. Even Paul's writings in the Bible were mostly letters to a certain church, usually pinpointing a problem there. The same was true for Luther. His writing either addressed error or fired back at direct challenges from opponents, mainly the papal authority. They would write scathing rebukes back and forth to each other. These writings were published and distributed throughout the country.

Let me comment further about the disposition that was developing in Luther at this time. He was getting bolder, rougher, stronger, more certain and surefooted. He may have started out in the monastery timid and defeated, but now he took on strongholds in a strength given to him by truth. What made him this way was his ever-growing revelation of the truth. As he was discovering freedom, he began provoking the source of the people's bondage—the Church.

Luther pursued the Word of God above everything. And the more he did, the more he saw things in black and white. Out of an indignation that came from heaven, Luther tore into the religious spirit that had taken all of Europe captive.

Along with preaching and lecturing, Luther attacked religious demons with his writings. Encouraged by his opponents, he challenged core doctrines that had been established for centuries.

A Message to Germany's Upper Class

Four thousand copies of Luther's *Address to the Christian Nobility of the German Nation* sold within eighteen days of its printing, and a number of reprints went to press. Almost the entire upper class of Germany read it. Luther would declare here that: (1) anyone who

Luther preaching. Roger Viollet/Getty Images.

has been baptized is a priest before God; (2) there is no special spiritual plan preferring any person over another; (3) there is no human mediator, namely, a priest, in a person's relationship with God; and (4) any and every Christian can proclaim the Word of God. [45]

Leaders tried to suppress the spread of this document. One leader described that what was initially offensive to him in the document began to ring true as he mulled it over. Eventually, he, too, became convinced of the truth and wrote to Rome: "What is written there is not altogether untrue, nor is it unnecessary that it should be brought to light. If no one ventures to speak of the evils in the church and if everyone must keep silence, the stones will eventually cry out." [46] (See Luke 19:40.)

Luther wrote,

> The pope or bishop anoints, shaves heads, ordains, consecrates, and prescribes garb different from that of the laity, but he can never make a man into a Christian or into a spiritual man by so doing. He might well make a man into a hypocrite or a humbug and blockhead, but never a Christian or a spiritual man. As far as that goes, we are all consecrated priests through baptism as St. Peter says in 1 Peter 2:9. [47]

Luther attacked the Roman Catholic rule that allowed only the pope to interpret Scripture. He found no scriptural evidence to support this, and no support for the idea that Jesus gave only St. Peter the keys to the kingdom. [48]

In his second writing, entitled *On the Babylonian Captivity of the Church,* Luther challenged the Roman Catholic idolatry of the sacraments. "Faith in the sacrament makes them effective," he wrote, adding that there was no power in the sacrament itself; only faith gave it power. Luther boldly declared that no one could be saved without faith, but that it was possible to be saved without the sacrament.

This was a most offensive statement to Rome. The sacraments and the priest's duty of turning communion into Jesus' actual body was a major tenet of the faith. And Luther had kicked it over by telling the people that the sacraments belonged to all men, not just to the priests.

Luther also attacked the Mass, as a whole, and the people's motives for attending. In the spirit of indulgences and storing up good works, the people had reduced what was supposed to be a worship service to a sacrifice that added merit to their life.

In the third book, *On the Freedom of a Christian,* Luther discussed what would seem like a paradox to the Roman Catholic world. People were so accustomed to performing good works with an agenda, there was little done from the heart of man. Luther tore into this by declaring that, unless a person's good works came from a disposition created out of faith, those seeming good works were evil in the sight of God. [49]

Works that appear wonderful on the outside may be the greatest sin before God. God does not judge the act, but the person's heart.

Luther wrote,

> Faith is not a work of man. It is a disposition produced by God, or, more correctly, the consciousness of new life which takes root in the soul when it has gained the assurance of God's favor through the glad tidings of God's love in Christ. What man does in response to this disposition or consciousness is good, trifling though it may appear outwardly—even walking, standing, eating, drinking, sleeping, and picking up a straw. On the other hand, what he does not, or cannot, do in response to this disposition is not good, no matter how magnificent and holy it may look outwardly. [50]

Luther used this writing to attack the idea of works. Works that appear wonderful on the outside may, in and of themselves—due to the condition of the person's heart—be the greatest sin before God.

Luther wrote, "Anyone who is not at one with God begins to search and to worry as to how he may make amends and move God with many works." But one who is established in faith, Luther added, "serves God without looking for a return, satisfied that it pleases Him." [51]

Facing the Enemy at Worms

These writings were all trumpet blasts in the ear of Rome, and Luther had set out with this blaring kind of declaration to uproot centuries of demonic strongholds, customs, and mind-sets.

Whereas the book written to the German nobility stayed within the nation, the work on the Babylonian captivity reached into all of Europe. With it, he attracted the hostility of King Henry VIII of England, who would write a scathing rebuttal and posture himself against Luther for the rest of his life. [52]

While leaders of nations had to decide what to do with Luther's influence, his personal friends were also choosing sides in the ensuing war. Some remained loyal, while others withdrew. Some stood in indecision while trying to formulate their own belief systems. One devout follower of Luther's struggled with the writings and threw one of the books down in anger, but then he picked it up and read on. In the end, he became convinced and stood with Luther as so many others did. He was recorded as saying, "the whole world has been blind until now." [53]

In response to these writings, a second attempt was made to silence Luther at the annual meeting of a secular court of judges called the Diet of Worms in the city of Worms. It was the year 1521, and

Martin Luther faces Emperor Charles V at the Diet of Worms in 1521.
Hulton Archive.

Luther was summoned there to answer for his writings. The emperor presided over the meeting. Frederick hoped this court would grant Luther favor because it was this emperor who deemed it illegal to charge a man with heresy without first hearing him. Luther was glad for the chance to explain his position but soon discovered that the agenda was the same as with Cajetan.

The emperor, Charles V of Spain, wasn't really interested in spending energy on Luther, so the meeting was short and to the point. Referring to a pile of books on a table, Luther was asked if he was their author and if he wished to recant any part of them. [54]

The court waited for Luther's answer as if he should respond immediately so they could move on to other business. Luther, not wanting this to be the end of it, begged for more time: "This touches God and his Word. This affects the salvation of souls....I beg you, give me time." [55]

He was given one more day. He spent the evening pondering the question, but he had his mind made up long before. The next day he stood before the court. A member of the court spoke, "You must give a simple, clear, and proper answer....Will you recant or not?" [56]

To this, Luther declared,

> Unless I can be instructed and convinced with evidence from the Holy Scriptures or with open, clear, and distinct grounds of reasoning...then I cannot and will not recant, because it is neither safe nor wise to act against conscience.
>
> Here I stand. I can do no other. God help me! Amen. [57]

Luther before the Council.

☆☆☆☆☆

Edict of Worms

Luther was condemned but was granted twenty-one days of safe conduct to get back to Wittenberg. On the heels of the Diet of Worms came the Edict of Worms in May 1521. This was the decision the pope and all of his associates were awaiting. Finally, Luther was legally condemned as a heretic, which made him open prey for anyone to murder him without consequence. If Rome could have found a way, he would have been burned at the stake like Jon Hus.

With the edict, Luther was told that his doctrine was a cesspool of old and new heresies and was banned from the empire. The edict forbade anyone to print, sell, or read his books. It also made it unlawful for anyone to help Luther in any way. But even with this edict, Frederick the Wise, Luther's elector and friend, intervened.

Frederick arranged for a fake arrest of Luther as he was making his way back to Wittenberg. He had Luther captured and taken to one of his castles, Wartburg. Luther hid there in a room behind a retractable staircase for ten months. He grew his hair out, grew a beard, and was referred to as "Knight George." His disguise was so good that later, when he left the castle, he was unrecognizable to a friend and painter for whom Luther had previously posed.

Luther's capture.
North Wind Picture Archives.

He hated his time at Wartburg. He wrote about it:

> I was in my prison in my Patmos, high up in the castle in the kingdom of the birds, but often plagued by the devil. I withstood him in faith, and answered him with the words: My God is the One who made human beings, and He has put all things under their feet (Psalm 8:6). Try if you have any power over Him! [58]

Even though he spent those days in torment, he made full use of his time. He was able to continue on with some of his writings, and probably the greatest feat was his complete translation of the New Testament from Latin to German. The common man had never had the Bible. The few Bible passages that were read to them at Mass were read in Latin. Now the whole face of Christendom would change. The common man would have the light!

Destruction, Chaos, and Revolt in Wittenburg

But even before the common man had access to the Scriptures, the Ninety-Five Theses, alone, had erupted into a movement. What was previously one man's war, Luther's, was becoming something called Lutheranism. One of his associates, Carlstadt, took the helm while Luther was in Wartburg. But he took the movement in a direction that angered Luther and brought him out of hiding to set straight the havoc in Wittenburg.

Under Carlstadt's direction, nuns were leaving the convent and monks the monastery. This didn't upset Luther—he wrote and preached against monastic vows. But the destruction of paintings and altars was not okay with him. Priests were stoned; the altar of the Franciscan Monastery was destroyed. Mass-reading priests were being ejected

Luther, translating the New Testmament from Latin into German.
Roger Viollet/Getty Images

forcibly from the city church. Riots broke out when the movement's followers were arrested. Masses were stopped, a rectory at Eilenberg was plundered, and the Augustinian monks solemnly burned all their pictures from the walls of the monastery.

Luther stormed back into town, rebuking Carlstadt. He reminded him that it is through love that people are won over. He asked those who had gotten caught up in the wildfire of the movement why they tore down the statues or pictures that might have meant something to another's devotion to the Lord. He encouraged them to consider the weaker ones who needed their monastic vows, their pictures, and their statues.

His feelings about the nature that the reform should take are best said in his own words.

> Give men time. I took three years of constant study, reflection, and discussion to arrive where I now am, and can the common man, untutored in such matters, be expected to move the same distance in three months? Do not suppose that abuses are eliminated by destroying the object which is abused. Men can go wrong with wine and women. Shall we then prohibit wine and abolish women? The sun, the moon, and stars have been worshipped. Shall we then pluck them out of the sky? Such haste and violence betray a lack of confidence in God. See how much he has been able to accomplish through me, though I did no more than pray and preach. The Word did it all. Had I wished I might have started a conflagration (a disastrous fire) at Worms. But while I sat still and drank beer with Philip and Amsdorf, God dealt the papacy a mighty blow. [59]

He was a Reformer, and reform he did. Though he did correct a wrong spirit, he stuck to many of Carlstadt's reforms and began making many of his own. He took his pulpit back and preached every day. He restructured worship, writing many hymns himself, and he printed his first German Mass.

Luther began his reforms in Wittenberg. He was safe there—the people loved, esteemed, and protected him. But he dared not step out of the territory of Saxony. Frederick, the elector there, didn't need to lift a finger to protect him because the people's favor was enough. To come against Luther was to come against the people. And no secular or Church official in the country was willing to draw that kind of backlash against himself.

Luther's reforms included public care of the poor. At that time, begging was prohibited. Money that was previously used by the monasteries was used for orphans, students at the universities, and poor girls' dowries.

The Mass was reconstructed. Evangelical preaching replaced the old stodgy routine. Carlstadt began an attack on celibacy, which Luther ultimately agreed with. Luther became personally responsible for the escape of nuns from their convents. Once the nuns were in his custody, he sought to marry them off to priests who had left the monasteries.

His Resolute, Redheaded Wife

Luther even married one of the nuns himself, though he tried in earnest to marry her to someone else. It began after he arranged for her rescue from a convent, something he felt was his duty before God, though it was a crime punishable by execution. Her name was Katherine von Bora, and she was one of many who had gotten ahold of Luther's writings inside the convent. Already discontented before reading his works, she wrote Luther on behalf of herself and eleven other nuns who wanted to leave the convent. [60] Luther devised a plan using the father of one of the nuns, who delivered smoked herring inside the convent walls weekly. He was trusted by the Church authority there, so his truck wasn't stopped and searched on the day he emptied twelve barrels of fish and left with those same barrels filled with twelve nuns. Katherine was one of them. [61]

Katherine had been at the convent against her will, as many of the nuns were. This was why Luther would write the fathers of nuns to get them to set their daughters free. But in Katherine's case, she was put there because of her stepmother. Katherine was born with a strong personality and quick wit. This was uncomfortable for her father's new bride, so she was sent away at the age of nine or ten. [62]

When the twelve nuns were safely outside the convent walls, three went home to their families and the other nine were delivered to Luther's doorstep. He found husbands for eight of them. They were all married, all but Katherine. She started doing domestic work at a neighbor's house.

She was twenty-six years old, a redhead with a high forehead, long nose, and powerful chin. One biographer said she was a "quick-witted Saxon with a ready tongue." [63] Even though society said she was past the prime age for marriage, she did fall in love with a man, who returned her feelings. But his parents refused the marriage because she was a runaway nun. The relationship ended, and she was left brokenhearted.

Luther, who by now was developing a strong friendship with Katherine, had recommended a few more men as possible mates for her. Still nursing the pain of her breakup, she refused. Luther doubted whether, this late in her life, she had the right to be so picky. Still, she refused, but recommended two men of her own choosing—one of whom was Luther himself! [64]

Luther was astounded by the suggestion! Absolutely not! Luther couldn't marry—or so he thought. He could be hanged any day as a heretic. It was a ridiculous idea.

This was his sentiment when he went to visit his family, but his father's encouragement to marry changed his mind. Already happy that Luther had left the monastery, his father wanted him to marry, have children, and carry on the family name.

Luther was beginning to see the benefits. He could, with this marriage, please his father, further infuriate the pope, and perhaps have a child to carry on his name in the event of his martyrdom, which he lived in expectation of daily. There was no romance for Luther or Katherine. He married out of duty, she on the rebound. But they had a strong admiration and mutual respect for each other. [65]

"I am not madly in love, but I cherish her," Luther said. On June 10 he wrote, "The gifts of God must be taken on the wing." On June 13, 1525 he married her. [66]

Pigtails on My Pillow

The suddenness of the marriage brought an onslaught of rumors. A rumor that Luther was living with Katherine was already circulating, when, in fact, he was just visiting her daily. For Luther, this was the only way he could proceed with the marriage. He wrote about it later: "If I had not married quickly and secretly and taken few into my confidence, everyone would have done what he could to hinder me; for all my friends said: 'Not this one, but another.'" Luther's friends wanted him to marry someone more distinguished. [67]

Marriage at forty-one years of age was an adjustment for Luther. Set in his ways, he said, "There's a lot to get used to in the first year of marriage....One wakes up in the morning and finds a pair of pigtails on the pillow which were not there before." [68]

Kate stepped into the marriage no holds barred. Her forceful personality and strong resolve brought order to Luther's life. For example, she changed the year-old mildewing straw in his mattress for fresh stuffing. In his relentless pursuit for reform, he used to fall exhausted into bed nightly without noticing the odor.

She also brought order to Luther's finances. Luther's bank account was frequently overdrawn because he was so generous. He said God gave man fingers that money might slip through them easily. Kate took hold of the purse strings and managed to save money enough for the purchase of more property. [69]

Luther's wedding.

☆☆☆☆☆

Kate found a new skill in marriage she hadn't known or learned in the convent. She learned she had the ability to be a manager, landlord, and administrator. She brought increase to everything, purposing to make their home self-sufficient. The Luthers lived in the Augustinian monastery, which the government deeded to them. It was a forty-room building, and sometimes every room was filled with people. Eventually the Luthers had six kids of their own, a half-dozen nieces and nephews, and some children Luther took in after their mother died. Kate's relatives moved in to help, including her Aunt Magdalena, who became "nanny" to the children. Tutors and student boarders also lived there. Luther and Kate had a great partnership—he *invited* the student boarders, and she charged them rent! [70]

It took Luther a while to adjust to living surrounded by so many people, but soon he was thriving in it. Speaking of his son Hans, he once wrote, "As I sit and write, he sings me a song, and if it gets too loud I scold him a little, but he goes on singing just the same." [71]

Table Talks

Out of this household of continual activity, a mentoring relationship between Luther and the students who lived there developed. Their time together became known as the famous "table talks." The students would swarm to him around the dinner table, asking questions and scribbling the answers in their notebooks. Kate wanted to charge them money for the revelations they were writing down, but Luther wouldn't allow it. In the end, many of these students published the information they gleaned during those times. [72]

Luther would sit at one end of the dinner table with the students and Kate at the other end with the children. She grew weary of their questions and of Luther not being allowed to eat his meal for all of his talking. During one table talk, Kate commented from her end of the table, "Doctor, why don't you stop talking and eat?" Luther replied, "Women should repeat the Lord's prayer before opening their mouths." [73]

Though she was something to get used to, Luther yielded his weaknesses to her strengths, handing over the affairs of the house to her. He called her "my rib," "my chain," and "my lord," referring to the way she managed the house. [74]

However, she did more than manage the house. She made the house prosper. She became a manager of two households—the Augustinian monastery, and then another she inherited in Zulsdorf, a two-day journey from Wittenberg. She had farms, gardens, cattle, pigs, pigeons, geese, a dog (which Luther loved so dearly he hoped he would see him in heaven), orchards, a fish pond, and a brewery. [75]

On a side note, don't let the fact that she had a brewery bother you. In that day, to own a brewery was a luxury, and to drink beer was to nourish your body. Beer was to them what our protein drinks and supplements are to us today. Even in Germany today, you see a people whose relationship to alcohol is very different from that of Americans'. Moderation was the key for them. In addition, beer was a particular benefit to the Luthers because Luther was frequently sick.

Kate preferred her land in Zulsdorf to Wittenberg, but, due to his frequent illness, Luther didn't like it when she was away. She was even going to add to her property by buying another farm, but Luther stalled her until someone else bought it. "Oh, Katie," he said, "you have a husband who loves you. Let someone else be an empress." [76]

Striving to please Luther, she would wait on him hand and foot. She became quite a doctor in her own right. Luther suffered from so much: gout, insomnia, catarrh, hemorrhoids, constipation, stones, dizziness, and ringing in the ears. She became very skilled in herbal medicine, poultices, and massage. And the beer she brewed, which Luther boasted of, was great medicine for his insomnia and stones.

In a letter Luther wrote to her concerning her watchful care over everything and everyone, he said,

> To the saintly, worrying lady Katherine Luther, doctor at Zulsdorf and Wittenberg, my gracious, dear wife. We thank you heartily for being so worried that you can't sleep, for since you started worrying about us, a fire broke out near my door, and yesterday, no doubt due to your worry, a big stone, save for the dear angels, would have fallen and crushed us like a mouse in a trap. If you don't stop worrying, I'm afraid the earth will swallow us. Pray and let God worry. Cast your burden on the Lord. [77]

Marriage was growing on Luther by this time and so was his love for Kate. Before he was married, Luther taught that marriage was a necessity for the flesh. But afterward, he said it was an opportunity for the spirit. "The first love is drunken," Luther said of marriage. "When the intoxication wears off, then comes the real married love." [78] And this is what he and Kate had.

He grew to love her so deeply that Luther renamed his most loved Pauline epistle "My Katharina Von Bora." He said once of her, "In domestic affairs, I defer to Katie. Otherwise, I am led by the Holy Spirit." [79]

Luther spoke and wrote a lot about marriage. Following are some of his most quotable sayings:

> Of course, the Christian should love his wife. He is supposed to love his neighbor, and since his wife is his nearest neighbor, she should be his deepest love. And she should also be his dearest friend.
>
> Marriage is no joke, it must be worked on, and prayed over.... To get a wife is easy enough, but to love her with constancy is difficult...for the mere union of the flesh is not sufficient; there must be a congeniality of tastes and character. And that congeniality does not come overnight.
>
> To have peace and love in a marriage is a gift that is next to the knowledge of the Gospel.
>
> Some marriages were motivated by mere lust, but mere lust is felt even by fleas and lice. Love begins when we wish to serve others.
>
> I will not take the vexation out of marriage. I may even increase it, but it will turn out wonderfully, as they only know who have tasted it.
>
> Nothing is more sweet than harmony in marriage, and nothing more distressing then dissension....Next to it is the loss of a child. I know how that hurts. [80]

✯✯✯✯✯

Loving and Losing Children

The Luthers knew the pain that comes with losing children. Together they had six children, of which they lost two. The loss of those children was probably the most painful experience in Luther's life. Luther found so much fulfillment in his children that their loss was torturous to his soul. He felt at times he might not recover. Luther was as passionate and as humorous about fatherhood as he was about being a husband. He once said, "The father ever learns from his experience of hanging out the nappies to the amusement of his neighbors. Let them laugh, God and the angels smile in heaven." [81] He viewed his role as a parent as one of the most powerful responsibilities he had, saying that there was no greater power given from God that what was given to parents.

Peasants' Revolt

As Luther passionately pursued reform, reform seemed to be pursuing him. As fast as he brought change to the church, he was being changed in his own heart and everyday life, first with his wife and then with his incredible love for his children. These emotions were opening him up to an abundance he hadn't known God had for him.

The peasant class's search for that same abundance for themselves created a stir that would eventually get Luther in trouble. Latching onto Luther's coattails, the peasant class used the Reformation as their platform for rising up against the noble class. The noble class owned the land, controlled government jobs, and took advantage of the peasant class. With no conviction about the Gospel, the peasants borrowed the Reformation's power to leverage their demands. They wanted to choose their own ministers, and they wanted to bring an end to serfdom, which was a system where a peasant was bound to the land and subject in some degree to the owner. They also wanted a fair rate of profit for the work they did in the fields.

Luther sympathized with the peasants, but he would later give advice to the higher class that would cause him to be blamed for some of the violence against the peasants.

Luther understood the peasants' reasons for revolting, but he warned them not to use violence and rioting. They did not heed his advice. The peasants went forth with their rebellion full throttle. They refused to pay any of their rates; then they plundered castles and monasteries. The noblemen used their force and cracked down on them—six thousand peasants lost their lives. Luther tried to calm them all and bring them to the Cross, but since their primary motivation wasn't the Cross, they certainly didn't want to change their focus at this point in the conflict. Luther responded to the situation by writing a message to the nobles.

He wrote *Against the Robbing and Murdering Hordes of Peasants.* In it, he told the noble class to admit their own guilt, pray for God's help, and offer terms to the peasants. Only if those terms were refused did Luther advocate harsh punishment of the peasants. He wrote,

> Smite, strangle, and stab [the peasants], secretly or openly, for nothing can be more poisonous, hurtful, or devilish than a rebel. It is just as when one must kill a mad dog; if you do not strike him, he will strike you and a whole land with you. [82]

The lords cracked down and brought the rebellion to an end.

Luther felt the lords misunderstood his heart and wrote to them a second message entitled an *Open Letter on the Harsh Book against the Peasants.* He wanted to make sure the lords knew their responsibility as Christians was not only to shut down the rebellion but also to turn in mercy toward the peasants with a heart of restoration after the victory.

The peasants blamed Luther for the lords' harsh victory, and the lords blamed Luther and the Reformation for stirring the peasants' uprising. Like many apostolic people, Luther became accustomed to receiving the blame. Some would say he had thick skin, but I have found that the makeup of a reformer gives him strength for this kind of pressure. The Reformers were remade from the inside out by their calling and by the cause they stood for. This enabled them to move forward while being misunderstood or, in Luther's case, hated and blamed—here by the peasants and the nobles, and in other cases, by his own family and other Protestant reformers.

The papacy's hatred for Luther continued to grow, and Emperor Charles V disliked him immensely after the Diet of Worms, though not for any particular conviction. It simply bothered him that one man should cause so much trouble for so many. Charles endeavored to enforce the Edict of Worms, but Lutheranism was too popular and escaped his attempts to quench it. Lutheran ministers were removed from their pulpits, but they took to the streets, preaching before throngs of people from the banisters of local inns. Entire German cities, like Strasbourg, Augsburg, Ulm, and Nuremberg, were turning into Lutheran strongholds.

Congress upon congress was called to deal with this heresy that challenged the unity of Roman Catholicism. It all culminated in 1530 with the Diet of Augsburg. Luther was not allowed to go and was kept again in another castle during the three-month deliberation. The princes of the territories of Germany were all present. These men were the secular authority in the nation under the Emperor. They held the same rank as Frederick the Wise, who ruled over Luther's territory and also was the man who hid Luther in Wartburg Castle after the Diet of Worms. These princes presented the Augsburg Confession, which was a Lutheran statement of faith. The Emperor did not receive it, demanded the stamping out of Lutheranism, and commanded the German princes to lead their country back into union with the Catholic Church. They refused; one prince knelt before the Emperor and said he would rather be beheaded than take the Word of God from his people. The princes' bravery equaled Luther's, and the conviction of the movement was not watered down in Luther's absence. The Emperor would not give them the acceptance they sought but could do little to stop what was already taking over in Germany—Lutheranism.

Reordering the Church

Thankfully, the Emperor was called away to the business of war, and Luther would never feel the weight of his opposition again. Luther continued to move forward and soon began his reforms of the church. He started with an inspection of the services as they were. It didn't take too long for him to see that a German Mass was needed.

Luther proceeded slowly with these reforms out of concern that moving too quickly from Latin to German would alienate those people who were weaker in the faith. He could see people knew very little about the foundational principles of the kingdom of God and wrote, with the help of his assistants, two catechisms in German for them to study—one for the adults and one for the children. After his translation of the Bible, Luther considered the catechism for the children his most important work. [83]

Luther ensured that the followers of the movement came into the knowledge of the Gospel and the kingdom by enforcing the study of the catechisms. Both the adults and the children were assigned the memorization of the catechisms. Failure to fulfill a certain assignment meant the withholding of food and drink by the employers or the parents of the guilty parties. [84]

Reforming Music

In his reforms, Luther brought music to the forefront of the Mass saying that, "Next to the Word of God, music deserves the highest praise." [85] This is another instance where he parted ways with other Reformers of the day.

Ulrich Zwingli, a Reformer of the church in Switzerland, was a trained musician, yet he banned all organ playing. Some of his followers took it further and smashed organs to reinforce their view. Another Reformer, John Calvin, allowed singing, but only in unison. All harmonies were outlawed. He felt that, though music was a gift of God, it was only to be used in the world and not in the Mass.

Luther at home, playing his guitar, surrounded by family.

✯✯✯✯✯

But Luther thought music was divine. He was an incredible musician himself, had a good singing voice, and was skilled on the lute, which he had given up upon entering the monastery as a young man.

Luther was part of a group of Reformers who thought music propelled the Gospel forward. He believed that God had created all things to be used in service and worship to Him and that it was the people's job to discover creativity within themselves and allow it to flow into every area of their lives, using it for God. Luther said,

> I am not of the opinion that all arts are to be cast down and destroyed on account of the Gospel, as some fanatics protest; on the other hand, I would gladly see all arts, especially music, in the service of Him who has given and created them. [86]

Luther even had music practices during the week. The congregation was expected to come and learn new songs so there could be uninhibited worship on Sunday mornings. Today, in general, the music team of praisers and worshipers has a midweek practice to prepare for Sunday. But this was not the tradition Luther followed. He expected the entire congregation to be at practice. He was definitely a director and a leader—Luther pointed the way and expected Christians to follow!

To support his arguments about music, he pointed to Moses and David. He showed the people how Moses praised God after passing through the Red Sea and how David wrote many psalms.

Luther felt so strongly about the place of music in ministry that he wouldn't ordain a new minister who didn't know the spiritual significance of music. A man seeking ordination had to be skilled in music or sensitive to the praise and worship it brings. Furthermore, he thought a schoolmaster who was not able to instruct in music should not be hired.

Luther wanted the people to experience the power of music. For this reason, Luther wanted to replace the Latin hymns with German ones so the people could understand what they were hearing and be edified by the Word of God as they sang it. So, he put out a notice calling for poets and musicians to produce German hymns. He told them to stay close to the Scriptures to preserve the pure teaching of the

Word. He wanted no mixtures or secular thoughts. He wanted every man-made idea removed from the Mass and was not afraid to insist upon it! He referred to the canon law, the papacy's written code for all of Catholicism, as "that abominable concoction drawn from everyone's sewer and cesspool." [87]

Luther soon began to write hymns himself. At first, his skills were shaky, but after many attempts, he developed the gift. He wrote more than twenty hymns in a year's time. By 1526, Luther had enough material in liturgy and hymns to produce his first German Mass.

Luther wanted the people to experience the power of music in German so they could be edified by the Word of God as they sang.

The classic hymn for which he is best known is "A Mighty Fortress Is Our God." He penned the song in 1527, his worst year, a year of great testing and trial. Two distressing conditions led to the writing of this hymn.

First were his disputes with other Reformers of the day. The arguments had left him angry, disturbed, and depressed. His ears began to ring from all the stress and pressure of the dissension. He lay down thinking it was his last night alive. But through it all, Luther surrendered himself to God afresh. Speaking of his condition when the hymn was written, Luther said,

> I spent more than a week in death and hell. My entire body was in pain, and I still tremble. Completely abandoned by Christ, I labored under the vacillations and storms of desperation and blasphemy against God. But through the prayers of the saints [his friends], God began to have mercy on me and pulled my soul from the inferno below. [88]

He survived. But that same year, the second inspiration for the song broke out—the plague. While everyone who was well was leaving Wittenberg, the Luthers stayed to care for the sick. Luther watched his friends die as he turned the monastery into a hospital. The monastery was so overtaken with the sick that the place was quarantined.

Out of this situation of pain and distress, Luther wrote the very potent words of "A Mighty Fortress Is Our God." Here are a few lines from one of the sixty English versions that are sung worldwide every Sunday morning to this day:

> And though this world with devils filled
> Should threaten to undo us,
> We will not fear, for God has willed
> His truth to triumph through us.
> The prince of darkness grim? We tremble not for him.
> His rage we can endure, for lo! his doom is sure
> One little Word shall fell him.

Luther at home in his study.
North Wind Picture Archives

His Greatest Work: The German Bible

Along with Luther's hymns, the most enduring work we still have today is his translation of the Bible into German. He had already translated the New Testament from Latin to German during his ten-month stay in Wartburg Castle, when he was hiding after the Diet and Edict of Worms.

In 1534, the great cap to all reform work came, the publication of the Old Testament, translated out of Hebrew into German. Luther was suited for this undertaking. He gathered his best scholars, a team of men the likes of which had never before been assembled.

Luther's goal was to put out a Bible that would be understood by all Germans, so he spent time in different regions talking with the older generations, hearing how they spoke, and then bringing it back to the translation table. He wanted the Bible to sound right to the ear. Speaking of the Old Testament prophets, Luther said,

> O God, what a hard and difficult task it is to force these writers, quite against their wills, to speak German. They have no desire to give up their native Hebrew in order to imitate our barbaric German.
>
> In rendering Moses, I make him so German that no one would suspect he was a Jew. [89]

Luther was a perfectionist, and, if it weren't for the help of his scholars, he might never have finished. He was known to spend a month rolling a single word around in his head to get the right translation.

The German Bible was nothing but a success. In some circles, it is considered superior to the King James Version that followed. It became prestigious to possess this Bible, which caused those who originally had no hunger for it to buy the Bible and actually read it. It was the "in" book for every German to have in his household. Luther's translation was later used in linguistics for the formation of the modern German language, and today it remains a popular translation used by Christians in Germany.

Anti-Semitic and Anti-Catholic

Luther was convinced that he was living in the last days, and he was violently against anything that was not Christian. That included the Jewish religion.

In earlier years Luther was sympathetic to the Jewish condition and blamed the papacy for the lack of Jewish converts.

> If I were a Jew, I would suffer the rack ten times before I would go over to the pope. The papists have so demeaned themselves that a good Christian would rather be a Jew than one of them, and a Jew would rather be a sow than a Christian. [90]

The Roman Catholic position taught hatred of the Jews. They referred to them as dogs and denied them work. Luther felt that, on the whole, the Jews were a stiff-necked people, but he had hope for their conversion if they were shown the love of Christ.

Luther hoped reform in the papacy would assure Jewish conversions. Luther first tried to convert the rabbis. In so doing, he found the rabbis were trying to convert him. He also heard rumors that in some countries, the Jews were winning converts to their side. This brought his sympathies to a halt. Now he wanted only for all the Jews to be shipped to Palestine. In his unrefined and straightforward manner, Luther dismissed their scriptural interpretations as Jewish garbage. [91]

Luther accused the Jews of killing Christian babies, poisoning wells, and murdering Christ all over again by stabbing Eucharist hosts. He eventually took on the Catholic opinion that Jews were dogs and said at his death, "We are at fault for not slaying them!" [92]

Luther, a Nazi?

Although Luther said his view of Jews was strictly theological, he became known as a racist and the father of the anti-Semitic church. Even Adolf Hitler would quote Luther, and the socialists of the nation called Luther "a genuine German who hated non-Nordic races." [93]

I believe Luther was mistaken in his thoughts about the Jews. Paul warned us in his letter to the Romans to consider ourselves, Gentile believers, as the wild branch that was grafted into a Jewish root. Luther's extremism was wrong, but it wasn't based on race. He despised the Jews for not accepting the revelation of God in Jesus. His hatred is inexcusable, but I wanted to make this distinction. The theory that argued Jews were biologically inferior, an argument Hitler stood on, didn't emerge until the nineteenth century. The twisted labeling involving Luther's name and beliefs had more to do with promoting the Holocaust than what Luther actually stood for.

A student of Luther can tell by reading his many statements concerning the Jews that he was troubled by their spiritual beliefs and not by their race. For example, when confronted by those who thought he abused the Jews, Luther didn't respond with questions about race. He answered, "What do you think of Christ? Was he abusive when he called the Jews an adulterous and perverse generation, an offspring of vipers, hypocrites, and children of the devil?" [94]

☆☆☆☆☆

Luther, an Anti-Papist!

Luther realized that Christ's condemnation wasn't directed solely at the Jewish religion. Just as he was dismayed with the Jews, he was equally disgusted with the papacy.

Luther was a prisoner of his own territory. A convicted heretic, he dared not leave the safety of his home turf. This left him with little else to use for fighting with except the quill in his ink well. So he wrote biting and often foulmouthed comments to the papacy. These comments were widely published throughout the world. [95] Luther's writings shook his enemies and thrilled his followers as he said things like, "We should take him—the pope, the cardinals, and whatever riffraff belongs to His Idolatrous and Papal Holiness—and (as blasphemers) tear out their tongues from the back, and nail them on the gallows." [96] Frequently, cartoons accompanied his writings. Sometimes a cartoon could say more—and say it better—than words. Luther was totally unrestrained in these cartoons. Because Luther thought the pope was the Antichrist, he felt foul language was an appropriate weapon.

Luther violently came against anyone who opposed his reforms. Like an Old Testament prophet, Luther walked the fine line between an attacking wit and prophecy. He constantly scolded his Catholic enemies, saying, "How often must I cry out to you coarse, stupid papists to quote Scripture sometime? Scripture! Scripture! Scripture!" [97]

Before you judge Luther as too coarse, too rough, or too rowdy, stop to remember that he was one man, attacking the head of a dark, deceptive, and hypocritical religion. This mind-set had been in the Church for centuries, and it was going to take an explosion to shake it. Luther gave his *entire* life for the reformation of the church world.

What are you giving your life for?

His Last Days

Luther was perhaps the most influential German who ever lived. Though he was sick much of his later years, he never stopped his efforts at reformation. He started a revolution, but with the revolution, the work had only begun. And work he did. His life was filled with accomplishments, whether he was deathly ill or feeling well. No matter how he felt, he preached. He once preached 195 sermons in just 145 days. [98] If he couldn't preach, he wrote letters and pamphlets. There seemed to be no stop to the amount of work he could bring forth.

Although he was greatly persecuted, Luther had an even greater sense of humor, which is the mark of a truly matured apostle. He had his own personal battles, but, in the end, Luther was always able to laugh at himself. He was often relaxed, cheerful, and extremely witty when everyone else around him was in a state of desperation.

His life touched the earth, and what it took several men in England to do, Luther did all by himself—for all of Europe and eventually the whole world. He made an everlasting impact on the nation of Germany. He called himself a German prophet, mostly to further anger the pope. His Bible translation was used to mold today's spoken German language, and his home life touched all the home lives in Germany.

Luther influenced the church worldwide. Lutheranism took over in Scandinavia, and it proliferates in the United States today. Even the Catholics owe many of their reformations to Luther.

Luther's God was Hebrew. He was the God Moses served. He inhabited storm clouds and rode the wind. Luther's God made him bold.

He also changed the face of religion. Luther despised the idea of a Greek God. His God was Hebrew. His God was the God that Moses served. His God inhabited the storm clouds, rode the wings of the wind, and caused the earth to tremble with a nod. His God was majestic, terrifying, devastating, and consuming. His God made him bold. Though he once trembled in a field, afraid of the thunder and lightning, fearful of the God whom he so misunderstood, now he was full of reverence, admiration, and love. [99] With spiritual strength and an undying loyalty, he took on the assignment of shaking all Christendom.

The last days of his life were met with strength equal to that demonstrated earlier in his life.

☆☆☆☆☆

On January 23, 1546, Luther set out on a journey to settle a dispute between various dukes and their subjects. He was so ill and weak that he had to stop and rest along the way. By the time he had reached his destination, Luther's condition had worsened—yet he preached four times, administered the Lord's Supper twice, and ordained two ministers. He commented about his journey, "If I can but succeed in restoring harmony amongst my dear princes and their subjects, I will cheerfully return home and lay me down in the grave." [100]

On February 17, his illness increased so greatly that Luther was confined to bed. A doctor came to assist him and even offered hope for a cure. But Luther wouldn't hear of it. For years Luther had felt he was close to the grave, mainly because of constant physical affliction. He once, humorously, wrote to Katie, "I am fed up with this world, and it is fed up with me." [101]

During the night of February 17, Luther prayed continuously and spoke of eternity to those around him. Late in the evening, while feeling a great constriction upon his chest, Luther prayed saying, "I beseech Thee, my Lord Jesus Christ, receive my soul. O Heavenly Father, though I be snatched out of this life, yet know I assuredly that I shall dwell with Thee for ever." [102]

Luther on his deathbed.

Between two and three o'clock on the morning of February 18, 1546, Luther closed his eyes and left the earth to be with the Lord. His body was conveyed in a lead coffin, and he was buried in Wittenberg with the greatest of honors. His body still rests at the foot of the pulpit of Castle Church, where he first nailed the Ninety-Five Theses to the door.

Castle Church became the Westminster Abbey of the Lutheran Church. In 1760, the original wooden doors were burned in the Seven Years' War. In 1812, bronze doors were erected in their place, and Luther's Ninety-Five Theses were cast within them. [103]

An "Increasing Church"

Today, we honor Martin Luther as one of the greatest Reformers ever to have lived. However, in all his dramatic exploits, in all his confrontational encounters, his great spiritual strength can be attributed to the simplicity of the Word of God. The revelation of the written Word of God birthed the ministry of Luther into a reforming fire, burning the hypocrisy of the Church and igniting the true spirit of it.

From the Word, Luther realized that he had forgiveness through Jesus Christ and that he was a friend of God's. Luther focused totally on forgiveness, and, from that premise, he continued to build an arsenal of revelation. With these weapons he began to pierce the dark heavens. Those dark heavens eventually opened for you and I. Because of this, we can learn in one service what might have taken believers in the Dark Ages seventy-five years to learn.

Luther believed that the sustaining power in the Word would keep the church alive and well, that it would be able to thresh out deceptions and hypocritical doctrines and find the truth. His vision for the church didn't end with his death.

So I close this chapter with Luther's continuing vision for the church. He knew the dark heavens had begun to open and that they would continue to open as people sought the truth of God. Let his words bring encouragement, because, today, *you* are Luther's fruit in the earth. He said, "I entertain no sorry picture of our Church, but rather that of the Church flourishing through pure and uncorrupted teaching and one increasing with excellent ministers from day to day." [104]

★★★★★

Build your spiritual strength. Know the Word and keep the truth planted firmly in your heart so that you can bear fruit in your nation, keep the heavens open, and bring reformation in the twenty-first century!

✯✯✯✯✯

Martin Luther's Ninety-Five Theses

Out of love and concern for the truth, and with the object of eliciting it, the following heads will be the subject of a public discussion at Wittenberg under the presidency of the Reverend Father, Martin Luther, Augustinian, Master of Arts and Sacred Theology, and duly appointed lecturer on these subjects in that place. He requests that whoever cannot be present personally to debate the matter orally will do so in absence in writing.

1. When our Lord and Master, Jesus Christ, said "Repent," He called for the entire life of believers to be one of penitence.
2. The word cannot be properly understood as referring to the sacrament of penance (i.e., confession and satisfaction) as administered by the clergy.
3. Yet its meaning is not restricted to penitence in one's heart; for such penitence is null unless it produces outward signs in various mortifications of the flesh.
4. As long as hatred of self abides (i.e., true inward penitence) the penalty of sin abides, viz., until we enter the kingdom of heaven.
5. The pope has neither the will nor the power to remit any penalties beyond those imposed either at his own discretion or by canon law.
6. The pope himself cannot remit guilt, but only declare and confirm that it has been remitted by God; or, at most, he can remit it in cases reserved to his discretion. Except for these cases, the guilt remains untouched.
7. God never remits guilt to anyone without, at the same time, making him humbly submissive to the priest, His representative.
8. The penitential canons apply only to men who are still alive, and, according to the canons themselves, none applies to the dead.
9. Accordingly, the Holy Spirit, acting in the person of the pope, manifests grace to us, by the fact that the papal

regulations always cease to apply at death, or in any hard case.

10. It is a wrongful act, due to ignorance, when priests retain the canonical penalties on the dead in purgatory.
11. When canonical penalties were changed and made to apply to purgatory, surely it would seem that tares were sown while the bishops were asleep.
12. In former days, the canonical penalties were imposed, not after, but before absolution was pronounced; and were intended to be tests of true contrition.
13. Death puts an end to all the claims of the church; even the dying are already dead to the canon laws, and are no longer bound by them.
14. Defective piety or love in a dying person is necessarily accompanied by great fear, which is greatest where the piety or love is least.
15. This fear or horror is sufficient in itself, whatever else might be said, to constitute the pain of purgatory, since it approaches very closely to the horror of despair.
16. There seems to be the same difference between hell, purgatory, and heaven as between despair, uncertainty, and assurance.
17. Of a truth, the pains of souls in purgatory ought to be abated, and charity ought to be proportionately increased.
18. Moreover, it does not seem proved, on any grounds of reason or Scripture, that these souls are outside the state of merit, or unable to grow in grace.
19. Nor does it seem proved to be always the case that they are certain and assured of salvation, even if we are very certain of it ourselves.
20. Therefore the pope, in speaking of the plenary remission of all penalties, does not mean "all" in the strict sense, but only those imposed by himself.
21. Hence those who preach indulgences are in error when they say that a man is absolved and saved from every penalty by the pope's indulgences;

22. Indeed, he cannot remit to a soul in purgatory any penalty which canon law declares should be suffered in the present life.
23. If plenary remission could be granted to anyone at all, it would be only in the cases of the most perfect (i.e., to very few).
24. It must therefore be the case that the major part of the people are deceived by that indiscriminate and high-sounding promise of relief from penalty.
25. The same power as the pope exercises in general over purgatory is exercised in particular by every single bishop in his bishopric and priest in his parish.
26. The pope does excellently when he grants remission to the souls in purgatory on account of intercessions made on their behalf, and not by the power of the keys (which he cannot exercise for them).
27. There is no divine authority for preaching that the soul flies out of purgatory immediately when the money clinks in the bottom of the chest.
28. It is certainly possible that, when the money clinks in the bottom of the chest, avarice and greed increase; but when the church offers intercession, all depends on the will of God.
29. Who knows whether all souls in purgatory wish to be redeemed in view of what is said of St. Severinus and St. Paschal?
30. No one is sure of the reality of his own contrition, much less of receiving plenary forgiveness.
31. One who, *bona fide,* buys indulgences is as rare as a *bona fide* penitent man (i.e., very rare indeed).
32. All those who believe themselves certain of their own salvation by means of letters of indulgence, will be eternally damned, together with their teachers.
33. We should be most carefully on our guard against those who say that the papal indulgences are an inestimable divine gift, and that a man is reconciled to God by them.

34. For the grace conveyed by these indulgences relates simply to the penalties of the sacramental "satisfactions" decreed merely by man.
35. It is not in accordance with Christian doctrines to preach and teach that those who buy off souls, or purchase confessional licenses, have no need to repent of their own sins.
36. Any Christian whatsoever, who is truly repentant, enjoys plenary remission from penalty and guilt, and this is given him without letters of indulgence.
37. Any true Christian whatsoever, living or dead, participates in all the benefits of Christ and the Church; and this participation is granted to him by God without letters of indulgence.
38. Yet the pope's remission and dispensation are in no way to be despised, for, as already said, they proclaim the divine remission.
39. It is very difficult, even for the most learned theologians, to extol to the people the great bounty contained in the indulgences, while, at the same time, praising contrition as a virtue.
40. A truly contrite sinner seeks out, and loves to pay, the penalties of his sins; whereas the very multitude of indulgences dulls men's consciences, and tends to make them hate the penalties.
41. Papal indulgences should only be preached with caution, lest people gain a wrong understanding, and think that they are preferable to other good works: those of love.
42. Christians should be taught that the people do not at all intend that the purchase of indulgences should be understood as at all comparable with works of mercy.
43. Christians should be taught that one who gives to the poor or lends to the needy does a better action than if he purchases indulgences;
44. Because, by works of love, love grows and a man becomes a better man; whereas, by indulgences, he does not become a better man, but only escapes certain penalties.

45. Christians should be taught that he who sees a needy person, but passes him by although he gives money for indulgences, gains no benefit from the pope's pardon, but only incurs the wrath of God.
46. Christians should be taught that, unless they have more than they need, they are bound to retain what is necessary for the upkeep of their home, and should in no way squander it on indulgences.
47. Christians should be taught that they purchase indulgences voluntarily, and are not under obligation to do so.
48. Christians should be taught that, in granting indulgences, the pope has more need, and more desire, for devout prayer on his own behalf than for ready money.
49. Christians should be taught that the pope's indulgences are useful only if one does not rely on them, but most harmful if one loses the fear of God through them.
50. Christians should be taught that, if the pope knew the exactions of the indulgence-preachers, he would rather the Church of St. Peter were reduced to ashes than be built with the skin, flesh, and bones of his sheep.
51. Christians should be taught that the pope would be willing, as he ought if necessity should arise, to sell the Church of St. Peter, and give, too, his own money to many of those from whom the pardon-merchants conjure money.
52. It is vain to rely on salvation by letters of indulgence, even if the commissary, or indeed the pope himself, were to pledge his own soul for their validity.
53. Those are enemies of Christ and the pope who forbid the word of God to be preached at all in some churches, in order that indulgences may be preached in others.
54. The Word of God suffers injury if, in the same sermon, an equal or longer time is devoted to indulgences than to that Word.
55. The pope cannot help taking the view that if indulgences (very small matters) are celebrated by one bell, one

pageant, or one ceremony, the Gospel (a very great matter) should be preached to the accompaniment of a hundred bells, a hundred processions, a hundred ceremonies.

56. The treasures of the church, out of which the pope dispenses indulgences, are not sufficiently spoken of or known among the people of Christ.
57. That these treasures are not temporal is clear from the fact that many of the merchants do not grant them freely, but only collect them;
58. Nor are they the merits of Christ and the saints, because, even apart from the pope, these merits are always working grace in the inner man, and working the cross, death, and hell in the outer man.
59. St. Laurence said that the poor were the treasures of the Church, but he used the term in accordance with the custom of his own time.
60. We do not speak rashly in saying that the treasures of the Church are the keys of the Church, and are bestowed by the merits of Christ;
61. For it is clear that the power of the pope suffices, by itself, for the remission of penalties and reserved cases.
62. The true treasure of the Church is the Holy Gospel of the glory and the grace of God.
63. It is right to regard this treasure as most odious, for it makes the first to be the last.
64. On the other hand, the treasure of indulgences is most acceptable, for it makes the last to be the first.
65. Therefore the treasures of the Gospel are nets which, in former times, they used to fish for men of wealth.
66. The treasures of the indulgences are the nets today which they use to fish for men of wealth.
67. The indulgences, which the merchants extol as the greatest of favors, are seen to be, in fact, a favorite means for money-getting;
68. Nevertheless, they are not to be compared with the grace of God and the compassion shown in the Cross.

69. Bishops and curates, in duty bound, must receive the commissaries of the papal indulgences with all reverence;
70. But they are under a much greater obligation to watch closely and attend carefully lest these men reach their own fancies instead of what the pope commissioned.
71. Let him be anathema and accursed who denies the apostolic character of the indulgences;
72. On the other hand, let him be blessed who is on his guard against the wantonness and license of the pardon-merchant's words.
73. In the same way, the pope rightly excommunicates those who make any plans to the detriment of the trade in indulgences.
74. It is much more in keeping with his views to excommunicate those who use the pretext of indulgences to plot anything to the detriment of holy love and truth.
75. It is foolish to think that papal indulgences have so much power that they can absolve a man even if he has done the impossible and violated the mother of God.
76. We assert the contrary, and say that the pope's pardons are not able to remove the least venial of sins as far as their guilt is concerned.
77. When it is said that not even St. Peter, if he were now pope, could grant a greater grace, it is blasphemy against St. Peter and the pope.
78. We assert the contrary, and say that he, and any pope whatsoever, possesses greater graces, viz., the Gospel, spiritual powers, gifts of healing, etc., as is declared in 1 Corinthians 12 [:28].
79. It is blasphemy to say that the insignia of the cross with the papal arms are of equal value to the cross on which Christ died.
80. The bishops, curates, and theologians, who permit assertions of that kind to be made to the people without let or hindrance, will have to answer for it.
81. This unbridled preaching of indulgences makes it difficult for learned men to guard the respect due to the

pope against false accusations, or at least from the keen criticisms of the laity;

82. They ask, e.g.: Why does not the pope liberate everyone from purgatory for the sake of love (a most holy thing) and because of the supreme necessity of their souls? This would be morally the best of all reasons. Meanwhile he redeems innumerable souls for money, a most perishable thing, with which to build St. Peter's Church, a very minor purpose.
83. Again: Why should funeral and anniversary Masses for the dead continue to be said? And why does not the pope repay, or permit to be repaid, the benefactions instituted for these purposes, since it is wrong to pray for those souls who are now redeemed?
84. Again: Surely this is a new sort of compassion, on the part of God and the pope, when an impious man, an enemy of God, is allowed to pay money to redeem a devout soul, a friend of God; while yet that devout and beloved soul is not allowed to be redeemed without payment, for love's sake, and just because of its need of redemption.
85. Again: Why are the penitential canon laws, which in fact, if not in practice, have long been obsolete and dead in themselves,—why are they, today, still used in imposing fines in money, through the granting of indulgences, as if all the penitential canons were fully operative?
86. Again: Since the pope's income today is larger than that of the wealthiest of wealthy men, why does he not build this one Church of St. Peter with his own money, rather than with the money of indigent believers?
87. Again: What does the pope remit or dispense to people who, by their perfect penitence, have a right to plenary remission or dispensation?
88. Again: Surely greater good could be done to the Church if the pope were to bestow these remissions and dispensations, not once, as now, but a hundred times a day, for the benefit of any believer whatsoever.

89. What the pope seeks by indulgences is not money, but rather the salvation of souls; why then does he not suspend the letters and indulgences formerly conceded, and still as efficacious as ever?
90. These questions are serious matter of conscience to the laity. To suppress them by force alone, and not to refute them by giving reasons, is to expose the Church and the pope to the ridicule of their enemies, and to make Christian people unhappy.
91. If, therefore, indulgences were preached in accordance with the spirit and mind of the pope, all these difficulties would be easily overcome, and, indeed, cease to exist.
92. Away, then, with those prophets who say to Christ's people, "Peace, peace," where there is no peace.
93. Hail, hail to all those prophets who say to Christ's people, "The cross, the cross," where there is no cross.
94. Christians should be exhorted to be zealous to follow Christ, their Head, through penalties, deaths, and hells;
95. And let them thus be more confident of entering heaven through many tribulations rather than through a false assurance of peace.

★★★★★

Notes

[1] "Martin Luther, The Later Years and Legacy," *Christian History Magazine* 12, no. 3, issue 39, (Carol Stream, Ill.: Christianity Today, Inc.): 10.
[2] Roland H. Bainton, *Here I Stand—A Life of Martin Luther* (Nashville, Tenn.: Abingdon Press, 1978), 18.
[3] Ibid., 19.
[4] Ibid., 25.
[5] Ibid., 21.
[6] Ibid.
[7] Ibid., 27.
[8] Ibid., 24
[9] Ibid., 25.
[10] J. H. Merle D'Aubigne, *The Life and the Times of Martin Luther* (Chicago, Ill.: Moody Press): 31.
[11] Heinrich Boehmer, *Martin Luther: Road to Reformation* (London, England: Meridian Books, Muhlenberg Press, 1957): 43.
[12] Bainton, 35.
[13] Ibid., 37.
[14] Ibid., 36, 38.
[15] Ibid., 41.
[16] Ibid., 41–42.
[17] Ibid., 44.
[18] "Martin Luther, The Early Years," *Christian History Magazine* 11, no. 2, issue 34 (Carol Stream, Ill.: Christianity Today, Inc.): 15.
[19] Ibid.
[20] Ibid.
[21] Bainton, 50.
[22] Ibid., 51.
[23] Ibid., 59.
[24] Ibid., 58, 60.
[25] Ibid., 63.
[26] "The Early Years," 49.
[27] Mike Fearon, *Martin Luther* (Minneapolis, Minn.: Bethany House Publishers, 1986): 128.
[28] Bainton, 67.
[29] Boehmer, 236.
[30] Ibid., 235–240.

[31] Bainton, 80.
[32] "The Early Years," 14.
[33] Boehmer, 361–362.
[34] Ibid., 362–363.
[35] "The Early Years," 14.
[36] Boehmer, 369.
[37] Ibid., 373.
[38] Ibid., 370.
[39] "The Early Years," 14.
[40] Boehmer, 371.
[41] Ibid., 196, 378–379.
[42] Ibid., 372.
[43] Ibid., 299.
[44] Ibid., 299–300.
[45] Ibid., 332–333.
[46] Ibid., 321.
[47] "The Early Years," 24.
[48] Ibid., 23–25.
[49] Ibid., 25.
[50] Boehmer, 307.
[51] Ibid., 308.
[52] Ibid., 323–325.
[53] Ibid., 324.
[54] "The Early Years," 16.
[55] Ibid.
[56] Ibid.
[57] Ibid.
[58] German Luther Society, 18.
[59] Bainton, 165–166.
[60] William J. Peterson, *Martin Luther Had a Wife* (Chepstow, Gwent: England, Bridge Publishing, 1984): 20.
[61] Ibid., 20–21.
[62] Ibid., 20.
[63] Ibid., 14.
[64] Ibid., 22.
[65] Ibid., 22–24.
[66] Ibid., 24.
[67] Ibid.
[68] Ibid., 14.

★★★★★

[69] Ibid., 26.
[70] Ibid., 26, 29.
[71] Ibid., 31.
[72] Ibid., 30.
[73] Ibid., 30–31.
[74] Ibid., 31.
[75] Ibid., 31–32.
[76] Ibid., 32.
[77] Ibid., 33.
[78] Ibid., 34.
[79] Ibid., 14, 35.
[80] Ibid., 34–35.
[81] Ibid., 34, 36.
[82] "The Later Years," 11.
[83] Henry Eyster Jacobs, *Martin Luther—Heroes of the Reformation* (Stationers Hall: London, England, G. P. Putnam's Sons, 1899): 274.
[84] Ibid.
[85] "The Later Years," 16.
[86] Ibid.
[87] Ibid., 17.
[88] Ibid., 19.
[89] "The Early Years," 36.
[90] Bainton, 297.
[91] "The Later Years," 35.
[92] Ibid., 39.
[93] Ibid.
[94] Ibid., 36.
[95] Bainton, 298.
[96] "The Later Years," 35.
[97] Ibid., 37.
[98] Ibid., 28.
[99] Ibid., 302.
[100] Back to the Bible Publisher, *Martin Luther, The Reformer* (Lincoln, Nebr.: Moody Press): 125.
[101] "The Later Years," 35.
[102] *Martin Luther, The Reformer,* 125.
[103] Jacobs, 408–409.
[104] Bainton, 286.

CHAPTER FOUR

John Calvin

1509–1564

"The Teaching Apostle"

"THE TEACHING APOSTLE"

When I consider that I am not in my own power, I offer my heart a slain victim for a sacrifice to the Lord....I yield my soul chained and bound unto obedience to God. [1]

This quotation was spoken by John Calvin late in his life and ministry, and I feel it best portrays the explosive yet deeply committed personality of this great Reformer. It illustrates the heart behind a great drama that will unfold in the following pages.

A Reforming Apostle

Though he made mistakes, and several of his theological positions remain in question, John Calvin truly portrayed the spirit of a Reformer. He is called one of the greatest Protestants who ever lived—some believe he surpassed Luther. Calvin took the truths that Luther unveiled and, driven by divine direction, used those truths to ignite further revelations from the Word.

Though each "general" in this book had his specific post ordained by God, none but Calvin had such a pivotal and monumental role in reforming the Church. He was not an earthshaking preacher, nor was he a fiery evangelist. Some have said that, in our generation, he would have been a world-renowned prophet. But I disagree.

I can say that he was an apostolic teacher, a reformed thinker and writer, unearthing the hidden truths that had been covered by ignorance, superstition, persecution, and religion. If anything, Calvin taught us how to unflinchingly stand by the Word, to unearth hidden treasures within ourselves, and to stand for the truth of God at all times and in any situation. He carried a divine torch that we must again discover, obtain within ourselves, and then bear to our generation.

A Prisoner of Truth

A thousand pens have written about Calvin's life. A highly controversial figure, Calvin was either passionately loved or vehemently hated by those who knew him and, later, by those who studied his life. The second attitude still prevails among people who do not understand this apostolic personality. Before we explore Calvin's life, it's important that we acquire a basic understanding of why he operated as he did.

Called one of the greatest Protestants who ever lived, none but Calvin had such a pivotal role in reforming the Church.

Calvin was an intricate and complex person. Most apostolic people are viewed as complicated because they do not fit the status quo. They won't "go with the flow" if the flow is heading in the wrong direction. They won't conform or keep quiet for the sake of peace. Apostolic people aren't peace*keepers*, like those who forsake principles and truth in order to keep everyone happy. Instead they are peace*makers*, ready and willing to take the necessary action for truth to prevail. To them, there is no peace if error is present. Calvin believed that to ignore error was grossly carnal. To him, those who hid from controversy or confusion were brutes.

An apostle thinks this way: If you don't have understanding, get it, and get it with truth. Once you get it, live it and voice it. If error is present, correct it; then do whatever it takes to change it, and live however you must in order to make the change complete.

Apostolic people are passionate for the truth; they are unflinchingly loyal to God. Because of those core passions, they are viewed by the uninstructed as odd or mean-spirited when they stand against those who violate His truths. To apostles such as Calvin, the greatest tragedy on earth is a life that does not follow God's plan. Because of that unflinching loyalty to God and His kingdom, apostles are sometimes labeled as having little understanding, little kindness, and little humor.

Actually, the opposite is true. In spite of how it seems, genuine apostles are our strongest advocates. We need to thank God for apostles who have little sympathy for the error that deceives and who have little kindness for the sin that destroys the fruitfulness of our lives. We need to understand that the apostles see little humor in the kingdom of God being hindered by the weaknesses and evils of mankind.

Calvin thought this way: If you don't have understanding, get it, and get it with truth. Once you get it, live it and voice it.

I ask you: Where would we be today if apostolic leaders had sympathized with error, evil, and weakness? Would they have achieved a monumental Reformation if they had sided with conformity and ignorance?

A Chapter Can't Tell It All

There have been hundreds of books written to portray every aspect of Calvin's life; this is only a chapter. In one chapter, I can only highlight certain specifics. My goal is to present great men as human beings who gave their lives in obedience to the call of God. The simplicity of Calvin's call is evident as one studies the passions of his heart.

Later in the chapter, I will highlight a few of Calvin's theological positions. My goal is not to present a theological exposition or debate on Calvin's beliefs, but to present the spirit by which he reformed the body of Christ. If you wish to study Calvin with a theological tone, there are volumes of books that have been written throughout the centuries that can amply educate you in that area.

Born into the Upper Crust

Noyon was a small yet influential town approximately sixty-five miles northeast of Paris, France. It was here on the summer morning of July 10, 1509, that the distinguished notary Gerard Calvin and his wife, Jeanne, gave birth to their fourth child, a son, whom they named John.

In the year that Calvin was born, whispers and waves of a new Reformation were already circulating throughout France. The leader of this Reformation, a German named Martin Luther, had received his baccalaureate degree in Bible and was giving lectures on obtaining salvation through a relationship with God.

John Calvin enjoyed a childhood of prominence and influence. Although he wasn't born into wealth, his mother was the daughter of a very successful innkeeper, and his father had a prominent position as a notary in the service of clergy and magistrates. Having a practical knowledge of legal matters, his father also acted as an attorney for the cathedral chapter and was a secretary to the bishop, overseeing his financial records and accounts.

There is very little information on Calvin's mother. She was known for her beauty and commitment to the Church, and she took young John to visit the shrines while he was a baby. On one of the visits, young John kissed the head of one of the statues.

After giving birth to five children (two of whom died young), John's mother died when he was only three years old. Gerard remarried, but nothing is known of John's stepmother except that she gave birth to two daughters, one of whom lived with her famous half-brother later in life.

Because of his father's influential position, young John made friends with the upper crust. His boyhood companions consisted of the wealthy, and he enjoyed an education by private tutors. He was granted the privilege to attend a private boys' school in Noyon.

John developed a warm affection for aristocracy. He referred to himself as a common person who was granted the luxury of good friends and an excellent education.

Due to his father's influence, John was only twelve years old when he was appointed as a chaplain in the cathedral. During this time, he was given a modest salary without having to perform any duties. Gerard Calvin was establishing his son for prominence.

It was not surprising that an education at the university in Paris was planned. Gerard arranged for the Church to provide the funds for his son to attend the university, promising that John would study for the priesthood.

When John was only fourteen years old, he left Noyon to live with his uncle in Paris and enrolled in the College de la Marche, an arts and theological college of the University of Paris. The university entrance records state the name "Cauvin" had been Latinized as "Calvinus," and deLatinized again; the name appears as we know it, "Jean (John) Calvin." [2]

Calvin enrolled in 1523, just three years after Martin Luther had burned the canon and the papal papers threatening his excommunication. By this time, the Reformation in Germany had reached a zenith, saturated by the ideas and actions of Martin Luther. The Reformation was exploding throughout Europe.

A Fourteen-Year-Old College Student

At a mere fourteen years of age, Calvin found himself in one of the greatest universities, located in the heart of the one of the greatest nations known at the time. The shallow ideologies of Noyon were left far behind, and Calvin now found himself in the midst of the intellectual, political, and religious excitement of the era.

Government and religion were tightly intertwined. In fact, rarely did any concept exist or any event take place in which both weren't deeply involved. France, however, was a monarchy, which meant that, officially, the king ruled, even at the protest of the Church.

The Roman Catholic Church was in sad shape. Immorality was rampant, and theological education was at an all-time low. The Church had no desire to pursue truth. Because of the Reformation's growing prominence, all kinds of unusual views and theories were circulating at the university. The Church was not interested in sorting through these views to find truth, preferring instead to defend its current traditions and doctrines.

Calvin was unusually brilliant and eager to learn. Because of this, he stood out to a very distinguished priest and teacher of Latin, Mathurin Cordier. Cordier spent many hours with Calvin, educating him in Latin and in the systems of government and church. Although the two were thirty-two years apart in age, they became lifelong friends. Cordier followed Calvin later in the Reformation and lived with him until death. Cordier's influence upon Calvin helped to establish a sense of style and brilliance in his future writings.

Molded for Destiny

Calvin soon left College de la Marche and enrolled in the College de Montaigu.

I believe Calvin made this move because of his hunger for purity. This university was known for its moral strictness, and a person attended this school only if he desired a life of discipline. I think Calvin was becoming disillusioned by the moral laxity he saw among the clergy and was searching for the best he could find within his own beliefs. At this time in his education, Calvin "ate little and slept little, but devoured books." [3]

Although Calvin was young, he had the mind of an old man. He was very mature for his age, and an air of studiousness surrounded him. Calvin loved books; he enjoyed dissecting a subject until he came to a thorough understanding of it.

Although he spent many hours studying, he was not a critical, condemning hermit, as many of his contemporaries claimed he was. Many of these writers didn't understand his personality, and rumors began because some were jealous that he attracted so many choice friends at such a young age.

Calvin remained close to these childhood friends from Noyon, and these same friends later joined Calvin in the Reformation. He also made new friends, many of whom were several years older than him. The fact that these friends were loyal throughout the years demonstrates his character and personality.

Calvin was a frequent guest in the homes of two of the greatest scholars in the university—one of whom was the king's physician. He became very close to the sons of these men, and both of their families were welcomed by Calvin as refugees during his Reformation years.

Relationships were very important to Calvin. No matter where the path of destiny took him, he never forgot his friends, nor the people who treated him with kindness. Within his superior mentality was a heart of gold. Calvin was softhearted, always willing to help those in need, even allowing them to live in his home if the need arose.

While a student at College de Montaigu, Calvin furthered his study of Latin and learned the art of debate, or vocal argumentation, as they called it. It's easy to picture the slender seventeen-year-old, brilliant in phrase, disrupting a debate and silencing the participants with his superior insight and knowledge. Debate was an art Calvin cherished, and I'm sure it fueled the fiery temperament he became known for.

At this time he also came in contact with a very famous Scotsman named John Major. Calvin was mesmerized by the scholastic philosophy of this Scotsman and spent every free hour he could with the instructor. Calvin would debate Major on the subjects he had learned in class, but Major's articulate knowledge would leave Calvin yearning to learn more. Major had previously written a commentary on the Gospels, which had been influenced by Wycliffe, Hus, and Luther. Calvin heard the undistorted details of Luther's life and theology from the lectures of Major. He embraced the information and buried it deep within his heart.

An Abrupt Turn in the Road of Destiny

In 1528, when Calvin was only eighteen years old, he received a master of arts degree. He was now fluent in Latin and proficient in philosophy and humanism. Just when it seemed that the road to priesthood had been paved for Calvin, an unexpected turn of events took place.

Gerard's job was threatened. Calvin's father had grown increasingly unpopular with the clergy at the cathedral in Noyon. They questioned Gerard about his accounting abilities and requested to review his books. Gerard was highly offended that his integrity was questioned and refused to turn the books over. His resistance resulted in excommunication.

Possibly fearing that the funds for his son's education would be cut off, or perhaps just angry at the Church establishment, Gerard was inspired to make an abrupt change in Calvin's education. Now Gerard wanted his son to be educated as a lawyer. He had been a lawyer and had enjoyed the wealth and social perks that accompanied it. Being excommunicated, he knew that his son's priesthood would not financially benefit the family. Gerard decided that his son should pursue the legal profession and sent word to him, commanding him to make the change to the college at Orleans.

The news was shocking to Calvin. He didn't have a close relationship with his father, but he felt bound by duty to obey. At nineteen years old, Calvin found himself migrating to Orleans and enrolling in the school of law.

Calvin Embraces the Renaissance

Although Calvin was not genuinely interested in law, being the ardent student that he was, he found his studies fascinating.

During the year-and-a-half study at Orleans, he became the pupil of Pierre de l'Etoile, one of the foremost instructors of jurisprudence in all of France. Calvin had great respect for Etoile, partly because he was a devout conservative who had become a priest after his wife's death.

Calvin moved to the front of the class. His promotion was not due to a love for law but to a passion for the study of languages, literature, and cultures. Calvin maintained such an iron discipline of study that he was regarded as a "rising legal scholar." [4] Calvin developed the ideals of the Renaissance here and began to delve into the outskirts of evangelical faith as well.

During this era, the effects of learning Greek as well as Latin saturated Europe. The Greek language was an uncharted field of study and was still linked to heresy. The timid avoided it and bowed to the Church's judgment. Concerning Greek, this warning was published, "We are finding now a new language called *grège.* We must avoid it at all costs, for this language gives birth to heresies. Especially beware of the New Testament in Greek; it is a book full of thorns and prickles." [5] But Calvin was a freethinker. If something increased or gave substance to his reasoning and thoughts, he embraced it. He cared little about the opinions of others, unless they gave validity to a thought he was processing. During his studies at Orleans, he openly thanked those instructors who dared to mix the Greek language with the law.

Intellectualism was at its peak. This era produced a revolution of the arts. For example, the printing press had been invented during the fifteenth century, and its use was becoming common throughout the known world. People saw the printing press as a vital way to spread their messages. The phenomenon of such an invention could be compared to the computer in our day. The printed word soon had great value because authors realized a book would reach much farther geographically than they were able to physically travel. Cheap editions of Greek and Latin classics were being printed rapidly, and people rushed to purchase them. Martin Luther had already taken advantage of distributing his books years earlier. Calvin would similarly take advantage of this great expansion.

John Calvin, French Protestant Reformer.
Hulton Archive/Getty

Calvin purchased the classics and read the works of Plato and Aristotle in every moment of his spare time. His hunger for philosophy was so great that he was never satisfied with his learning in political and humanistic writings.

Calvin was always searching for something to satisfy his hunger and his discontent with the status quo. Many of the law students decided to transfer to the college at Bourges. The king's sister had appointed a radical Italian instructor to teach Roman law at the school, and Calvin's classmates were wild with excitement at the thought of learning from him. After hearing their reasons and watching the finest of his classmates transfer, Calvin soon joined them. At the end of 1529, Calvin became a student in Bourges.

The Threat of Lutheranism

Although Calvin was absorbed in his own studies, Lutheranism loomed all around him. If a proponent of this theology was caught, he would be given a trial by the Church and, if found guilty, with the nod of the government, be either burned at the stake, lynched, or beheaded. This happened quite frequently in Paris, and even though it seemed Calvin's life was filled with other distractions, he was aware of each verdict as it happened. He was also aware of the rapidly rising Protestant movement—of both the Reformers and the Lutherans.

Before I continue, it's important to explain the differences between the Lutherans and the Reformers, two branches of Protestantism.

Reformed theology (i.e., New Testament, grace, faith, etc.) had been circulating for years before Martin Luther stepped on the scene, but his life's work forced it to the forefront. With his Ninety-Five Theses, Luther separated Reformed theology from Roman Catholic theology, and the Roman Catholic Church proceeded to label everyone who was associated with these truths as Protestants.

Since Luther believed a little differently than the Reformers, chiefly in the area of communion, Lutheranism became a segment of Reformed Protestant theology. There were many Protestants who would not call themselves Lutherans because they didn't believe as Luther did. In fact, Ulrich Zwingli, the great Swiss Reformer, claimed to have preached the true reforming Gospel long before Luther came on the scene, and he resented being designated as a Lutheran, as if that was the only branch of Protestantism. At that time, there were many different segments of belief that claimed the name of Protestant, as there are today. In this chapter, I will label both Lutherans and Reformers as Protestant unless a clarification is needed.

Because Calvin had a mind for reason, he often discussed with fellow students the passion and ideas these Lutherans and Reformers had. One of the most famous heresy burnings took place in Bourges just as Calvin arrived. One of Luther's followers, who had been vastly instrumental in penetrating France with books on his ideas and opinions, had finally been caught by the Church just as Calvin arrived. They burned him at the stake, but this man's death did nothing to stop the spread of Lutheranism throughout France.

★★★★★

The college at Bourges was a disappointing experience for Calvin. Calvin was an admirer of the conservative Etoile, and the new Italian instructor who was brought in by the king's sister openly condemned him. Calvin had already come to the conclusion that the Italian instructor was pompous, vain, and irreverent. In fact, Calvin was so disdainful of the man's prideful personality that he hated the thought of sitting under him.

The first preface that Calvin ever wrote for a book was birthed from his disgust for this man. One of his classmates had written a book in Etoile's defense, and Calvin was honored to write its preface. As a slap in the face to the famed Italian instructor, Calvin wrote in his published preface of Etoile, "for his penetration, competence, and expertness in law is the unrivaled prince of our age." [6]

At a young age, Calvin demonstrated that he would never flinch at controversy if it meant defending what he believed to be truth.

A Mark That Couldn't Be Erased

Shortly after his first preface was published in 1531, Calvin was summoned to Noyon with the news that his father was dying. Calvin was at his bedside when Gerard met his death. Calvin spoke of his father's death with a strange indifference. Possibly, he resented the change of professions that his father had commanded of him.

With his father gone and the details of the estate in the hands of his brother Charles, Calvin took a break from law school and spent the rest of the summer and fall in Paris, attending lectures on Greek and Hebrew. He was now free to make his own choice of profession. Although he had no intentions of becoming a lawyer, he was not finished with his studies at the law school. Paris was a dangerous place to live since it was grossly infected with the plague, but Calvin was not one to leave a task unfinished. He reluctantly returned to Orleans and, in 1532, obtained his doctorate in law.

An Unshakable Lutheran Impression

Bursting with knowledge, Calvin felt inspired to take advantage of the printing press and write a book of his own. The plague had now been subdued in Paris, and, longing to see his vast circle of friends,

Calvin returned to the bustling city later in 1532. This time, he paid little attention to the lectures going on around him and, instead, gave himself to the task of writing his first book.

Loving politics, he was obsessed by the ideas of an ancient philosopher named Seneca. Calvin took this man's ideas and formulated a book filled with academic reasoning, attempting to provide some insight as to why Nero ruled as he did. The book was entitled *A Commentary on Seneca's "Of Clemency."* In the book, Calvin agreed that kings have a high authority by a divine right, yet he condemned the pride, sins, and reasonings that led them to inhumane actions.

Calvin published the book himself, and it was a miserable failure. However, two good things came out of what seemed to be wasted time and money. First, there are elements in this book that became a permanent foundation in his political doctrine during his leadership in the Reformation. Second, in order to write the book, Calvin secluded himself in the home of a devout Lutheran. As a result, he came under direct and constant Protestant influence.

Why did he seek refuge with this particular man? Perhaps Calvin felt that none of his Catholic peers would bother him there to question or influence his writing. It could have been that Calvin felt comfortable with the heart of this man and secure that it would be a haven for his thoughts to run freely. Or maybe the Holy Spirit led him there.

While Calvin was hard at work with his secular writings, this man would sit in the next room and devour the books and writings of Luther, commenting on the inspiration he received. Calvin's thoughts would be interrupted by Protestants, French and foreign, constantly knocking on the man's door, seeking refuge in his home. Calvin was probably an interested listener as the refugees sat around the table, discussing their strong beliefs and dangerous exploits. Calvin would often find himself alone as his host visited the poor and the sick, handing out food, tracts on Lutheranism, and Scripture passages. This kind, fearless man was later burned at the stake for his Protestant passion and involvement.

Having such a genuine and earnest heart himself, there is no way that Calvin was unaffected by the kindness, passion, and true Christian service that this man showed to others. Calvin witnessed this man die willingly for what he believed. The events that went on in that house made a mark on Calvin that would never be erased.

☆☆☆☆☆

The Inner Conversion

Portions of Calvin's life are unclear because he himself gave no significant details concerning them. Sometime between 1529 and 1533, Calvin was converted to the beliefs of Protestant salvation by faith, yet he remained a Catholic. No one can pinpoint the date of his conversion. Some records say that Calvin was preaching as early as 1529, in stone pulpits, in villages, and "in a barn near the river."[7] It isn't clear what Calvin was preaching, although one hearer commented, "At any rate he tells us something new."[8] It is possible that he could have remained a Catholic and preached, although the practice of open-air preaching was not common among them. He could have been preaching his philosophies. It is also possible that he embraced the evangelical position for some time before he openly spoke of it. His sympathy to the cause developed as early as his stay in the Protestant cloth merchant's home while writing his first book.

Calvin described an experience of his in one of his published manuscripts entitled, *A Commentary on Psalms* (1557). He said,

> God drew me from obscure and lowly beginnings and conferred on me that most honorable office of herald and minister of the Gospel....What happened first was that by an unexpected conversion He tamed to teachableness a mind too stubborn for its years—for I was strongly devoted to the superstitions of the Papacy that nothing less could draw me from such depths of mire. And so this mere taste of true godliness that I received set me on fire with such a desire to progress that I pursued the rest of my studies more coolly, although I did not give them up altogether. Before a year had slipped by, anybody who longed for a purer doctrine kept on coming to learn from me, still a beginner and a raw recruit.[9]

Similar to Luther, Calvin never gave the exact date of his conversion. These Reformers were more interested in the corporate expansion of the Reformation than they were in the individual details of their lives.

The early Reformers were selfless individuals. They truly had the distinction of giving their lives for what they believed. They understood persecution, and they never backed away from it. The Reformers were absolutely fearless individuals who voiced their convictions without trembling and without remorse. They lived what they believed and drew a very clear line between right and wrong as they knew it.

Some believe Calvin's conversion took place in 1533 because of the events that followed him that year. Up to this particular time, lynching and burning for heresy took place all around him, but neither touched Calvin nor even challenged him, perhaps because he kept an alliance—though loose—with the Catholic Church. That alliance protected him from being counted among the Protestants.

But that safe, unspoken alliance changed dramatically after a speech by Nicolaus Cop.

The Speech That Shattered

The year was 1533. Calvin had returned to Paris only to find the atmosphere of the city marked by tension. Europe had been wrestling with the new Christian faith sparked by the writings of Martin Luther.

Calvin mainly returned to the city because his very close friend, Nicolaus Cop, had just been appointed as the dean of the University of Paris. He made sure to be present when Cop gave his inaugural address to the academic community. Calvin was seated among the inner circle of friends and also honored for his own academic achievements.

On November 1, the auditorium was packed with Catholic clergy and honored students. The mood was tense as Cop climbed the stairs and stood at the pulpit.

The inaugural address was designed to review institutional goals and affairs, and each instructor and honored student was to use the speech to plan his vision of education for the coming academic year.

Cop opened the address by announcing his theme: Christian philosophy. Calvin's mind must have turned to the long nights that he and Cop had sat and discussed their views of Christian faith. He probably held his breath, wondering if Cop would use this platform to voice his views.

Calvin didn't have to wonder for very long. Cop spoke as though the entire audience consisted of Reformers.

Cop began his speech with a presentation of Christian philosophy. Many of his ideas came from the original Greek, a language that the Catholic Church classified as heretical. Some of the points Cop used were taken directly from a published work by Luther. He showed his indebtedness to Luther by saying, "The law drives by commands, threatens, urges, promises no good will. The Gospel drives by no threats, does not force by commands, teaches God's utmost goodwill toward us."[10]

As if that statement wasn't enough of a challenge to the Church, Cop went further. He said, "A faithful son may serve his father while the father lives and then receive an inheritance upon the father's death. The inheritance may be seen as a reward of faithful sonship, but it is in no way a debt owed the son by the father. So it is that we may be faithful to God, serving Him and obeying the law as His children. The blessings of God are not the reward of that service. They are instead the benefit of our salvation received by grace."[11]

Cop went on to praise those who had been persecuted for God and called for an end to the theological differences that are "practiced through fear of those who kill the body but cannot harm the soul."[12] (These very words would be turned against Calvin later in his life, when he was blamed for the execution of a man.)

Cop intended his address to open the minds of the students and faculty to consider the Protestant ideas as a part of the new learning that was knocking at the doors of the university. They didn't see it that way. Instead, they viewed Cop as an undercover Lutheran and saw his ideas as a threat. They interpreted his speech as an attack against those who persecuted the Protestants. Needless to say, shortly after the opening address, Nicolaus Cop fled Paris.

Being such a close friend of Cop, Calvin's name was grouped with the Protestants. In fact, for years after Calvin's death, many still believed that he was the one who actually wrote the speech! Among Calvin's personal papers, an exact copy of the speech, written in his own handwriting, was found. [13] If this is true, Calvin had definitely embraced the Protestant belief of salvation years before, though he remained a Catholic. During the many years he spent in studious seclusion, it is believed that Calvin was the ghostwriter for Protestant sermons preached by others, as well as speeches such as Cop's.

After Cop fled Paris, Calvin was not far behind him.

Breaking an Addiction to Religion

Calvin went into hiding in the small town of Nerac throughout the winter of 1533–1534. He greatly wrestled within himself during this period of seclusion. Scores of young Protestants sought him out, desperate to receive his knowledge and wisdom. But Calvin considered himself merely a novice; besides, he was still connected with the Catholic Church.

Calvin's internal struggles led him out of hiding in the spring of 1534. He returned to Paris for one reason: to seek out the wisdom of the famed Bible scholar Lefevre D'Etaples.

Calvin had heard of Lefevre since his formative years and had been friends with several of his students. He had heard how this greatly respected man, once ordained as a Catholic priest, had instead become the leader of the French Reform movement. Lefevre searched the Scriptures for himself and came to the conclusion that the Bible was the sole source of authority. He coined the phrase, "literal-spiritual," meaning that only the Holy Spirit could interpret the meaning of Scripture.[14]

Lefevre and Calvin emphasized that man was saved by grace and not works. Grace spoke of the love and goodness of God toward mankind.

Lefevre also came to understand that man was saved by grace (faith) and not by works, nor by human merits established by the Church. He spoke more of grace than faith, as did Calvin in his later years. This was a product of the religious era and error in which they lived: Grace spoke more of the love and goodness of God toward mankind—something that the Catholic Church had deleted.

A strong advocate of the very strict doctrine of predestination, Lefevere's interpretation of Scripture influenced Luther greatly, and the two men's works complimented each other.

In the year 1534, Lefevre was nearly one hundred years old, and Calvin knew he needed to move quickly if he wanted to have audience with him. Living to that age in the current day is quite a feat, but in those days it was especially amazing; most were fortunate to live into their fifties. Calvin made the journey from Nerac and, being a fellow Frenchman, was granted an audience with Lefevre.

There is no record of their conversation, but I would have loved to have heard it. Lefevre prophesied to Calvin that he would be "an instrument in the establishing of the kingdom of God in France."[15] I believe that the Holy Spirit was present in their discussion and that Calvin found revelation and understanding. Lefevre encouraged Calvin to take a bolder stand than even he himself had taken. Coming to Lefevre as a confused and questioning young man, Calvin departed with a clear understanding of the task ahead and what he had to do. Whatever was spoken between the two was never discussed by Calvin, but his life clearly demonstrated the transformation.

The meeting with Lefevre took place April 6, 1534. Despite his father's excommunication, Calvin had remained in good standing with the Church in Noyon. In fact, he was scheduled to be ordained as a Catholic priest just two months after his meeting with Lefevre.

What had once been painful to Calvin was now his only course to peace. Calvin came away from the meeting with Lefevre convinced that reform would never take place as long as he remained within the Catholic Church. No matter the price, the hypocrisies of the Catholic Church must be refused and cut off by his personal denunciation.

Calvin's meeting with Lefevre showed him that God had His hand on Calvin's life. Calvin knew he could no longer compromise.

Calvin had wrestled with this fact for years. He later confessed that he had been "stubbornly addicted" to the papacy and to the religious system in which he had been raised and expected to obtain leadership.[16]

Calvin described his love of the Church as a "barrier of resistance" that had protected his ministry plans and financial security. But this barrier now appeared to him a hypocritical heresy against the will of God. Understanding had broken through his passive protection, and the hindrances had been removed. Calvin no longer viewed his life as one of the many in a compromising multitude. Now that he knew his course, there could be "no postponement, no rationalized evasion. The hand of God was laid upon him."[17]

On May 4, 1534, less than one month after his historical and divine meeting with Lefevre, Calvin journeyed to Noyon and turned in his ministerial papers with the Catholic Church. The questions were over and the truth was clear. He had decisively and forever made his stand against the institution of the Catholic Church and for God.

The Placard War

Calvin decided to remain in Noyon for a season and visit with his family. He must have underestimated the uproar that occurred when he broke ties with the Catholic Church.

In a matter of days, Calvin's brother Charles was arrested for heresy. On May 26, Calvin himself was arrested because he failed to report Charles for heresy. After two short periods of imprisonment, Calvin was told to leave Noyon. He wasn't held for heresy himself.

Throughout 1534, Calvin moved from place to place, making his whereabouts unpredictable. He never spoke publicly during this time, but he constantly held Bible studies for those who were entering the arena as Protestants. People from all walks of life sought Calvin out, from a paralyzed shoemaker to nobles and professors. These were the first "Calvinists."[18]

At this time, Calvin risked his life to enter the streets of Paris for a meeting with Michael Servetus. Servetus was a Spanish radical who had just published a book seeking to reform the Church. The book was written in a confused and heretical fashion, and Servetus had agreed to meet Calvin to discuss and correct the errors. Calvin hoped that his meeting would cause Servetus to become a powerful voice in the Protestant Reformation.

Servetus never showed for the appointment. Calvin had to leave Paris for safer surroundings, but he had marked the unpredictable character of Servetus as trouble. Calvin had no idea at the time just how much trouble Servetus would prove to be later in his life.

Although remaining in France seemed safe enough for Calvin, this was soon to change. The Protestant radicals in Paris began to launch a massive campaign against the Catholic Church. It culminated on October 18, 1534. The campaign came to be known as the Affair of the Placards.

Before I discuss the Affair of the Placards, it is important to first discuss the main character of the event: King Francis I.

Francis I was the king of France during Calvin's early Reformation years. He had been tolerant of the Protestant cause, mostly because his sister was sympathetic toward and friends with many Protestants. But that all changed with the placards.

The Protestants published tracts denouncing the Catholic Mass and worship of saints, stating that they were blasphemous and that the pope, his cardinals, bishops, priests, and monks were hypocrites and servants of the Antichrist. [19] These famous placards were posted on virtually every street, building, and church in Paris—even on the bedroom door of the king!

No one knows how a placard made it to the king's bedroom door, but he was outraged by the audacity of it. Feeling belittled and mocked by this action, Francis I now cared little what his sister thought, and he waged an unprecedented response to the placards. He felt the words on these placards posed a threat to France as a Christian nation, so he staged a procession, which marched through the streets of Paris with the purpose of purging the city of this defilement.

The procession ended at the Cathedral of Notre Dame, where a Mass was performed to atone for the Protestant defilement. At a public celebration meal, the King stood and declared that he "would not hesitate to behead any one of his own children if found guilty of these new, accursed heresies, and to offer them as a sacrifice to divine justice." [20]

To demonstrate his intentions, Francis I summoned the citizens of Paris to witness the burning of six Protestants. Twenty-four Protestants were burned at the stake over the next six months.

With such intense persecution, Calvin was forced to leave the nation of his birth and seek refuge in Switzerland. Little did he know that, from this small nation, a worldwide Reformation would grow—a Reformation that continues to shape Western civilization.

A Plea for the Martyrs

After making several stops in various cities along the way, Calvin found himself seeking refuge in Basel, Switzerland, deep into the Swiss Alps. His friend Nicolaus Cop had already settled there. The date was January, 1535. At this time, Calvin had no desire for public work or ministry; he only wanted to give himself to study and writing. Basel was a very obscure and peaceful town, settled mainly by Germans and far from the perilous tension in Paris.

Calvin had just received word that his cloth merchant friend (who had housed him while he wrote his first book) had recently been burned at the stake. Calvin's heart nearly broke at the loss. He began to write the first edition of the famous Institutes, *Christianae Religionis Institutio.*

The first edition of this classic was not primarily written to provide or explain Protestant doctrine, although it did include instruction. Instead, the main reason Calvin wrote it was to vindicate the martyrs whose deaths were *"precious in the sight of the LORD"* (Psalm 116:15) and to ask for help from other nations to end the murder of those deemed heretics by the Church.[21]

In August of 1535, the 520-page first edition was completed. It contained only six chapters; four of which contained Protestant instruction concerning the law, the creed, the Lord's Prayer, and one chapter divided between the Lord's Supper and baptism. The remaining two chapters were arguments stating why the Church should be reformed.

Calvin saw himself as bringing the Church back to its original divine perspective and mission.

On a side note, over the years, Calvin continued adding chapters filled with his insights to the original base of this first edition. The Catholic Church felt so threatened by one of the versions that it burned the book in a ceremony at Notre Dame. Today, theologians enjoy the final edition of the Institutes, which grew to be five times greater than the first, with eighty chapters of very small print.

I also want to point out a key element of Calvin's motivation and logic. He always stressed reform rather than rebellion. He never allowed himself to be labeled as a revolutionary, although many tried to proclaim it. Calvin believed that a revolution always involved the invention of something new—and he emphatically stated that the creation of a new church was not his intention. He called himself a Reformer because he was determined to reform what had been lost or changed. He saw himself as bringing the original purpose of the Church back into its divine perspective and mission. That was the primary reason he continued to nurse the additions to the Institutes.

In 1536, the first edition of the Institutes was published in Basel. It was sent directly to King Francis I with a letter exposing his murderous spirit and exonerating the martyrs.

No one in Basel knew that Calvin was the author, because few even knew he was there. He had been living under the assumed name of Martianus Lucanius because he wanted to be left alone to write without interruption. A fervent group of young Protestants was searching for Calvin, hoping for an opportunity to sit at his feet and learn from his knowledge.

Soon, this first edition was on bookshelves everywhere, famous for its boldness in being directed to Francis I and because John Calvin authored it. The book was an overnight success, putting Calvin high on the list of influential Reformers.

God's Plan for Calvin

Soon after the book was published, Calvin and his friend Louis du Tillet left Basel and headed for the city of Ferrara in the Italian Alps. The reason Calvin decided to leave Basel is unclear, but many believe he had found employment with the Duchess Renee as a court secretary. In this position, he would have financially security, use his legal skills, and have freedom to pursue his studies and writing. Calvin preferred the life of a scholar and writer to that of a public speaker.

But soon after Calvin arrived in Ferrara, trouble began. First of all, although the Duchess Renee was giving shelter to Protestant refugees, she was still the sister-in-law of Francis I. That direct relationship kept some of Francis' attention in Ferrara. Within weeks of Calvin's arrival, a French clergyman was arrested, and a hunt for the French in Ferrara began. Calvin and du Tillet immediately departed from the town. Calvin later wrote that he only entered Italy to leave it.

After their brief stay in Ferrara, the two friends went their separate ways. Francis I had granted six months free passage to anyone charged with heresy. So Calvin returned to Paris. While there, he obtained a power of attorney for his younger brother Antoine to sell the family land in Noyon. Not trusting the conditions in Paris, once the land was sold, the two brothers, along with their sister Marie, found themselves again on the road. Calvin had intended for them to travel to Strasbourg, Switzerland, where they could settle down and live in peace. There, Calvin thought he could continue his writings to influence the Reform.

But the plans were altered. Francis I and Emperor Charles V were in the opening stages of their third major war, and the road to Strasbourg was blocked. Calvin, his brother, and his sister were forced to head for Geneva, but they planned to remain there only one night.

The events of that night would change the course of Calvin's life.

The Radical Redhead

The year was 1536, and it was late August. Calvin was spending the night in a little inn nestled in the heart of Geneva. He had been traveling under an assumed name, but his friend du Tillet had earlier settled in Geneva, and he discovered Calvin was there. Du Tillet disclosed Calvin's location to a wild, redheaded evangelist named Guillaume Farel.

Farel had been born in an elite family and was granted the privilege of studying under Lefevre. In fact, Farel was his most aggressive student. Lefevre prophesied to Farel in 1512, "God will renovate the world, and you will live to see it."[22]

Farel was not a teacher; his scholarly abilities were minimal. But he was an explosive evangelist who spread the Gospel of Reform wherever he could. Farel had been so radical that he had been forced to flee France as early as 1523. He had written three small books and had converted a Paris-trained scholar by the name of Pierre Viret, who would later be an instrumental Reformer and close friend to Calvin. Under his influence, the prosperous city of Bern had become Protestant, and Farel had other cities on his list.

Being an evangelist, he was a very persuasive and dramatic preacher. Because of his fervent and radical nature, Farel easily ignited many angry mobs against him. In spite of many death threats, he managed to escape with only a few scars.

Farel entered Geneva in 1531 and set his heart on the city becoming Protestant. The city was experiencing both political and religious revolution. Having been expelled from Geneva several times because of his dramatic preaching, Farel made sure that others invaded the city in his absence, Viret being one of them. Finally, in 1533, after Viret had made additional progress toward reform, Farel reentered Geneva and attempted to organize the Protestant believers in order to form a school and church. He made significant steps in discipleship, worship, and education; but he wasn't a teacher or an administrator. Farel lacked organizational and administrative skills, so confusion began to brew. The people were willing and ready, but Farel was a visionary with very little ability to distill it all into long-term leadership. He openly confessed his inability and lack of skill in this area.

Because of Farel's influence, Geneva became a Reformation city two years later. The government and the church would work closely together to see that Protestant beliefs prevailed. If someone refused Protestant instructions or caused trouble for its leaders, the person could be expelled from the city.

The setting was perfect, but Farel found himself exasperated. Who would lead the movement? Who had the ability to instruct the new converts and organize the budding church?

As these questions burned within him, Farel heard John Calvin was in town for the night, and his heart leapt at the opportunity.

The sovereign hand of God works in the lives of those whose hearts are committed to Him. We may have our own plans, but God sets the course.

The Famous One-Night Stay

When speaking of that fateful night in Geneva, Calvin said, "God thrust me into the game."[23] I love that statement because it speaks of the sovereign hand of God working in the life of one whose heart is totally committed to Him. We may have our own plans, but God ultimately sets the course.

Calvin was enjoying a peaceful summer night in the heart of Geneva. Suddenly, someone was pounding on his door. He opened it to find a passionate veteran of the Reformation—Farel—begging him to stay and help establish the work in Geneva.

Calvin saw the flaming zeal of this man. Then, longing for the quiet library and a life of study, Calvin refused Farel's request to remain in Geneva. He told Farel that he wanted to remain free, on his own, to study and write as he willed. Calvin continued, stating that he had no intentions of organizing a church or school because he had no desire for a public life. He wished to remain in seclusion. After all, he was only going to be there for one night.

Calvin had already planned his life, and Farel's offer didn't match Calvin's desires.

Obedience Is the Issue

Not long ago, I saw a television interview with a popular Christian figure in children's ministry. The man had once been a successful actor in Hollywood. He now makes videos as a Christian action hero, exposing and conquering the demon villains that try to deceive us.

The interviewer asked this man, since he was in such high demand in his field, if he would say that he had a heart for children. His answer got my attention. Without hesitating, the actor answered, "No."

Shocked, the interviewer was at a loss for words. The Christian action hero quickly responded something along these lines, "Don't get me wrong; I love children. But I don't think that God is interested in what we have a heart to do; and by that, I mean in our own desires. The Bible clearly states that there is no good thing in the heart of man. I think God is more interested in our obedience than what is in our hearts to do. The questions will always be, Will we do His desire? Will we demonstrate His heart?"

Obedience is what God is looking for in our lives. The questions will always be, Will we do His desire? Will we demonstrate His heart?

Looking straight into the television camera, he continued. "If it was my desire to do a certain ministry or a certain thing," he essentially said, "and I said 'no' to God when He asked me to do something else, then I might be sitting on the sidelines for the rest of my life."

I enjoyed this man's honesty and the straightforward way he disarmed a popular, yet perverted, doctrine that exalts personal desire. Obedience is what God is looking for and what He expects from our lives. When we are obedient to do what He asks of us, then His desire fuses into our own. Obedience produces a submitted life, a life that says "God, this is all about You; it's not about me." Obedience is the only force that can tame a heart and produce that attitude. John Calvin discovered that vital truth and, from his obedience, entered into a new level of leadership.

Claimed or Cursed?

Feeling that the meeting between the two was divine destiny and believing that Calvin was deserting the cause of the Lord, Farel pointed his finger in Calvin's face and rebuked him sternly. He thundered, "If you refuse to devote yourself with us to the work...God will condemn you."[24]

Calvin's friend du Tillet was also in the room—probably hiding in a corner! At that moment, he was doubtless sorry that he had been the one to tell of Calvin's whereabouts.

Calvin looked Farel in the face. The tall, redheaded man spoke with the surety of an Old Testament prophet! Farel's words shook Calvin to the core. He later admitted that Farel terrified him, and he felt as if God had looked down from on high and laid His hand upon him.

Farel adjourning Calvin.

Farel stood his ground and refused to take back his words. He could not understand why someone would want to retreat in seclusion when the world so needed his services. Geneva was primed and ready for reform, and Farel believed that Calvin was the man to lead it.

Calvin felt the hand of God upon him, melting away his own desires and fears and molding them into the strength to obey. He resigned the comfortable plans he had made for himself. Calvin became a new man, a "man God had claimed." [25] After staying only one night in the city, he left for Basel to gather his personal belongings and leave his family. By September 1, Calvin was in Geneva, ready to begin the work.

Geneva: Round One—Pastoring

Calvin began his leadership role in the new church as "professor of the sacred Scripture." At the time, Farel was considered the "preacher," and Calvin taught and gave lectures on the Scriptures. Within a year, Calvin assumed the role of "senior pastor."

His life as a pastor was very different from what it had been. Calvin was used to seeing people on his terms then retreating to his solitude. Not any more! Now, he was baptizing, officiating at weddings and funerals, organizing the church services and preaching in them, as well as heading up the church administration and board meetings. As soon as he got involved in one area of church life, he would get a revelation about another and start organizing and leading in that area. The same diligence he had given to his studies was now apparent in his ministry to others.

Prior to Calvin's famous one-night stay in Geneva, the citizens there had voted to "live by the Gospel." [26] The political powers of Geneva supported Farel in the complete reformation of the religious and moral life of the community. Farel was fiery and brash, and Calvin didn't waste any time organizing what Farel's zeal would produce. He unleashed what he had bottled up within himself—all the years of academic study, his understanding of Greek and Hebrew, the philosophy of Reformation and government, and his discernment in theological debates. Calvin flooded every area of the community with his insight and wisdom.

The city and the attitude of the people were a Reformer's dream. The Reformers had complete authority to restructure a city whose morals were extremely loose. Calvin tackled the feat by serving the people and bringing them knowledge of the Scriptures to help them live godly lives. Even with all Calvin's knowledge, he never taught over the heads of the people but always brought his lessons down to their level, identifying with their personal struggles.

You may not think that this was anything new, but remember the century in which they lived. The Catholic Church had kept everyone in darkness. The only advocated service was by the people to the Church; it was a bold reformation to turn the tables and have the Church serve the people. It was even bolder to actually teach the people the Word of God so that they could understand it.

Although it seemed idyllic, there were struggles. Calvin had a strong personality, and the political powers, although they wanted reform, struggled with Calvin to maintain their own base of strength. Their struggle became a central opponent of the reform.

Calvin created a confession of faith, which was to be proclaimed by all who wished to be citizens. The confession stated that the Word of God was the ultimate authority; that natural man had no good in him; and that salvation, righteousness, and regeneration were in Jesus Christ alone.

This confession of faith introduced musical praise into the Church. Calvin stated that the singing of psalms would be done, in order to give life to the words of the Scripture, bringing revelation to those who sang them. Since there was no music in the Church at that time and no one knew any tunes, Calvin established a children's choir and taught them particular tunes by which to sing psalms. The choir would sing during the service, and the adults would listen. As the congregation learned the tune, they were invited to join in the singing. Calvin intended for several well-known songs to be sung during each service so that a heartfelt worship could erupt. Up to this time, no one understood the songs during Mass because the lyrics were all in Latin.

Calvin then planned an educational program that everyone was required to attend and established a rule of excommunication, particularly from the Lord's Supper, for those who failed to live by God's standards. It wasn't that Calvin believed we could live above sin. This rule was for those who continually practiced an immoral lifestyle with no remorse or dependence upon the Holy Spirit.

Struggles and arguments over this strictness continued for about a year, and the situation became quite tense. Finally, in January of 1538, the political powers forbade Calvin and Farel to preach because Calvin had called them "a council of the devil" [27] in one of his sermons; they ordered Calvin and Farel to allow everyone to take Communion.

Calvin and Farel preached anyway and continued to turn away immoral people from the Communion table. A mob erupted in the streets outside the church, threatening Calvin and Farel with death.

By April, the government was enraged. They ordered Farel and Calvin to leave the city of Geneva within three days.

Calvin gladly left Geneva; he and Farel headed straight for the city of Bern to represent their cause to the Council there. When Bern failed to act on their behalf, the two traveled to Zurich and again pleaded their case.

The Council at Zurich felt Calvin was much to blame for his untamed zeal and lack of tender-heartedness toward undisciplined people. Nevertheless, they asked Bern to mediate between the two and Geneva in order to restore Calvin and Farel.

In May of 1538, a delegation was sent to Geneva on behalf of Calvin and Farel, but it failed in its negotiations. Calvin felt a strong hostility toward Geneva and believed that God had released him from the assignment.

Now, without a home, personal possessions, or any signs of ministry, Farel and Calvin turned again to the peaceful city of Basel.

Pain Yields to a Plan

By now, Calvin and Farel had become very close friends. Once in Basel, the two stayed in different homes, pondering their next move.

Adding to Calvin's depression, which was a result of the way he had been treated in Geneva, he received news that one of his friends had been poisoned and had died as a result. Deeply grieved, Calvin tossed and turned at night, trying to find answers to the injustice of it all. He was embarrassed and humiliated at how his ministry had turned out in Geneva. Feeling that he might be a failure in public life, he imagined how Basel could be his retreat for a life of study and writing. He decided he wanted nothing more to do with public ministry. He didn't feel that anyone should have to live that way—constantly serving and constantly under scrutiny.

It was a hard summer for Calvin. He sold books for income. As if his emotional pain wasn't hard enough, his old friend du Tillet wrote to say he had returned to France and to the Roman Catholic Church. The letter questioned whether the new Protestant movement could be considered as the true church or if it was just the latest movement, blowing by with the wind. His old friend then questioned if Calvin's banishment from Geneva had been a sign from God that He was displeased with the Protestant Reformers. The letter was a dagger in Calvin's heart.

Du Tillet then offered financial support, but Calvin flatly refused it. He realized that if he accepted the money, he would be linked to the Catholic Church again, and whatever the cost, whatever discomfort he would have to endure, Calvin wanted no ties with the Church.

Feeling alienated and betrayed, Calvin buried his pain and continued on, although he had no idea where he was going.

Farel received a call to help with the ministry in Neuchâtel and asked Calvin to come with him, but Calvin declined. Farel accepted the position and left.

Fearing Failure

Now, Calvin was alone, thinking his life in public ministry—and possibly the reputation he had studied most of his life to attain—had ended. His thoughts were confused, and he felt a sense of injustice that evil motives had been exalted over pure ones. He had given his life to God, and now what did he have to show for it? It seemed everyone else was doing well, and he was the one who suffered. He felt alone, abandoned with his problems. The hot and parched winds of testing and patience were blowing from every side during this hour of hardship. But Calvin had not yet come into his greatest hour.

In July, Calvin took a break from the surroundings of Basel and visited the city of Strasbourg, where he was introduced to a very well-respected Reformer by the name of Martin Bucer. Bucer invited

Calvin to move to Strasbourg and pastor the five-hundred-member French refugee church there. The French refugees were welcome in that city, but they felt isolated because it was a German-speaking area. A French pastor would be just the thing they needed.

Martin Bucer had quite a history. He had been converted to Protestantism when he heard Martin Luther's defense at the famous Heidelberg Disputation in 1518. Shortly afterward, he and three others took leadership of the Reformation at Strasbourg. Bucer became well-respected when he reconciled Ulrich Zwingli and Luther on their differences with the Lord's Supper. And now, Bucer was urging Calvin to come to Strasbourg and use his gifts for the Reformation there.

Calvin's fear of failure returned, and he adamantly refused the offer. Although there would be no city council to deal with, the memories of pastoring were too painful. Quickly returning to Basel, he found a renewed invitation by the Strasbourg group waiting for him. However, this time Bucer resorted to Farel's method of winning Calvin. He wrote, "God will know how to find the rebellious servant, as He found Jonah."[28]

There it was again—that sense of calling and destiny. This stern rebuke struck a chord of truth within Calvin, and he reversed his decision. In spite of his pain, Calvin had a healthy fear of the Lord.

By the first of September, Calvin sailed down the Rhine River to the city of Strasbourg, where he once again assumed the role of pastor.

Three Years of Bliss

Strasbourg was the opposite of Geneva. The city had adopted evangelical worship fourteen years previously. Bucer and the others had done a splendid job of organizing the churches with a well-rounded program promoting group participation. It was a flourishing center of reformation, and it seemed Calvin and the French church were an immediate match.

Calvin remained in Strasbourg for the next three years, from 1538–1541. He matured during this time and was able to rest from continually fighting opposition, as he had done in Geneva.

The people were thankful to have a French-speaking pastor, especially one as well-versed as Calvin. Within months, he applied for and was granted citizenship, something he never did in Geneva.

Calvin's time in Strasbourg became a period of healing. The open atmosphere and the warm reception of the people began to mend and heal his heart. Bucer, eighteen years his senior, became his mentor and one of his closest friends. Calvin often spent his free time sitting at the feet of Bucer and learning his views on predestination and church organization.

Since the people received Calvin with such open hearts, there were no factions in the town. Unlike Geneva, Calvin didn't have to spend his time fighting opposition; now he had time for personal relationships with the people.

In addition to his roles in baptizing, performing marriages, and preaching, Calvin introduced pastoral counseling. Up to this time, counseling from a minister was virtually unheard of.

Calvin encouraged his parishioners to come to him for counsel and consolation when in trouble. He kept the counseling appointments private and never spoke of their conditions or outcomes.

The church at Strasbourg was already operating the way Calvin had desired the Geneva church to operate. He preached each day and twice on Sunday. He was involved in a Protestant school, teaching biblical principles to the young. And to top it off, they sang lively and high-spirited psalms during the services. One refugee visited the church and commented that he couldn't help but weep for joy when the congregation began to sing. One year later, Calvin took these psalms and published them in a book. Now, everyone could have his or her own songbook to use in worshipping the Lord. Calvin's design of public worship from Strasbourg was of great historical significance. He passionately taught it as a way to restore the features of worship in the early church.

While meeting regularly with Bucer for those three years, Calvin solidified and matured his teaching on Communion. The subject was very close to his heart and, for years, had been the main controversy between the Reformers and the Lutherans. Martin Luther insisted that Christ was physically present at Communion; Zwingli, a leading Swiss Reformer, stated that Communion was only a memorial of Christ's death. The Protestant Reformation lay in division over the issue until Calvin wrote a little book entitled, *Little Treatise on the Supper of Our Lord.* In it, Calvin simply explained that Christ was truly present in the celebration of Communion, but that His presence was spiritual rather than physical.

The book was popular with the people and the ministers. Martin Luther was said to have read the book, as well, and to have stated that if Calvin had been there to give his view twelve years earlier, he and Zwingli would have come to an agreement. [29]

Into the Highways and Byways

While Calvin was enjoying his office as a pastor, another segment of the ministry began to open. Bucer had recently installed a man by the name of John Sturm to be the rector of the old Strasbourg convent, with the mission of turning it into a Bible school. Sturm soon turned this school into one of the most renowned and successful schools of the Reformation.

Sturm also became a close friend of Calvin's. God was placing the most matured Reformers of the period in Calvin's path, and Calvin embraced their friendship. Soon, Sturm appointed Calvin as a chief instructor at the school. With Calvin's involvement, the school expanded into an academy with a wide curriculum. Calvin and Bucer groomed and prepared students for the ministry. Calvin called the students the "new teachers."

This church school was a prototype, the first of its kind. Its mission was to raise up a new breed of teachers who would go out and spiritually reproduce themselves in other cities and nations.

The new school's mandate and purpose made Calvin feel like he was in heaven. Everything flourished around him; he couldn't even begin to satisfy the immense spiritual hunger of the group. His involvement in this school would serve as a pattern for something he would pioneer later—a school that sent its ministers to every corner of the known world.

During this time, Calvin's influence began to spread. Strasbourg was his place of training and maturity, but he was constantly called out to lecture and speak at conferences in surrounding cities and nations. He was particularly popular with the Holy Roman Emperor, Charles V, who sponsored a series of conferences regarding religion. Calvin was always an invited speaker.

He also continued to use his writing skills. (I have listed the dates and titles of all his works at the close of the chapter.) During his three years at Strasbourg, Calvin authored four books and a very famous letter that rescued the destiny of Geneva.

Attempted Spiritual Coup D'Etat

The year was 1539. Since Farel and Calvin had been banished from Geneva, it appeared to the Catholic Church that the hopes of reform in the city had been banished as well. Without Reformation leadership, the town seemed ripe and ready for the Catholic Church to take advantage of a swift return to power.

Roman bishops and cardinals in northern Italy looked for ways to regain their influence. They had recently installed a new cardinal by the name of Joseph Sadolet. He was a man of high moral character and eloquence. Very respected among the people, Sadolet was the man the Church needed. They collaborated with Sadolet to formulate a letter to the government of Geneva, inviting the government to retain its political control but to return to the Catholic Church. The letter promised security from Rome, along with their unity and alliance, asking Geneva if it "be more expedient for your salvation to believe and follow what the Catholic Church has approved with general consent for more than fifteen hundred years, or innovations introduced within these twenty-five years by crafty men."[30] With that, Sadolet cast shadows of suspicion against the motives and character of the Reformers.

When the government of Geneva received the eloquent letter, they promised a response. The letter was written in Latin, so it escaped a wide circulation among the citizens. The government in Geneva sensed evil behind the letter, but they had no one capable to respond to this degree of pressure. The only thing to do was send Calvin a copy of the letter and pray he would forgive them and respond on their behalf.

The Letter Heard 'Round the World

When Calvin received the letter, I don't believe he even considered how badly he had been treated in Geneva. Calvin saw the letter as a threat to the cause of Christ, the true Gospel, and the true church; he never entertained the self-gratifying thought that Geneva could fend for itself.

Calvin cleared his schedule and sat down to write a response. In a matter of six short days, Calvin had written a letter that was such a masterpiece, it still circulates and stimulates the world. It became so famous that it was given a title: *Reply to Cardinal Sadolet.*

Calvin answered Sadolet's letter point by point. With accurate facts, examples, and arguments, he illuminated, then disarmed, the abuses and corruption of Rome. He identified himself as one of the reformers whom Rome had denounced. "If you had attacked me in my private character, I could easily have forgiven the attack in consideration of your learning....But when I see that my ministry, which I feel assured is supported and sanctioned by a call from God, is wounded through my side, it would be perfidy [treachery], not patience, were I here to be silent and connive."[31]

Calvin claimed the Word of God as his only source and said that the Word, combined with the Spirit, shapes the Church.

Although he was no longer with them, Calvin claimed a fatherly oversight of the Geneva church. His letter was aimed at protecting the innocent from the jaws of a wolf. Calvin told Sadolet, "Had I wished to consult my own interest, I would never have left your party."[32] He claimed the Word of God as the only source of conviction for the Reformers and said that the Word, mixed with the Spirit, was what shaped the true church. He beautifully illustrated that the preaching of the Gospel was the scepter by which the Father ruled the kingdom—not a Latinized liturgy or the tyranny of a papacy. "You either labour under a delusion as to the term *Church,* or...knowingly and willingly give it a gloss."[33] With great passion and conviction Calvin wrote,

> As to your assertion that our only aim in shaking off this tyrannical yoke was to set ourselves free for unbridled licentiousness [wanton lust] after casting away all thoughts of future life, let judgment be given after comparing our

> conduct with yours. We abound, indeed, in numerous faults; too often do we sin and fall. Still, though truth would, modesty will not permit me to boast how far we excel you in every respect, unless, perchance, you except Rome, that famous abode of sanctity, which having burst asunder the cords of pure discipline, and trodden all honor under foot, has so overflowed with all kinds of iniquity, that scarcely anything so abominable has ever been before.[34]

Sadolet never replied to Geneva's expansive response written by John Calvin. In fact, the Catholic Church never bothered Geneva again.

The reply remains one of the most outstanding vindications given during the Reformation. In it is the true spirit of reform.

In the Market for a Wife

You'll notice throughout this chapter that Calvin rarely, if ever, spoke of his private life or personal feelings. We are left to imagine how he felt based on the common trials of humanity and life in general.

Sometime close to the age of thirty, Calvin began to consider marriage. Up to this point, he was never too concerned with the thought. His mate was the Gospel, and he gave most of his time to nurture its expansion.

He never wrote of the reasons for the change in his desired marital state, but many have assumed it came as a result of living in the Bucer household.

Bucer and his wife, Elizabeth, had a vibrant, wonderful marriage. Their home was called an "inn of righteousness,"[35] filled with laughter and warmth.

Reformers and refugees all over Europe would retreat to the Bucer home to be blessed and ministered to. Bucer also encouraged his ministry friends to each find a wife and enjoy the comforts of marriage. Calvin's closest friends in Strasbourg were also happily married.

His living conditions might also have had something to do with it. Calvin was able to rent a large home in Strasbourg; so he sent for his brother and stepsister in Basel, and they moved in with him to help with the rent. He also took in several ministry students. But Calvin's time, patience, and money were all put to the test. I believe he longed for a personal life that would be enjoyable to him. He had always been taking care of everyone else, and he was weary of it. As suggested in the following letter that he wrote to several friends, Calvin wanted someone to help take care of him. He asked for his friends' help in finding him a wife. He wrote,

> Always keep in mind what I seek to find in her, for I am none of those insane loves who embrace also the vices of those with whom they are in love, where they are smitten at first sight with a fine figure. This only is the beauty that allures me: if she is chaste, if not too fussy or fastidious [oversensitive], if economical, if patient, if there is hope that she will be interested about my health.[36]

Calvin considered three women that his friends had suggested. The first was wealthy, but she didn't know French and didn't care to learn. Calvin was concerned about having wealth because, at that time, a wealthy minister was connected to the hypocrisy of the Catholic Church in the eyes of the people. Besides, what good would she be as a companion if she didn't know French?

The second was French and committed to the Protestant cause—but she was fifteen years older than Calvin. He reasoned that she didn't have long to live. The third one seemed right in every area and the couple planned to marry. But for unknown reasons, the opportunity fell through.

Frustrated, Calvin wrote to Farel saying that he had just about decided to call off the search and forget the idea entirely. That was when Bucer suggested that he consider Idelette Stordeur.

Idelette was a widow with two children, a daughter and a son. Her former husband, Jean, had pastored the Anabaptist church in Geneva while Calvin was there. Jean and Calvin were once at odds, because the two publicly debated and Calvin soundly defeated him. But harsh situations moved the Stordeurs to Strasbourg, and they met up with Calvin once again. This time, they shared a friendly relationship. The Stordeurs came to believe as Calvin did and became faithful members of his church. Calvin even baptized their young son. Jean died of the plague while in Strasbourg. Idelette grieved her husband's death, and Calvin felt he had lost a friend.

Idelette was an attractive woman from an upper middle-class family. Her personal faith had grown very strong. She was a student of the Word and prayed fervently for God's purposes to be done in Strasbourg.

Idelette responded to Calvin's intentions, and the two were married in August of 1540. Farel performed the ceremony, and Calvin finally had a wife. His local ministry schedule was pressing, and he was constantly called away to speak at conferences. During the first forty-five weeks of their marriage, Calvin was gone for thirty-two of them.

But Idelette wasn't distraught about it. She knew of Calvin's demands before she agreed to be his wife. In Calvin's absence, she managed the home and the residents. When the plague briefly struck Strasbourg, she moved the family away to safety until it passed. She was respected for her quiet force and dignity.

After their first year of marriage, Calvin received a surprising yet very gracious invitation from Geneva to return to their city and become the pastor there.

Geneva, the Second Time Around

It took Bucer's counsel to convince Calvin to return to Geneva. Although he loved to further the work of God, Calvin loathed the thought of returning to such a difficult place. Farel had written letters urging him to return. Calvin wrote him back a heartfelt vow, including the statement that I opened this chapter with, but he also included a statement asking who could blame him for not wanting to return to such a place of danger and destruction.

Strasbourg had been almost a utopia for him and his family. Bucer counseled Calvin to come to Geneva for a season, then return to Strasbourg later. That was probably the only comfort Calvin could find in the decision—the hope of returning to Strasbourg. Calvin was only planning to stay for a few months to set the church in order; he died there twenty-three years later.

Unlike his first entrance as a mere traveler, Calvin returned as a highly sought-after preacher, with great prestige and influence. Even with all the pomp, Calvin still grieved at the thought of returning. He called his return a "sacrifice to the Lord."

Geneva spared no expense to retrieve and secure Calvin. The city sent a distinguished herald and a two-horse carriage to Strasbourg. They packed the family and secured them a beautifully furnished home near the cathedral with a view of the lake. Even with all this attention, Calvin still arrived at the gates of Geneva in September, 1541 with tears in his eyes.

As he and his family pulled through the fortified front arch, his friend Viret was reading a letter from Calvin, describing his thoughts of returning to Geneva. One sentence reads, "There is no place under heaven that I am more afraid of." [37]

Calvinism Grows Up

The tremendous praises and compliments of the people and the government comforted Calvin little. Three days after his return, he told Farel, "As you wished, I am settled here: May God direct it for good." [38] When Calvin took the pulpit that first Sunday morning in September, he continued in the same passage he had left off from three years earlier.

Calvin speaking at the council of Geneva.
Getty Images

☆☆☆☆☆

The Calvin that Geneva had previously known had an explosive and uncontrolled temper. But being associated with mature men in Strasbourg helped Calvin to curb his dramatic emotions. Writing Bucer from Geneva, Calvin assured him that he would operate in moderation and brotherly kindness.

Numbing his immense dread of being there, Calvin immediately set to work. Calvin felt his first task was to organize the church. Again, his experience in Strasbourg was a tremendous help. The government in Geneva consisted of the Little Council, the Two Hundred, and the General Council.

Using the Word of God as his pattern, Calvin outlined four permanent orders of the ministry—pastors, teachers, elders, and deacons—and around these, he formed his organization. These four primary areas covered the entire church life—worship, education, soundness and moral purity, and works of love and mercy.

This pattern of organization has designated the administration of Protestant churches from the sixteenth century until today. It is especially prevalent in Baptist churches; although the office of a teacher is not specifically recognized or titled within them today. The only ministries Calvin did not recognize were those of the apostle and the prophet. (See Ephesians 4:11.) Calvin placed his role primarily under the function of a pastor, though he was more accurately an apostolic teacher.

Under his guidelines, Calvin reformed the Church: The Catholics had no operation like this. Calvin's reorganization was the closest to biblical truths in its day. Although he chose to ignore the apostolic and prophetic offices when defining the duties in a church, he thoroughly followed Scripture. From his organization and method of doctrine, this segment of Protestant followers became organizationally known as Calvinists. Calvinism has influenced thousands of great preachers such as Charles Spurgeon, Jonathan Edwards, William Carey, and David Brainerd. Its principles continue in the lives of countless ministries today.

First Order—Pastors

Pastors were to preach the Word, instruct, admonish, administer the sacraments, and, with the elders, make structural changes within the church. They were to be given to prayer and fasting so the Word could be preached to the people purely and accurately. They were not to burden themselves with the everyday maintenance of the system, nor were they to wear themselves out visiting and taking care of the many needs of the people. They could pray for the sick throughout the community, as they felt led by God to do so.

Calvin felt very strongly about the pastors only giving themselves to the Word and prayer, because he felt that preaching was like a "visitation from God, through which He reaches out His hands to draw us to Himself." [39] Calvin would not tolerate anything less in his pastors, or they would be severely disciplined.

If a man wished to be a pastor, he gave proof of his calling and lifestyle. Then, passing a test of his conduct, he was tested for his knowledge of doctrine and Scripture. He had to go through several stages of presentation from the ministers then acceptance by the council and the people.

The pastors were to have a weekly meeting to promote church life, discuss doctrine, and resolve problems. If there were arguments or contentions that could not be solved among the ministers, the elders were called in to settle them or pronounce any judgment.

The pastors were also required to attend quarterly meetings where officers were elected. These meetings primarily discussed administration, salaries, and any noted discipline. This quarterly assembly was called the Venerable Company, and it was established for accountability among the new churches.

The Venerable Company eventually became known as one of the most powerful groups of ministers in the world. From them, Geneva's missionary agency was formed, which sent missionaries of Reform to Italy, Germany, Scotland, France, England, and non-European nations across the ocean. In that day, sending missionaries was a complicated matter; many were killed on arrival. Some of Calvin's missionaries who traveled to South America were killed on their way there. For that reason, these men formed an underground church wherever they went, meeting secretly in barns, open fields, or secluded caves.

Calvin's Academy was the first organized school of ministry that sent missionaries throughout the world with a mandate to reform the church to its original state. In this area, we can see that Calvin specifically operated in the apostolic anointing.

The apostolic anointing creates a hub environment, or a central headquarters, from which come many different facets of ministry that spread throughout the world. The people sent out from these hubs are trained to confront territories that are adverse to the Gospel. They are trained to discern and to operate in various spiritual climates that have been hardened by demonic, cultural, or religious oppression. They are equipped to change and subdue those spiritual atmospheres for God so that residents can be productive through the Word and the Spirit.

Calvin created that atmosphere in his school. He taught his students the vitality of the Word; he raised up a new breed of believers who stood on raw faith, for which many gave their lives. He ignited their hearts with a mission and a plan to instigate radical reconstruction wherever the Spirit of the Lord sent them.

Calvinism spread further and was implemented in stronger fashion than Lutheranism. Why? Because of the organizational skills that Calvin possessed. Luther spread his message through the printed word, public debates, and radical demonstrations, which inspired the faith of others. Calvin methodically organized a radical reconstruction of doctrine by teaching the reasons for it, revealing the true meaning of what destiny means to a believer, and then implementing that teaching segment by segment. His apostolic abilities built a firm foundation within his students that gave reason and substance to their boldness and faith.

Second Order—Teachers

The teachers were also called doctors, and they were chosen from the company of pastors. They were charged to guard the purity of the Gospel and to secure a good company of well-equipped ministers for the various teaching tasks. Theology was the primary function of the teachers, and to know both language and science was a prerequisite. Therefore, the new churches established a school to teach their young Hebrew and Greek, as well as doctrinal material. In the social order of the day, the girls had a separate school from the boys. This famous school became known as the Academy of Geneva. A Frenchman by the name of Theodore Beza was chosen as dean. He would later become one of Calvin's best friends, even assuming Calvin's mantle and taking full leadership of the Venerable Company.

Teaching lectures for adults were held each Monday, Wednesday, and Friday. These lectures were given to educate the congregation on the precise meaning of the Scriptures and to equip prospective pastors.

Third Order—Elders

Elders were chosen by their conduct. They were to be persons of good moral report, known for their wisdom, dependability, and reputation as people not easily swayed into sin or corruption. These men were appointed by the head pastors and given the responsibility of overseeing the moral and spiritual life within the community.

Each church had one or two elders who personally watched over the individual lives of families within their jurisdiction. If they noted disorderly conduct, their job was to correct and instruct, then see to it that repentance came. The elders were to report undesirable conduct only if they could not help to remedy it. The behavior would then be reported to the board, and the person would be exhorted to repent. If that effort failed and the sin continued, the person would be excommunicated until repentance was offered.

Based on Hebrews 3:13, the elders had the primary responsibility of exhorting their members daily, encouraging them to good works and spirituality that was pleasing to the Lord.

Fourth Order—Deacons

Based on the moral guidelines in 1 Timothy 3, deacons were chosen to serve in one of two divisions: to oversee and manage the funds of the church, or to oversee the social welfare of people within the church.

Geneva boasted that it had no beggars, nor were there any sick or afflicted who didn't have the utmost of care. Each deacon established a hospital management board for his individual community. If a member fell sick, the deacons appointed their choice for a physician or surgeon. Depending on which was needed, the appointee would either attend to the member in the hospital or in his or her home. This was especially designed for the poor of Geneva. In unprecedented displays of care and concern, members received the best of medical and spiritual care, and Geneva became known as a city of the true Gospel.

What Does the Gospel Mean to You?

You've just read that Geneva was known as a city of the true Gospel. Calvin's organization of the elders and deacons portrayed the true heart of an apostle. The true apostle lives and works for the heart of God to be manifested throughout the world. And what is the heart of God all about? One word: People. Hear me well: The Gospel was given to take care of the needs of humanity, of which salvation is only part.

The Gospel is not given to feed your own personal ego or to give you status in society. It is not given for the eyes of the world to be focused upon you. The heart of God will always be for the needs of the people. It will always be for the hurting to be comforted, for the broken to be restored, for the hungry to be filled, for the lost to be saved, for the depressed and deceived to be delivered, and for the sick to be healed.

Some truths God has brought to the earth through amazing men and women of God have been twisted and misrepresented in some circles. I believe wholeheartedly in the prosperity message. But God gave it to show His people his priority in financing the kingdom. Second to this priority is the truth that you will be blessed as a result of living a surrendered life—heart, body, soul, and, yes, wealth. God wants you to be prosperous, but He'll only trust great wealth with someone who has paid a price over a period of time in giving toward the expansion of His kingdom.

There's a fine line that ministries can cross trying to raise money; across that line is error and deception. If God truly spoke to you to do something, He will supply. But to invent your own vision and then apply pressure on the people to supply for it can open your ministry up to a wrong spirit.

I have found that people really do want to give. But they may be worn out on your building project. I've taken up a lot of offerings for a lot of different things. Sometimes it was for the new sanctuary. Sometimes it was for new chairs. And I'm not saying that is wrong. The Bible tells us to give that there would be meat in His house. (See

Malachi 3:10.) But the easiest offerings I ever took were taken for the missionary program God branded in my heart to start.

People gave like crazy. All I did was share the vision of putting five hundred missionaries in the toughest parts of the foreign field and people gave without hesitation. People will give into your building project, and your new sound system, but they really want to feel like they are directly involved in lifting the burden of society.

People who are hurting don't care about your money. What they want is the relief that only an anointed, spirit-led person can give them. Money is just a tool that will facilitate that.

We must stand for God and speak the truth so that His plan won't be aborted in this hour. May we say again, like the city of Geneva, that our city—and church—is known for being an example of the true Gospel.

Our Inheritance from Calvin

Calvin introduced many things to the Church that were virtually unheard of in his day. You might be surprised to find that some of the things you've taken for granted in your church or ministry were actually instituted by Calvin.

1. He introduced personal counseling according to the Word of God.
2. He set in order the pastoral office, with inspired preaching of the Word.
3. He set in order the office of the teacher, whereby the simple and basic principles of the Gospel were broken down for every person to understand, from children to adults.
4. He outlined the requirements and functions for the elders and deacons.
5. He introduced congregational worship in corporate form so that everyone could enter into the presence of God through song.
6. He presented the original Greek language behind the New Testament, giving his listeners an accurate understanding of what the Scriptures literally meant.
7. He reintroduced the Hebrew language for accurate interpretation of the Old Testament. Until Calvin, the Jews were the only

ones who incorporated Hebrew in their understanding of God.

8. He reintroduced the commission for ministers to pray for the sick as they felt led to do.

Calvin organized many other segments of ministry, but I believe the facts you've just read are the highlights. You can see how his radical reconstruction of the true Gospel exposed the many disguises that the Catholic Church had deceived the people with.

Character Assasination

Even though everything seemed to work in an orderly fashion, things didn't operate as smoothly as it sounds. While Calvin was pioneering his part in Geneva for the Gospel, the government continued with their interruptions, including arresting people for offenses without contacting the elders. The government wanted to support the church, but the interaction between civil and moral laws was hazy and unclear. As a result, confusion continued between the two entities.

The personal life of Calvin also suffered. In 1542, during his first summer in Geneva, Idelette gave birth to a premature son who died two weeks later. Both she and Calvin were heartbroken. Three years later, a daughter died at birth, and in 1547, another child was delivered prematurely and died.

Calvin's enemies took advantage of these tragic occasions to persecute his family. They held that the Calvins' inability to have a child was God's hand of judgment on their lives for hidden sin and disobedience. Calvin's most violent persecutors searched for evidence to prove their accusations, finding that Idelette had been the former wife of an Anabaptist. The Anabaptists believed that marriage came under the sanctity of the church, so there was no need for a civil ceremony. Their enemies began to gossip that Idelette was an immoral woman who had borne her previous children out of wedlock, which wasn't true. They represented her to the community as a woman with serious heretical beliefs. Calvin's name was slandered for marrying Idelette, demeaning his spiritual position and authority.

His enemies were known to sic their dogs after him, turning the animals loose to nip and bite at Calvin's feet as he walked past them.

Many times the church was plastered with rotten vegetables, which bitter or unbelieving people had thrown. Often these people would stand outside making loud noises to disrupt the services inside the cathedral.

Calvin's main enemies were a religious sector within the city called the Libertines, who interpreted the Gospel as they wanted to hear it. They felt that since they were under the grace of God, they could live any way they chose. Many were notorious for their adultery and fornication; many were guilty of drunkenness and brawls. Yet, these same people would be in their church on Sunday, listening to a perverted Gospel that agreed with their lifestyles. Based on their beliefs, you can see why Calvin's strict doctrine and ethics of accountability infuriated them. They sought to discredit him any way they could, especially with taunting accusations that Calvin was the dictator of Geneva.

The opposite was true. Calvin was appointed by the council to return to the city and establish the Protestant church. He was paid a salary and could have been relieved of his position at any time. The Libertines were outraged because their lifestyle was being challenged by the atmosphere of righteousness that Calvin established.

"No Common Grief"

Although Calvin never slowed in his reformation of Geneva, his health did. He was constantly plagued with stomach problems and kidney stones. Idelette's health also deteriorated. Never able to regain her full strength after her last premature delivery, Idelette contracted tuberculosis.

On her deathbed, Idelette's main concerns were that Calvin's ministry not be hindered by her condition and that her children be taken care of. Calvin assured her that he would take care of the children as if they were his own. She replied, "I have already entrusted them to God."[40] When Calvin responded that her statement didn't relieve him of his responsibility to care for them, she acknowledged that she knew he would take care of that which was given to God.

That's the way Calvin was. Everything he did for the Lord was done from a conviction, and not just by mere human will. His wife knew him best. If Calvin thought something was the will of God, he would guard it with his life and perform it until his death.

★★★★★

In 1549, eight years after their return to Geneva, Idelette died so quietly and calmly that those present could barely tell something had happened.

As I've already stated, Calvin spoke very little of his personal life. But he wrote several letters that told of his deep and sorrowful grief at losing Idelette. Just days after her death, Calvin wrote his friend Viret, saying, "Truly mine is no common grief. I have been bereaved of the best friend of my life, of one who, if it had been so ordained, would willingly have shared not only my poverty but also my death. During her life she was the faithful helper of my ministry. From her I never experienced the slightest hindrance."[41]

Calvin was married to Idelette for only nine short years. He kept his promise and raised her two children as his own. He was only forty when she died, but he never married again.

Everything Calvin did for the Lord was done from a sense of conviction. If Calvin knew something was God's will, he would guard it with his life.

Calvin's Reforming Personality

Burying his grief and loss, Calvin's ministry efforts went into full swing. He moved his immediate family back into his home, although their individual lifestyles kept him in a flurry of personal controversy.

Calvin was a good and faithful friend. We know that he took himself very seriously. And although he never met Martin Luther, he felt he was Luther's successor. Calvin carried an incredible presence, noted by all when he walked into a room.

Even though he took his mandate as a Reformer very seriously, Calvin was very warm and trusting of his associates. He reminded them constantly that they were to receive the good and beautiful things around them as gifts from God, as testimonies of His love for them. He visited their homes, shared their jokes and laughter, officiated at the marriages of their young, and grieved at their personal tragedies. He was a wonderful dinner companion, full of thought and conversation. And though he was skillful at the games he did play, it's not likely he delegated too much spare time for recreation.

His home was also the center of church activity; many refugees ran to it as a haven from the world. One visitor wrote of Calvin's busy lifestyle, saying,

> I do not believe there can be found his like. For who could recount his ordinary and extraordinary labors? I doubt if any man in our time has had more to listen to, to reply to, to write, or things of greater importance. The multitude and quality alone of his writings is enough to astonish everyone who looks at them, and even more those who read them....He never ceased working, day and night, in the service of the Lord, and heard most unwillingly [sic] the prayers and exhortations that his friends addressed to him every day to give himself some rest. [42]

Mentoring John Knox

One of his most famous refugees was John Knox, the future Scottish Reformer. Calvin placed Knox as the pastor of the English-speaking refugee church in Geneva. When the time came for Knox to return to Scotland, he did so having been groomed and trained by Calvin. Those efforts and the call of God upon his life caused Knox to become a renowned Reformer in Scotland. There, he established a national church that was patterned after Calvin's church in Geneva. Knox boasted of Calvin's academy. He said that not since the days of the apostles was there ever a finer school for Christ. [43]

Knox also testified to many enjoyable hours with Calvin, when the two of them would share in laughter as well as debate theological thoughts. The two great Reformers had a game they played. Both would stand at the end of a table and see who could slide a key the furthest down the table without it falling off the other end.

Calvin also instituted an accountable and highly diligent work ethic among the congregations. He taught that everything belonged to God—their employment, their possessions, their lives, and so on. When classifying possessions, he found no division between secular and Christian. If you were a believer, everything was centered around God. Calvin convinced the people that to be slothful in their employment was disrespectful to God. He also taught the people to charge interest on their loans, stating that it was good, diligent business and to not do so was wasteful. This strong work ethic was so established among the people of the day that it helped form the strong capitalistic mind-set that was to characterize the coming centuries.

Many loved what Calvin's life demonstrated through the Word, but his persecutors accused him of being harshly unkind and cruel. He was known to debate and hotly argue his point until the other person agreed or was worn defenseless. His debates weren't isolated to Protestants; he debated the Jews as well. Joseph Gershom, a famous Jewish controversialist, once wrote that he debated a Protestant controversialist who attacked him with a "violent, angry, and menacing" speech. [44] Jewish theologians believe this man to have been John Calvin.

Calvin taught his congregation that if they were believers, everything they had belonged to God—their employment, possessions, and lives.

This part of his personality is somewhat ironic, because, unlike Luther and Knox, Calvin didn't enjoy conflict. Those closest to Calvin knew that, even though he appeared steely to his opponents, he was very sensitive and apprehensive inside. His disposition was usually far from composed but rather boisterous against annoyance and persecution. Calvin despised his temper and was constantly in remorse over his weakness in that area. Before we accuse him, let us remember that few have endured such persecution, and few have instituted such a comprehensive reform in such a violent setting. So, it could be said that, although he was sensitive, he carried an invincible spirit that refused to quit.

When Calvin set his direction, he pushed ahead so forcefully that few could follow him. If he understood a principle, only death could silence him. It wasn't that he didn't understand compromise; it was that Calvin saw truth so clearly that compromise was an unforgivable error to him.

One of my favorite stories about Calvin shows his sensitive and compassionate side. Once he wanted to send a letter to Viret, and a pair of Bible students approached him to deliver it. When Calvin gave the letter to one of them, he noticed how disappointed the other student seemed at not being chosen as the messenger. So Calvin acted like he forgot to write something in the first letter, sat down to write another quick sentence or two, folded the paper, and gave it to the second student. The letter said only for Viret to pretend the words said something important!

In 1547, an era of hardship dawned upon Calvin. A Libertine movement would bring Calvin face-to-face with the most controversial period of his life and ministry. The movement was ignited by the man who had stood him up many years earlier: Michael Servetus.

Calvin and the four syndics in the courtyard of the college of Geneva.
Hulton Archive/Getty

The Mistake That Made History

Calvin's affairs with Servetus brought him not only heartache but also a condemnation that still follows him today. Servetus, the rebellious Spaniard, had been a noted theologian, then a lawyer and respected physician. He had written a book years earlier attempting to discredit the teachings of Calvin. Calvin had attempted to reconcile, but Servetus failed to show for the appointment.

Through the years of ministry and reform, Servetus had been a constant and plaguing enemy with gaining notoriety, especially among the Libertines who hated Calvin. He was also a hunted man among the Catholics as well as the Protestants for his heresy. In fact, no one had a greater price on his head than Servetus.

Calvin could tolerate almost anything except what he considered heresy. Even Jewish theologians, although not fond of his ministry style, stated, "With all this fury, Calvin showed himself somewhat more merciful toward Jews, as well as the Muslims, than toward Christian heretics."[45]

Servetus taught that the Trinity was foolishness and that Jesus was not God in the flesh but became God's Son after He triumphed over temptation. Calvin categorized these beliefs as blatant heresy under a penalty of death.

After a long road of trials and mishaps, Servetus, now a fugitive backed by the Libertines, appeared in one of Calvin's church services. Calvin recognized him and called for his arrest. Servetus was hauled to prison to await trial.

At the trial, the Libertines worked their plot to free Servetus, and Calvin maintained a violent stance against them all. When the ruling went in favor of Calvin, the council also agreed with his penalty and sentenced Servetus to burn at the stake.

Servetus asked for an audience with Calvin, and it was granted. Servetus asked for reconciliation and begged Calvin to implore the courts for a lesser sentence. Calvin earnestly pointed out his theological errors, asking him to retract them. Servetus only laughed.

Calvin did ask for a different sentence. He asked for Servetus to be beheaded instead of burned. Some were shocked at Calvin's request, but he had no mercy for heresy.

The council denied Calvin's plea, and on October 27, 1553, Servetus, escorted by Farel to the stake, was burned for heresy. Because of his lobby for the death penalty, Calvin became a subject of controversy and criticism.

Earlier in this chapter, the story of Calvin and his friend Nicolaus Cop was told. Cop's opening speech as the dean of the University of Paris so many years earlier was controversial because he attempted to open the Roman Catholic eyes of the university system to the ideas of freedom that prevailed among the Protestants. In that address, Cop rebuked those who, through fear, killed the body but could not kill the soul.

Now, those very words, which some believe were written by Calvin for Cop, became the words Calvin's enemies used to persecute him. They charged him as a tormentor of religious freedom who stooped to the ranks of the Roman Catholic persecutors in the Inquisition. The news of Calvin's strong stance traveled into the Jewish and Muslim communities. They called the event the "first inquisitional act of faith on the part of Protestant believers."[46]

Throughout history, many have tortured and killed others for what they believed to be heresy. We can all think of murderous events from long ago, but it happens even today in many areas of the world; the Sudan and the Middle East are prime examples. When a man kills another for his wrong beliefs, he has acted under demonic delusion.

Calvin was directly responsible for the death of one man; if he felt remorse over it, history doesn't state it. Calvin evidently believed that he was protecting the multitudes from the evils that a man such as Servetus would inflict upon them. However, the judgment of such action can be made only by God Himself.

Death Wasn't the End

The year was 1564. The churches in Geneva had been established as an example for Protestant churches throughout the known world. The academy was flourishing with young students seeking the ministry; many were planning to be missionaries carrying the message of reform to dangerous or uncharted territories. Calvin's writings, which were continuing to be a source of enlightenment to the multitudes who read them, were in the highest demand. Five years earlier, Calvin had finally become a citizen of Geneva, the city to which he humbly referred to himself as a servant.

The burden of work and responsibilities were taking a toll on his health. Apart from stomach problems, he was now tortured with migraines. His lungs were constantly inflamed and hemorrhaging, arthritis had settled in his knees, and he had a continuing problem with kidney stones that caused him tremendous pain.

Amid all these hardships, Calvin never missed a day when he was scheduled to preach. When he couldn't walk to the church on his own efforts because of pain, he was carried in a chair to the platform. When his physician denied Calvin the privilege to leave his bedroom, an audience would come and pack into the room, listening to him for hours. During the times when he couldn't move his body because of illness, he would dictate letters from his bed. As the onlookers would beg him to rest his body, Calvin would rebuke them and say, "What! Would you have the Lord find me idle when He comes?"[47]

The last time he preached in the cathedral was February 6, 1564. His last attendance was the Easter service, where he received Communion from Beza, his dear friend. When April came, Calvin bid farewell to the council and the ministers in a letter recounting his goals, his struggles, and his faults. He dictated with great composure, stating, "My sins have always displeased me and the fear of God has been in my heart."[48]

Calvin preaching at St. Peter's in Geneva in his old age.
The Banner of Truth Trust

He also had letters written to his closest friends, calling Farel his best one. He asked Farel to always remember their friendship and what they did together in the ministry. He reminded Farel that a reward would be waiting for them both in heaven.

By the middle of May, Calvin's health was depleted. He was near death and in a coma when those present in the room began to lament over what would happen when he died. Without opening his eyes, Calvin told them if they would look to the Lord, they wouldn't have to worry about it.

After that, Calvin never spoke to another person; his voice was heard only in prayer. On May 27, 1564, at the age of fifty-four, Calvin departed this life and went to meet the Lord.

His close friend Beza was present at his death. Of the event, he wrote, "On that day, with the setting sun, the brightest light that was in the world for the guidance of God's church, was taken back to heaven."[49]

The next day, Calvin's body, which had been an invincible physique standing in the face of error and deception, was wrapped in a simple shroud and placed in a wooden box. He was buried in an unmarked grave in a common cemetery. To this day, as executed by Calvin's last wishes, no one knows where the great Reformer is buried. His cause and goal was always to point to Jesus Christ; in his death, he wanted nothing less.

Beza assumed Calvin's role as moderator of the Venerable Company. The day he took the role, he stated of Calvin, "I have been a witness of him for sixteen years and I think that I am fully entitled to say that in this man there was exhibited to all an example of the life and death of the Christian, such as it will not be easy to depreciate, and it will be difficult to imitate."[50]

The government and citizens alike greatly mourned the death of Calvin. In a special session honoring Calvin, they made a statement, proclaiming, "God marked him with a character of singular majesty."[51]

Today in Geneva, one will find a monument erected to the cause of the Reformation that transformed the city. Four men—John Calvin, Guillaume Farel, Theodore Beza, and John Knox—have their names engraved in stone there.

It is somewhat strange to stare at those names, now only engraved remembrances, and to think that they were once actual lives, with real heartaches, tragedies, persecutions, and victories. Although the stone binds their names, their voices continue to echo throughout the centuries. The truths these men stood for continue to disarm perverted doctrines and unearth divine treasures within the men and women who hear their cry. These men are not just a memory; they are eternally alive, cheering us on from the portals of heaven as we receive our mandate in this hour and run to transform nations to the Gospel of Jesus Christ.

I can think of no words better than Calvin's to close his chapter: "It is enough that I live and die for Christ, who is to all His followers a gain both in life and in death." [52]

Calvin's Doctrine

What follows is a brief look at Calvin's theological beliefs. Again, allow me to stress that these samples are in no way complete, as volumes of his doctrine are written in tribute to him. If you wish to explore any of the few that I've listed, I encourage you to do so.

Predestination

Probably the most popular of all Calvin's thoughts is the doctrine of predestination. Before I go into a summary of what Calvin believed, it's important that I place a fact in historical context.

Contrary to contemporary belief, the doctrine of predestination did not begin with Calvin. Calvin is not the "father of predestination."

This doctrine began before Calvin's ministry, but he was the one who made it famous. Actually, the belief was introduced by Augustine, a man who had once been a pagan philosopher before he turned Christian. In his youth, Calvin had attended the university that Augustine founded, and he was greatly influenced by Augustine's method of thought. Later, Martin Luther and countless others firmly held to his beliefs concerning predestination. Calvin followed his predecessors.

When Calvin became a pastor, he noticed that different people responded in different ways to the preaching of the Gospel. He gave the example that if the same sermon was preached to a hundred people, twenty would embrace it and grow, while the others laughed or were bored. He was troubled by it, and in Calvin's analytical mind, he pondered over the reason for it. He searched the Scriptures and stated that the reason why some received with obedience while some firmly rejected was explained by the doctrine of predestination.

Calvin made the doctrine famous when he was called upon to defend it. Augustine's doctrine was viciously attacked and, given Calvin's outstanding skills in debate, he was chosen to respond. His response was so thorough that he soon became known as the main proponent of it. In fact, when the Roman Catholic Church began to accuse Calvin of inventing this theology, he rebuked the accusation by reminding them of their ancient Bishop Augustine. Arguing that he was hearkening back to the teachings of Augustine, Calvin stated, "Augustine is so completely of our persuasion, that if I should have to make written profession, it would be quite enough to present a composition made up entirely of excerpts from his writings." [53] When asked why he defended the doctrine so strongly, Calvin responded, "Even a dog barks when his master is attacked: how could I be silent when the honor of my Lord is assailed?" [54]

Calvin went through two separate controversies for the doctrine, one with the Catholic Church and the other with a Carmelite monk turned Protestant named Jerome Bolsec. Until these two blatant attacks, Calvin had only mildly mentioned his stand on the issue. But after these controversies, he decided to clarify his beliefs and began to write very strongly about it. Many have wondered, if these two controversies had not happened, would Calvin have been so paired with the doctrine as he is today?

It should be noted that not all of Geneva shared in Calvin's views on predestination; but, most assuredly, all his ministerial students and associates, such as John Knox, soundly shared his belief.

In a nutshell, Calvin said predestination was like walking a tightrope—fearful and wonderful at the same time. He cautioned that all should keep their balance of it by holding firmly to the Scriptures.

He said that God "does not indiscriminately adopt all into the hope of salvation but gives to some what he denies to others." [55] Based on Scriptures such as Romans 9:18, which says, *"Therefore hath he mercy on whom he will have mercy, and whom he will he hardeneth,"* Calvin believed God decreed within Himself what would become of each man. Some were created for eternal life, some for eternal damnation. He believed that predestination was like a coin with two sides. One side showed God's mercy, the other His judgment. Calvin felt that God must manifest both attributes toward mankind or else He would be incomplete. The ones with the favor and eternal life of God are called the elect.

So, how did the mercy of God fit in? Calvin believed that the mercy for mankind was given through Jesus Christ and His sacrifice on the cross. It would seem that mercy would not have a place in this doctrine, but the contrary is true. Calvin viewed the Word of God according to Romans 10:8, as the Word of faith. "Faith can have no stability unless it be placed in the divine mercy."[56] In other words, a person will have no faith and cannot believe in the Word of God as the truth unless he is in the mercy of God, and mercy is only bestowed on the elect. If you have faith in God, you are the elect.

Calvin believed that revelation was progressive. If one progressed in the revelation of God and His goodness and mercy toward them, he or she was one of the elect. A person's election was discovered and verified in his progressive comprehension of Christ's sacrifice, which overcomes the malignity of sin.[57]

Calvin believed the elect should also be full of joy, knowing that the blessing and favor of God were upon them and nothing could change that. Although everyone deserved condemnation, the elect instead received the mercy of God and carefully tried to live through that mercy each day. They were never to be found idle or without dedication. The nonelect didn't care about it and wanted nothing to do with God and His principles.

What about evangelism? It played a vital part in Christianity. Although a man might believe in predestination, he never knew whom God had chosen. Therefore, the Gospel had to be given to every man, and the outward results would eventually manifest themselves.

Calvin never attempted to understand why the doctrine of predestination existed and warned others against attempting to understand its existence. He knew he was agreeing with statements that have no moral explanation. He said that the reason of divine righteousness is higher than man's, and we would never be able to understand God's depth of wisdom. He did not attempt or pretend to understand it fully, for, to him, that would require that he fully understand God.

The Church

The doctrine of the church held high importance to Calvin. Like Luther, he referred to it as the "catholic" church, meaning universal, not because it was tied with the Roman Church.

He believed the true church was invisible, not bound by walls. The members consist of God's elect, whose membership is regarded by their confession, love, lifestyle example, and participation.

Calvin believed that there would be hypocritical and defective teachings within the true church, but one should not sever himself from the body because of it. As long as it was preached that Jesus Christ is the Son of God and that one must be born again and depend upon His mercy; that the Scriptures were esteemed to be the written Word of God; and that the sacraments were offered in honor of Jesus Christ, then other defective doctrines should be tolerated and worked out. He observed that no one was free from ignorance or misinterpretation.

He also believed that the true church should practice discipline, including the right to excommunicate a disorderly person. Calvin felt that discipline was the muscle and ligaments of the church and should be exercised so that the sanctity of Communion could be maintained.

He viewed the universal church as the nurse of Christian life, writing that it keeps us under its protection and guidance, teaching us the things of Christ, and that we may not leave its school until we have spent the course of our lives as its pupils. Calvin believed it was the ministry within the church that groomed its children.

Calvin saw the Reformation as the restoration of the true church, which, up to that time, had been almost completely suppressed and undiscoverable. He saw himself as one who never had any other purpose other than the church's advancement.

Communion

Calvin wrote of Communion in various tracts because it held high importance to him. Unlike Luther, Calvin believed that the spiritual presence of Christ was to be found in Communion. For that reason, he denounced any questionable behavior taking part in it, as it would surely be arrogant and disrespectful to Jesus Christ; it crossed the border of blasphemy. He believed that those who took part in Communion and refused to cleanse themselves by repentance would encounter physical hardship and affliction, even death. He believed that when Communion was taken on behalf of a repentant and respectful believer, it produced a power within his life that enabled him to walk a victorious Christian life. He also believed in using wine, not grape juice. He felt that alcoholic wine symbolized the invigorating power of the Holy Spirit that was present in the cleansing blood of Christ.

★★★★★

Works

Calvin believed that all good works come from faith. The Christian life was not only marked by faith and knowledge but was also filled with responsibilities. No realm in life was exempt from the obligation of service to God and man.

Adding to his strong convictions of sacrifice and service, Calvin emphasized the necessity of humility in this service, which required the abandonment of superiority and self-love. He believed that those in the ministry had a high calling to answer to God, and he was appalled at those who placed themselves upon a pedestal above others. Calvin believed that Christians were to love and serve their neighbors whether good or bad, attractive or repulsive!

With regard to service that stretched beyond one's church and neighbors, Calvin made no distinction between secular responsibilities and church responsibilities. He viewed materialistic possessions as belonging to God and said that they must be held in diligent stewardship. He firmly denounced prosperity as the sole sign of God's favor and compared such a belief to that of the Sadducees, who did not believe in the life to come. No doubt, this adamant belief had to do with the financial abuses and excesses of the Catholic Church of the day. He actually believed that excessive prosperity was an occasion for anxiety, rather than the cure for it, and that only the ungodly thought otherwise. While he did believe that good success could be a blessing of God, just as calamity could be His curse, it cannot be established as the sole rule. Calvin saturated his writings in this area with Scriptures and commentaries.

*****

If you wish to study Calvin's core beliefs in greater detail, I suggest that you take time to read his *Institutes of the Christian Religion,* which fully explains his line of thought.

A Chronology of Calvin's Writings

1532 Commentary on Seneca's De Clementia

1536 The Institutes, first edition

1539 The Reply to Cardinal Sadolet
The Institutes, second edition

1540 Commentary on Romans

1541 The Institutes, French edition
A Short Treatise on the Lord's Supper

1546 A Commentary on First Corinthians

1547 A Commentary on Second Corinthians

1548 A Commentary on Galatians, Ephesians, Philippians and Colossians
A Commentary on First and Second Timothy

1549 A Commentary on Titus
A Commentary on Hebrews

1550 A Commentary on First Thessalonians
A Commentary on Second Thessalonians
A Commentary on James

1551 A Commentary on First and Second Peter
A Commentary on Jude

1552 A Commentary on Acts, first volume

1553 A Commentary on the Gospel of John

1554 A Commentary on Acts, second volume
A Commentary on Genesis

★★★★★

1555 Harmony of the Gospels

1557 A Commentary on Psalms
A Commentary on Hosea

1559 The Institutes, major revision
The Minor Prophets
A Commentary on Isaiah

1561 A Commentary on Daniel

1563 Harmony of the Pentateuch
A Commentary on Jeremiah and Lamentations

★★★★★

Notes

[1] John T. McNeill, *The History and Character of Calvinism* (New York: Oxford University Press Inc., 1954): 159. Excerpts from the History and Character of Calvinism by John T. McNeill, © 1967 by Oxford University Press, Inc. Used by permission of Oxford University Press, Inc.

[2] Ibid., 95.

[3] Ibid., 99.

[4] Ibid., 102.

[5] T. H. L. Parker, *John Calvin: A Biography* (Louisville, Ky.: Westminster John Knox Press, 1975): 21.

[6] McNeill, 103.

[7] Parker, 21.

[8] Ibid., 22.

[9] "John Calvin," *Christian History Magazine* 5, no. 4 (Christian History Institute): 8.

[10] Dr. William Lindner, *John Calvin* (Minneapolis: Bethany House Publishers, 1998): 44–45.

[11] Ibid., 45–46.

[12] McNeill, 111.

[13] Lindner, 46–47.

[14] "John Calvin," 16.

[15] Ibid.

[16] McNeill, 115.

[17] Ibid.

[18] Ibid., 119.

[19] Lindner, 49.

[20] Ibid.

[21] McNeill, 121.

[22] Ibid., 97.

[23] Ibid., 131.

[24] Ibid., 136.

[25] Ibid., 118.

[26] Lindner, 79.

[27] Parker, 66.

[28] McNeill, 144.

[29] Ibid., 153.

[30] Lindner, 122.

✯✯✯✯✯

[31] John Dillenberger, *John Calvin: Selections from His Writings* (Garden City, N.Y.: Anchor Books, 1971): 82.
[32] Ibid., 86.
[33] Ibid., 90.
[34] Lindner, 123.
[35] Ibid., 97.
[36] Ibid., 98–99.
[37] McNeill, 158.
[38] Ibid., 159.
[39] "John Calvin," 10.
[40] Lindner, 103.
[41] Parker, 102.
[42] Ibid., 103.
[43] Lindner, 132.
[44] Encyclopedia Judaica (Jerusalem, Israel: Keter Publishing House): 67.
[45] Ibid.
[46] Ibid.
[47] "John Calvin," 35.
[48] McNeill, 227.
[49] Ibid.
[50] "John Calvin," 19.
[51] McNeill, 227.
[52] Parker, 155.
[53] *Christian History Magazine* 19, no. 3: 31
[54] "John Calvin," 24.
[55] Ibid., 25.
[56] McNeill, 214.
[57] Ibid., 211.

★★★★★

CHAPTER FIVE

John Knox

1514–1572

"The Sword Bearer"

"THE SWORD BEARER"

O God, give me Scotland or I die! [1]

Of all the Reformers, John Knox has been the most unjustly despised, criticized, and hated. Even in our generation, writers have bluntly written of their dislike for him. He has been criticized by many for his crude prophetic strength, his boldness, and his thirst for the blood of those who deceived the people. The name of John Knox was used much like that of the boogie man—a harsh and frightening figure used to keep small children from wandering off into the woods. [2]

For generations, Knox has been compared to the outspoken Old Testament prophets—Elijah, Jeremiah, and, repeatedly, John the Baptist. It's amazing how soon these critics forget that John the Baptist was esteemed by Jesus. (See Matthew 11:11.)

If Jesus called John great and contemporaries think of Knox as crude, then it seems to me that, in our intellectual study of history, we have missed the treasures that heaven esteems. My purpose is to reveal those treasures—along with his mistakes—in the life and ministry of John Knox so that we may realize and understand that the spirit of reform has never been birthed in peaceful ivory towers.

John Knox was a wild, yet focused, Scottish patriot. Sometimes as I studied him, I thought of his resemblance to the Scottish warrior William Wallace. Wallace died over two hundred years before Knox was born, but the two shared a passionate dedication to their causes.

★★★★★

In a different arena than Wallace, Knox was a swashbuckling, prophetic preacher, who at one time carried a two-edged sword, willing to die for his Scotland before he would allow the heresy of the Catholic Church to dominate it. He fought three queens and a host of the Catholic hierarchy, experiencing the pain of prejudice and a persecution so brutal that it would make your skin crawl. When the Protestant cause would weaken, the people looked to Knox to rally their strength with his firey messages. He was a trumpet in the loudest and brightest form, and the message he blared shook Scotland, England, France, Germany, and John Calvin's Geneva. He was a man for his generation—and he rose to meet every second of it. Even when it seemed like he sat idle, Knox wrote tracts and pamphlets so searing that they stirred persecution and hatred for his message generations after his death.

Get ready for a wild adventure as we explore the ruthless and passionate ministry of the greatest Scottish Reformer to date, John Knox.

Knox was a wild yet focused Scottish patriot who has been compared to Old Testament prophets and John the Baptist.

The Affray in the High Church, Edinburgh.
Private collection,
Bridgeman Art Library, N.Y.

★★★★★

Barbaric Scotland

Knox was born in 1514, in the town of Haddington, located just south of Edinburgh, Scotland. [3] The inhabitants of Haddington consisted mainly of merchants and craftsmen, all residing within a nation that was considered barbaric, wild, and savage to the rest of Europe.

Little is known about the early life of Knox. His mother's first name is unknown, but her surname was Sinclair. His father, William, was a respected merchant and craftsman. William's family had owned lands in several Scottish regions. William, along with his father (Knox's grandfather) and grandfather (Knox's great-grandfather) held an honorable position with the Earls of Bothwell, the most powerful family in the region. [4] It would be unfair to state that young Knox lived in luxury or that he was a noble's son, but the ties his family had with the Bothwell clan gave them certain privileges—and one was education.

Knox's parents weren't wealthy, but they were able to put their son through grammar school in Haddington where young Knox mastered the basics of Latin. After he had completed grammar school, Knox became a tutor to a nobleman's children. When the children were sent to the University of St. Andrew's in 1529, Knox was able to attend with them, learning philosophy. [5]

A Bomb About to Go Off

At St. Andrew's, Knox studied under the famous Scottish theologian John Major, [6] the same teacher John Calvin had learned from earlier in Paris. Unlike Calvin, Knox wasn't mesmerized by Major's theology. Major criticized Luther and condemned practices in the Roman Catholic Church, depending on his own intellectual, scholastic opinions. Knox rejected Major's intellectual way of interpreting Scripture. To Knox, the Scriptures meant what they said and didn't need to be analyzed or shied away from. Unsettled, Knox went back to the original sources of Scripture and studied the early church.

Part of his quest for the truth came as the result of an event that happened a year earlier, in 1528. Scotland had burned its first martyr, a man named Patrick Hamilton. Knox had heard the story of how Hamilton preached a simple Gospel and, captured by his Catholic enemies, was indicted as a heretic. On the day of his execution, the martyr openly rebuked and held accountable before the Lord a friar heard loudly heckling him. Only a few days after Hamilton's death, the friar died from a mental frenzy. [7] When several of the Catholic laity began to question Hamilton's death, the general answers they received didn't satisfy them. Knox had heard these disturbing discussions and began to search for the truth himself.

In his search, he studied the church fathers who came before him, chiefly Jerome and Augustine. From Jerome, he learned that the Scriptures alone held the truth, not the words of men. From Augustine, Knox came to understand that a man might be greatly honored for his name or position, but his character or spiritual strength could be weak and overlooked by others, diminishing his effect on the world.

John Knox's house.

To Knox, these two truths became very simple. First, if it was written in the Scriptures, then it was truth. Anything else was simply an additive. Second, a man's popularity meant little if his character didn't strengthen his ministry. These principles became the foundation for Knox's life and ministry.

When Knox came to this understanding, he was still a Roman Catholic. In fact, in 1536, he was ordained as a priest, but he wasn't given a parish because Scotland was already overrun with priests. Although he had no real calling to the Catholic Church, he was given a job as a papal cleric in 1540 and began tutoring young students. All this time, the revelations of his studies began to accumulate and grow within him. As one author put it, "He was a reformation waiting to happen." [8]

Knox's Conversion

In the 1500s, the Catholic Church owned over half the land in Scotland, and the Catholic hierarchy gathered an income almost eighteen times that of the Scottish royalty.[9] There were no spiritual prerequisites to become a priest or archbishop in Scotland; they were appointed by political status. As a result, the character and ability of those to interpret Scripture was utterly blasphemous. They were barbaric, lustful, deceptive, conniving, and murderous. Most of them kept mistresses and were routinely caught in acts of adultery.

The Reformation in Scotland had been going on for several years before Knox joined it.

Knox found two truths. First, if it was written in the Scriptures, it was true. And a man's popularity meant little if it didn't strengthen his ministry.

The king of Scotland, James V, and his wife, Mary of Guise, had had a baby daughter—Mary—the future Mary, Queen of Scots. When she was only one week old, King James V died. As an infant, Mary was pronounced the queen of Scotland.

Of course, she was unable to reign, so a regent for James V was established. The regent established a pro-Protestant policy. He encouraged Bible-reading and promoted preaching by Reformers. Thomas Guilliame, a converted friar, and John Rough, a converted monk, were established as his chaplains. These two preachers went throughout Scotland, taking full advantage of the opportunity to proclaim the Gospel. When Guilliame came to central Scotland in 1543, Knox—still a papal cleric—was tutoring young students.

Always interested in an alternative viewpoint, Knox made his way to the streets to hear Guilliame. Listening to the simplicity of the dramatic preacher, coupled with years of intensive searching, Knox was hurled into another dimension. Guilliame's message had a profound effect upon him. God had been preparing him for this time; his research met the Spirit. Knox cut his ties with the Catholic Church and fully embraced the Protestant belief. He had now crossed the line.

The Protestant with the Sword

In the mid-1540s, the Protestant regent died. Mary of Guise assumed the role of regent, acting for her daughter. She was extremely

Catholic. She established new guidelines abolishing the Protestant policies, and death threats for those who opposed her or Catholicism began to circulate throughout Scotland.

At this time, a wonderful Protestant evangelist named George Wishart made his way into history. Ignoring the threats from the Catholics, he continued to travel throughout Scotland, preaching Reformation to all who would hear. Knox had heard the touching stories of Wishart's messages, so he went to hear him. Listening to his message, Knox saw the simple truth that Wishart proclaimed and was very moved by the evangelist's character. Before long, Knox joined Wishart's team—but not as a fellow evangelist. Instead, Knox was given a job as Wishart's bodyguard and, with his new position, was handed a two-edged sword, which he wore at all times at his side.

I can just see Knox standing beside Wishart with his sword gleaming, his arms folded, and his eyes darting back and forth among the crowd, looking for any aggressive movement. What a sight that must have been!

Wishart Dies in Knox's Absence

For five weeks, Knox followed Wishart as his bodyguard and, over time, became his friend, confidante, and student. Though Knox wanted to stay with Wishart, Wishart insisted, "Nay, return to your bairns [pupils], and God bless you. One is sufficient for one sacrifice." [10]

But in Knox's absence, the corrupt archbishop of St. Andrew's, Cardinal David Beaton, ordered the arrest of Wishart. The evangelist was tried and found guilty of heresy. On March 1, 1546, he was led to the stake to burn to death. Considering Knox's disposition, it is unlikely that these events would have taken place if he had continued as Wishart's bodyguard.

But Wishart didn't go quietly. With hands bound behind his back, a rope around his neck, and an iron band around his waist, he preached in the streets as the crowds gathered to see the spectacle. He encouraged the people to love the Word of God and to continue in what he had taught them. He reminded them that he had not taught man's doctrine or fables, but the true Gospel. He consoled them, saying that although he would be briefly pained in his body, he would shortly be kneeling at the feet of Jesus, safely in heaven with Him for eternity.

His last message was so moving that the hangman fell upon his knees, asking for forgiveness. Wishart forgave him and kissed his cheek, encouraging him to do his job. The hangman strapped him up, and hung him on a stake by the metal band around his waist until the flames consumed him. As he burned, Wishart cried out for the forgiveness of those who murdered him. The event was so moving that the crowd could not "withhold from piteous mourning" [11] at Wishart's slaughter. The air was heavy with death and the atmosphere thick with grief as one of God's servants was burned to ashes before their eyes.

The people began to cry for vengeance. Their voices only echoed the grief and outrage in Knox's own heart. He was not a man who cowered in a corner. If he believed in something, Knox found it revolting not to act upon it. Because he acted on what he believed, Knox eventually found himself involved in a full-fledged rebellion.

The pompous Cardinal Beaton began to be targeted with death threats, but he only laughed at them. After all, the queen regent was Beaton's friend (and widely believed to be one of his mistresses), and he was protected by the best that Scotland had to offer. [12] He hid within the fortified walls of St. Andrew's Castle under heavy lock and key. "What danger should I fear?" the cardinal vainly asked as he toasted the lord governor's son and made evening plans with another of his mistresses. [13]

"We from God Are Sent to Revenge..."

Two months later, on a foggy May morning before dawn, an armed group of men hid behind the bushes until Cardinal Beaton's mistress had slipped out from his room and left through the gate of St. Andrew's Castle. One of the men emerged from the group and approached the watch guard, inquiring if Beaton was awake. Looking at the man, the guard became suspicious and started to pull out his sword when the cloaked intruder buried his dagger deep into the guard's chest. The guard was thrown into the foggy moat below the wall.

The group of men hurried down the stone-walled path and up the stairs to Beaton's door. They awoke Beaton with their loud knocking.

Alarmed, he called for his aide to barricade the door with heavy chests while he ran to hide his gold. But the chests were no match for the fury of the group. With a heaving blow, they broke the door down, trampling it under their feet. As they rushed toward Beaton, the cardinal fell backward into a chair, screaming, "I am a priest! I am a priest! Ye will not slay me!"

Beaton's words could not deter the men. In fact, by protesting, he only infuriated them even more. Two of the men slapped him across the face and hit him repeatedly. One of the cloaked intruders stopped the beating, stating that the execution should be done with more dignity. He approached the white-faced, trembling Beaton, pointed his sword at Beaton's stomach, and said, "Repent thee of thy former wicked life, especially of the shedding of the blood of that notable instrument of God, Master George Wishart, which, albeit the flame of fire consumed it before men, yet cries its vengeance upon thee; and we from God are sent to revenge it." The cloaked man went on to state that neither Beaton's wealth nor fear of his power motivated this execution—the only reason was that Beaton had been and still remained an obstinate enemy to Jesus Christ.

Beaton refused to repent, so the cloaked executioner took his sword and thrust it through Beaton's body three times, as Beaton moaned, "I am a priest! I am a priest...all is gone." [14]

The cloaked men continued to beat and kick Beaton's corpse, slipping several times in his blood before urinating in his mouth and covering his body in salt (to preserve the evidence of their execution). Then they tied a rope around Beaton's neck and hung him out the window of the castle for all to see. The men made sure to dangle Beaton's body just above the place where Wishart had been held prisoner a few months earlier.

The Courageous Castilians

The group of men that executed Beaton didn't leave St. Andrew's Castle but stayed and held the castle under siege. The execution was carried out as both a religious and political protest. Beaton represented French intervention in Scotland, as well as Catholicism. In this obscene manner, the men staged a protest in both realms, calling themselves the "Castilians."

★★★★★

The news of Beaton's murder spread throughout Europe, arousing little sympathy since almost everyone hated France. This silent support only motivated the Castilians to continue their siege.

Knox wasn't present for the execution, but he supported it because he believed evil men would suffer the judgment of God. Knox was serving as a tutor at this time, but he was only a small player, not yet the leader we know him as today.

The Castilian revolt caused immediate pressure from the Scottish government on all Protestants. Now fearing for his life, Knox moved from house to house to avoid capture. He thought of fleeing to Germany, but the fathers of his pupils felt that Knox would be safer joining the rebels in the castle and that the students would benefit from the experience. Several of the prominent Scottish lords were sending supplies to the castle, and an English ship sailed into the harbor with a load of goods for them. Almost a year later, in April of 1547, Knox joined the Castilians at St. Andrew's Castle. [15]

Knox's Passionate Call

Knox soon rose to a prominent position within the walls of the castle. John Rough would listen as Knox lectured his students on Protestant doctrine, and he was impressed by Knox's strength and ability to verbalize his beliefs. The Catholics had commanded Rough to present a list of arguments against their beliefs, so he asked Knox to write it for him. Rough took Knox's presentation to the Catholic priests. On his return, he asked Knox to become the chaplain of the castle. Knox refused, stating he had not received such a "lawful vocation." [16]

Rough soon took care of that. The next Sunday, Rough preached on the election of ministers and then pointed to Knox in front of the congregation, charging him to receive his call as a minister. He then looked to the congregation and asked them to voice their approval. They did so with overwhelming agreement.

Surprised, Knox broke down and cried unashamedly before the people. Unable to contain himself, he got up and left for his room.

This shows the heart, the respect, and the great passion that Knox had for God. Yes, he was stout and crude with his words, but the Protestants of the day expected that. They didn't listen if a preacher wasn't outspoken, because there was no passion to tear at their hearts. They weren't moved by a mushy presentation of the Gospel. People have severely criticized Knox for his boldness, but that boldness was only a minor point in his life—it stemmed from his devotion to a greater cause.

What do I mean by a "greater cause"? Today, being a Christian is secondary in many lives, referring merely to the place where we worship on Sundays. Instead, skin color or nationality is what motivates our modern-day cultures and lifestyles. How we act, think, or carry out our lives revolves around nationality and culture.

God is not moved by our perfection. He is moved by the passion we have for Him, which is rooted in our faith.

It wasn't that way with the Reformers. To be called a Protestant in Knox's time spoke of one's culture—the title defined their entire lives, their total beings. How they thought, how they acted or reacted, and how they carried out their day-to-day lives was based upon whether they were Protestant or not. Being Protestant consumed them. A person was either a Protestant or a Catholic, each with a corresponding lifestyle. Many in that generation died for what they believed.

It was a very big responsibility to be called a Protestant minister. Knox knew that and accepted it with great passion, and I admire him for that. He made some great mistakes, and sometimes he carried out the vengeance of God through his own flesh. But God is not moved by our perfection; He is moved by the passion rooted in our faith.

Knox was a man totally consumed by his passion for God. He was a prophet, and there were no gray areas with him—only black and white. He didn't want to be a self-appointed revolutionary. He saw himself solely as a servant of God who would fight for the truth until his last breath. While he didn't carry out his ministry with perfection—as none except Jesus have done or ever will—he did have great passion. And I believe that's a great treasure we have overlooked. Our measure of success and God's scale of it are weighed on two different balances. Many times our scale of success is measured by the praise and respect of men, but God measures success based on our passion for Him and how much fruit we bear for the kingdom.

His First Sermon: A Catholic Fillet

For days, Knox pondered his call to the ministry. He kept to himself and spoke very little to anyone. But that was soon to change.

While he was still deliberating whether or not he had a public ministry, Knox heard that a priest he strongly disliked would be holding a service at a parish church. He felt compelled to go and witness what this priest was teaching to the people.

Sure enough, the priest infuriated Knox as he proclaimed that the Catholic Church had the ultimate authority over whether or not to condemn someone of heresy. Unable to tolerate these words, Knox stood up in the middle of the sermon and blurted out that he could prove that the Catholic Church had degenerated more from the early church than the Jews did from the Law when they condemned Jesus. Flustered, the priest refused to publicly debate Knox, but the crowd demanded that Knox prove his claim. Knox heartily accepted the challenge.

The news of Knox's upcoming sermon was heralded throughout the community. The following Sunday, many distinguished citizens and university peers sat eagerly awaiting Knox's sermon. Stoic friars and many priests from different sections of Scotland also crowded into the small parish church, hoping their presence would intimidate him. John Major, the celebrated theologian, was also present—out of respect for Knox.

Knox entered the room with confidence, climbed the steps to the pulpit, and delivered his first sermon, absolutely filleting the Catholic doctrine. He took his text from Daniel 7:24–25. He explained the vision with eloquence, describing in detail the Babylonian, Persian, Grecian, and Roman symbolisms. The last—the Roman—he unveiled as none other than the Catholic Church and the papacy. He labeled the Church the synagogue of Satan, pronouncing the Catholic regime as anti-Christian. He attacked the heresies of papal power and unveiled the scandalous lives of the popes from records that had been published elsewhere. Based on New Testament Scriptures, he renounced the heretical invention of purgatory, labeled praying for and to the dead as sorcery, and proclaimed the practice of abstinence from meats and marriage as cultic. Knox then dissected the ceremony of Mass, identifying it as blasphemous to the cause of Jesus Christ. Then he struck at the very root of the Catholic system, denouncing the pope as the Antichrist—not only him, but all who followed him as well.[17]

Not one person dared to interrupt his message. When the sermon was over, its message caused great celebration among the Protestants. Although many Protestant preachers had spread the Gospel and several had given their lives as martyrs within Scotland, up to this time, not a single person had ever delivered such an accurate and detailed message explaining the cause for reform. Some said that Wishart never spoke as bluntly as Knox, yet he was burned at the stake. They fully expected Knox to be the next martyr.[18]

Several Catholics later called for a meeting to question Knox regarding the sermon. He answered their accusations with such resolute accuracy that his intimidators were speechless. Knox calmly took it upon himself to close the session with these words:

> Of this Church if you will be, I cannot hinder you; but as for me, I will be of no other Church but that which has Jesus Christ for pastor, hears His voice, and will not hear the voice of a stranger.[19]

He had obviously accepted and acted upon his call into the ministry. Knox was no longer a small player.

Condemned to the Galleys

Early in his ministry, Knox had already delved deeply into the Roman Catholic infrastructure in Scotland. He was such a threat to them that they issued a command that only priests and distinguished university professors could preach on Sundays. Knox sidestepped their command by preaching other days of the week, drawing large crowds of people who, after hearing his message, denounced Roman Catholicism and became Protestants.

Feeling doomed, the Scottish Catholics called on the military help of France to come and lay siege on St. Andrew's Castle, driving out the Protestants and taking them prisoner. Knox was forced to surrender with the others inside the castle. In July of 1547, the Castilians made an agreement with the French that, if they went peacefully to France, they would be granted their freedom.

But when the ship of Protestants reached the shores of France, the agreement was not honored. Instead, the entire group was boarded onto ships and confined to the galleys. Now a captive and loaded with chains from his neck to his feet, Knox was sent out to sea and into hard labor for the next nineteen months.

Next to execution, to be made a galley slave was considered the most severe punishment given to a heretic or a criminal. Since the Castilians had not appeared before a court, they had no idea how long their punishment would last.

The galley slaves were chained to their benches in the belly of the ship, where they would row the heavy wooden oars for hours a day, unable to stop for fear of a whip across their backs. When not rowing, they performed other menial duties. The food was decent in the galleys, but aboard a hot ship, maggots and other infestations plagued their supply.

No Kisses for a Statue!

At this time, Knox was thirty-three years old and extremely healthy and robust. With the exception of one serious bout of sickness with an ulcer and with his kidney, Knox tolerated the galleys very well. He didn't cause any trouble by provoking the officers, but he didn't tolerate any unjust abuse either. The officers respected Knox's passionate will to live. He also kept his faith alive by believing that God would deliver him to preach in his beloved Scotland. Knox's passion grew into an iron will as he focused on his determination to perform the work of God when his day of freedom came.

Knox believed that, one day, God would deliver him to preach in Scotland. He focused on his determination to perform the work of God.

Knox continued to show his gumption even while a prisoner. One of my favorite stories happened after a Mass aboard the ship. The crew, officers, and galley slaves were all ordered to sing "Hail, Holy Queen" and to kiss a statue of Mary.

As the statue passed by each galley slave, Knox refused to kiss it. Amazingly, he got away with it. But that didn't satisfy him. Knox grabbed the statue and threw it overboard, declaring, "Now let our Lady save herself; she is light enough, let her learn to swim!" [20] No more attempts were made to force the galley Protestants into idol worship after that incident!

Although life in the galleys was difficult, Knox was allowed to receive letters and manuscripts while on board. He had the time to divide some of the manuscripts into chapters for other readers, as well as to write exhortations of his own.

One particular letter came from one of his students being held prisoner in Scotland. The young man had wanted to attempt an escape, but his father advised him not to try for fear of endangering others' lives. The young man wanted to know what Knox thought.

Knox answered him with a quotation that has become one of my favorites. He told the young man to go ahead with the escape and not to be afraid because fear was simply a love of self. [21] He then gave some advice. He warned the young man not to kill an innocent guard in the process. Knox seemed to be able to distinguish who should be killed and who shouldn't. According to Knox, the guards should live, while Cardinal Beaton deserved to die.

There's Strength in the Wilderness

Knox's wilderness experience in the galleys formed the leader we know him as today. It seemed he was a slave in a place of weakness, but the most tormenting time of his life produced an invincible strength within him. We may think thirty-three years old is a young and healthy age, but people in his day rarely lived past their fifties. The fact was, he was running out of time, and, coupled with the reality that the group had no idea when they would be released from the galleys, this could have caused hopelessness or thoughts of defeat in his mind. But Knox wasn't one to quit.

Even when it seemed that Knox was going to die of a serious illness before walking free again, he looked through a porthole as they sailed past St. Andrew's Castle and prophesied,

> I am fully persuaded that however weak I now appear, that I shall not depart this life till that my tongue shall glorify His godly name in that same place.[22]

In the hardest and weakest times of our lives, if we keep our faith ignited the best we can and fix our eyes on heaven, God will build a place of strength, character, and understanding within us that will carry us into our destiny. Moses emerged from the desert as a leader. Joseph came out of prison as a leader. Prisons and persecutions could not weaken the spirit within the apostle Paul. The spirit to never give up and to plow ahead, despite the circumstances around us, is another treasure that heaven honors. And Knox had it.

When Knox left the ship a free man, he was an invincible force that hell could not slow nor stop.

"Spare No Arrows"

The interest of the British government, and probably the specific interest of King Edward VI, allowed Knox and the Castilians to have their freedom. In February 1549, Knox stepped off the ship onto British soil as a free man. Around the same time, the young boy who had written Knox escaped from the Catholic prison in Scotland along with his father and others. The tide of hope had turned.

The religious and political authorities of England were eager to establish Protestantism within their nation, so they were thrilled to have someone like John Knox at their disposal.

For the next five years, Knox remained in England as an honored guest. The British government awarded him the honor of being a Protestant preacher. This time, Knox readily accepted the position. It wasn't safe for him to return to Scotland yet, so Knox took the opportunity before him to further the Protestant cause.

His first pastoral assignment was in the town of Berwick. The church here was filled with burly Scottish immigrants, and many of the British soldiers there were at odds with them. Knox's leadership was so successful that he managed to gain the favor of both groups and to unite them. His wild experiences at St. Andrew's Castle, along with the roughness of the galleys, gave him the fortitude to handle both groups with ease and confidence.

✯✯✯✯✯

True to form, Knox's robust and straightforward sermons left the crowds speechless. He concentrated on the spirit behind a doctrine, rather than the ritual of it, and expected his congregation to clearly discern the difference.

Here's an example of how he dissected the Catholic Mass in one of his sermons:

> In the papistical Mass the congregation getteth nothing except the beholding of your duckings, noddings, crossings, turning, uplifting, which are all but a diabolical profanation of Christ's Supper. Now duck, nod, cross as ye list—they are nothing but your own inventions....What comfort have these men taken from us, that the sight of it should be considered sufficient! [23]

His searing and honest words proved that Knox didn't fit in with the intellectual philosophers of his day—he was a man of action. He had a passion for the truth, a passion for the people to follow the truth, and a passion to personally experience Jesus Christ. If it took that kind of bluntness to expose error, he was the man for it!

Knox taught his Berwick church the three classic Protestant doctrines:

1. The supremacy of Scriptures (over traditions and man made church laws).
2. Justification by faith alone.
3. The priesthood of all believers.

While Knox was happily pastoring in Berwick, he heard the news that the Protestant cause in Scotland was winning against the Regent Mary and that the Castilians' land had been restored. It was very encouraging news, but for now, Knox had no intention of returning to his homeland. Instead, he was dramatically preaching throughout the region of Berwick, forcefully exposing error and calling into check any wrong thinking concerning the Lord.

He became famous for the motto, "Spare no arrows"—and spare none he did. His sermons shot straight up the middle, attacking every avenue of blasphemy, totally silencing and disarming the bishops and priests of England. [24] He saw himself as a battle-ax for the Protestant cause in the English Reformation. They might not like to admit it, but one of the most important fathers of the Church of England was John Knox. [25]

The Rumors about Mrs. Bowes

By 1551, Knox had such influence in England that first he was offered a position as bishop and then the pastorship of All Hallows in London. He refused them both. Knox was content to remain in Berwick, where a controversy arose that still agitates the enemies of Knox today.

A woman in the church by the name of Elizabeth Bowes had gained much of Knox's attention. She was not an ordinary woman.

Mrs. Bowes had been married for thirty years to a Catholic man who was very influential in England. She had borne this man fifteen children. Her fifth daughter, Marjory, traveled with her to hear Knox. They were mesmerized by the strength of his preaching and never missed an opportunity to be near Knox.

The fact that Mrs. Bowes suddenly changed from her husband's Catholicism to Protestantism shows that she was very liberated for her time. Her status gained her an audience with Knox, and, over a short course of time, the two developed a very close friendship.

Even today, there are all kinds of stories that circulate about the relationship between Knox and Mrs. Bowes. His critics accuse him of an adulterous affair, attacking her character as well. It is true that the two wrote repeatedly to each other for well over a decade.

Although Knox walked the thin line of controversy with her at the beginning, I don't believe there was any misconduct between the two. Letters from Mrs. Bowes are filled with spiritual questions for Knox, and his letters merely reply to her questions with some of his own thoughts. It was not uncommon for a Catholic-turned-Protestant to continue to use the minister as a confessional. It's also not uncommon for a person with deep spiritual insight—male or female—to gain the attention of a passionate prophet. However, since Mrs. Bowes was a woman, I do believe that if Knox had followed stricter rules of etiquette and ethics, this nagging rumor of their relationship would not have trailed him through history.

✯✯✯✯✯

A Personal Note on Relationships

I do want to say that this kind of relationship is where many ministers find themselves trapped by the devil, and, if left unchecked, they will fail morally. If you are a married minister, hold to your mate as a precious gift; allow your spouse to boost your confidence and make you feel special.

Let me state that every couple has some kind of difficulty or trouble to deal with and overcome in their marriage/ministry relationship. If you are having trouble in this area of your marriage that you can't work out, don't make the lethal mistake of waiting, thinking things will change. Seek godly, mature counsel. If you don't, deception will come in to crush your relationship, causing you to believe you were never supposed to be married in the first place. Don't allow pride to keep you from seeking help or cause you to think that no one can help you. In all my years of ministry, I've never seen pride that the devil doesn't delight in—instead, it's a feeding ground for him. I've seen so many sad examples where couples who were truly anointed by God lost everything because they waited to get the help or deliverance they needed, and full-blown deception consumed them.

Engaged to be Married

Knox soon extended his pastorate into the city of Newcastle as well. By the end of 1551, Knox was so celebrated in England that he was appointed as a royal chaplain, which involved preaching before the king of England. In this capacity, he was assigned to help rewrite the *Book of Common Prayer* into a second edition. True to form, Knox revolted against the prayer book's instructions for the congregation to kneel at Communion. He insisted that an excerpt be added to the prayer book, stating that kneeling did not mean the person believed the Communion elements actually turned into the body and blood of Jesus. Although it caused great controversy, Knox got his way.

Knox was busy with his ministry, but he also made space for his personal life. In 1553, although little was said about it, he proposed to and was promised in marriage to Mrs. Bowes' daughter, Marjory. However, Mr. Bowes was not at all impressed with Knox and refused permission for the marriage. Knox respected Mr. Bowes' wishes. He and Marjory remained engaged, but their marriage was on hold for a time. He was now living in London, itinerating to his churches in Berwick, Newcastle, and throughout the region. It was an ideal situation with many model converts to Protestantism.

Prophecy Fulfilled: Bloody Mary's Assault on Protestants

In the first half of 1553, all appeared rosy for Knox. He had several influential Catholic enemies in England, but this didn't phase him—his ministry was thriving. His role as a itinerate preacher enabled him to effectively spread the cause of Protestantism.

In his sermons, he continued to blast vain traditions and even went as far as exposing the names of those he considered traitors. Although he couldn't marry yet, his personal life looked promising with his engagement to Marjory. But the events of that year soon brought massive devastation to jolly old England. Knox's reaction to it so blackened his reputation that future queens loathed the mention of his name.

On July 6, King Henry VIII died. Knox sensed trouble in the air—he knew that Protestant maturity in England was shallow from a lack of preaching and frequent error in teaching. He publicly prophesied the desolation of the Protestant movement there.

By the end of the month, Mary of Tudor was crowned queen. Being a strong Roman Catholic, Queen Mary immediately began to undo all the Protestant reforms that her father had instituted. Change came quickly. By November, Parliament had revoked all of the Protestant laws and restored Catholicism as the national religion. Protestants were informed that they had until December 20 to change their beliefs or else they would be treated as heretics.

Knox soon saw the danger for himself. His enemies attempted to seize one of Knox's aides as he carried letters to Marjory and Mrs. Bowes. They had hoped to find information that would lead to Knox's arrest and execution.

Because of this treachery, Knox's followers begged him to leave England. In a letter to Marjory and Mrs. Bowes, Knox stated that his brethren "partly by admonition, partly by tears, compelled him to obey."[26] Reluctantly and wisely, Knox fled for Dieppe, France, in

January, 1554. Later, he wrote that he was not sure he should have left England, for "never could he die in a more honest quarrel."[27] Not wishing to arouse suspicion, Marjory and Mrs. Bowes remained in England, but they made it a point to correspond with Knox on a regular basis. The privileges of the Bowes family protected them for now. With Knox gone, the Catholic hierarchy felt they now had a clear reign in England, and their terrible acts continued on a wider scale.

Knox was correct in his prophecy concerning the desolation. Queen Mary held her first execution—a Protestant Bible translator by the name of John Rogers—in February 1555. In her reign of terror, she executed more than three hundred people, including the first author of the *Book of Common Prayer*, Thomas Cranmer. She shed so much blood in her effort to restore Catholicism that she was given the nickname "Bloody Mary."[28]

Safe in another country, Knox was described as a "warhorse being kept from the battle." He was uneasy about leaving England and wrote of his only assurance in the matter, saying, "My prayer is, that I may be restored to the battle again."[29]

"Let Them Go Quick to the Hells..."

Remaining in Dieppe for about a month, Knox couldn't sit still any longer. He traveled to Switzerland and met with Heinrich Bullinger, a strong and noted leader of the Reformation. One of Knox's main questions to him was whether he was obliged to obey the rules of a monarchy that enforced idolatry. Bullinger could not answer to Knox's satisfaction.

Frustrated, Knox briefly returned to Dieppe, writing to the believers he left behind in England, encouraging them and telling of what he had heard in Switzerland. It is very clear that Knox was pained for those left in England and that he constantly thought of and prayed for their welfare—and, probably, for his return.

As the late summer of 1554 came upon him, Knox sat in Dieppe staring across the English Channel, knowing that on the other side was England with all its idolatry going unchecked. He thought of how he had been stripped as a minister there, how the martyrdom was rampant, and how he had been separated from Marjory and Mrs. Bowes—all because of the queen.

He could no longer contain his passionate hatred for the heresy. In this mood, he sat down and wrote *The Faithful Admonition unto the Professors of God's Truth in England.* It was his longest and sharpest letter to date. In fact, it called for blood! He attacked the Catholic bishops, calling them the "Devil's Gardeners," and the priests, or "blind buzzards," declaring that they all deserved death. He unveiled the hypocrisy of Bloody Mary's court, writing how they were once unified in an opinion that she was an "incestuous bastard who would never reign in England," but they were now kneeling at her feet.

Knox further unleashed his fury by writing that, had Bloody Mary been put to death before she had the chance to be queen, her cruelty would have been avoided. He wrote, "Jezebel, that cursed idolatress, caused the blood of the prophets to be shed...yet I think she never erected half so many gallows in all Israel as mischievous Mary hath done within London alone." He ended with a chilling prayer on behalf of England: "Delay not Thy vengeance, O Lord, but let death devour them in haste; let the earth swallow them up and let them go quick to the hells. For there is no hope of their amendment, the fear and reverence of Thy holy name is quite banished from their hearts." [30]

With a few more strokes of his pen, Knox sealed the letter and sent it to England, knowing it would be published throughout the kingdom.

Knox and Calvin Meet

With no congregation to pastor, and seemingly no revolution to fight, Knox had nowhere to turn but Switzerland. But during this period of banishment, there was another vital element that needed to be added to his life. After making sure his letter left Dieppe, Knox traveled to the city of Geneva specifically, to meet with John Calvin. It was here, in the autumn of 1554, that the two men finally met.

Although they were fighting for the same cause, the methods of Calvin and Knox were vastly different. Calvin was a methodical thinker, a brilliant intellectual scholar and debater, silencing his enemies by his immaculate intelligence. Knox was a brawler who believed in action over words, a fighter with such passionate articulation that he silenced his enemies by presenting the raw truth. I would describe Knox as "Calvin with a sword."

Calvin admired Knox for his courage and embraced him, though somewhat loosely. You can imagine how a person of such intellectual capacity would view someone with such a coarse personality. Knox did things that Calvin might not ever have dreamed of, and Calvin possessed the knowledge that Knox wanted to further fuel his cause. The two became good friends in the name of the Protestant cause.

While in Geneva, Knox finally acquired a mastery of Hebrew. He sat in and observed Calvin's school of theology, calling it, "the most perfect school of Christ that was ever in earth since the days of the apostles."[31] The two men spent hours together, discussing theology and the exact meaning of the Scriptures.

By now, the persecution in England was so terrible that scores of Protestants had fled to Europe. Some of them had gone to Frankfurt and were graciously given a church to worship in. This band of refugees wrote to Knox in Geneva, asking him to come and be their pastor. Knox had only been in Geneva for a few months and was enjoying it so much that he really didn't want to leave, but Calvin felt it was a good idea. Knox accepted the invitation and made his way to Germany. He arrived in Frankfurt in November.

The Frankfurt Fight

All did not go well in Germany. In the church that Knox was sent to pastor, a heated debate broke out over which liturgy to use; some wanted to hold on to the old customs of the Anglican Church, while others wanted to move on to the next step. Unable to solve the dilemma, the group wrote to Calvin, asking his opinion. He responded with disappointment that they would argue over such a trivial issue and said that they should all move ahead to the next phase God had for them.

Calvin's response didn't resolve the issue. Knox was forced to step in and make peace between the two parties. The group compromised, agreeing to follow the liturgy as closely as they could. But the agreement was short-lived. A new company of exiles arrived, and soon those who wanted to worship the old way won out under the pressure of a new majority. Finally, in February 1555, Knox and a group of men drew up a new order of service. In the coming years, it would become the official worship book of the Church of Scotland, *The Book of Common Order.*

Wearied by the immature bickering of this refugee congregation, Knox challenged their shallowness in one of his searing messages. In it, he attacked the sin of governmental leaders, claiming that Emperor Charles V was the same enemy to Christ as Nero was.

This unnerving assertion was sounded throughout Frankfurt. What made matters worse, Charles V was only one hundred sixty miles away! The magistrates feared what might happen to their city if Knox remained. Because of all the controversy, they voted to expel him as the pastor. Knox gladly gave them their wish. He and several others left the church.

Wanting Calvin's approval of their actions, they wrote him of the situation and awaited his response. It wasn't what they were hoping for. Calvin wrote back to the congregation, "I cannot keep secret, that Master Knox was, in my judgment, neither godly nor brotherly dealt withal."[32]

A Return to Scotland

Knox was cordially received by Calvin when he returned to Geneva in April of 1555. For the second time, he tried to settle down into a life of scholarship and study. Deeply impressed with the way Calvin ran Geneva, Knox wanted to learn all he could from it. He wrote of it, "In other places, I confess Christ to be truly preached; but manners and religion so sincerely reformed, I have not yet seen in any other place."[33]

Back in Scotland, it was clear that Protestantism would be unofficially tolerated for the time being. The Protestants there were taking advantage of the occasion, spreading the Gospel wherever they could. There was such high hope among them that they even believed that the Regent Mary might someday convert. Her young daughter, Mary, was now being educated in France and would return someday soon to Scotland as the queen. The Regent Mary had obtained the services of a Protestant to represent Scotland to France in hopes of opening trade. She was now growing older and, by her actions, it seemed that she had weakened in her stand for Catholicism. Compared to Bloody Mary next door in England, anyone looked good! Many Protestant refugees had fled England and taken refuge in Scotland, thinking it was safer. But they still desperately needed preachers and pastors.

In the meantime, Knox was busy organizing a radical English congregation in Geneva. He was grooming them and rallying them to eventually return to England for a Protestant takeover.

All this time, he was still receiving letters from Mrs. Bowes, telling him of the increasing pressure on her family to attend Mass. Their lack of conformity to Catholicism was placing her husband in danger, and, though he was unwilling to convert from Catholicism, Mr. Bowes reluctantly agreed that she and Marjory could leave England. Mrs. Bowes wrote that she and Marjory wanted to join Knox in Geneva so they could worship as they believed.

One after another, she wrote these urgent letters to Knox. Finally, Knox arranged for Marjory and Mrs. Bowes to meet him in Scotland. Initially, he regretted leaving Geneva to go back to Scotland. But he soon became glad when he finished a successful preaching tour there. He would credit Mrs. Bowes for encouraging him to go.[34]

Knox's Marriage to Marjory

Mrs. Bowes and Marjory had a web of contacts in Berwick, making it easy for them to slip into Scotland. When Knox arrived in Edinburgh in the late summer of 1555, he and Marjory were married.

Now Knox not only had a mother-in-law with him, but a new wife as well. There isn't much written about Marjory, except for the fact that she was eighteen years old when she married him; he was thirty-eight. She was levelheaded and charming, and their marriage seemed to be a happy one, proving again that Knox and Mrs. Bowes were never romantically involved. Marjory bore him two sons; the first, Nathaniel, was born in 1557. She also performed secretarial duties for Knox's ministry.[35]

His Short Blast in Scotland

Knox was encouraged by the Protestant advancement he found in Scotland—those who had remained had doubled their efforts. Protestant congregations were now in Edinburgh, St. Andrew's, Dundee, Perth, and other strategic cities throughout the region. The Protestants urged Knox to remain as an inspiration to them all. He did.

★★★★★

For the next nine months, Knox served as an itinerate preacher throughout Scotland, delivering his hard-hitting, explosive sermons wherever he went. His preaching style left the masses in awe. Knox would usually spend about thirty minutes calmly explaining a Scripture passage. Then, as he applied the Word to a current situation the Scottish people found themselves in, he would become "active and vigorous," [36] violently pounding the pulpit. One person in the congregation noted, "He made me so to grew [quake] and tremble, that I could not hold [a] pen to write." [37] Knox was a tremendous success for the Protestant cause.

The Scottish bishops were so afraid of Knox's popularity that, in May 1556, they summoned him to Edinburgh to face legal proceedings. But the Protestants wouldn't stand for it. Hundreds of them gathered to rally in his support. Hearing rumors of their gathering and remembering the St. Andrew's siege, the Regent Mary wisely canceled the proceedings.

Encouraged by her action, the Protestants were again hopeful that they might sway the Regent Mary to their cause. They begged Knox to write her a letter that would persuade her to hear the Word of God. He agreed with them.

Sitting down to write, Knox tried to clear his mind of the disgust he felt toward the Catholic royalty. He began the letter mildly; then he would write something harsh. Frustrated by his written outburst, he would again contain himself and write something nice. But after two or three sentences, he couldn't help but blast the hypocrisy of her government, stating that if she didn't change, she would be in pain and torment forever.

The completed letter was presented to the regent. After she read it, she casually, with no thought or care, handed it to the archbishop of Glasgow, saying, "Please you, my lord, to read a pasquill (a fairy tale or satire)." [38] Knox's efforts had been considered a joke. However, it obviously had some affect on her. After she read it, the regent became less tolerant of the Protestants and their cause.

By now, letters from Geneva were coming to Knox, commanding him to return and continue pastoring the English congregation there. Realizing that Scotland was not quite ripe for change, Knox returned to Switzerland in July 1556.

He had scarcely arrived in Switzerland when he received a summons from Scotland, demanding he return to Edinburgh to face charges. When Knox didn't appear, the Catholics molded a sculpture and painted it in the likeness of Knox, then burned it on a public cross.

When Knox heard of it, he was outraged. Amazingly, he didn't retaliate. Instead, he remained in Geneva for another two years, nursing his rage. He never forgot that the Regent Mary had ridiculed him and allowed him to be publicly condemned to death. From that day on, Knox considered her murderous, sly, and deceitful.

History's Shady Mark: Mrs. Anne Locke

In Geneva, Knox found himself in the midst of some of the greatest minds of the Reformation. But he also found himself surrounded by women. Not only did he have his wife and Mrs. Bowes, but a host of other women had also taken to him, and daily he received their letters from England and Scotland asking him questions.

While it was true that Knox despised queens and that he considered most of the men he knew to be two-faced, he felt differently about women in general. In fact, with his affectionate relationship with Mrs. Bowes and others, it is evident that he considered women as his primary aids in the Reformation.

He had two particular women friends in London who shared much of his confidence. One was named Mrs. Hickman, and his favorite was a woman by the name of Mrs. Anne Locke. In her mid-twenties, Mrs. Locke was the very educated and talented wife of a London merchant. When Knox was forced to flee to France, Mrs. Locke continued her friendship with him through letters. He encouraged her to stand strong under the terror of Bloody Mary and many times gave her instructions and messages to pass on to the Protestants in England. She was also the main fund-raiser for his work. She alone had the authorization to open his mail and read it. He sent her manuscripts to study, asking for her opinion of them, and constantly asked her to send him the latest books on theology. She eventually published her own translation of Knox's sermons, along with material from other Reformation writers, and had them distributed to further the Protestant cause.

One of the main reasons Knox admired her was that Mrs. Locke didn't try to govern a man, though she was equally educated. Believing that it was totally unscriptural, he had no patience for any woman who tried to exercise her authority over a man. According to Knox, Mrs. Locke clearly stayed behind that line. [39]

Because of his dramatic and passionate personality, Knox did several things that would raise an eyebrow. His friendship with Mrs. Locke was one of them. While Knox was in Geneva, he wrote to Mrs. Locke, asking her to come to Geneva and live there—without her husband.

Now, up to this time, several women had written to Knox, complaining about their husbands, asking if they could leave them and come to Geneva. Knox turned them all down and, instead, encouraged them to live peacefully with their mates. Perhaps he sensed a wrong motive with them. But he did just the opposite with Mrs. Locke.

Only a few months after he had settled again in Geneva with his wife and Mrs. Bowes, Knox wrote to Mrs. Locke, saying,

> Ye wrote that your desire is earnest to see me. Dear sister, if I could express the thirst and languor which I have for your presence, I shall appear to pass measure. Yea, I weep and rejoice in remembrance of you; but that would evanish [vanish] by the comfort of your presence, which I assure you is so dear to me that if the charge of this little flock here, gathered in Christ's name, did not impede me, my presence should anticipate my letter. [40]

Knox wrote in another letter that, though she was doubtful about joining him and God willed her to remain in London, he still wished in his heart God would lead her to Geneva. [41]

Perhaps Knox's letter was motivated by the persecution raging in England during this time. But many critics like to point out that the persecution was the same for all the women he knew in England. Why didn't Knox ask them to move to safety? Perhaps Knox didn't fear any hidden motives with Mrs. Locke and felt comfortable asking her to move. Perhaps her husband was very settled in his trade and to move would cause financial disaster. In those days, unless he was a preacher, a man usually remained where his business was.

In May of 1557, Mrs. Locke found the courage to leave England—without her husband—and move to Geneva. She arrived with her son, her daughter, and her maid. Sadly, her daughter died just a few days after she arrived. Later, Knox wrote that he knew he would "be judged extreme and rigorous" [42] by encouraging her to leave her husband and move to Geneva.

I believe her husband, fearing for her safety, let her move. He was a Protestant as well and probably couldn't bear the thought of her being harmed. When Bloody Mary died, Mrs. Locke returned to London in 1559 and lived with her husband until his death in 1571.[43]

Knox was unethical in his passionate words to her, but I still believe her safety was the issue.

Black and White

Some historians write that Knox had a great need to be mothered by sensitive yet intelligent women.[44] Although it is not pleasant to write about, it was probably true in Knox's case. No one ever insinuated that he and Mrs. Locke had any kind of relationship besides a deep friendship. Knox had a hard life, a hard ministry, and he had the ability to be a hard man. Very few men would embrace Knox as a close friend—most of them were jealous of him, feared him, or, even worse, wanted to use him or betray him for their own political gain. In the early days of his ministry, those closest to Knox seemed to be intellectual women whom he grew to respect. Realizing that in his day women had no status in society (except royalty by birthright), I believe he trusted their genuine concern for his ministry and the truths that he taught. History never mentions any woman, except for royalty, ever publicly subverting Knox's message. But men constantly challenged him.

I'm sure it was very dangerous to have John Knox as a close friend. Because he cherished his friendship with these women and wanted their safety, the only obvious answer was for them to move to Geneva. He once wrote to both Mrs. Hickman and Mrs. Locke in a joint letter asking them to come for fear they would be tempted to idolatry if they remained in England.[45] But his singular letters to Mrs. Locke gave a more personal tone, and those are the ones that history accents. You can understand how his words attracted rumors.

I want to make a side note here. Most great people in history have done something to raise an eyebrow, something to make someone feel uncomfortable. When I write about God's generals, I make it a goal to speak of their successes and their failures—their bright moments and their shady ones. I don't do it slanderously, and I would never touch the marks that the great men and women of God have left on the earth for Him. But I do want you to realize that God will operate through anyone who passionately loves Him, in spite of occasional controversies. You must be very aware of your own faults and weaknesses—and don't ever excuse them. Work on what is not right. You might not think God could ever use you if I only spoke of the greatness in these men and women or presented them as perfect vessels. When I write of successes and failures—comfortable and uncomfortable—it gives us all hope that we too can be used by God to change the world.

Waiting: The Ingredient for Controversy

Knox made a tremendous impact every place he went. Even his little English congregation in Geneva eventually became responsible for producing the famous Geneva Bible.[46] The marginal notes in the Bible came from Knox's writings and political beliefs. Although he was miles away in Switzerland, his presence was still felt so strongly in Scotland that he received regular letters from the congregation, updating him on the progress of the Reformation.

It was a peaceful time for him. Geneva was absolutely beautiful in the spring. In May of 1557, his first son, Nathaniel, was born. His church was thriving, and Knox had the luxury of immersing himself in studies and speaking freely with Calvin any time he needed to.

But necessity came crashing into his utopia near the end of that same month. Knox received an urgent letter from the Scottish Protestant leaders, asking him to return. They promised him that not only would the faithful be ready to hear his messages, but they would also be ready to give their lives and goods for the Reformation of Scotland.

Knox gave the letter to Calvin and asked his opinion. He stood before his English congregation and asked what they thought of his return to Scotland. They all agreed that Knox could not turn down such a request. Even so, he waited until the end of September before he left.

Arriving in Dieppe, France, in October, Knox intended to take the first ship to Scotland. But instead, he found another letter for him there, asking him to delay his journey. The letter stated that now the leaders were discussing if it was good for him to make an entrance at this time. He was asked to remain in Dieppe for further instructions.

Annoyed, Knox wrote the Scottish leaders, rebuking them for inconveniencing him in such a manner. He'd had to travel eight hundred miles to Dieppe, leave his wife, his new son, and his congregation. In addition, he could be arrested as a heretic while he was in France—and they were telling him to wait for further instructions! Knox was most troubled about the lack of stability in the Scottish leaders. He wondered how a Reformation could be possible in Scotland if the leaders said one thing one day and changed their position the next. The Scottish leaders didn't send a reply.

When December came, Knox was still waiting in Dieppe. He composed a second letter but received no reply. In the middle of December, he wrote a third letter to the nobles of Scotland. By now, Knox had no intention of returning to Scotland. He preached from time to time at a Calvinistic church in Dieppe, but for the most part, he fumed with disgust.

Knox would sit in the port at Dieppe and look across the channel. He realized that the two Marys were the cause of his problems: Bloody Mary in England and the Regent Mary of Guise in Scotland. One had caused him to flee, the other tormented his fellow Protestants and hindered his return. He concluded that these two women were the main enemies of Protestantism and the champions of persecution in two countries.

Stewing with anger, Knox sat down and began to vent his thoughts. Realizing he was creating an unprecedented masterpiece, he tucked away his manuscripts and decided to return to Geneva before the end of winter. Once there, he would then decide what to do with the written material.

Finally back in Geneva, Knox kept busy with his pastoral duties, yet he had plenty of time to write. In 1558, he wrote at least six books and pamphlets. In a pamphlet aimed at the Regent Mary of Guise, he wrote of God's displeasure with her and called her crown as fitting as "a saddle upon the back of an unruly cow." [47]

★★★★★

However, the pamphlet directed toward the Regent Mary was nothing compared to his manuscript against Bloody Mary. This manuscript created a "greater uproar than anything that had been published in Europe since Luther's three great treatises." [48] This was the one he had written in Dieppe and tucked away.

The controversial ministry of John Knox was about to begin!

The Blast against England's Jezebel

The First Blast of the Trumpet against the Monstrous Regiment [unnatural government] *of Women* put Knox on the map as a revolutionary Reformer. Its ammunition came from years of unethical executions, unresolved conflicts, and unanswered anger against the Catholic queen of England, Mary of Tudor—Bloody Mary. Unfortunately, future generations branded Knox as a woman-hater based on this manuscript. This is not a fair accusation: Any anti-women feelings Knox portrayed were a product of his generation and its beliefs concerning women.

Moreover, the manuscript wasn't written in a moment of rage. It had some history behind it.

Before the manuscript was written, Knox repeatedly tried to find the answers to this female tyranny through Calvin, Bucer, and other Reformers. But no one gave answers to soothe his disgust. Calvin had already been a player in heretical executions (Michael Servetus), so there was little he could say to justify the means. He told Knox that a female ruler must be a deviation of God's order, resulting from the fall of man. The queen's rule had been imposed upon them like slavery, as a punishment for sin. Calvin said that queens could be the "nursing mothers of the Church," and therefore their role should be carried out as such. But then he warned Knox not to touch what was obviously the providence of God. [49]

This answer certainly didn't satisfy Knox. If the queen was to "mother the Church," he didn't understand why the Protestants should passively allow her to kill them and destroy their work. Unable to pacify his anger through the Word of God, Knox took matters into his own hands without telling Calvin about it. Believing he was an instrument of God, he detailed his beliefs.

The foundation of the *First Blast* stated that it was against the law of God, as well as the law of nature, for a woman to rule a kingdom. If man was prepared to submit himself to the government of women, he would do what no other species of creation did, for no male animal was prepared to be dominated by his female. Knox went on to state many reputable facts of the day as to why a woman should not be the chief ruler, his main reason being that the ruler was to lead the army into battle. It was basically an attack on the cruelties of Bloody Mary, and an appeal for the British to revolt against her and overthrow her regime.

Using the illustration in which the apostle Paul stated that man was the head of the woman, Knox went wild with imagination. Comparing Paul's figurative body with the woman as a head to a monster, he said, "...who would not judge that body to be a monster, where there was no head eminent above the rest, but that the eyes were in the hands, the tongue and mouth beneath in the belly, and the ears in the feet." [50]

About women, he said, "Nature, I say, doth paint them forth to be weak, frail, impatient, feeble and foolish; and experience hath declared them to be unconstant, variable, cruel, and lacking the spirit of counsel and regiment [government]." [51] I will say that he was very hard with some of his adjectives defining women, but we must realize these descriptions were ammunition in his argument against the evils of Bloody Mary.

He marveled at the greatness of the people of England, then asked why they stooped to such an evil ruler. Knox concluded the manuscript with a warning to Bloody Mary:

> Cursed Jezebel of England, with the pestilent and detestable generation of papists, make no little brag and boast, that they have triumphed...against all such as have enterprised anything against them or their proceedings. I fear not to say that the day of vengeance, which shall apprehend that horrible monster Jezebel of England, is already appointed in the counsel of the Eternal. And therefore let all men be advertised, for the first trumpet hath once blown. [52]

When Knox finished the manuscript, he decided not to show it to Calvin. He felt it was too inspired and too important for anyone to shelve it. Amazingly, Knox managed to have the *First Blast* printed in Geneva without Calvin's knowledge. He did not print an author's name, nor did it have any publisher's name. Secretly, the manuscript was packed in crates and shipped to England.

With the labor of it behind him and with the realization that he had written what he had always wanted to say in person, Knox probably sat back and smiled. He intended to be controversial. The passivity of the British people had wearied his last nerve, and he wanted to jolt them into action. As he looked out over the mountains surrounding Geneva, Knox could imagine firing his cannons of rage through the atmosphere.

Tearing Down the Veil of Vain Excuses

It took a few months, but just as Knox expected, the *First Blast* produced an uproar from everyone—even the Protestants. The English Protestants in Geneva complained about it to Calvin, who was outraged. The book was condemned and, by royal proclamation, anyone who had it in his possession would be punished with death. Not long after the *First Blast* reached the shores of Britain, Bloody Mary died, and her sister, the Protestant Elizabeth I, took the throne as queen.

Knox couldn't be anonymous for long. In the summer of 1558, he wrote several other pamphlets in which he declared himself as the author of *First Blast*. These pamphlets served as an appeal against the Scottish bishops who burned his likeness on a public cross and condemned him in his absence. He wrote one to the nobility of Scotland, one to the common Scottish people, and one to the Regent Mary, publishing them all in his own name.

To the Regent Mary, Knox revealed that he knew of her statement calling his former letter a "pasquill." Then he bluntly declared,

> My duty to God (who hath commanded me to flatter no prince in the earth) compelleth me to say, that if no more ye esteem the admonition of God nor the cardinals do the scoffing of pasquills, that then He shall shortly send you messengers with whom ye shall not be able on that manner to jest. [53]

To the nobles, Knox wrote that he didn't expect them to take a passive role in protecting the Protestants; he expected the "idolaters," the Catholics, to be put to death. He compared them to the British people when he wrote,

> It had been the duty of the nobility, judges, rulers, and people of England, not only to have resisted...Mary, that Jezebel, whom they call their queen, but also to have punished her to the death, with all the sort of her idolatrous priests, together with all such as should have assisted her, what time that she and they openly began to suppress Christ's Evangel, to shed the blood of the saints of God, and to erect that most devilish idolatry.[54]

Knox wrote to the Scottish commoners, bluntly stating that they were wrong to be passive with their government. Seeing through the veils they hid behind, he wrote what they were privately saying to each other:

> "We were but simple subjects, we could not redress the faults and crimes of our rulers, bishops, and clergy; we called for reformation, and wished for the same; but lords' brethren were bishops, their sons were abbots, and the friends of great men had the possession of the Church, and so were we compelled to give obedience to all that they demanded." These vain excuses, I say, will nothing avail you in the presence of God.[55]

As a true Reformer, Knox was in rare form as he chose to "spare no arrows." He uncovered the deception of passivity. How easy they could moan about reformation yet put no action behind it. The same is true today. God has given us everything we need to bring about godly change in our nations, but until we stop simply talking about it and start acting on it, He will watch from heaven, allowing us to continue in our choice of dull and suppressed lives.

Was It All a Mistake?

Elizabeth I and her adviser knew that Knox was with Calvin, so they wrote Calvin, questioning him about *First Blast*. He vehemently denied having any association with the book or its contents, and he had it banned from the city of Geneva.

Did Knox make a mistake in writing it? I believe his timing was a little off. As he wrote, England already knew that Bloody Mary was near death and that a Protestant would soon be reigning. They were ready and waiting for their moment, which was sure to come. Knox's *First Blast* seemed out of touch to them. However, although the timing may have been a little late, I believe his words against this evil queen were right!

Knox had no idea that Bloody Mary's health was failing, but he did prophesy accurately to her in the book, stating that she would reign for fewer years in the future than she had already reigned in the past.

Although the book was written against the former queen, it severely hurt any friendship that Knox might have had with Queen Elizabeth I. A relationship with her might have opened the doors to the English Reformation. Instead, she slammed the doors of England on Knox. Elizabeth I never forgave him for his cruel words against women in general, and certainly not toward women rulers, since she was one. It would be years before Knox would be allowed to visit England again.

Knox was highly criticized for *First Blast* by almost everyone, even his friends, but he never backed down or apologized for what he had written. Knox defended it until his last breath. His feelings on Queen Elizabeth were contradictory. She was a Protestant, but had publicly attended Mass so as not to draw Bloody Mary's fury. Knox counted her as an idolater for these actions. His only regret was that his traveling papers to England were denied.

However, his pamphlets to Scotland had a different effect. There was no doubt that before the Scottish Reformation could happen, a revolution would have to take place. The Scottish people received his words, and his voice grew daily in their hearts. They were ready, and Knox was their leader.

The criticism seemed to strengthen Knox's stand, so he decided to hit back with another punch. He wrote a pamphlet to the common British people as well. In it, he told the citizens that all who bowed their knee to the Catholic Mass were accountable for the bloodshed of Queen Mary's reign and would answer to God for it. He cursed them, saying that he counted them as idolaters, murderers, and guilty with the queen because none of them did their duty to God by remembering their callings. He told the clergy that they should have been as bold for God as they were in parading their titles and robes before the people.

Needless to say, Knox was his own man—one who followed what he believed God wanted, despite what his critics said or what the respected religious hierarchy believed. He was one of the most powerful men of his day. His voice commanded respect and action from those who believed—and it terribly polarized those who were against him.

The Long-Awaited Return to Scotland

When Elizabeth I became queen, and the heretical, terrorizing reign of Bloody Mary had ended, many of the English refugees began to leave Geneva and return to England. By the end of January 1559, less than a handful remained in Switzerland. As his congregation disbanded, Knox decided to leave as well. Calvin was still very annoyed with him, and their relationship was strained. Marjory had another son, Eleazer, so it was decided that she, the two boys, and her mother would remain in Geneva until Knox knew where they would all live.

As usual, Knox headed for Dieppe. Twice, he asked for permission to enter England—and was denied. At first, it disturbed him, but he decided that he didn't need England to get to Scotland. He wrote, "England hath refused me; but because, before it did refuse Christ Jesus, the less do I regard the loss of that familiarity. God grant that their ingratitude be not punished with severity, and that ere they be aware."[56]

What seemed like a tide changing against him didn't phase Knox. Temporarily stranded in Dieppe, he used it to his advantage.

Before Knox came to Dieppe, the Protestants there worshipped only at night for fear of being arrested as heretics. Knox decided to change that. His ministry and preaching in the city made a big impression: The Protestants were infused with the boldness of God and began meeting and worshipping during the day!

★★★★★

Knox remained in Dieppe for three months, waiting on a signal to return to Scotland. In his time there, he fought the Anabaptists (who attacked Calvin and Knox's belief of predestination/election) and continued to denounce the queens.

The Anabaptists were probably his greatest religious enemies outside Catholicism. They were constantly rising up against the doctrines of Calvin and his belief that heretics should be executed. Knox saw the Anabaptists as soft Christians who didn't stand up for the commandments of God.

Knox's doctrine consisted of unquestioning obedience to God, which would only be found by knowing His commandments and following them.

Predestination is a hard and complicated doctrine, but it is easy to see why Knox would be a follower of it. His doctrine consisted of unquestioning obedience to God. That obedience could only be found by knowing His commandments and following them literally, word for word, from the Bible. Knox didn't worry about the context or customs in which certain verses were written. It was not a question of how someone interpreted it. To him, if it was found in the Bible, it was truth—case closed.

He accused the Anabaptists of totally relying on their reason instead of on what God stated. In short, Knox found no use for them and denounced them soundly. Before he had left for Dieppe, he had published his largest book, a refute against them entitled, *An Answer to a Great Number of Blasphemous Cavillations Written by an Anabaptist and Adversary of God's Eternal Predestination*. The book contained over one hundred seventy thousand words, and he used much of this material against them while in Dieppe. [57]

Believing he had won the "war of words" against the Anabaptists and feeling he had inspired the Protestants there to continue, Knox felt a release to set sail for Scotland in April 1559. He arrived on the Scottish shores of Leith in May.

He found Scotland in greater turmoil than he had imagined—but his greatest hour had come.

✯✯✯✯✯

"I See the Battle Shall Be Great..."

Scotland was very different from the way Knox had left it years before. It had become a backward country, far from the affluent city of London and the intellectualism he had known in Geneva. Many roads were impassable because of the rough terrain.

The Regent Mary had succeeded in getting British soldiers out of her country, but it was a political move. Her young daughter (the future Mary, Queen of Scots) was living in France and had now married a French prince, so the French army made its presence and power known in all of Scotland. The French army had become an enemy to Scottish freedom.

Meanwhile, Protestant Reform had been growing in Scotland. When Knox arrived, he immediately set out to preach in Dundee and Perth. When the news reached the authorities that Knox had returned, the government branded him an outlaw.

Coincidentally, the Regent Mary had just begun her suppression of the Protestant preachers. Unlike the British people, the Scots sent the regent word that they would force her out of Scotland if she stood in the way of Reform. Trying to keep the upper hand, she set a date for them to appear in Stirling for a court trial. Knox surprised them all when he arrived on the Scottish shores just in time to hear about it. He wrote, "I see the battle shall be great, for Satan rageth even to the uttermost; and I am come (I praise my God) even in the brunt of the battle....For my fellow-preachers have a day appointed to answer before the queen-regent...when I attend also to be present."[58]

On the appointed day, Knox joined with the preachers, but a great multitude of unarmed people also traveled with the group. They stopped in a city outside of Stirling and sent word they were coming in peace. When the Regent Mary heard that Knox was with them, along with a great group of people, she was alarmed and sent word that the preachers didn't have to appear.

The people rejoiced; yet, when they failed to show, the judges declared them all outlaws in rebellion to the government.

A Sermon That Ignited a Civil War!

When Knox heard of the judges' injustice, he retaliated by preaching one of his famous sermons against the Mass in Perth. He called the

Mass idolatry and bluntly called on Christian men to do their duty to God in response. This famous sermon started a civil war in Scotland. [59] Only nine days after his arrival, Knox caused a national revolution!

The people were incredibly stirred by his preaching. They already had the fight in their hearts—Knox's words caused their passion to ignite! When Knox dismissed the group, only a few stayed behind in the tense atmosphere. One of them was a priest. In defiance to Knox's message, he boldly—and ignorantly—proceeded to uncover an altar and hold a Mass. Knox made a derogatory comment to the priest; the priest turned around and hit him across the face.

A young boy who witnessed the attack picked up a rock and furiously threw it at the priest. The priest ducked just in time for the rock to hit an image by the altar, smashing it to pieces.

A riot broke out. The priest ran for his life, but all the sacraments of the Catholic Mass, and the building itself, were broken into bits. Unsatisfied that all they had to break was stone, the mob ran toward a monastery, hoping to find people! The other friars and priests fled, and the monastery was soon destroyed, leveled by the outraged mob. In two days, the silver, gold, lead from the roofs, meat, wine, and every personal belonging the mob could find had disappeared. Bonfires were made of the Catholic images, and death threats were made to the priests; even the trees around the monasteries were pulled up by the roots!

Surprisingly, Knox denounced the actions of the mob. He wanted the idols destroyed, but not this way. He also knew that the Regent Mary would use it against him, and his life would be in further danger. He was right.

The Standoff in Perth

Hearing of the mob, the Regent Mary declared a war on the city of Perth, vowing to leave the town in rubble. She wasn't ready for the response. The citizens cheered at her threat and asked Knox to represent them through a letter to the French soldiers, the nobility, the Catholic clergy, and to Mary herself.

To the soldiers and the regent, Knox wrote that the citizens of Perth were loyal to Scotland and meant it no harm; they only wanted the freedom to worship as they chose.

To the Protestant nobles that served in the regent's court, Knox was stronger. Threatening them with excommunication, he wrote, "Doubt ye nothing but that our church and the true ministers of the same, have the power which our Master, Jesus Christ, granted to His apostles in these words, 'Whose sins ye shall forgive, shall be forgiven, and whose sins ye shall retain shall be retained.'"[60] The "true ministers" of the Protestant church at that time only numbered about five or six! Yet they spoke with the spiritual strength of David to Goliath!

The taunting letter to the Catholic clergy began, "To the generation of antichrist, the pestilent prelates and their shavelings within Scotland, the congregation of Jesus within the same saith...."[61] It ended by announcing that the Protestants would arrest them all as murderers if they continued in their cruelty.

The regent continued in her march toward Perth. Using the sly treachery she was known for, she stopped outside the city and offered a negotiation. The citizens again announced their loyalty but stated they wanted the freedom of worship. Knox went a step further. He told the nobles to give the regent a special message from him.

They were to tell her that those she so blindly persecuted in her rage were God's servants and her obedient subjects; that her religion was contrary to Christ's; that her designs would not succeed; that, though she might humble some for the time being, she was really fighting against the almighty God; and that her end would be confusion if she did not repent. He required them to tell her the message "in the name of the eternal God," and to say that he (Knox) was a better friend to her than those who flattered her.[62]

Despite the words of Knox, the regent felt she must punish the citizens with treason for their mobbing. She sent a message ordering the people of Perth to abandon the city. They did not.

Two days later, twenty-five hundred Protestants marched to Perth from western Scotland, on foot and horse, coming to the aid of their fellow believers. When they were six miles from the town, the regent decided to formulate an agreement with Perth, giving them freedom of worship.

The Protestant nobles informed Knox that if the regent did not keep this agreement, they would leave their positions in her court and join with him and the Reformers. Knox assured them that she would break her word. He was right.

A few days later, the regent marched into the city. The first shot fired killed a child standing in a window. From there she divided soldiers to hold the citizens under restraint as she had a Mass prepared in the desecrated monastery sites.

It was a deadly mistake on her part. The Protestant nobles that had served in high offices of her court did what they promised Knox. They denounced her and refused their support. Instead, they joined Knox in his efforts and used their skills to further the cause of the Reform.

"My Life Is in the Custody of God"

The Protestant nobles once again took over St. Andrew's Castle. In the meantime, Knox continued his itinerate ministry throughout Scotland and preached the message of Reform to each town.

The nobles wanted to call a meeting at St. Andrew's, and issued the date of June 3 to all the Protestant ministers. As Knox began his entrance into the castle grounds, he was immediately met by Hamilton the archbishop and his men, who were pointing a hundred spears at him. Grinning, Hamilton informed Knox that if he entered to preach, he would be met with "a dozen culverins (long cannons), whereof the most part should light upon his nose."[63]

Years before, Knox knew he would return to St. Andrew's to preach. Queens, armies, and the torment of the galleys couldn't stop him.

Knox had not been stopped by murderous queens, by barbaric executions, by expulsions, by armies, or by the torments of the galleys. Besides, years before he had prophesied that he would again stand in St. Andrew's and preach. No man could stop that from happening—especially a heretical archbishop!

The Protestants began to shout that Jesus would be preached in spite of Satan. The nobles had a host of horsemen at Knox's back. But none of this moved him. Knox was moved only by the fact that God had given him his wish to preach again at the Castle. It was thirteen years in coming, but the day was here.

He answered the archbishop, "As for the fear of danger that may come to me, let no man be solicitous, for my life is in the custody of Him whose glory I seek. I desire the hand nor weapon of no man to defend me."[64]

His words caused the archbishop's boldness to weaken. Hamilton looked around him and saw hundreds of eager Scottish Protestants, with wildly barbaric eyes, eager to pounce upon him at any signal from Knox. He thought better of his threat and called off his spearmen.

Knox entered St. Andrew's, untouched, and preached the next day to a crowded room of listeners. Many of the Catholic clergy were also in attendance. They had come ready to snare Knox in his words, but the tables were turned against them.

Knox entered the pulpit with a great anointing upon him, ever mindful that he was fulfilling prophesy. His theme was from the New Testament incident when Jesus drove the money changers from the temple. He applied the Word so skillfully to the current situation that the Catholic clergy sat almost hypnotized. The strength in Knox's words was so great that not even a sigh was heard from the congregation. They were all defenseless.

Knox planned an encore to his message, which was unrivaled in Scottish history. To show how strongly he felt that Catholic images were a form of what Jesus drove out of the temple, Knox set fire to the images and burned them before their eyes. The priests were still so dumbfounded that they were unable to move!

Knox preached for three more days, and, by the time he was finished, all the other Catholic churches in the area were dismantled!

Men Rained from the Clouds

When the regent heard of Knox's latest victory, she was beside herself with rage. Rallying her army, she marched from her palace in the Falklands to St. Andrew's.

But the nobles had already gathered over three thousand men to meet her. Knox wrote of it, "God did so multiply our number that it appeared as men rained from the clouds."[65]

When the regent and her army reached St. Andrew's, they saw a miserable defeat for them. There was no course left but for the regent to retreat. In one last stand, she stated that she would grant amnesty to the Protestants if they would promise not to destroy any more Catholic property and to stop their public preaching. The Protestants were indignant and refused both conditions.

After a week's worth of negotiating, a truce was declared. While a truce was agreed upon, the conditions were still unresolved. The Protestants began wrecking more monasteries, overthrowing altars, and burning images while the monks and priests helplessly watched. City after city became subject to this kind of looting. Knox and the other nobles tried to intervene and stop it, but the Protestants had been suppressed and endangered for too long. Momentum was on their side, and they seized the opportunity.

Realizing he could do little to stop their physical looting, Knox simply wrote, "The Reformation is somewhat violent, because the adversaries be stubborn...."[66]

Many times, Knox would stand by and watch the sacking and looting of the monasteries. His assurance that all would be well came from an old woman's testimony. She walked over to Knox as a monastery burned to the ground and told him,

> Since my remembrance, this place hath been nothing else but a den of whoremongers. It is incredible to believe how many wives hath been adulterate, and virgins deflowered, by the filthy beasts which hath been fostered in this den; but especially by that wicked man who is called the bishop. If all men knew as much as I they would praise God; and no man would be offended.[67]

After her statement, Knox held his peace, believing it was the just judgment of God.

The people had held a mystic reverence for the beautiful statues and images throughout Scotland, and the Protestants wanted to kill that misplaced reverence. They marched on to Edinburgh to continue their destruction, but the citizens there had beat them to it. Every Catholic work of art, every statue, and every image that stirred the affection of the people toward itself instead of toward God had already been destroyed.

Up until now, Knox had been the only Reformer of wide reputation who allowed the destruction of images and works of art. Like the prophets of old, Knox was a Reformer who believed in passionate action. He didn't just suggest that the altars of Baal be destroyed, and he didn't merely write about it; he destroyed them. Like David, he didn't stop with merely knocking Goliath down to the ground—he cut the head off!

"Where Is Now John Knox's God?"

By now, Knox was greatly missing his family. He wrote repeatedly to Geneva, asking Marjory and the children to meet him in Scotland. By the end of 1559, Marjory and their two sons joined him at St. Andrew's. Because of the violence, Mrs. Bowes had been granted admission into England and remained there for the time.

France had been an important religious and political ally to the regent, and she certainly needed France's help now. The French answered the Regent Mary's cry and came sailing toward Scotland to intervene in the civil war. Embarking upon the Scottish coast in January of 1560, the Protestants and the French fought a guerrilla war in the deep snows.

John Knox preaching before the Lords of the Congregation, June 10, 1559.
North Wind Picture Archives

Knox sent urgent letters to Elizabeth I, begging her to protect her interest in Scotland. Without knowing of the letter, she had already sent a fleet of fourteen ships with one of her most experienced sea captains.

Meanwhile, the French were wreaking havoc in Fife. They were ransacking the houses and hanging the inhabitants. The Protestants could do very little against the massive French army. The regent, by now very ill and weakened with gout and dropsy, laughed when she heard the news, saying, "Where is now John Knox's God? My God is now stronger than his."[68]

She was despised by the Protestants for her ruthlessness. Once, a troop of French soldiers had killed some British soldiers, stripped their bodies, and then hung them over the wall to glisten in the sun. The regent complimented the sight by saying that she had never seen such a fine tapestry and wished that the entire field was laced with such a sight.

For the next six months, the battle for Scotland raged between the British and the French, and it seemed the French were gaining ground. Knox was not completely inactive during this time. There weren't many people to preach to, since they were all fighting the war, so Knox continued with his writing and began building a church system and policy based on the Calvinistic beliefs of the men within the castle of St. Andrew's.

It soon became mandatory for every Protestant to attend church at the castle each Sunday. The law was strictly enforced. From this mandatory attendance, Knox preached and rallied the dejected troops back into strength. He preached with a fury that they were losing ground because they had placed their trust in man and not in God. Knox thundered, "Yea, whatever shall become of us and our mortal carcasses, I doubt not but that this cause (in despite of Satan) shall prevail in the realm of Scotland. For, as it is the eternal truth of the eternal God, so shall it once prevail...."[69] His words and his spirit infused life back into the Protestant troops.

When it looked the worst for Scotland, deliverance came. The British plundered Scotland with a host of troops, driving the French back into their holds. The Regent Mary, who was by now very ill, asked for refuge in Edinburgh Castle, a neutral zone. It was granted.

A short time later, Knox was preaching in Edinburgh when he heard the news that the Regent Mary had died on the morning of June 11, 1560. The struggle for Scotland abruptly ended with her death. In July, both the French and the British left Scottish soil.

It was later said that Knox felt he had finally gotten even with the regent by his prayers for her death. [70]

Setting Things in Protestant Order

Immediately following the French and English evacuation, the Scottish Parliament began meeting in regular sessions. A treaty had been signed giving both them and Mary, Queen of Scots (when she returned from France) a say in the direction of the nation. Knox was asked to hold a thanksgiving service for them. Afterward, he was asked to preach to the Parliament on a regular basis.

In August of 1560, the Parliament voted to abolish Catholicism and establish Protestantism as the national religion. The papal authority was totally relinquished. Gone were the bells, the chalices, the Latin services, the statues, the crucifixes, the worship of Mary and the saints, the prayers for the dead, the belief in purgatory, and the elaborate rituals. In their place came a simple church service with passionate preaching, Bible study, prayer, and psalms sung by the entire congregation to common melodies.

It was a tremendous victory for the Reformation, but now guidelines had to be established to lead the nation in its faith. The people looked to Knox for the answer. He had no trouble helping them.

In the same month, Knox and other ministers presented a confession of faith, which basically combined the Protestant and Calvinistic beliefs. The Parliament read it and voted it in.

Next, they wanted a common discipline book, and Knox presented his *Book of Discipline.* Not everyone was able to agree with it, so he was asked to modify it, and he did. It stated that the moral discipline of the church members would be handled solely through the church and not the government. It explained where the tithes of the people should go and how the ministers should be supported. Each local church would elect its own ministers from a list provided by the core leaders. Superintendents would be installed and would be required to travel throughout their districts, preaching at least three times a week and watching over the behavior of the local ministers. Although he modified the *Book of Discipline,* it was not presented as law. It would be voted on at a later time.

The Death of Marjory

Knox was now able to settle down into his pastorate in Edinburgh. The ministers wanted to appoint him as a superintendent, but he refused, stating his health was bad. As pastor in Edinburgh, Knox held a very honored position, complete with financial and social privileges. He lived in a large house—a mansion in its day—complete with a beautiful garden and lavish furnishings, and totally paid for by the council in Edinburgh.

Knox had just settled into his new home when tragedy struck. Marjory, who was in her mid-twenties, died. Her cause of death was never stated. Some have assumed that overwork caused her to become weak and vulnerable to sickness. They base this upon Knox's statement, "The rest of my wife hath been so unrestful since her arriving here, that scarcely could she tell upon the morrow what she wrote at night."[71] Marjory had, with great energy, thrown herself into the work as vigorously as Knox had.

She left behind two small sons who were only two and three years old. Knox tried his best to raise them alone, but he eventually sent for Mrs. Bowes to live with them and help.

Marjory's death was a great personal loss to Knox, and he struggled with the emotions of it as he tried to nurse himself back to health. He buried himself in the work of the Reformation and relied on the Lord for consolation. Knox wrote how her death devastated him. His fond memories of her were expressed in his words about her "whose like is not to be found everywhere."[72]

The years they lived before their season of comfort in Edinburgh had been extremely taxing on them all.

Another Murdering Mary

The only hope that the Catholics had for Scotland was the return of Mary from France. She had been sent away when she was only six years old to be educated in the finest Catholic schools of the era. She had married a French prince in 1558, but he had died suddenly in

1560. Mary was now single once again, very beautiful, very witty, and very spoiled. If anyone tried to cross her or change what she wanted, she was extremely impatient and emotional with them, demanding her own way, or else.

Several Scottish nobles had traveled back and forth to France, advising her of how she should return to Scotland. She had heard of Knox's *First Blast* and had already decided that he was the "most dangerous man in her realm." [73] Fearing that he would start a revolution against her, Mary demanded that Knox be banished from Scotland or else she would not live there.

Her threats didn't work. Elizabeth I, the queen of England, was advised to protect Knox's solitude in Scotland—all for the political interest of England. Knox's influence was weakening the strength of the Scottish royalty. This helped assure Scotland's submission to England. Though Mary was determined to have her own way once she returned to Scotland, she left Knox alone because of her fear of Elizabeth I.

Mary was a devout Catholic and was fiercely against the Reformation. She gave an ultimatum that she would return as queen on two conditions: that she could remain a Catholic and have Mass held only in her royal court and that she would have the same lavish and extravagant court that she was used to in France. The nobles agreed. On August 19, 1561, Mary, Queen of Scots, arrived on the shores of Scotland, heartily welcomed by the people of Edinburgh. She was only nineteen years old.

When she arrived, it was raining heavily, there was a thick fog, and visibility was reduced to only a few feet. The weather was unusual for that time of year, and Knox took it as a prophetic sign. He wrote,

> The very face of heaven, the time of her arrival, did manifestly speak what comfort was brought into this county with her, to wit [that is to say], dolour [sorrow], darkness, and all impiety [irreverence]. In the memory of man, that day of the year, was never seen a more dolorous [sorrowful] face of heaven....The sun was not seen to shine two days before, nor two days after. The forewarning gave God unto us; but alas, the most part were blind! [74]

A New Foothold for the Catholic Regime

The first Sunday that Mary arrived, she arranged for a Mass to be held in the court for herself, her court, and her relatives. As the ceremony was about to begin, a group of Protestants tried to force their way into the court, yelling that the priest was an idolater and should die. They succeeded in wounding one of the servants who carried a candle but were then overpowered and forced to leave the premises.

At the same time, Knox was preaching to an unusually large gathering of Protestants, denouncing the queen and her plot to destroy what the Reformers had built. A British ambassador, who wanted to give Mary a chance, was very upset by the sermon. He wrote that everyone in Scotland had been impressed with their new queen, "saving John Knox, that thundereth out of the pulpit, that I fear nothing so much that one day he will mar all. He ruleth the roost, and of him all men stand in fear." [75]

It was true. Knox had the ability to discern the motives of Mary, and he saw through her before she even arrived. One man said that Knox was the only man who had ever met Mary and was neither charmed nor deceived. [76]

After the disruption of Mary's Mass, a proclamation was issued from the court that stated if anyone tried to hinder or hurt any part of royalty, the penalty would be death. The political heads attempted to reason with the Protestant nobles, asking why they wanted to chase Mary out of Scotland. They wanted the Protestants to give Mary a chance, because it seemed sure that she would eventually be swayed to believe as they did. The Protestants were assured that, when a large part of Mary's relatives returned to France, they would be able to rule as they pleased.

Knox didn't fall for it. He saw that the Protestants' fervor was beginning to fade and that they were compromising their stand. The next Sunday, Knox preached with even greater force. He soundly denounced the Catholic idolatry that was attempting to invade them and, step by step, repeated the plagues that befell other nations that had tolerated it. He then gave his famous statement, "One Mass is more fearful to me than...ten thousand armed enemies." [77]

He continued, "In our God there is strength to resist and confound multitudes if we unfeignedly depend upon Him, whereof heretofore we have had experience." He asked, What would become of them all if the presence of God left them? What would be their defense? Prophetically, he added, "Alas, I fear that experience shall teach us, to the grief of many." [78]

Although he saw the struggle and the grief in store for them, Knox never abandoned his fight or fell victim to a weakened spirit. He didn't run, and he didn't desert the cause. Knox didn't give up, nor did he resign from the front lines to hide in the back. The battle was on—and the sight of it gave Knox his reason for living.

A "Common Threat"

The personality and tenacity of the Scottish people is found nowhere else. They have an unbreakable backbone and incredible audacity. Their ability to unite against a common threat spells disaster for anyone daring to stand against them. Trust me, you wouldn't want to be counted among those who threatened their welfare!

Seeing this tremendous quality within them, I've often wondered why their nation is not leading a current Reformation for God. They have the ability to unify and rally like none other; but the problem now is that they've not seen the "common threat" against them, and that's their key.

What glory and deliverance will come if we rally together and put an end to the evils that hinder us. We can stand against our "common threat."

The "common threat" now—just as it was in the past—is spiritual. The enemy has pacified their nation, keeping them subdued and passive toward God. They, like other nations, have become absorbed with their own personal interests and quests for intellectual status instead of focusing on the Holy Spirit and His power to deliver their nation. If they could only again see the complacent devastation that their "common threat" has produced and that the enemy is responsible for the lullabies of their passivity, then that great Scottish spirit and fervency for God would rise again, and their nation might lead the way for others to experience and know God. What glory and deliverance would come if they would rally together and put an end to the evil that hinders their nation so that God could truly come and live among them with continual power!

The Reformation in Scotland couldn't have come through written material or passive gestures. Restoration wasn't their answer. Restoration returns something that has been lost or taken. Reformation stops the abuse to make something better. Reformation must come before restoration. The two forces—restoration and reformation—are similar, yet different; don't confuse them. We can't have one without the other. Since the terminology is important, I'll discuss it thoroughly at the end of this chapter.

True to the Scottish personality, the Reformation could have only come through a revolution that would open people's eyes to the truths of the Gospel. Knox felt that, as a prophetic ambassador of God, he was the one to spearhead this. He viewed his assignment as threefold: to purify the national religion, to hold to His covenant, and, finally, to resist and continue to resist any and all authorities who promoted idolatry (anything contrary to the Word of God).

What is the "common threat" that continually hinders God from getting totally involved in your church, your home, your nation, or your life? To a Reformer of any generation—in any nation—the "common threat" is a call toward confrontational action and change toward God.

Face-to-Face Confrontation

Mary, Queen of Scots, was furious at the latest preaching tactics of Knox. Feeling she must confront him, Mary summoned Knox to appear before her—the first of five times.

The first meeting was September 4, 1561. Mary had been in Scotland less than a month. She asked him why he had written *First Blast*, why he had incited a revolt against her mother and herself, and if it was true that he was a magician. (In an attempt to instill fear, the Catholics had invented the rumor that Knox practiced magic.)

Knox eloquently stated that in Scotland he had only rallied against the Catholic faith so that the true faith could be defended; that what he had written in *First Blast* against Bloody Mary, her court, and her supporters was true; and that he was not a magician.

She then asked his position under her government. Knox responded that he would be as content to live under her rule as the apostle Paul was under Nero. He then pointed out that if he had wanted to stop her, he could have done it much easier while she remained in France. He had no intention of overthrowing her government—her religion, however, was another issue. He denied her the right, as queen, to dictate her faith to the people.

She sharply attempted to insult him, saying, "But ye are not the Kirk [church] that I will nourish. I will defend the Kirk of Rome for I think that it is the true Kirk of God."

"Your will is no reason, madam," countered Knox, "Neither doth your thought make the Rome harlot to be the true and immaculate spouse of Jesus Christ." He then went on to explain, just as in all his sermons, how the Catholic Church had degenerated and to the point of opposing the early church.

"My conscience says that is not so," Mary stubbornly replied.

"Conscience, madam, requires knowledge; and I fear that right knowledge ye have none." [79]

When she asked whom she should believe, Knox told her she was to believe God, who plainly spoke in His Word. She abruptly cut him off and ended the meeting. Knox dismissed himself, saying that he prayed she would be as successful in Scotland as Deborah was in Israel.

After their first meeting, one of Knox's friends asked what he thought of her. Knox replied, "If there be not in her a proud mind, a crafty wit, and an indurate heart against God and His truth, my judgement faileth me." [80] He later wrote to the adviser of Elizabeth I, "In communication with her, I espied such craft [slyness] as I have not found in such age." [81] To Knox, it was a battle between light and darkness.

The Unbridled Spirit

In the beginning, it seemed that Mary was winning over Scotland. A large part of the Protestants were mesmerized by her beauty and youthfulness and grew quiet about her Catholic faith.

However, those Protestants who remained true to the Reform terrorized her at every turn. When she appeared in public, they greeted her by burning the likeness of a priest on a cross. The Edinburgh Protestant nobles issued a proclamation ordering all drunkards, adulterers, priests, monks, and nuns to leave town. When she celebrated a Catholic holy day in one town, the priests there were mobbed and driven from the choir with bloody heads. Mary watched and cried helplessly. Knox was also there, watching her every move and preaching against any violation Mary might have done in opposition to Scripture.

A sympathetic Protestant noble wrote England's advisers of the trouble Knox was making for their new queen. The letter stated, "You know the vehemency of Mr. Knox's spirit which cannot be bridled, and yet doth utter sometimes such sentences as cannot easily be digested by a weak stomach. I would wish he should deal with her more gently, being a young princess unpersuaded."[82]

The controversy grew into such a peak that soon the majority of the nobles denied that the Protestant church had any right to meet without Mary's consent.

Knox wouldn't hear of such a backward injustice. Raging against them with his eloquent and decisive sermons, the nobles soon backed down and decided that their meetings could remain as they had been as long as Mary's interest was represented as well.

Knox's *Book of Discipline* now came up to be voted on as law. The book did not pass on the issue of where the money would go. The nobles and the royalty wanted the excess of the tithes and the property. They got their way.

Hearing of the news, Knox lamented, "O happy servants of the devil, and miserable servants of Jesus Christ, if after this life there were not hell and heaven!"[83]

Knox wearily settled back into his pastorate in Edinburgh. As the only Protestant preacher in the city, his audience was huge. He preached twice on Sunday and three times during the week. The rest of the time he was preaching in distant parts of Scotland and presiding over Protestant councils and general meetings. He continued to write letters to his friends and to Mrs. Locke.

During the winter of 1562, after hearing the news of a successful massacre of Protestant Huguenots in France, Mary held a grand ball and danced late into the evening. Knox violently attacked the frivolity of Mary and her court and again condemned her efforts to restore Catholicism to Scotland. He was summoned to appear before her a second time.

A Second Meeting with the Queen

Mary received Knox in her bedchamber. Present with her were the court maids and several nobles. She questioned Knox on the authority he had to preach against the dancing of royalty, charging that he was exceeding his limitations as a minister.

Knox answered that he didn't mind dancing as long as it didn't cause people to neglect their duties; those who danced in celebration of the tribulations of God's people, however, would drink in hell.[84]

Mary answered, "If you hear anything of myself that mislikes you, come to me and tell me, and I shall hear you."

Knox gave her an astonishing rebuke for an answer.

> I am called, madam, to a public function within the kirk [church] of God, and am appointed by God to rebuke the sins and vices of all. I am not appointed to come to every man in particular to show him his offence; for that labor were infinite. If Your Grace please to frequent the public sermons, then doubt I not but that ye shall fully understand both what I like and mislike, as well in your Majesty as in all others.

In other words, Knox let Mary know that, in the eyes of God, she was the same as every one else. Knox preached scriptural truth from the pulpit and allowed every person to judge themselves. He viewed his calling and his ministry office higher than her royal regime and openly declared it to her. If she wanted to come to his church services, then she, like everyone else, would hear what was right in the eyes of God. Knox was submissive as a Scottish subject, but he held his ground as a spiritual ambassador for God.

Insulted, Mary snapped, "You will not always be at your book," and turned her back to him. Knox smiled, then left.[85]

Knox realized Mary would never attend a Protestant service, but that wasn't the issue. The real victory of this meeting was that he held the dignity of his calling in the face of intimidation and disrespect. Before Knox, the Catholic priests had always treated royalty differently, catering to their every need and meeting with them for private admonition.

Knox refused to do this. He believed that both royalty and subject were the same in the eyes of God, and in his position as a Protestant minister, he refused to treat one more highly than the other. In the sixteenth century, this kind of ministerial attitude was scandalous! But Knox never bothered with pointless etiquette; he bowed to no one but God. To him, the highest position on the earth was to be commissioned by God as a preacher of the Reformation, and he let Mary know that in no uncertain terms.

Despite Mary's efforts, Knox's thunderous sermons on dancing did have a fearful effect in Scotland. Her musicians, the French as well as the Scots, refused to play for her Mass on Christmas Day! [86]

A Third, Face-to-Face Blast

Famine greeted northern Scotland in the beginning of 1563. Knox strongly believed that the famine was a direct rebuke from the Lord because the people had allowed Mary to defile their land with the Catholic Mass. By now, Protestant preachers were praying that God would either convert Mary from Catholicism or cut her off—however it pleased Him—while she was yet young. Priests were still being attacked in the night, cut in the face and head, or beaten. Knox wasn't part of these attacks, but neither did he condemn them. He believed God would use any means possible to rid Scotland of Catholicism.

On Easter, in April 1563, a number of prestigious Catholic leaders defied the law and celebrated a public Mass. When the government took no action against them, several prominent Protestants took matters into their own hands, arresting the priests and hauling them off to prison for breaking the law. The Protestants issued a proclamation of their own, stating to all Catholic priests that if this kind of outbreak continued, they would not protest to the queen or any other authorities but would themselves seize the offenders and put them to death—just as the law required.

Mary panicked and summoned Knox for his intervention. Knox calmly stated that if the queen would abide and enforce the laws, he promised the Protestants would be quiet; but if she continued to ignore the problem, then he was sure that the papists would be punished for violating the majesty of God. He reminded her that if the government did not do its duty, then it was in the hands of the people to enforce the law.

Mary was again insulted by Knox's tone, but she agreed the next day to have all the offenders tried in court. She briefly kept her word, and all the defendants were tried and imprisoned; the archbishop himself, greatly mocked and insulted by spectators during the trial, was imprisoned in Edinburgh Castle.

The Fourth Encounter: A Divine Warning

The fourth confrontation between Mary and Knox was probably the worst. Mary was a prime candidate for marriage, and it was rumored that she would marry the prince of Spain. Knox was outraged! This Spanish prince was the son of one of the greatest Protestant persecutors, and Knox vehemently preached that if the marriage succeeded, it would bring the vengeance and plague of God upon Scotland. [87]

Again, Knox had taken the Reformation past the personal arena and brought it to a national level. His searing message made everyone accountable for their thoughts concerning the upcoming marriage. It was an uneasy moment for Catholics and Protestants alike.

His proclamation caused Mary to summon him once again. When he entered her courtyard, Mary began to cry. With the outburst and emotional raging of a child, she swore her revenge upon him.

Knox calmly replied that when she was delivered from doctrinal error, then she would no longer find his words offensive.

Mary snapped, "What have ye to do with my marriage? Or what are ye within this commonwealth?" She tried to belittle him, but Mary didn't realize that she had just asked a Reformer a loaded question! She set herself up for his answer.

> A subject born within the same, madam. And albeit I neither be earl, lord, nor baron within it, yet has God made me (how abject that ever I be in your eyes) a profitable member within the same; yea, Madam, to me it appertains no less

> to forewarn of such things as may hurt it, if I foresee them, than it does to any of the nobility; for both my vocation and conscience crave plainness of me. [88]

Knox once again upheld his calling and his office as a prophet to the nation of Scotland. He humbly, yet resolvedly, informed the queen that because of his position with God, he would continue to disarm perverted doctrines and warn of the devastating evils that attempted to deceive his countrymen and his nation.

His response to Mary's demeaning question reduced her to uncontrollable tears. Her aide rushed to assist her, reassuring her. Knox was commanded to leave the room and wait outside.

After he had waited for over an hour, he was told to leave.

A Fifth Encounter Weakens Mary's Foundation

Month after month brought much of the same—Catholics attending unlawful Mass and Protestants taking matters into their own hands. August of 1563 was no different.

Mary was away and the priests of the city of Edinburgh decided to attend Mass in the Royal Chapel instead of attending Knox's Protestant service. A band of Protestants heard of it, broke into the chapel armed with pistols, and defied the priests. Twenty-two Catholics were prosecuted by the Protestants. [89]

When Mary returned, she was outraged at the news and ordered the prosecution of the Protestants who broke into the Royal Chapel. Their trial was set for October.

Knox immediately wrote to all the Scottish Protestants, reminding them of how, in the past, they had rallied together for the common good of the Reformation. He was asking them to do it again—this time to assemble in great numbers at the Protestant trial set for October.

In an attempt to snare Knox, a bishop retrieved one of the letters and gave it to Mary. Hoping she had at last caught him, Mary was thrilled and devised her plan. Instead of prosecuting the Protestants who attacked, she and the council took action against Knox on the grounds of treason for commanding the queen's subjects to assemble against her without lawful authority.

Summoned to stand before the council, Knox defended himself against the accusation of high treason. True to form, Knox made a powerful speech in his defense—he did not accuse the queen of cruelty, only the Catholics. As a representative of the church, there was no treason in that. He operated with such precision that the queen herself became confused, her most searching questions seeming silly and out of context. Mary lost total control of herself and began to cry. The council told Knox that he was excused to return to his home. Then they voted that he was not guilty. To add to Mary's misery, even the bishop that had given her the letter voted with the majority! [90]

Observing her undignified behavior, the Protestant nobles of Mary's court began to turn against her. From this point on, the reign of Mary, Queen of Scots, began its downward spiral.

Knox Married Royalty!

Despite all the trouble this fight drew, Knox obviously had time for his personal life. On March 25, 1564, Knox married again. Now, Mary had another cause for outrage. Her offense wasn't because Knox married; it was because of whom he married—a distant cousin of hers!

It seems a little bizarre that his new wife, Margaret Stuart, was only seventeen years old and Knox was in his fifties. Marriages like this were not unusual in his day, though Calvin had firmly denounced them for Protestant leaders. But Knox never allowed the man-made rules of etiquette or ethics to stop him from what he believed was God's will. His new marriage was no exception, and he didn't hide his relationship with Margaret. He would ride to her home on a beautiful horse, his jacket adorned with ribbons and gold. [91]

Although Margaret was of royal blood, she was very unlike her cousin, Mary, Queen of Scots. She proved to be a loving and faithful wife, working with Knox in his ministry and giving him three daughters from their marriage.

In 1565, Mary, Queen of Scots, weary from her fight with the Protestants, also married. She chose the empty-headed, vicious Henry Stuart (Lord Darnley), an English Catholic. Her downfall came quickly after that.

The Protestant ebb was at an all-time low, and Knox called for a fast. During the fast, Mary's immoral lifestyle began to come to a head. Although she was now pregnant, she hated her husband and instead found consolation in her Italian secretary, David Rizzio. Darnley was jealous and, with a pack of Protestant nobles, rushed in upon Rizzio (while he was with Mary) and murdered him. The small group of murderers imprisoned Mary inside her room.

Two days later, she wooed her husband over to her side, and he helped Mary escape by horseback to Dunbar.

Knox continued to pray as never before. He knew that Mary would return with a vengeance against the Protestants as he prayed, "Lord, put an end to my misery." [92]

What he feared soon became a reality. Mary returned in greater power than she had ever had, the people siding with her in anger at the Protestant murder. Knox took solitude in Kyle, being slowed by his decreasing health. Here, he resumed writing his *History of the Reformation within the Realm of Scotland*, the first and only book written by a Reformer at the time of the events. He began writing the book in the summer of 1559, and worked on it until his death. It wasn't published until 1644. [93]

By 1566, things had quieted down, and it was safe for Knox to return to Edinburgh, but he didn't. His health was so depleted that another minister had to be assigned to his pastorate to help him. In 1567, Knox was granted the privilege of returning to England to visit his sons, who were being educated there. Knox's visit was timely; Scotland erupted from Mary's immorality while he was away.

Mary's Scotland: The Den of Lust

Mary had given birth to a son, who later became James I, King of England. During all the celebrations of his birth, Mary's husband, Lord Darnley was noticeably absent.

Mary's fickle affections again wandered until they landed on the Earl of Bothwell. The two had an obvious adulterous relationship while Bothwell's wife sat at home.

Darnley was presumed to be ill, and, as he rode into Edinburgh, the presumptions became a reality. His face was covered with festering sores, proving him to be a victim of syphilis. Mary came to his bedside and comforted him into the early hours of morning. As soon as she left him, Darnley's house was blown into a thousand pieces by a charge of gunpowder, and Darnley was found strangled in the garden. Obviously he was murdered, and all the Scots looked to Bothwell for the answer.

Three months later, Bothwell staged a siege (with Mary's consent) on Mary's traveling entourage. Before them all, he kidnapped her, carried her off to Dunbar, and staged a rape. Of course, it was all planned. With so many witnesses to the scene, the two of them "had" to get married. Bothwell's wife protested to the Catholic priests, hoping that she could stop the marriage. But Bothwell conveniently paid the Catholic hierarchy to "discover" that his wife was actually a cousin, so their marriage was not legitimate. With all the roadblocks out of the way, Mary and Bothwell married in May 1567. It was a fatal mistake.

The entire Scottish nobility was appalled at her immorality and united against Mary and Bothwell, seeking their arrest. In June, Mary surrendered to the nobles. Bothwell fled on a ship and eventually escaped to Norway.

Mary was brought back to Edinburgh in the midst of a howling mob who demanded her death. The next day, Mary, Queen of Scots, was imprisoned in a castle on Lochleven. The government of Scotland, now in the hands of the nobles, called a Council of Lords. [94]

Beheaded!

The capture of Mary coincided with the end of Knox's visit to England; hearing the news, he returned to Scotland like a lion on the prowl. He immediately called for a meeting of the General Assembly of Protestants, but the nobility had been almost torn apart by the atrocious events of Mary and Bothwell, so the attendance was small. It was decided that the Protestant ministers in attendance would branch out all over Scotland and bring the remaining nobles in for another meeting in July.

Knox daily thundered throughout Scotland that Mary must be executed as a murderess and an adulteress if the wrath of God was to be averted from them all. When the assembly met in July, the attendance was small once again. The small group of ministers was not listened to, and the government decided not to execute Mary but instead to force her to abdicate her throne to her infant son.

Knox felt that the Protestants were in error not to execute Mary. He knew that, although she was imprisoned, she would somehow be freed.

Sure enough, in May of 1568, Mary escaped from Lochleven and assembled a small army of nobles to fight for her cause. Hearing of it, the Protestants were terrified and proclaimed a fast. Weary of them not listening to him, Knox wrote the Protestants telling them that Mary's escape happened because they showed mercy to a murderess, an idolatress, and an adulteress. He believed that whatever terrors they were all to suffer would be a just punishment for their error.

The terrors did not come. Mary was easily defeated and fled to England, hoping to find aide from Queen Elizabeth I. But Elizabeth viewed Mary as a rival to the throne of England and threw her into prison where she remained for the next nineteen years. Later, while still in prison, Mary was accused of aiding in a plot to kill Elizabeth. Still maintaining her innocence, Mary, Queen of Scots, was declared guilty and beheaded February 8, 1587.[95]

"Lying in St. Andrew's, Half Dead"

By the end of 1568, Mary was gone and Knox focused his attention upon the advancement and establishment of the Protestant church in Scotland. Once again in Edinburgh, Knox felt the majority of his fight was over, writing to a friend that he had "quietness in spirit, and time to meditate upon death."[96]

In autumn of that year, Knox had a stroke that temporarily paralyzed the use of his tongue. For a few days, he was powerless to speak, and his enemies were greatly relieved. Rumors flew wildly that Knox would never preach again or that he was dead.[97] But in a matter of days, Knox returned to the pulpit and preached as before.

Even though Mary had fled to England, Knox continued to preach against her. This disturbed many people, and, for a time, Knox was very unpopular because of it. One night, a shot came through his window and would have struck him had he been sitting in his usual place. His friends set guard around his house and begged him to leave Edinburgh. Knox resisted their advice for a while but eventually left for St. Andrew's, reluctantly.

But St. Andrew's offered no peace for the elderly Knox. The city seemed to be filled with enemies and supporters of the abolished Queen Mary. For the next fifteen months, he argued back and forth with them concerning his stand for God and their idolatries.

Knox was now so feeble from the stroke that, when he walked, he leaned on his ministry assistant, Richard Bannatyne, and supported himself with a cane. Sometimes, while he leaned on Bannatyne's arm, Knox would walk in the courtyards and talk with the students, encouraging them to continue standing in the cause of Reformation. On Sundays he had to be lifted up into the pulpit. Although he was feeble in body, Knox became another man in the pulpit. One student wrote that Knox was so active and vigorous that he was likely to beat the pulpit into shreds and fly out of it! [98]

During this time, Knox began showing the signs of age in his letters. He mixed his exhortations with complaints about his bodily weakness. He signed his letters as, "lying in St. Andrew's half-dead." [99]

Although he saw himself as "half-dead," Knox became involved in a struggle that, after his death, had a profound effect on the future church of Scotland. The struggle was over the appointment of bishops. Knox arranged it so that when the old Catholic priests died off, new Protestant bishops were assigned to take their places and their churches. What Knox helped put into place in 1571 still exists in Scotland today!

Though Weak, He Thundered!

In 1572, Knox was very ill. However, he continued to write and succeeded in publishing his last pamphlet, entitled, *An Answer to a Letter of a Jesuit Named Tyrie*. He wrote the pamphlet from his bed, getting up only once a week.

In his feeble condition, Knox managed to travel from St. Andrew's back to Edinburgh. In August, he preached in his old pastorate for the first time in sixteen months, but his voice was so weak that he couldn't be heard. He decided to hold the rest of his services in a smaller room. For the next two months, he continued to preach there every Sunday. One man stated that although Knox's voice could barely be heard even in the smaller room, he still preached with as much vehemence and zeal as ever. [100]

★★★★★

About this time, the news of the Protestant Massacre of St. Bartholomew in France had reached the shores of Scotland. The French ambassador just happened to be visiting in one of Knox's church services at that time. The opportunity was too great for Knox to let slip by. In a voice barely audible, Knox told the ambassador to tell the king of France that he was a murderer and that God's vengeance would strike him and his descendants.[101]

In September, Knox resigned his office as pastor of Edinburgh, and James Lawson, the assistant principal of Aberdeen University, was chosen to take his place. In November, Knox ordained Lawson as pastor. When the service was completed, Knox left the doors of his church for the last time. His congregation accompanied him from the building to the door of his home.

The Death of a Hero

Two days later, Knox had a coughing attack which left him extremely weak. His mind started slipping—on Friday he got out of bed to dress himself, thinking it was Sunday. When Sunday came, he remained in bed and refused food, thinking it was the start of a fast that had been proclaimed. Surprisingly, the very next day his mind was clear and sharp, so Knox called the elders and deacons to his bedside and gave them all a long sermon. The ninth Psalm was read, and Knox commended them all to God. The group left his bedside in tears.

Every day, his wife, Margaret, or Bannatyne read to him out of John 17. Sometimes, Knox asked for Calvin's sermons to be read to him; other times, he wanted to hear from the Psalms. Many times Knox seemed so unresponsive that they inquired whether he heard them as they read. He would reply, "I hear and understand far better."

His mind and body were very feeble, but Knox's will was still unbroken. While he could speak, he continued to denounce the Castle of Edinburgh. He called for the undertaker and ordered his own casket to be made.

Sometimes, as he lay sleeping, he muttered phrases, such as "Live in Christ! The kirk [church]! Now, Lord, make an end of the trouble!"[102]

On the morning of November 24, 1572, Knox tried to get up from his bed but was unable to stand. He asked his wife to read certain

Scriptures to him. In the late afternoon, Knox specifically asked her to read John 17, the chapter where he said he "first cast his anchor." This was obviously the chapter that, in his early years, solidified his walk with God after he was born again.

Late in the evening, the group that was with him knelt down to pray. Knox remained unmoved. Someone asked, "Sir, heard ye the prayers?" He answered, "I would to God that ye and all men heard them as I have heard them; and I praise God for that heavenly sound." Then Knox suddenly cried, "Now it is come!" and he released a shuddering sigh.

Bannatyne sat down by his bed and urged him to remember the promises in the New Testament. Wondering if Knox had heard him, he asked for a sign. For the last time, Knox gathered all the strength he had and lifted one hand—then he passed away. [103]

Scotland was still in a religious turmoil at his death, but Knox felt peace that he had run the race as well as he could and had kept the faith. His portion in the Reformation of Scotland was complete.

Two days later, on November 26, Knox was buried in the yard of his church in Edinburgh. All the nobility in Scotland attended his funeral. The presiding regent of Scotland read his epitaph, which stated, "Here lies one who neither flattered nor feared any flesh." [104]

A Catalyst for Presbyterianism

I don't know if I've ever studied a man so passionate and incredibly unflinching in his stand for God as John Knox was. Battle after battle, hit after hit, victory after victory, John Knox remained the same. Despite any weaknesses or failures in his personality, his uncompromising stand is a great tribute to the cause of God. That is a tremendous treasure that many have overlooked.

I think it's sad that John Knox's life and dramatic ministry has been so greatly misunderstood. Scotland (and the world) owes so much to this great leader, yet his grave has been covered by a paved parking lot. Until this century, when a statue was finally erected in his memory, there was no memorial whatsoever to his work in Scotland. [105]

It takes several great leaders of God to establish a work, and Knox was by far one of the most important leaders of the Reformation as a

Knox's statue outside St. Giles' Cathedral, Edinburgh.
Banner of Truth Trust

whole. Although Knox laid the foundational stones for the modern-day Presbyterian faith, I believe he was only the catalyst of it—not the father of it. I believe that Andrew Melville (1545–1622), Knox's successor, was the Father of Presbyterianism. Similar to Knox, he also caused a great uproar in Scotland and England—even going several steps further than Knox.

The Reformation that Knox ignited in Scotland exported Presbyterianism throughout the world. That early Presbyterian fight had a great impact on various parts of the world, including America. It has been said that the American Revolution was a Presbyterian revolution. Many leaders of that war were Presbyterians who felt the common threat of unjust dictatorship, absorbed that fierce Scottish sense of independence, and fought against all odds for the freedom of the American colonies. [106] I believe Knox would have been proud of them.

✯✯✯✯✯

After all, history credits Knox for being a great contributor to the struggle for human freedom. He taught the people that they had a duty to fight for what was right, regardless of national allegiance or the order of governments. History has stated that "modern democracy is grounded upon this principle which Knox deduced from the texts of Exodus and the book of Kings." [107]

When it came to the call of God, Knox was a passionate man who dearly and totally loved the church and prayed for the work to continue.

The Greatest Reformer

It's important to note that Knox succeeded where no other Reformer had. He totally rejected the rule of the papacy without leaving the church members subject to a monarchy. That didn't happen in any other nation but Scotland.

Although he refused to acknowledge holidays and events such as Christmas, Easter, and birthdays, it was only because he failed to find them celebrated in the Bible. The Word had the final authority in his life. I've heard many people criticize him over his resolve on certain issues, but these immovable positions, along with violent preaching, is what moved age-old national strongholds. Some people aren't destined for popularity on earth, but these people will be popular with the countless who will be in heaven because of their ministry. I believe Knox would be horrified if he were to see what is going on in churches today.

I don't compare Knox with John Calvin. Although Calvin was his mentor and they agreed theologically, Knox was much bolder than Calvin and vehemently taught that Christians should resist unjust authority or rulers. Calvin didn't like confrontation or persecution; Knox thrived on them both. Calvin mainly worked out of one city; Knox took on the national canvas, making his work far more expansive.

Although Knox was, and still is, looked upon as mean and crude, he was only that way toward the enemies of God. When it came to the call of God, Knox was a passionate man who dearly and totally loved the church and, even on his deathbed, prayed desperately for the work to continue.

As Knox lay dying, he was heard to pray,

> Be merciful, Lord to Thy church, which Thou has redeemed. Give peace to this afflicted commonwealth. Raise up faithful pastors who will take the charge of Thy church.
>
> Lord, grant true pastors to Thy church, that purity of doctrine may be retained. [108]

"Lord, Grant True Pastors"

The deathbed prayers of Knox echo in my heart. Our generation needs true pastors, true prophets, true apostles, true evangelists, and true teachers. We need men and women like the children of Issachar—people with spiritual understanding of the times and who, through the Holy Spirit, know what the church should do. (See 1 Chronicles 12:32.)

I am somewhat disturbed by the popular Christian theory of restoration because I feel its true application has been misplaced and sometimes abused. Some have even come to me and said that *restoration* is the word for today, not *reformation*. As I've stated earlier in this chapter, the two words are similar, yet they have different applications and meanings. Don't get them confused.

Knox's pulpit. Now in the National Museum of Aniquities, Edinburgh.

Webster's *New World Dictionary* defines the word *restore* as "to give back something taken, lost; to return to a former state or to a position, rank; to bring back to health, strength."

I have no problem with the restoration that heaven speaks of; I believe in it, cry out for it, and, as the Holy Spirit leads, I minister it in my meetings. I believe that God has shown us what is to come. But just like every new whisper we receive from heaven, we have a tendency to instantly run for it, producing excesses and extremes.

I believe that many are "putting the cart before the horse" in their pursuit of restoration. Its true application has been misplaced in the atmosphere of our selfish, self-centered generation. We've limited its true strength because we've believed it was simply a quick fix for the pain and sadness in our personal situations. Many times, calling for restoration has been easier than destroying the root of what is causing our problems.

Webster's *New World Dictionary* defines *reform* as "to make better as by stopping abuses."

Human nature will drive us to emphasize messages of restoration that pat us on the back. But these sugar-coated messages, often preached out of a fear of man, are preached to a congregation of people who may all go to hell if someone like Knox doesn't tell them that the lies of religion can't save, deliver, and change their lives.

New Age humanism has led us into preaching a different message. If Knox returned to the earth, I'm sure he wouldn't know if some of our houses of worship were churches or social clubs.

Jesus was our Teacher for reform. Throughout His ministry, He taught us how we should be acting, how we should be operating, and the way we should be thinking. He was getting the thoughts of restoration planted in our hearts. But before what He taught could come to pass, He had to be a Reformer by dying on the cross, snatching the keys of hell and death from Satan to stop the abuse, and then being resurrected from the dead so that our divine right of inheritance could be restored to us.

Jesus won the war, and we have the final victory, but we also know that the attacks still come in an attempt to hinder the Gospel and halt our growth in the Lord. That means that every generation must experience some type of reform. We may be the last generation—no one knows for sure. Let's be declarers so no one can say, "no one told me."

The spirit of reformation is the spirit of truth. It is the strength to stop abuses in our personal lives, our churches, and the life of our nation. It must come before we will ever see the power of a true restoration. Heaven has shown us what is to come, but we must take the vital steps for our generation and our time. We must call for the spirit of truth to live in our homes, in our churches, in our lives, and in our nations.

The spirit of reformation, birthed by the Holy Spirit of God, must be cried for and grasped. It then must be carried to every area of society so that room can be made for heaven's restoration. We must have men and women of God who will rightly discern what they are hearing from heaven; see what they've heard in the entire Word of God (not just a Scripture or two); and birth the will of God into our generation through prayer and demonstration.

So, I close the chapter of John Knox with one of his last prayers, believing the spiritual strength of his passionate words still vibrate throughout the earth. Those who have an ear to hear, let them hear:

> Lord, grant faithful pastors, men who will preach and teach, in season and out of season. Lord, give us men who would gladly preach their next sermon even if it meant going to the stake for it. Lord, give us men who will hate all falsehood and lies, whether in the church or out of it. Lord, grant to Your struggling church men who fear You above all. [109]

Notes

[1] Douglas Wilson, *For Kirk and Covenant: The Stalwart Courage of John Knox* (Nashville, Tenn.: Highland Books, Cumberland House Publishing, Inc., 2000): 3.
[2] Ibid., Introduction, X.
[3] Jasper Ridley, *John Knox* (Oxford, England: Oxford University Press, 1968): 1–2.
[4] Thomas M'Crie, *The Life of John Knox* (Edinburgh, Scotland: Wm. Blackwood and Sons, 1865): 304.
[5] Ibid.
[6] Wilson, 11.
[7] John Knox, *The History of the Reformation in Scotland* (Edinburgh, Scotland and Carlisle, Pa.: The Banner of Truth Trust, 2000): 6.
[8] Wilson, 13.
[9] "John Knox, The Thundering Scot," *Christian History Maganize* 14, no. 2, issue 46 (Carol Stream, Ill.: Christianity Today, 1995): 2.
[10] Ibid., 58.
[11] Ibid., 64–65.
[12] Ridley, 46.
[13] Knox, 66.
[14] Ibid., 68–69.
[15] Stewart Lamont, *The Swordbearer—John Knox and the European Reformation* (Kent, England: Hodder and Stoughton Ltd., 1991): 32, 35.
[16] Ibid., 36.
[17] Ridley, 56.
[18] Ibid., 57.
[19] M'Crie, 32.
[20] *Christian History Magazine,* 12.
[21] Lamont, 44.
[22] Ibid., 45.
[23] Ibid., 50.
[24] Wilson, 39.
[25] Ibid., 40.
[26] Ibid., 44.
[27] Ibid., quoted from Thomas McCrie, 69.
[28] "Mary I," *The World Book Encyclopedia* 13, (Chicago, Ill.:World Book, Inc., 2003): 239.
[29] Wilson, 44, quoted from *John Knox* by Henry Cowan, 135–136.

☆☆☆☆☆

[30] Lamont, 76.
[31] Ridley, 215.
[32] Wilson, 47, quoted from *John Knox* by Henry Cowan, 131.
[33] Ridley, 215.
[34] Edwin Muir, *John Knox: Portrait of a Calvinist* (Freeport, N.Y.: Books for Libraries Press, 1971): 88–89.
[35] Lamont, 59.
[36] *Christian History Magazine,* 3.
[37] Ibid.
[38] Muir, 94.
[39] *Christian History Magazine,* 38.
[40] Muir, 119–120.
[41] Ibid., 120.
[42] Ibid., 120–121, 157; Ridley 248.
[43] Lamont, 89; Ridley, 248.
[44] Muir, 120.
[45] Ridley, 247.
[46] Wilson, 55.
[47] *Christian History Magazine,* 36.
[48] Ridley, 264.
[49] Ibid., 268.
[50] Muir, 132.
[51] Ridley, 270–271.
[52] Muir, 132.
[53] Ridley, 273.
[54] Ibid., 276.
[55] Ibid., 277.
[56] Muir, 158.
[57] Ridley, 290–291.
[58] Muir, 170; Wilson, 60, quoted from Thomas McCrie, 49.
[59] Muir, 171.
[60] Ibid., 172–173.
[61] Ibid., 173.
[62] Ibid., 173–174.
[63] Ibid., 176.
[64] Ibid.
[65] Ibid., 177.
[66] Ibid., 178.
[67] Ibid., 179.

★★★★★

[68] Ridley, 364.
[69] Muir, 207–208.
[70] Ibid., 213–214.
[71] Ridley, 383.
[72] Ibid., 384.
[73] Ibid.
[74] Knox, 267.
[75] Ridley, 390.
[76] Wilson, 65.
[77] Knox, 269–270.
[78] Ibid., 270.
[79] Muir, 237.
[80] Ridley, 393.
[81] Muir, 238.
[82] Ibid., 240.
[83] Ibid., 241–242.
[84] Ibid., 247.
[85] Ibid., 247–250.
[86] Ridley, 422.
[87] Ibid., 425.
[88] Ibid., 426.
[89] Ibid., 428.
[90] Muir, 264–265.
[91] Ibid., 268.
[92] Ibid., 275.
[93] Ridley, 453–454.
[94] Ibid., 465.
[95] "Mary, Queen of Scots," *The World Book Encyclopedia* 13, 239.
[96] Muir, 281.
[97] Ibid., 284.
[98] Ibid., 292–293.
[99] Ibid., 293.
[100] Ridley, 511.
[101] Muir, 294.
[102] Ibid., 297.
[103] Ibid., 298.
[104] Ibid., 299.
[105] *Christian History Magazine,* 3.

★★★★★

[106] Ibid., 42.
[107] Ridley, 530.
[108] Wilson, 223.
[109] Ibid., 226.

CHAPTER SIX

George Fox

1624–1691

"The Liberator of Spirit"

"The Liberator of Spirit"

I had been brought through the very ocean of darkness and death, and through and over the power of Satan, by the eternal, glorious power of Christ;...that darkness...which covered over all the world, and which chained down all, and shut up all in the death. The same eternal power of God, which brought me through these things, was that which afterwards shook the nations, priests, professors, and people. [1]

I have long wondered if our generation knows of or even realizes that many of the freedoms we enjoy today are largely due to the dramatic ministry of one of the greatest prophets to have ever lived—George Fox.

When his name is mentioned, many rightfully acknowledge that Fox was the founder of the Quakers, or Society of Friends. Some see that denominational group as a small, isolated community of mild-mannered believers who wear hats, live on rural farms, and have a reputation of fairness and integrity. But George Fox gave his life to far more than establishing a dress code and an agricultural lifestyle. In fact, Fox was so extreme in his efforts to further the cause of the Gospel that, over two hundred years later, the Salvation Army (founded by William Booth) was greatly influenced by Fox's ministry. An early spokesman for the organization stated that if the "Quakers had remained true to their first principles and evangelical mode of work, there would never have been any need for a Salvation Army!" [2]

★★★★★

Fox was credited in leading the "Radical Reformation." [3] In my opinion, that simply means Fox took the Reformation to the next level—he combined the Spirit with the Word.

George Fox did what the early apostles did, and the Revivalists later did the same. He revived the combination of the Spirit with the Word and, in doing so, crossed Calvinistic and religious mind-sets, making the Christian lifestyle attainable and reachable for everyone who believed. The Friends broke ground for a return to the daily work of the Holy Spirit in every believer's life, which I believe prepared the way for ministries in the eighteenth and nineteenth centuries. The Holy Spirit became a personal Friend to those who followed Fox.

We don't realize that many freedoms we enjoy are largely due to the dramatic ministry of one of the greatest prophets who ever lived—George Fox.

Because of their relationship with the Holy Spirit, the Friends revolutionized many areas of Christianity that had been dormant or forgotten. They were one of the first groups to encourage women's ministries, and they strongly supported these women as they preached and taught the Word throughout the world. They are also credited for being one of the few known groups of their era to cast out demons, heal the sick, and work miracles by the power of God. While a few isolated groups might have understood spiritual warfare, George Fox demonstrated it on a daily basis. Fox fervently taught Romans 8:14, which says, *"For as many as are led by the Spirit of God, they are the sons of God,"* and practiced that verse in every area of his life. He emphatically taught that the leading and the help of the Holy Spirit was first and foremost in every venue of life.

He stood on the truth that being a Christian was not something one was born into or something that came as a result of church attendance or baptism. It was not bestowed upon someone because a degree was obtained from a theological seminary or school. To Fox, a Christian was one who personally knew Jesus Christ as the Son of God and daily relied on the help of the Holy Spirit to interpret the Bible and live by its principles in a very corrupt world. In short, Fox believed a true Christian lived out the values that he or she confessed.

All that may seem very simple to you, but Fox paid a tremendous price for it. As this chapter progresses, you will be surprised to see that some of the freedoms you enjoy today were birthed by the steel principles and repeated imprisonments of George Fox.

Several dates in Fox's life are a little hazy because many records were lost or are believed to be unreliable. But the circumstances of the events are accurate. So, in this chapter, I will speak much about his character and his spiritual motivation. He was such an intricate and fascinating man, I could never record all the bold and sometimes extreme confrontations that played a part in his life as he fought for his beliefs. Again, I encourage you to find all the resources you can on George Fox, and saturate yourself with the incredible spirit of Reform that motivated him.

Fox believed that a true Christian personally knows Jesus Christ and lives by the Bible and its principles—he lives what he preaches.

A Reformer Is Born

The year was 1624. The place was Leicestershire, England. Mary Fox, probably in her early twenties, was thrilled to be carrying her first child. Her husband, Christopher, a man of strong, honest character and religious Presbyterian belief, was several years older than her. The name *Fox* was well-known in the region. Several centuries earlier, a Fox had been mayor, and another displayed a coat of arms, or heraldry. Heraldry was a system where families could show their reputation for bravery and the importance of their lineage, proving their name's social status. The Fox heritage had also been known to support the Lollards, a group of people living throughout Europe who vowed to read the Bible for themselves and expound on its Scriptures within an established church, despite opposition from state authorities.[4]

As a weaver, Christopher Fox had set himself up well in Leicestershire, obtaining a home for himself and his wife. His skilled occupation had placed him near the top, both financially and influentially, in their town, called Drayton-in-the-Clay. It was a small, rural town, nestled in rolling hills, located in the center of England.

The month of July finally arrived and, along with it, the birth of their first son. They named him George. The couple had other children, perhaps four, but most of the records are unreliable. In fact, legend says that the parish clerk's wife used the page that would have recorded the birth of George Fox "for kitchen use."[5] However many children the couple had, it is sure that the weight of the family was placed on their oldest, George Fox.

"Of Another Frame of Mind"

If someone expected young Fox to be like all the other children, they were in for a surprise. He never played the games that other children played, nor did he take part in their jokes and pranks. He was probably awkward to be around because he was so different, yet he was not disagreeable. Young Fox would sit in a corner and think. Even as a small boy, he could size up people with his discerning eye. When he would observe the character of men who came to sit around the fire and visit with his father, he thought to himself, "If ever I come to be a man, surely I shall not do so or be so wanton."[6]

As a boy, Fox was not like other children. He would often sit in a corner and think. He could size up people with his discerning eye.

William Penn, whom we'll discuss later in the chapter because he played a vital part in Quaker history, gave a vivid description of Fox's childhood: "He appeared of another frame of mind from the rest of his brethren; being more religious, inward, still, solid, and observing beyond his years, as the answers he would give and the questions he would put...manifested, to the astonishment of those that heard him, especially in divine things."[7]

Although she never understood her strange and unchildlike little son, Mary Fox was satisfied that he was very smart and competent, so she nurtured him and never attempted to force him into typical little-boy behavior. Fox had a good relationship with his mother, although she never fully understood his cause and rarely saw him when he was an adult. She lived to a ripe, old age; when she died, Fox, in his fifties, grieved deeply.

☆☆☆☆☆

His Resolute Character

Although the Fox family had an upright reputation and was financially sound, life in the seventeenth century was difficult. People of this time were illiterate, narrow-minded, rude, and rough. Society was filled with social and economic ills. Because the economy was drastically unstable, the Drayton villagers turned inward, caring little about the affairs outside their own town. Little did that sleepy town realize there was one among them who would shake all of England.

Fox didn't fit in with the society, and he really didn't care to. At age eleven, he had his first encounter with what he later repeatedly termed as "the inner light" of Jesus Christ. This profound understanding taught him how to walk in purity in the midst of surrounding evils. It so affected his life that, from age eleven, Fox followed this inward leading and continued to build upon it until his death. During this young age, he made four resolutions by which to conduct his life:

1. He would live a pure and righteous life.
2. He would be faithful in all things, inwardly to God, outwardly to man.
3. He resolved to always keep his word.
4. He would not commit excess in eating and drinking. [8]

"The inner light" of Jesus Christ taught Fox to walk in purity though surrounded by evil. From age eleven, he followed this inner leading.

When his relatives saw that Fox was so spiritually disciplined, they insisted that his parents send him to school for training as a minister. I believe Fox had no intention of being trained in the manner of the ministers he saw around him as a child. His discernment was already so keen that he realized the clergy he knew were morally loose, hypocritical, and deceiving. Although he couldn't quite put what he was sensing into words, he soon realized that many ministers had been given their offices because of education and social status and not because of spiritual calling from God.

Fox's parents sent him to work in an apprenticeship less than half an hour from their home when Fox was somewhere around age fifteen. Fox went to work for a shoemaker who also dealt with sheep and cattle.

Although a deep thinker, Fox never allowed it to interfere with the duties of his job. His experiences dealing with sums of money, going to market, and interacting with all kinds of people helped prepare him for the many diverse personalities he was yet to face. It also trained him to make shoes, which would come in handy in the coming years as he walked thousands of miles. Fox was diligent in business, and his employer was very successful the entire time that Fox worked with him. Fox prided himself in being able to get the highest dollar for his employer while not misleading customers.

Apprenticeships such as this were to last for seven years. But in 1643, a life-changing event happened to George Fox that caused him to abruptly end his employment training and follow a different path.

The Prophetic Call

As Fox grew into a young man, he was keenly aware of the hypocritical moral looseness around him. He had come from a village that promoted religious reform, so watching his friends and their parents so willingly engage in excessive drinking—and love it—probably repulsed him all the more. He couldn't understand why the people who believed in moral purity before God would drink until they couldn't stand, or why they would spend their hard-earned money fulfilling their other lusts. It was revolting to him.

Fox stayed away from these kinds of people, earning him a reputation as a loner. Instead, he drank and ate only for his health and set aside special days to fast and read Scripture. He was a total oddity to his fellow townspeople.

It was not surprising that he had such a dramatic reaction to an event he encountered at age nineteen. In fact, it changed his life forever.

In late summer of 1643, Fox was representing his employer at a market when he ran into a cousin and his friend. Like Fox, these two young men supported the reforming faith, so when they asked Fox to share a jug of beer with them, he agreed. The weather was hot, he was thirsty, and he was thrilled at the opportunity to see his cousin and talk with the two young men.

Understand this: Drinking beer or wine was not a sin to them. In the seventeenth century, beer was a common drink, like soda is to us today. As with anything, it is excess that damages a person.

So, Fox entered the tavern with his cousin and friend; but after the first pint was consumed between the three, the other two wanted to continue drinking as a game to see who could drink the most. They wagered that the first to stop drinking had to pay for all the rounds.

Fox was astounded. Here were two Christians, supposedly against self-indulgence, yet they were willing to drink until they couldn't hold their heads up. It was no temptation to Fox. Instead, he abruptly stood up and stated, "If it be so, I'll leave you." With that, he plopped money on the table and walked out of the tavern, never looking back. [9]

Fox hurried through the rest of his business at the market and then left for home. The event troubled him. He was appalled by the attitudes he had encountered and the perverseness of his generation.

He couldn't sleep that evening. Instead, he cried, walked, and prayed. During his prayer time, Fox began to see that if there was any hope for the world, it would have to come from the younger generation. [10] The older generation had become too set in their ways, too content with the status quo, and too docile to attack the evils of formal religion. Yes, it would have to come from young people like him who would stand up for what was right, people who would proclaim the life of God and righteously confront those, young and old, who were inwardly dead.

As he walked and prayed late into that summer night, he heard the voice of the Lord speak to his heart: "Thou seest how young people go together into vanity, and old people into the earth; therefore thou must forsake all, both old and young, and be a stranger unto them." [11]

The words he had heard were the basis for his prophetic call. It was to be the foundation on which he based his future ministry. For a brief moment, Fox had a sense of peace. For the first time in his young life, he realized he was called to walk a different path. He didn't stop to ponder why he wasn't like the rest. Instead, I believe at that moment he knew that, from his birth, the hand of God was upon him for a purpose, and it would be something he could never escape. The beautiful thing was that Fox never tried to escape it, but instead submitted to it.

Does Anyone Know God?

Just a few short weeks after that fateful night, Fox began pursuing his call. Realizing that he was still very young and inexperienced, Fox broke off all his relationships and left home, wandering the countryside in search of answers to his questions.

Fox knew that the hand of God was upon him for a purpose. He could never escape it. But Fox didn't try to escape. Instead, he submitted fully.

As with all prophets, whether mature or not, Fox recognized right and wrong. Prophets view every issue in life in either black or white—there are no gray areas. There is no "maybe"; it's either "yea" or "nay." Sometimes, a prophet will swing all the way to the right to avoid the evils on the left, and that's why they get the reputation of being overly dramatic. How do you react when you see something very clearly? Prophets are the same, except that they see into or hear from the spirit realm usually before others see it or hear it. Their clear-cut insight causes them to act or react in an absolute, passionate manner because they love God and want His will to be done on earth above all else.

Fox hated the fashionable class society of his day because it unjustly separated some people from others. He was determined to make a statement. So, refusing to cut his hair and sporting a hat, Fox's five-foot-seven, stocky build trudged through the countryside, wearing a grayish leather outfit that got immediate attention wherever he went.

He traveled around the Midlands, heading ultimately to London. He was desperately grieved within himself, wrestling daily with his dissatisfaction and unanswered questions. He protected his heart so much that he would have little to do with anyone—heathen or Christian. He would pass through town after town, never staying long, earnestly searching for someone whom he felt was a genuine believer. In his journal, he wrote, "For I durst not stay long...being afraid both of professor [Christian] and profane, lest, being a tender young man I should be hurt by conversing much with either."[12]

Entering the city of London, Fox was certain he would find someone who could answer his questions and end the desperate spiritual battle that was raging within him. While there, he listened to the great preachers of the day, but no one had a word for him. Others he spoke with suggested that he find a good girl and marry her, and she would surely end his turmoil. Another suggested that he enlist as a soldier, for then he would have no time to brood. All these suggestions caused young Fox to run away even faster.

Leaving London, he encountered one of the clergymen from his village. Surely, he could answer Fox's restless, probing questions. But it seemed the minister had more questions than him, and Fox ended up solving all the minister's problems only to hear of the minister using Fox's answers as his message the next Sunday.

Discouraged, he visited another minister in a nearby town. After hearing Fox's spiritual anguish, the minister suggested that he use tobacco as a tranquilizer and sing psalms. On top of that poor advice, Fox discovered that the minister had spoken of their private discussion with the inhabitants of the town, and now everyone laughed when they saw him.

Still not giving up, Fox visited yet another minister in another town. Before he could even speak of his plight, the minister flew into a rage, shouting because Fox had accidentally stepped into his flower bed.

The last minister Fox went to told him that his discouragement came from an illness and that he wanted to "bleed him" to rid him of it. A popular medical remedy in that time, "bleeding" someone meant making an incision in his body for the blood to drain the ailment or infection out of his system. Although this medical procedure was attempted on him, Fox wrote in his journal that his body was so dried up with sorrows, grief, and troubles, that one drop couldn't be produced from him. He wished he had never been born.[13]

A Word about Prophets

I want to make a side note here. It is interesting to me how the books of different camps of the Society of Friends represent Fox during this time of his life. Today, the denomination is split into different categories, and I'll elaborate on that later in the chapter. But one of them—the Liberites—is basically a secular segment, denying the Virgin Birth and depending upon reason; they seem to write the largest books on Fox.

George Fox, Founder of the Sect of the People Called Quakers, from an original painting done by Hanthorst, done in 1654.
Friends Historical Library, Swarthmore College

After visiting Fox's modern-day headquarters in London, I can sadly say that today it consists mainly of Liberites. It seems they have forsaken the truths of their leader concerning the working of the Holy Spirit and biblical principles, and, instead, they rely totally on the intellect, rationalizing everything. If you spoke to them about this period of Fox's life, they would probably attribute it to a mental melancholy or psychological depression. I believe they felt it was a deficit in his mental and physical abilities. It wasn't.

Prophets can experience times of anguish, but normally it's not a mental weakness. They see differently than others and, many times, intensely feel the heart of God in a given situation. If a prophet can't find the correct outlet for what he sees or feels, it can cause anguish. Feelings of anguish are usually caused when prophets fail to understand the balance between timing and practical living. Sometimes the situation they see is so large to them, they feel it's the only message that needs to be preached. When others don't see it as the prophet does (because they weren't the ones to hear it from heaven), their responses—their words and reactions—can hurt an immature prophet. A prophet must deliver the message of the Lord, but he must leave the results of that message with the Lord. Prophets can never allow their message and their dramatic, passionate concern for souls to interfere with the will of the person or the work of the Lord in the lives of others. A prophet's job is to tell it like he heard it, then leave it to the Lord and the audience to follow through.

Is Your Soul Mature?

Fox was experiencing some of this prophetic anguish. I believe the main reason he went through all of this trauma was to develop the strength of his soul for future ministry. He was developing what I call "soul maturity."

Here's what I'm referring to. No matter how many dead ends Fox hit because of the backslidden state of ministers, he continued on. Sure, he felt depressed and hopeless at times, but he never stopped. He kept searching for the answers he needed, and he kept reading the Word, saturating his heart and listening for the help of the Holy Spirit. That's how you build maturity in your soul against persecution and criticism.

Fox learned that, in a Reformer's life, only God can be the source of strength. Man can encourage, but God gives the strength.

The Lord had already instructed Fox to guard his heart, and he did. To build maturity against the things that negatively affect your soul, you must guard your heart well. Like Fox, saturate yourself in the Word, especially Scripture pertaining to areas that are sensitive to you. As you allow the Holy Spirit to guide you and help you, soon you'll walk right through the thing that tried to capture you in the past. The Word, the Holy Spirit, and your tenacity to keep going will build a spiritual strength in that area of your soul.

It happened the same way with Fox. Soon these ministers that he wanted to run from became the targets he searched for. To be a leader, he couldn't depend on man to always furnish the answers or to give comfort to his soul. In a true Reformer's life, only God can be the main source of daily strength. Man can encourage you, but God gives the strength. Fox learned this lesson well.

✯✯✯✯✯

His First Revelation: The New Birth

Fox, still greatly disillusioned and without answers, returned home in 1644. He was determined to find God, and he wasn't going to pursue Him in anything that caused further unrest or depression to him. As if leaving home to find God wasn't dramatic enough, he now refused to attend his boyhood church with his Presbyterian parents. His parents and fellow villagers were horrified that Fox had turned his back on the religion in which he'd been raised. While others attended the service, Fox retreated with his Bible to a quiet hillside to meditate on various Scriptures.

This sort of stand became a way of life for him. He constantly roamed the open fields and orchards during church services, reading his Bible, praying, and wrestling with the evil forces that tore at his heart. He wrote of various "openings" or insightful experiences where he suddenly had divine revelation regarding the Scriptures he had read.[14]

Church membership, good works, baptism, or birth into a certain religion does not give a person the power to live according to the will of God.

During these times of searching and communion with the Lord, Fox began to understand what appeared to be a new revelation in that day. In fact, the revelations that Fox received during this time became the foundational stones of his life and ministry. These pivotal foundations became the primary beliefs that eventually launched the formation of the Quakers.

His first revelation was understanding the new birth. In spite of what was being taught in the church (that all Christians were believers), Fox realized that one could only become a Christian if he was converted from within, giving the person eternal life. Thus, the new birth. Church membership, good works, baptism, or natural birth into a certain religion did not qualify, nor did it give the power to live according to the Word of God. Only the new birth, the transformation from within, qualified a person to be a follower of Jesus Christ.

If one experienced this new birth, then the person would possess—or live—what he or she professed. The beliefs of the day did not cover this teaching at all.

His Second Revelation: True Authority

His second revelation was directly connected with the new birth. Fox had been troubled with the "authority" question: Where did it come from, who acquired it, and who possessed it? As he read the Scriptures, the Holy Spirit illuminated them, and Fox realized that, contrary to the popular and accepted belief of the day, an education at Oxford or Cambridge—or any college—was not enough to make a man a minister. When he tied this revelation with the first one, he saw that if a minister didn't have the new birth, he couldn't be a true minister.[15] A college education didn't make the difference. Just like church membership didn't make one a Christian, college didn't make one a minister. A true minister was born again from within, sensitive to the help of the Holy Spirit, ever searching the Scriptures for edification and advice. A true minister sensed that calling in his heart, and God enabled him to perform it. He didn't rely on his education or his intellect as prerequisites for that calling.

Fox believed that no man could approve an ordination; only the divine action of God's grace could set the man apart and accomplish it. To this day, Quaker ministers show their papers as "recorded" by the church; they are not ordained or licensed. They believe that only God ordains; the people merely record it.[16]

Fox's revelations were revolutionary. They totally undermined the social and religious precepts of the day. The pulpit had been used as a controlling power, giving the minister an air of superiority and all others a sense of inferiority. Fox would see other truths that had been hidden or distorted by man's greed and lust for control, but, for now, these two main themes—the new birth and the true call of God—would remain the central mark of his ministry.

Once the Holy Spirit revealed these first two truths, Fox set his face like a flint, vowing to shout them from the housetops. He immediately cornered his parents and relatives and, citing Scripture after Scripture, stung them with the accusation that their Presbyterian minister lacked the qualifications to hold his position.

His parents were shocked at the behavior of their son. Embarrassed by his adamant statements, they tried to console him and make excuses for him, hoping to weaken his boldness. But Fox never wavered from these revelations nor backed away from their truths; instead, he grew bolder. This word from God would eventually cause him severe persecution, including years of torturous imprisonments.

His Third Revelation: "Steeple Houses"

Fox continued to discuss his revelation with his parents and family, hoping to persuade them. Instead of seeing it his way, they continued to be appalled that he would cause such havoc within their close community. The family minister felt extremely threatened by Fox and denounced him to his parents, saying their son was one of these "newfangles" that was claiming new light on old truths. [17]

Fox now stood apart from his community, his family, and his friends. But instead of backing down because of the pressure, he pressed further into the presence of God, seeking Him daily, relying on the Holy Spirit to reveal His truth.

His third revelation was, like his first two, not accepted in the circle of popular opinion. In that time, the church building was considered a holy place, where everyone whispered and tiptoed because God lived there.

Fox thought the temple of God consisted of flesh-and-blood believers. They were the spiritual church, and their bodies were the temples of God.

Fox understood it differently. According to Scripture, God had no need for a special material structure; His temple consisted of flesh-and-blood believers who had experienced the new birth and looked to the Holy Spirit for guidance and direction. Fox believed that true Christians were the spiritual church and that their bodies were the temples of God. So, he began calling the church buildings *steeple houses,* a slang term, which led to great fury among the pious and religious. This revelation eventually caused him tremendous persecution, because he developed and acted upon a righteous indignation for what these church buildings represented—or more appropriately, misrepresented.

His Fourth Revelation: The Holy Spirit Teaches

The third revelation led yet to a fourth: The Lord would teach His people Himself. Fox was ushering in the ministry of the Holy Spirit to the dry churches that had used the Word of God only, without the Spirit, creating a self-righteous, letter-of-the-law mentality. Fox realized that one must depend on illumination (revelation) by the Holy Spirit, not merely on the written sentences within Bible. His insight into certain verses had been quickened by the Spirit within him, making them come alive with understanding.

Fox was beginning to understand the necessity of mixing the Spirit and the Word together. Now the Bible was exciting, filled with wonder, with answers and opportunity! He asserted that, just as Jesus Christ had died for everyone, so the Spirit of God was available to teach everyone, not just the clergy. But he also believed that every leading of the Holy Spirit would be validated by the Word.

This revelation was revolutionary in his day for two reasons. First, the clergy had made it clear that only they could interpret the Bible, and they used that self-righteous control as a hammer over the heads of the people, forcing them to do and to live however they said.

The second reason it was revolutionary was because the people had been categorized into a class society. That meant that, up to this point, the lower-class citizens had little say in the social realm, and they were certainly scorned by the clergy and the elite if they felt the Lord could show them something. But Fox's revelation was to prove that anyone, no matter his or her rank in society, was capable of hearing from God and being taught by Him.

You can see that Fox not only spoke to the religious section of his day but also to the social ranks of his society. Like all Reformers, he refused to remain in an isolated corner, only affecting those who believed like he did.

Give Me the Disgruntled, Disillusioned, and Disheartened

Like Luther and Calvin, Fox also believed that the church was much like a nursery for believers, but he went beyond their beliefs by

Fox preaching in a tavern.
Hulton Archive/Getty

supporting individual offshoot groups that were filled with dissenting believers.

In 1646, he began his wanderings once again, finding these offshoot gatherings and preaching his revelation to them. The groups he preached to were very encouraged as Fox spoke with authority, answering the questions of their hearts—both their political questions and their spiritual ones.

This practice of searching out dissenting groups would be extremely unpopular with ministries and churches today, just as it was then. I can just hear the fires of God being extinguished with cautious and fearful advice. But here's the vital difference that made it work for Fox: He never looked for ministers who were on the rise. He wasn't interested in climbing a political, religious ladder in hopes he would be noticed. Instead, Fox sought out the disgruntled and the disillusioned. And he had a keen insight to locate them, because his heart was truly after God. He had finally learned that man could never answer or remedy the questions of his heart. While he was searching for a man to be his teacher, he heard the voice of the Holy Spirit say to him, "There is One, even Christ Jesus, that can speak to thy condition."[18]

☆☆☆☆☆

He realized that only Jesus Christ can truly speak to a heart, change it, and give spiritual strength, and that He alone should have the glory for it. That revelation became an incredible restraining factor all the days of his life, which kept him from seeking to please man, become popular, or try to get along with everyone.

Whenever he would hear of a gathering where political dissenters would be, Fox made sure to be there, using the occasion for the Gospel. He took their social grievances, addressed them, then gave an answer according to the Word and the Spirit. People were gratified, and as he spoke they saw the issues clearly.

This is another valuable lesson that Fox demonstrated. Even though he thought way ahead of his time, he was a man of his generation, a man who was totally involved with his culture. It makes me think of David, as described in Acts 13:36: *"He had served his own generation by the will of God."*

Fox realized that only Jesus Christ can truly speak to a heart, change it, and give it spiritual strength, and that He alone should receive the glory for it.

Fox wasn't a closet Christian. Although he demonstrated true holiness, he wasn't so afraid of touching the world that he hid in some secluded corner with those who believed like he did. Reformation will never come from Christians who act that way. No, Fox went after the people, winning them to God and, at the same time, tackling the evils and ills of society. He felt that both were his divine duty, and he brashly addressed his audiences with the tongue of an angel.

I believe every great Reformer knew how to blend their authority in several worlds—political, social, and spiritual. After all, the Gospel is given to meet the needs of people, and the government many times affects those needs. Reformers understand that men can't remedy the evils of society, but changed hearts can and will. As they work to bring spiritual reform to the hearts of men, political and social reform ensues.

Today our nations and societies are ripe for another reformation. Are you one who has the thread of God running through you? Or are you more concerned with how you would look to others if you obeyed

God, more concerned with popular opinion? Are you one struggling to climb a political, religious ladder, hoping to be recognized? Are you more comfortable staying isolated with your Christian friends and churches, or do you dare to be the extended hand and voice of God in the earth, at whatever cost? I hear the voices of the multitudes crying, even pleading for reformation and change.

Do you?

The Mantle to Confront

While traveling through Manchester, one of his early converts, if not the first, was a woman by the name of Elizabeth Hooten. She became one of the strongest missionaries whom Fox ever had. Her home was one of his bases in the early years of his ministry.

As Fox traveled from village to village in 1647, he came to the town of Mansfield, where an elderly prophet by the name of Brown lay dying. This prophet's full name is unknown; he was just Brown. He asked to speak with Fox and prophesied many wonderful things concerning his future—mainly that Fox would convert many sinners.

When Brown died, a great mantle of anointing came upon Fox. For two weeks, people came from everywhere, hoping to speak with him. His prophetic anointing had come into a full operation, and he could see into the lives of the people that stood before him. As he prayed in a meeting, the power of God came down so strongly that the very building seemed to rock. Some of those present declared, "This is like that in the days of the apostles, when at Pentecost the house where they met was shaken!"[19]

After that tremendous outpouring, Fox returned to his own region, Leicestershire. He came just in time for a gathering of all denominations, called to dispute various issues. Several spoke, and then a woman, with unusual boldness for that day, stood to ask a question.

The presiding minister, flustered with rage and determined to humiliate her, announced that he did not permit women to speak in church.

Religious guidelines of the day held that a woman shouldn't be allowed to speak or teach in church but should just sit quietly. But this society also took that doctrine a step further. Filled with pagan notions and mysterious hearsay, some believed that women didn't have souls! Of course, Fox ran into this crazy belief several times during his travels and always refuted it by reminding them that the mother of Jesus exclaimed how her soul magnified the Lord. He knew that this kind of thinking was ridiculous.

But Fox heard another word in the minister's response that infuriated him. It wasn't the word *woman*. It was the word *church*. Knowing what the Holy Spirit called a true church, Fox couldn't let the minister's abusive, religious comment go unchecked. Feeling the unction of God, he stood up and met the man head on.

"Dost thou call this place a church, or this mixed multitude a church?" he asked in an attempt to bait the minister.

"What do you call a church?" asked the minister, thinking he had control.

"The church," began Fox, "is the pillar and ground of the truth, made up of living stones and lively members; a spiritual household of which Christ is the head. But He is not the head of a mixed multitude, or of an old house composed of lime, stones, and wood."[20]

At that, the red-faced minister ran down from the pulpit, heading straight for Fox! The entire congregation burst into a yelling match, and Fox was ousted from the building!

From that day on, he became a dreaded target to established religion. Fox made it a point to enter the churches of the villages he visited. He would stand up in their services, condemn the ministers, and preach to the people of their deception.

This may seem totally out of order, but in those days it was a common practice for people to stand and speak their minds at the end of every service. The services weren't dismissed until that opportunity was presented.

Fox took full advantage of those times. But every now and then, he couldn't contain the strong stirring of the Holy Spirit—especially when the minister was grotesquely wrong or self-righteous in his ministry. At these times, Fox would stand up in the middle of the sermon and blurt out the truth! Sometimes he called the minister a deceiver, exposing how he was growing wealthy off the tithes of poor people. Other times he denounced the minister's interpretation of Scriptures, shouting out his error. Whatever the occasion called for, Fox delivered. He always spoke what he discerned, whether it be that the minister was a hypocrite or that he was a wolf in sheep's clothing sent by the devil to ravish the flock—it didn't matter to Fox. All that mattered was that deception be revealed and truth be proclaimed!

The priests or clergy would stand red-faced and speechless or fly into some wild rage while the other members of the church beat on Fox with their fists, rods, and canes until he was covered with knots and bruises. Some pulled knives and tried to slash him. They threw him in the streets, over hedges, and down steep stairways, or pelted him with stones and rocks.

Some of his newly won disciples also began to make it a practice to enter churches and attack the empty traditions. They were all absolutely fearless because they had one great goal in mind—to destroy religion and usher in the true Spirit of Christ. There are so many great stories of these church encounters, one chapter can't contain them all.

Persecution Meant Success!

During those physical, violent attacks, Fox would simply stand (when he could), brush off his leather pants, and walk away, deeply satisfied that persecution meant the hand of God was upon him.

It was a good thing that Fox viewed persecution as a motivation because, as we continue, your heart will break at the suffering he and those who followed his teachings endured. No one in his right mind would love to be beaten upon. Persecution only motivates a person when he understands it by the Spirit.

Fox judged the success of his ministry by one of two ways. Either sinners would be converted, and that meant success, or he would be thrown out and many times beaten, which meant success because his message had made the devil mad. Either way he couldn't lose. Fox's mind-set regarding persecution was more than just positive thinking. Fox was a prophet, who, like the apostles in the book of Acts, rejoiced at being counted worthy to suffer for the sake of Christ. Persecution and suffering motivated him into knowing he was following the right path.

They Quake at the Word of God!

In 1649, Fox's famous description for the direction of the Holy Spirit as the "inner light" became a common cliché. He based that terminology on John 1:4, which says, *"In him was life; and the life was the light of men."* In fact, Fox didn't stop with that one Scripture. The books of John and 1 John specifically tie the light of God to Jesus Christ and the Holy Spirit. Fox believed that the inner light would lead anyone into truth, as long as the person followed it, and he based that belief on many Scriptures. There was nothing New Age or spooky about the way he interpreted it; it was biblical. But it made the Calvinists wild with rage!

By now those who had been converted by his itinerant teachings had grown into quite a group, and they began to hold their own meetings. His followers and converts began to assemble together, and, sitting in silence, they would wait until the Holy Spirit moved one to witness in prayer or speech or song. If the Holy Spirit didn't move, the group would disassemble, reflecting quietly upon their relationship with the Lord.

During this time, it was the furthest thing from Fox's mind to begin another denomination. Still, his followers were called certain titles to distinguish them from the others. "Children of the Light," "People of God," "Royal Seed of God," or "Friends of the Truth," were some of the names they were labeled. In the end, the latter name won the most favor, hence the modern name, "Religious Society of Friends" or "Friends Society."[21] This name was again based on Scripture. John 15:13–15 says, *"Greater love hath no man than this, that a man lay down his life for his* ***friends****. Ye are my* ***friends****, if ye do whatsoever I command you. Henceforth I call you not servants; for the servant knoweth not what his lord doeth: but I have called you* ***friends****; for all things that I have heard of my Father I have made known unto you"* (emphasis added). You can see from these verses how strong the foundation was within the group for the leading and direction of the Holy Spirit. In the early days of the Quakers, the Holy Spirit was given total preeminence.

Throughout Fox's life, he would be imprisoned nearly a hundred times. In 1650, Fox was imprisoned for the first time on the sole charge of blasphemy. Questioned by a group of clergy, he was cursed for saying that he and his followers had no sin. Fox corrected them by stating that through Jesus Christ all were made free from sin if they learned how to follow the Holy Spirit. Refusing to hear him, they threw him in jail for six months.

✯✯✯✯✯

During this imprisonment, Fox rebuked a justice, telling him he should tremble at the Word of God. The justice scornfully mocked Fox and his followers, calling them Quakers in reference to Fox's rebuke about trembling. The label, Quaker, stuck—partly because they were known to shake or tremble in their meetings. This was due to the intense presence of the Holy Spirit coming upon them strongly.

No Stone Unturned

During this time Fox also ventured further into his calling, challenging the social and economic society of the day. It was one thing to know about the light, but living in the light was another. Remember, to Fox, if you called yourself a Christian, you had better possess what you profess. Fox invaded every area of society with this belief and understanding.

He would ask questions like the following: If you were a craftsman, did you turn out quality work? Were you offering fair wages? If you were a trader, were your prices fair? If you had the chance to sell poor goods for profit or overcharge a customer, did you? If you were a magistrate, did you deal justly with the poor and unpopular?

He scolded the lawyers who were out for their own gain, and the doctors because they failed to give God the credit for making and healing the human body. No one was left out. He instructed the teachers to take care of children's behavior and parents to be responsible. He scolded innkeepers for giving too much to drink for the sake of money and astrologers, with their popular, misleading predictions, for causing people to be unaccountable for their own lives. He berated entertainers for getting a laugh from crude jokes, causing the mind to think of sin and temptation. Of course, these probing questions stirred social hatred against him—something that the religious ministers were glad to see.

Their hatred toward his message meant little to Fox. He believed that God meant equality for all, and he catapulted a lifelong campaign to see that it happened. Unfortunately, he lived in a time, much like today, when people were obsessed with status. In that day, social rank was acknowledged through elaborate language and gestures. For example, "thee" and "thou" were still used, but only to inferiors or lower class people—and also to deity and lovers. To Fox, this was inexcusable. He felt that no person should be humbled as a servant or flattered as a superior through speech.

The elaborate custom of dress was another social evil. Class rank required not only bows and curtsies but also elaborate and dramatic raising and sweeping down of hats. Everyone wore a hat, and there was a certain etiquette dictating when and why to wear one. In the midst of this starchy attitude about proper etiquette came the bullish Fox, with his hat firmly on his head, refusing to lift it whether he met king or pauper. He wore his hat in defiance, for the sake of the Word of God, declaring that all stood on the same level with Jesus Christ and that there were no class rankings with Him.[22]

He even took on the area of clothing, which he believed needed to be sensible, free of extravagance and attention. Thus, today, the Friends are still known for their simple dress and hat-wearing, no matter where they are or who they meet.

The mind-set of George Fox could be summed up best by this: In the entire course of his life, he couldn't see anything sinful, oppressive, or undermining without feeling a burning desire to remedy it. He went after the remedy with great vigor, regardless of the pain, suffering, or persecution it caused him.

Meetings, Swine, and a Moldy Communion

It seemed that the people of every independent group that had broken from established religion were coming out in droves to see and hear George Fox. By 1652, Fox had perfectly blended his spiritual message, appealing to the social conditions and aspirations of his audiences as well. Fox appealed to them all—Baptists, Independents, Presbyterians, Puritans, and those who had no special group to which they belonged. He continued to interrupt church meetings, and each time the entire building seemed to thunder with his voice of conviction.

Fox spared no one's feelings in his attack on religion. He called the church of his day, "the false church ruled upon the beast and dragon's power."[23] He didn't hesitate to declare that his followers were members of the true church. He thoroughly welcomed the opposition, loving the "wonderful confusion it brought among all professors and priests."[24] Many times, those who heard him blast a church service would be convicted, leave that church, and become his followers.

Meanwhile, in his own camp, Fox refused to call the gathering of his followers a church service, so he simply called them meetings.

Prayer was a very vital part of the meetings, and intercessory entreaty was common. Fox and the early Quakers believed in being filled with the Holy Spirit, with the evidence of speaking in other tongues. An early Quaker by the last name of Burrough wrote several times in his book, *Preface to the Great Mystery,* these words: "Our tongues [were] loosed and our mouths opened, and we spake with new tongues as the Lord gave us utterance."[25] This outpouring of the Holy Spirit came often as the Quakers waited in silence.

In these meetings, a witness stated that the presence of the Holy Spirit would be so intense that it felt like the soul was in desperate agony, so painful that it had an external effect. Frequently, the people in the meetings would be shaken with "groans, sighs, and tears" much like a "woman in labor." Some would swoon as "with epilepsy," and while lips quivered and hands shook, the worshippers might lie on the ground in this condition for hours at a time.[26]

Some who attended these meetings would erupt in violent opposition when the presence of God would manifest itself like that. Once, when the Holy Spirit fell on a meeting, a man ran toward Fox to challenge him—to which Fox bluntly commanded, "Repent you swine and beast."[27]

Onc of my favorite stories has to do with Fox crudely challenging the Communion tradition—the belief of transubstantiation. Transubstantiation is the idea that the bread and wine are actually transformed into the actual body of Jesus during Communion. Fox encountered a Jesuit priest who believed it to be that way. He dramatically challenged the Jesuit to divide the bread and the wine, to bless or consecrate only half, and to allow the people to see if the portions that were the body and blood of Jesus resisted molding. Of course when the Jesuit priest refused, Fox was vindicated.[28]

Home, Sweet Prison

Fox was put in jail for everything from refusing to take off his hat to refusing to take an oath. Sometimes, a Quaker was put in prison for simply walking down the street. The magistrates called it loitering. Quakers were easy to spot because of their style of clothing. It may sound strange to put it this way, but the majority of Fox's ministry consisted of extreme and bold confrontations, physical beatings, and imprisonment. These harsh punishments insured many of the freedoms we enjoy today.

Since prison was a large part of Quaker life, I want you to understand what an incredible trial it was. The prisons of that day were absolutely deplorable. Open sewage ran through the middle of these dark dungeons, which were located under the city streets, making the conditions filthy and the fumes toxic. Most of the time, there was only a small opening that allowed light and air. The summers were stifling, and prisoners would faint, become severely ill, and sometimes even die because of lack of air and circulation. The prisons didn't provide food. If a prisoner did get food, it was because a relative or friend brought it and found favor with the keeper of the prison. This was also the case for fresh straw to sleep upon. It had to be provided by a prisoner's family or friends. If family and friends failed to bring it or if favor wasn't found with the prison authorities, the prisoners lay on hard, wet floors.

Since the Quakers were extremely hated, many times the prison keepers would crowd them into a chamber where an infectious disease was raging, hoping death would claim them all. In spite of this inhumane abuse, there is no record that even one Quaker denied his faith.

Fox in prison.
North Wind Picture Archives

There was a saying in that day that went something like this: "Wherever you see a Quaker, hit it; and if you don't meet one, go look for it." [29] If they were seen praying over a meal in public, they were thrown into prison. If they didn't remove their hats or take an oath (because they would not swear), if they denied playing a game, or if a woman was rumored to have spoken in a meeting, they were imprisoned. By 1656, over a thousand Quakers had been imprisoned for non-criminal actions such as these.

If a Quaker visited another in prison, he could be whipped. It didn't matter the age or the gender; every Quaker was severely persecuted. Women would be snatched from their homes, labeled as witches, and thrown into the dungeons or publicly whipped and beaten until their backs were a bloody mess; children would be taken from their parents and sold into slavery. Even if some were sick in bed, they could be arrested in their rooms and dragged through the streets to be thrown into prison.

All this atrocious action was taken because the Quakers dared to oppose organized, dead religion, because they dared to stand by the Word of God, and because they dared to proclaim that every person was equal. Still, through all this hatred, not one Quaker denied his faith or his stand for God.

One time, Fox was imprisoned in Scarborough Castle by the sea. It was a very cold winter, and the salty water from the sea constantly sprayed into his room until his bed was soaked, and the water stood in the floor of his cell. He had no fire to keep warm. He lay in the cold dampness with no relief, night or day, until his hands swelled to twice their normal size.

Sometimes in the cold chill of the evening, I look around at the comforts of my home and think of George Fox and how horrible it must have been to suffer so much for what he believed. I wonder about what he was thinking during those times, how he kept his mind occupied and strong, and how he must have struggled against the physical discomforts and hardships, never succumbing to them. I find myself sizing it up against my own life and the lives of those in my generation. My heart grows heavy as I think of the hardships Fox endured for us, and yet I can almost sense the sweetness of experiencing God's love and mercy that has to be present at times of suffering and martyrdom. I know that, although he was physically alone at those times, he was not alone. There must have been a divine opening from heaven during those times. There must have been a security and strength that is beyond human description poured into the lives of those suffering.

☆☆☆☆☆

The Height and Depth of His Spirit

During one of Fox's imprisonments, a sheriff by the name of John Reckless heard him speak at the trial. Impressed, he sent for Fox to stay at his home. Realizing the hand of the Lord was involved, Fox agreed. As he entered their home, the wife of the sheriff met him and, with shaking hands, cried, "This day is salvation come to our house!"[30] The wife had been present in a church when Fox had reprimanded a minister and was greatly touched by all she had heard.

The couple kept Fox through the night, listening intently to all he had to say about the Holy Spirit. The next day, as the sheriff was sitting alone in the room with Fox, he suddenly jumped up and exclaimed that he must go into the market and preach repentance to the people. With that, he ran out of the room, still in his slippers, and began to preach in the streets! There was such an uproar that soldiers had to be called in to disperse the mob. Immediately, the magistrates went to the sheriff's house to get Fox and put him back in prison, hoping to stifle any further action like this.

How did Fox's one-night stay so strongly affect this household? What did Fox possess that could move upon a prestigious man such as the sheriff and cause him to instantly change professions? Why was it that every place Fox went, he was either violently hated or passionately loved?

You and I weren't alive then, and we can't speak to him or ask questions so that we might understand. Books that have been written about him can only provide a slanted point of view. Only his personal journal can give the insights we need.

Believing so strongly in the ministry of the Holy Spirit, Fox constantly gave himself to the Lord, and visions were a very common occurrence in his life. His physical surroundings never moved him, because he was always challenged and motivated by what he had seen in the Spirit.

The following is a portion of several excerpts from Fox's journal. It shows his great depth as a believer, his character, and his maturity as a prophet of God. It also gives us insight as to why he did the things he did and why he remained strong and faithful to the Reforming cause. When you read these few portions, you will understand the spiritual thrust behind George Fox.

Excerpt 1—My Life in His Blood

"As I was walking by the steeple-house side in Mansfield, the Lord said unto me, 'That which people trample upon must be thy food.' And as the Lord spoke, He opened it to me that the people and professors did trample upon the life, even the life of Christ; they fed upon words, and fed one another with words; but they trampled upon the life; trampled underfoot the blood of the Son of God, which blood was my life, and lived in their airy notions, talking of Him. It seemed strange to me at the first that I should feed on that which the high professors trampled upon; but the Lord opened it clearly to me by His eternal spirit and power."[31]

"I saw the harvest white, and the seed of God lying thick in the ground, as ever did wheat that was sown outwardly, and none to gather it; for this I mourned with tears."[32]

Excerpt 2—A Vision of Revival

"I saw there was a great crack to go throughout the earth, and a great smoke to go as the crack went; and that after the crack there should be a great shaking: this was the earth in people's hearts, which was to be shaken before the seed of God raised out of the earth. And it was so; for the Lord's power began to shake them, and great meetings we began to have, and a mighty power and work of God there was amongst people, to the astonishment of both people and priests."[33]

Excerpt 3—The Deceit of Priests, Physicians, and Lawyers

"The Lord opened to me three things, relating to those three great professions in the world, physic [doctors], divinity (so called) [ministers], and law. He shewed me that the physicians were out of the wisdom of God, by which the creatures were made; and so knew not their virtues....He shewed me that the priests were out of the true faith, which

Christ is the author of; the faith which purifies and gives victory, and brings people to have access with God, by which they please God; which mystery of faith is held in a pure conscience. He shewed me also, that the lawyers were out of equity, and out of true justice, and out of the law of God,...which went over all sin, and answered the Spirit of God, that was grieved and transgressed in man. And that these three, the physicians, the priests, and the lawyers, ruled the world out of the wisdom [no knowledge or agreement with God]...the one pretending the cure of the body, the other the cure of the soul, and the third the property of the people. And as the Lord opened these things unto me, I felt His power...by which all might be reformed, if they would receive and bow to it. The pries ts might be reformed and brought into the true faith....The lawyers might be reformed and brought into the law of God....The physicians might be reformed and brought into the wisdom of God by which all things were made and created." [34]

Excerpt 4—An Unruly Prisoner

"There was also in the jail, while I was there, a prisoner, a wicked, ungodly man....He threatened how he would talk with me, and what he would do to me; but he never had the power to open his mouth to me. And on a time, the jailer and he falling out, he threatened that he would raise the devil, break his house down, so that he made the jailer afraid. Then I was moved of the Lord to go in His power, and thresh him in it, and say unto him, 'Come, let's see what thou canst do; do thy worst'; and I told him the devil was raised high enough in him already; but the power of God chained him down so he slunk away and went from me." [35]

Excerpt 5—An Experience in Paradise

"Now was I come up in the spirit through the flaming sword, into the paradise of God. All things were new; and all the creation gave another smell unto me than before,

> beyond what words can utter. I knew nothing but pureness, and innocency, and righteousness, being renewed up into the image of God by Christ Jesus, to the state of Adam, which he was in before he fell. The creation was opened to me; and it was shewed me how all things had their names given them according to their nature and virtue.
>
> "He let me see...the mystery that had been hid from ages and generations...."[36]

From reading these portions of his journal, it is clear that the hand of God was upon Fox for a specific work.

Healings, Demons, and Spiritual Warfare

As Fox continued his itinerant ministry through the Midlands and expanded north, he not only confronted lethargic ministers and preached to his growing followers; divine healing and the casting out of demons also became a trademark of his ministry. Fox believed every believer could and should walk in the spiritual authority and power given to him, and his life demonstrated it.

It was a common occurrence for a sick person to be healed by simply standing in Fox's presence. One man in particular had been suffering from either acute arthritis or neuritis in his arm and hand. Having seen many physicians, no one could offer a cure. Growing worse and suffering tremendous pain, the man was soon unable to dress himself without help. One night, he had a dream that he and Fox were together, and he was healed after spending time with Fox. With great determination, the man made his way to Fox. When the man showed Fox his arm and hand, Fox asked him to take a walk. While they were conversing, Fox laid his hand on the man's shoulder and the man was instantly free from pain, moving without difficulty. By the next day, he was fully recovered to the "former use and strength, without any pain."[37] God healed what doctors could not.

Fox's mother also received healing through her son. She had experienced some sort of stroke, which had affected one side of her body, making movement and stability difficult. For many years she suffered, for as the muscles would suddenly paralyze, she would fall down. Once when Fox came to visit her, she had a paralysis attack and fell. When Fox took her by the hand, the paralysis left her. She arose and could easily go about her business. [38]

There was also a lame woman who couldn't walk without crutches. While other Friends prayed silently, George Fox spoke to her in the "power of God and bid her stand up." [39] Not only did she stand, she also walked without the crutches.

Once, Fox visited the house of an eleven-year-old boy who was very dirty, still lying in a cradle. Fox told his parents to get him up, wash him, and bring the child to him. After they obeyed, Fox spoke to the boy, laid hands on him, and told his parents to dress him. Fox then left for the next town.

A short time later, he came in contact with the boy's mother, who was beaming. She told Fox how the doctors had given her son up to death, but "after you were gone," she said, "we came home and found our son playing in the streets." The boy grew to be a fine adult, and the news of that miracle spread through the countryside. [40]

It was a common thing for Fox to wage spiritual warfare, casting down dark spirits in the heavens so the way could be made clear. He would feel the presence of darkness and take immediate authority over it. In his day, this kind of teaching was unheard of. Spiritual warfare was taught to him by the Holy Spirit and no one else. Yes, Jesus Christ had won the overall war, but evil principalities and powers still tried to get in the way by hindering work in believers who didn't know what was going on. But demons never prevailed with Fox.

There was one story in which Fox found a man's wife in severe mental anguish, even to the point of trying to kill her husband and children. Fox was brought to her and spoke to the demons in her. She fell to her knees, crying, and was delivered. She then begged to go and help bring reform to others through the Gospel that Fox knew and preached.

Another woman who hadn't been able to eat or drink for some time was brought to him. Fox addressed the demon spirit that had her bound; she then ate, spoke, and was made completely well. [41]

Fox stated throughout his journal that people suffering from insanity, mental imbalances, and deliriums were brought to him many times, and each one was delivered and restored to his or her right mind while in his presence. He also spoke of several cases where men and women were near death, and he was brought in to give them comforting words. But Fox's words went past comfort; they produced the life of God. Each time these deathbed cases were raised and restored to health, entire towns were astonished at such great power.

Although he strongly believed in divine healing, Fox never ignored the use of natural remedies for healing as well. He combined prayer and the use of medicinal herbs for many of the people he ministered to. We've read from his journal how God gave him the knowledge of how mankind and animals were created. From that divine knowledge, Fox had an incredible insight whereby he concocted herbs to use medicinally, depending on the ailment. We know that many healings also came as he prescribed the use of certain herbs to aid or strengthen the physical body. Later in his ministry, he planned for the medicinal use of herbs to be included in the Quaker education.[42]

Enough Is Enough!

As the teachings of Fox spread throughout northern England, the number of his followers grew at an alarming rate. Quakers were forming more and more congregations and holding meetings of their own. Out of these came several men and women who felt they were called of God to be ministers. They all devoted their time—even the women with children—to wandering around the country where they felt led by the Lord, preaching and teaching as Fox had been led to do.

Unlike Fox, who had a family inheritance, most of the Quaker preachers were poor and uneducated. But they all succeeded in stirring up crowds wherever they went because of the power of God within them. They had all learned how to listen to the Holy Spirit and follow His leading. They all experienced the same kind of persecution that Fox had endured, and many times they were beaten so severely they could barely walk. But all of them considered it a glory to suffer for the sake of Christ and for the sake of truth.

The Quakers viewed their imprisonments as seasons of missionary labor. Since prisoners were thrown into a common dungeon, the Quakers always had a congregation! They looked for every opportunity, no matter what the hardship, to preach and teach about Jesus Christ. Because of their astonishment at not being able to break the

Quaker spirit, many prison keepers would end up being saved while watching and listening to the Quakers preach in prison.

When Fox heard of Quaker women being imprisoned and beaten and their children being sold into slavery, he couldn't bear it. He himself could suffer all things, but he couldn't stand the thought of the women and children being tortured and suffering. For their sakes, Fox didn't spare himself from trouble or pain. He forced his way into the houses of those high in office to tell of the injustices that Quakers were suffering. He wrote to the leader of England, Oliver Cromwell, a great military genius, who, through a strong conviction, moved against the oppression of the monarchy of the day and ended up reigning as the uncrowned king of England for a time.[43] I'm sure Fox's plea on behalf of the Quaker people struck a note in Cromwell's heart that rang true, Cromwell having been one to stand up for liberty in the past. He granted Fox an immediate meeting.

A People That Couldn't Be Bought

The first meeting Fox had with Cromwell was in London. Fox made a dramatic impression from the very beginning. Cromwell sent a colonel to bring Fox to him, but Fox refused to go at that time, stating that the Lord had ordered him to go to a meeting instead. The colonel was surprised that Fox would refuse such an honor and returned for him the next morning. When Cromwell heard of this, he was intrigued.

As Fox entered Cromwell's chamber the next morning, he announced, "Peace be to this house."[44] He then proceeded to give Cromwell excellent advice as to his personal conduct and the conduct of the nation. They talked about various religious subjects, and Fox answered all of Cromwell's questions regarding the Quakers.

As Fox was leaving, Cromwell grabbed his arm and, with tears in his eyes, asked Fox to visit him as often as he could. The colonel then took Fox into a large dining hall where he was to dine with Cromwell—a great honor among people of the day. Fox, however, declined. He said, "Tell the protector I will neither eat of his bread nor drink of his drink." When Cromwell was told, he responded, "Now I see that there is a people risen up that I cannot win either with gifts, honors, offices, or palaces; but all other sects and people I can."[45]

After that meeting, most of the charges were dropped against imprisoned Quakers, and all charges were erased from Fox's record. Cromwell became a friend of the Quakers.

Two Different Generals

Cromwell, the high-ranking figure who never lost a military battle, became intrigued with George Fox, so much so that any time Fox wanted an audience with him, it was granted. Cromwell was politically championing what Fox was doing spiritually. I believe the two had a similar spirit, and it created a bond between them. Cromwell had the boldness and aggressiveness to do what he felt was right, but he also said that if he were ten years younger, "there was not a king in Europe he would not make to tremble."[46]

Fox felt the same way, yet in a different arena. Both ministers and townspeople trembled when Fox came to town. Sometimes the sheriffs would stand outside the city limits to stop Fox from entering, because the people were so afraid of him. Other times, when he would enter villages, people would run and hide under bushes, fearing that Fox would look upon them!

Fox began writing Cromwell regularly, admonishing him to stand strong in his efforts to politically reform England. The most impassioned letter ever read by Cromwell was written by Fox when it was apparent that Cromwell slacked in his promises toward religious reform.[47]

Although Fox rebuked Cromwell, he loved him. The Lord told Fox of Cromwell's death months before it happened, and Fox mourned over the foreknowledge as one would weep for a dearly loved relative.[48]

True to prediction, Cromwell died in 1658. His son Richard was the chosen protector in his place, but he didn't possess the strength of his father. Scotland invaded England, and Charles II became the ruler in 1660.

Fox lived through incredible changes, both spiritually and politically. Aside from the changing tides of religion, Fox lived through eight rulership changes in British government, each with their own very drastic alterations to England, and he flourished through them all.

★★★★★

Bloody Lichfield!

Unlike other Reformers, Fox's ministry wasn't built by earth-shaking events or through man's favors. His ministry foundation came at the beginning through his four revelations, and, from there and only there, Fox continued to build and publish. He never deviated from those four foundational truths, and, because he wouldn't, his ministry life became a dramatic adventure.

Part of that adventure included countless visions. My favorite one caused quite a stir. Sometime around 1651, having just been released from one of his many bouts in prison, Fox veered west in his journey home. Here, he had the famous Lichfield vision.

It happened like this. While walking near the village with other Quakers, he looked up and saw three church steeples—and you know what he thought of steeple-houses! Being grieved, a mile outside the town he pulled off his shoes and gave them to some nearby shepherds for safekeeping. Then, entering the city barefoot, Fox walked the streets shouting, "Woe unto the bloody city of Lichfield," seeming to see "a channel of blood down the streets, and the market place like a pool of blood." It seems he was having an open vision, which is a vision from God that comes while the eyes are wide open.

Amazingly, no one harmed him as he walked down the street hollering. His Quaker friends took him aside and began speaking to him, asking where his shoes were. As the burning sensation left his feet and body, he found his way back to the shepherds and paid them for watching his shoes. After he washed his feet in a ditch, he put the shoes back on and continued on his way.[49]

Pondering the open vision, Fox knew the inhabitants there weren't guilty of bloodshed. Researching more deeply, he discovered that a massacre had happened there during Roman times. I believe Fox was responding prophetically to something that was over the city, which was put in place by the spirit of the enemy through that massacre so many years earlier. You can see this today. Whole cities and even whole countries carry the nature of the principality that rules over them. And there is usually something in the history of that place that explains how a certain stronghold came into place. You can see this over people's lives as well. Rejection and other dispositions among men and women can always be traced to something in the history of the development of those individuals. The good news is that those bondages can all be broken, too, whether over a nation or over a person. There are curses over people and over lands. Some are generational and some territorial, but God gives us power over the enemy and strategies for victory. Fox was walking in a strategy from heaven to break a curse over a geographical area.

Hatless with a Bloody Nose!

Another of my favorite incidents involves a bloody encounter with a certain priest. It happened sometime in 1652. Fox had left a group of Quakers at a meeting to confront this priest. Normally, Fox got his say. But this time, just as he was starting to speak, the priest ran up and hit Fox in the face with his Bible. The blood gushed from Fox's nose so profusely that it splattered on the walls of the steeplehouse. He was then punched, beaten with books, fists, and sticks, and thrown over a hedge, losing his hat. However, the hatless Fox still got up and rebuked them, wiping the blood from his face.

He continued speaking so loudly to the crowd from over the yard wall that the priest began to shake! Seeing the trembling priest, the people started teasing him saying, "Look how the priest trembles and shakes. He is turned a Quaker also." Later, the priest trembled even more when the justices sought to examine what happened. He was afraid of having his hand cut off for striking Fox, but Fox comforted the priest quietly and forgave him.

Fox was not upset by the beating or the blood; he was only upset at losing his hat because it represented his social protest! [50]

Silence on the Haystack

The more prestigious Fox became, the more he attempted to smother his popularity. When it was noised abroad that Fox would be preaching at a village, hundreds gathered to hear him. Troubled, feeling the attention was upon him rather than God, Fox climbed to the top of a haystack and just sat there. As the throng of people waited for him to speak, he said nothing. Time passed, and still, he did not say a word.

Some gave up to go home, and that was fine with Fox. He must have felt they had only come to see him instead of hearing from God. When it seemed as if hours had passed, he slowly began to speak, and the power of the Lord fell.

The story of it was published far and wide, many wondering at the oddity of it. But they still didn't understand. Fox wanted all eyes upon the Lord instead of him. If they had come just to hear him, he would have rather they stayed at home.

His confrontational preaching, coupled with his visions and prophetic operations, all worked together to win over the North. From his influence in the North came some of the Quakers' greatest leaders.

James Nayler, Richard Farnsworth, and William Dewsbury were three of them. The groups led by these men caused so much of a stir in northern England that they were compared to the rough and rowdy Scottish army!

James Nayler became George Fox's right-hand man and grew to be nearly his equal in boldness. Farnsworth and Dewsbury were trusted friends who carried the work of the Quakers throughout England and beyond. By the end of 1652, Fox arrived at the destination that brought him into the divine connection for the rest of his life.

The Stage Is Set: Swarthmoor!

Probably the most important event since his foundational revelations was Fox's arrival at Swarthmoor.

Swarthmoor Hall was owned and occupied by the family of Thomas and Margaret Fell. Its grayish stone mansion loomed on the horizon, surrounded by the dismal moors. The Fell's were very affluent and well-known in the area. Thomas was a magistrate, judge, vice-chancellor, and high-profile parliamentarian. Margaret was also very respected, known for her wisdom and efficiency in running a household filled with seven children, while constantly opening their home to visitors and travelers.

It was the very place that Fox had set his sight. Earlier, he had been given an open vision at a place called Pendle Hill. The commoners dared not go there. Usually shrouded in fog, the strange hill that rose in the middle of the moors was rumored to be the home of witches. But Fox had been traveling in the North, and, as they passed by Pendle Hill, he was inspired to climb to the top. Standing alone at its peak, Fox received an open vision in which he saw a harvest of people in white, waiting for the Word of God.

Thrilled by what he had seen, Fox bounded down the hill and traveled further North to explore what the Lord wanted done. He had heard of the hospitable reputation of the Fells at Swarthmoor, and now he was within sight of the mansion. I'm sure he had no idea that he was walking into a divine relationship as he approached the Swarthmoor mansion.

As the road crossed in front of the mansion grounds, Fox met William Lampit, the minister of the local town where the Fells attended church. Realizing that they were both going to the same place, they walked along together and, at first, spoke together cordially. At the door of Swarthmoor, they found that Thomas Fell was away in London. Margaret was also absent, so the Fell children invited them both inside.

That Filthy Minister!

As the two men waited for the Fells, they found they didn't get along. After all, Lampit assumed that Fox was an irresponsible roughneck who called himself a Christian yet refused to obey the traditions of Christianity. Fox saw Lampit as so full of filth that he could barely speak to him without antagonistic overtones.

When Margaret returned home that evening, she was shocked to see the leader of the Quakers in her living room! Instead of the usual bows and social etiquette, Fox simply related his reasons for being there. Listening kindly to him, Margaret invited Fox to be a guest in her home that evening, while Lampit returned to his home.

Early the next morning, Lampit returned, knocking at the door. The ongoing argument between him and Fox resumed, and Margaret listened patiently, but she secretly leaned toward the assurance in which Fox spoke.

Fox remained a guest there for several days. Margaret's church had set aside a lecture day, and she asked Fox to attend with her; of course, he declined.

Instead, Fox walked around outside the church, listening to what was going on inside. All he could think of was how foul, false, and filthy Lampit was. Sensing a divine command to go inside, Fox entered the church and jumped up on a seat, lashing out at the minister and the congregation!

He claimed that they were using words they did not understand, though they pretended to, and that they had denied the true Spirit and life. He begged them to come out of their dead traditions and come into the light of Jesus Christ.

An incident like this had never happened in their small church. Soon the congregation was in an absolute uproar, and someone yelled for Fox to be thrown out. To the surprise of everyone, Margaret Fell stood up from her private pew to stare them down, defending Fox. They hushed at her response out of respect for her and the family's social position.

Fox continued in his convicting exhortation to them. He asked if they inwardly knew God, or was it all a show? At his words, Margaret began to melt. Looking around at those she had known for most of her life, she realized that all their outward religious lifestyles had been false, traditional, and dead. She began to cry openly and sat down in her pew, unable to hear the rest of what Fox was preaching.

As he went on, the congregation again began to be stirred against him. They finally escorted him out of the church and left him alone in the graveyard. As the congregation walked away and reentered the church, Fox continued to preach to them.

"A Man in a White Hat"

Later that night, Fox returned to Swarthmoor. The uproar continued as he preached to the household, converting them all. Margaret knew the truth inside, yet she feared what would happen when her husband returned. What would he think? How could she tell him that she had changed? How would he treat George Fox once he heard the news? She was fearful that if her husband opposed the newfound truth, she would not be able to stand with it.

Over the next few days, she and Fox carefully reviewed the entire history of the Quaker movement and how God had led Fox from his youth. Being ten years Fox's senior, Margaret wanted to know the details of the group she was willing to become involved with. She saw that Fox was not only an anointed preacher with great spiritual insight, but that he also had common sense.

Much later, Margaret confessed to Fox that before he had come, she "had a vision of a man in a white hat that should come and confound the priests."[51] Fox was very willing to answer any questions she had. I believe he sensed she would have a deep involvement in his ministry and life.

Soon, Fox had to leave for a short preaching mission in another town. Margaret was still waiting for her husband to return, knowing she had entered a situation that he knew little about.

"...If All in England Had Been There..."

Before the judge returned home, Margaret had already invited Farnsworth and Nayler to Swarthmoor as guests. The children were excited about their guests, but the household was unsettled, waiting for the return of the judge.

To the judge, it was always an exciting time to see those last few miles that stretched to his home. I'm sure his thoughts were on Margaret and the children, when suddenly he noticed the minister and a group of prestigious men riding out to intercept him in his journey. Fearful of their news, he assumed that someone must have died or become seriously ill.

To the men riding to meet him, their news was worse than death or illness. They were bearing the news that his wife had been involved in witchcraft while he was gone and that she had been seduced by a wandering preacher who had been staying in his home. They told him how this insane preacher had caused havoc in the church and disrupted the entire community. They pleaded with the judge to send these preachers, Nayler and Farnsworth, on their way before it could get any worse.

The judge was a man of character, a man who would never blindly believe ill reports about his family.[52] He continued on his journey, but I'm sure his mind was racing.

When the judge reached his home, the atmosphere was tense as Margaret warmly greeted him, then introduced Nayler and Farnsworth. Fell said very little but just stared at the men, judging their intent. They tried to assure him, but sensing the awkward moment, they made a decision to leave. Margaret, however, begged them to stay until Fox arrived once again.

The silence continued even during dinner. In fact, Margaret wrote of the deafening silence:

> And then was he pretty moderate and quiet, and his dinner being ready, he went to it, and I went in and sat me down by him. And whilst I was sitting, the power of the Lord seized upon me; and he was stricken with amazement and knew not what to think, but was quiet and still. And the children were all quiet and still and grown sober, and could not play on their music that they were learning, and all these things made him quiet and still. And then at night George Fox came: and after supper my husband was sitting in the parlor, and I asked him if George Fox might come in; and he said, "Yes!" So George came in without any compliment, and walked into the room, and began to speak presently, and the family and James Nayler and Richard Farnsworth came all in, and he spoke very excellently as ever I heard him; and opened Christ and the apostles' practices which they were in, in their day, and he opened the night of apostasy since the apostles' days and laid open the priests and their practices...if all in England had been there I thought they could not have denied the truth of those things. [53]

Judge Fell was obviously very moved by what he heard. He said no more for the rest of the night and went to bed.

Early the next morning, Lampit was at the house to see the judge, urging him to get rid of Fox. But his intentions did just the opposite with Judge Fell. Later in the day, when he heard the Quakers discussing where to have a meeting, Judge Fell spoke up and gave them his permission to hold it at Swarthmoor.

Judge Fell never joined the Quakers, but he stopped attending the local church. He allowed the Quakers to have consistent meetings in his home, and, although he wouldn't come into them, he remained outside the door in his study where he could hear all that was being said.

As long as he lived, no one dared to touch Margaret as she propagated the Quaker beliefs. No one persecuted Swarthmoor Hall as it soon became the central hub for the Quaker movement that eventually spread throughout the world. By his death in 1658, the judge had been a vital support and six-year friend to Fox, and the movement was too strong to be diminished.[54]

The Quakers owe much to this man who joined them in all but name.

Margaret Fell, the Lady

There is no portrait of Margaret Fell, yet from the many letters written about her, there's no doubt she was a beautiful woman. She was always praised for her virtue and honor, and she generously opened her home to any Quaker who traveled through the area. Many times, Swarthmoor became a hospital, nursing Quakers who had been beaten or severely abused. Fox would return to the hall many times to find Margaret bandaging heads, arms, and legs, caring for and feeding the injured.

As the lady of a large household, the wife of a distinguished judge, and the manager of a large estate, Margaret knew how to carry herself and deal with business affairs. Her experience proved vital for the organization and structure of the Quaker movement. Only three months after her conversion, leading Quakers already regarded her as the person they should inform about the direction the movement was taking.[55]

She was also a writer who never failed to pen long letters of appeal to high-profile figures on the treatment of her fellow Friends, and especially for Fox. She was constantly dispatching books for itinerant Quakers to distribute. Fox soon assigned her the task of taking handwritten material gathered from the meetings and mission exploits and turning them into books.[56] Because of her strong spirit, her understanding of the Word and the Spirit, and her common sense, the Quakers sent women to her who were doctrinally unsound or rebellious so she could groom and instruct them correctly.

The First Guidelines

By 1653 the Quakers had multiplied so greatly that some sort of order was needed. Fox had never intended for the group to become a denomination, but it was clear that guidelines had to be established. Remember, the people of this day had come from generations of Roman Catholic suppression. Many had no idea exactly what the Word of God stated about certain situations. Some had gotten confused by the movement's terminology. The term "inner light" was used to qualify strange leadings through people who weren't willing for that leading to be judged. The only way the Quakers could get a message of stability across to the people of this growing movement was through books or through credible leaders who visited villages to bring instruction.

Fox called the leaders together and organized the guidelines for the movement. Here's what they determined:

1. The term *minister* wouldn't be used; instead, one or two people were to oversee the needs of the flock. They were not to do it out of constraint, but by willingness; not for money or gifts, but because they wanted to further the work and mature the believers. The overseers would manage the needs of the people and arrange for two meetings a week—one on Sunday, the other on another day. (The term *minister* was introduced in 1654.)
2. A lay ministry was developed that differed from those with oversight. It was their job to hold others accountable, to see that material needs were met, and to discuss any problems with the overseer.
3. If a disorderly person failed to repent at the overseer's admonition, that person would be expelled until he or she repented. Until then, all association with the backslider, even eating with them, was forbidden.
4. Women were allowed to preach and prophesy, but only under the direction of the overseer. Since communities were raving about how preaching women seduced men, Fox admonished a tight rein on their mode of dress and manners. But he never backed down from their right and mandate from God to further the Gospel. In fact, he maintained that women had the right to serve in areas of responsibility, including those of administration. He instituted a separate series of meetings, run entirely

by women, to deal with their practical, personal needs. He believed that, through these meetings, women would be inspired to carry out tasks beyond what they thought possible.

5. Marriage was honorable among the Quakers, yet it had been a problem because Quakers did not recognize any authority to sanction their union except God. So the guidelines for marriage were as follows: When a couple decided upon marriage, before anything could be concluded, they were to confer privately with the overseers and followers to determine if the union could stand in the light. Then, with the couple present, the marriage could be declared to the meeting of people to make sure there were no other engagements or frivolity. If anyone opposed, the couple would have to be referred to a general or regional meeting. When all was cleared, the couple's intentions would be announced. All being satisfied, an assembly of Friends would be held at which those in attendance would be free to speak and the couple would also speak as they were moved at how their marriage should be joined together. A certificate would then be signed by those in attendance. The couple then had the choice to declare it to the government or not.

Fox reproves the women.
North Wind Picture Archives

After these five general guidelines were established, a move of God's Spirit swept over the gathering. Among the leaders nearly seventy felt the call of God to go to the mission field. [57]

Fox, the Writer

Although the Quakers had now grown into many thousands throughout England, persecutions still abounded on a daily basis. Many times, Fox was beaten so badly by those who hated him that he was too sore to even ride his horse.

Fox was a unique man. Even though the Holy Spirit showed him many things to come in the future, he still lived one day at a time. His journal proves that he continued to give every idea equal attention, no matter how minor or major the idea might have been. Despite his lack of formal education, he is credited for sheer genius and skill in being able to speak to the needs of his generation. He is said to have written well over two hundred pamphlets, based upon whatever inspiration got his attention at the moment. He constantly affirmed that the Quakers had been raised up by God to live with a new mission within an old society. [58]

One of his pamphlets, *The Lamb's Officer*, published in 1659, was written after the death of Cromwell but was inspired by his political position. Fox agreed with Cromwell, though his position was spiritual, demanding the clergy of the day plead guilty or not guilty to the questions in his book. He reminded the readers not to be found stained by the heretical practices of the Catholic Church that had left its residue around them. Here are some of the questions he posed:

> Have you not been standing [by], when the martyrs, and prophets, and saints' blood has been drunk?...did not the whore set up your schools and colleges, this false church, whereby you are made ministers?...Has not all this swearing since Christ been set up by the false church, the Church of Rome?...Have you not cast many into prison...until death?... And where did Christ or the apostles or the true church preach by the hour glass?...Are you not such as go in long robes, fashions and lusts of the world,...wearing gold rings? [59]

Remember, the Quakers refused to swear or take an oath; and for that, many were thrown into prison before they could even speak in their own defense. They strongly adhered to this from the words of Jesus in Matthew 5:34–37 which says,

> *But I say unto you, Swear not at all; neither by heaven; for it is God's throne: nor by earth; for it is his footstool: neither by Jerusalem; for it is the city of the great King. Neither*

> *shalt thou swear by thy head, because thou canst not make one hair white or black. But let your communication be, Yea, yea; Nay, nay: for whatsoever is more than these cometh of evil.*

Solely because of their stand against this issue, thousands were tormented, beaten, and even put to death. Today we have gained the legal right to "affirm" instead of to swear.[60]

Fox wrote books ranging from the evils of fashion to warning governmental authorities and kings. His writings were dramatic, filled with insight and emotion. His words are so descriptive and Spirit-filled, you can almost feel that you are in the midst of the situation he is writing about. Fox may have been hated by theologians and historians, but they could not deny that his accurate, spiritual insights cut them to the bone since he possessed a dimension they didn't, even with all their formal and extensive educations combined.

Trouble in the Ranks: The Nayler Crisis

Through all the severe treatment of the Quakers, I believe the emotions and heartache of Fox were only shown twice: when women and children were tortured and at the falling away of his faithful friend, James Nayler.

Nayler, who rose to prominence while Fox was conducting the meetings in the North, had been one of the most promising Quaker leaders. He was a better preacher than Fox in that he could articulate and hold attention as a great orator. To some in authority, Nayler was more visible and more important than even Fox himself. This was mainly due to the fact that Nayler had remained in the populated city of London while Fox had been out of sight in the North.

Overwork, coupled with the pressures of his audience's exuberant praise, and Fox's level-headed absence had caused Nayler to fall into a dangerously unbalanced emotional state. He had been reacting to all the extravagant excitement and praise of his successful preaching and to the flatteries of a group of women who clung to him as a kind of messiah. These crazy women had surrounded him, chanting and bowing like he was a deity.

Nayler had been imprisoned for visiting another Quaker when Fox heard of the trouble. Once in jail, Nayler committed to a long fast. Instead of helping him to gain a clear mind, however it only made things worse, weakening his physical condition.

Fox arrived to visit Nayler, not only to support him but also to rebuke him, hoping Nayler would return to a sensible way of thinking. But Nayler wouldn't reason with Fox. When Fox stood to announce his departure, Nayler attempted to kiss his cheek, but Fox turned away. The incident brought great grief to both of them. When the Quakers heard of it, unrest spread among them as they wondered what would happen if the two leaders couldn't reconcile.

When an order came from the government to release all Quakers from prison, Nayler was freed. You would think that the problem could then be solved, but it only grew worse. Still involved with these women, Nayler emerged, allowing the women to reenact with him Christ's entrance into Jerusalem on a donkey.

Lashed, Branded, and Bored through the Tongue

The magistrates were outraged and called for Nayler's immediate arrest. Although they couldn't make some of the charges stick, they did succeed in making him serve a short sentence. But the news of his flamboyance had reached Parliament, and they vowed to make a lesson of it to the public.

Nayler avoided the death penalty, but he was ordered to walk through the city being whipped as he walked for a total of two hundred and ten lashes. His tongue was to be bored through and he was to be branded on the forehead. If he survived the first set of tortures, it was to be repeated in the next city he came to. If he survived the treatment in both cities, he was to be placed into solitary confinement where he would be subjected to hard labor until released by Parliament.

He survived. In spite of various petitions asking for his release, nothing turned the heads of Parliament until Nayler's wife wrote a wrenching appeal. But then, they would only allow her to bring candles, fire, and food to the suffering Nayler.

The punishment not only attracted attention because of who the victim was, but also because it was brutally illegal. Quakers throughout the country were in a state of shock, and all eyes turned to Fox.

But Fox was unrelenting, making it clear that he disapproved of Nayler's extravagance. Many Quakers blamed Fox, saying he was too hard on Nayler and that his intervention might have released the suffering comrade. However, Fox seemed to feel that Nayler had cast a dreadful shadow upon the entire Quaker movement, possibly placing its future growth in jeopardy, having slapped the face of God by his outrageous behavior.

Nayler remained alive in prison until the next Parliament came into session, when they granted his release. Still, it was another three months after his release before he and Fox finally reconciled.

Despite his humiliating injuries and the damage to his reputation, Nayler found the courage and strength to begin once again as a Quaker leader. This time he was marked for his renewed spiritual reverence and devotion, working throughout the countryside with a marked personal humility.

In the autumn of 1660, while walking home, Nayler was apparently mugged. He died from his wounds in the home of a nearby Quaker.[61]

Although the torture of Nayler had been found illegal, Fox's imprisonment continued, one year after another. Margaret Fell had also been jailed several times, along with her daughters. The stories of imprisonment seem endless, but instead of wearing down the growing Quakers, it only strengthened them more. Whenever a local crackdown occured, the Quakers immediately gathered together, whether it be in a house, a barn, a workshop, an orchard, or any open space. Fox continually called for the Quakers to meet persecution in the peaceful confidence that if they were faithful and persistent, the power of the Holy Spirit would break it.[62]

The Great Fire, the Plague, and Missions

Sometime in the late 1660s, Fox began referring to himself as an "elder brother." Since the Quakers were becoming established with good leaders in the communities, he took the role of an adviser and was a welcome visitor to meetings that were very capable of carrying on without him.[63]

Though he was still being imprisoned on a regular basis, the work of the Lord continued to thrive through him since it could not be bound by concrete or bars. During one of his imprisonments, the Lord foretold a great plague that was to ravish London and of a great fire that would come to the city shortly after the plague.

From this foreknowledge, Fox became depressed, mourning and praying for the people, knowing that many would be lost in death without knowing Jesus Christ. While he was imprisoned in 1665, a terrible epidemic of the bubonic plague attacked London. Thousands of people died within a few months. Fox's stay in prison may have been what shielded him from the deadly disease that so freely permeated the streets of London.

The day after Fox was released from this prison in 1666, the Great Fire of London broke out just as he had seen. As flames roared through the wooden buildings, most of London, including St. Paul's Cathedral, more than eighty churches, the Royal Exchange, the halls of forty-four craft and trade guilds, and about thirteen thousand houses, was left in ashes.[64] The extreme hardships of his past, the constant imprisonments, and the strenuous travel didn't slow Fox down at all. Instead, greatly encouraged, he set out with his efforts redoubled. Now he was ready to visit Ireland, desiring to witness firsthand how it had been ignited with the Quaker message.

Some Quakers had already departed for foreign lands as missionaries. Fox wrote in his journal, "Several friends were moved to go beyond the seas to publish truth in foreign countries."[65] A flourishing Quaker community had rooted itself in Barbados, West Indies. Jamaica was also seeing a Quaker Reformation. Some had spread out to the East, and into Malta. Amazingly, these missionaries returned alive!

The missionaries would feel drawn to a particular country; then they would take this feeling to the Lord and wait in quietness until He revealed His will concerning it.

One of the greatest attributes of the Quakers is their ability to be quiet before the Lord and listen for Him. They were taught to never be hasty but to try and prove all things before the Holy Spirit. When they were confident that their concern for a particular land was from the Lord and not an idle prompting, they looked for the way to be opened. As soon as it opened, they were off, male or female, despite any obstacles that tried to block them.

Due to this consistent, trustworthy way of life, the Quakers came to be known as honest, upright people in business as well. By now, most English merchants would have rather done business with Quakers than with any other because of their integrity. This resulted from the teachings of Fox, where, early on, he taught the people to deal justly with every man.

The Emblem of Unity: Marriage

Margaret Fell was constantly involved with the many facets of the Quakers, and she and Fox met as regularly as possible. I stated before that the two had great admiration for one another. Margaret was now a widow, and Fox confided in his journal that, for some time, he had wished to marry her. He had left the matter with the Lord, fully persuaded that the time would "come for accomplishing that thing whereof I had long sought."[66]

I believe Fox and Margaret's admiration had grown into a genuine love; but true to their beliefs, they waited and kept it before the Lord. Up until then, the growing cause of the Quakers had been the only mate necessary for Fox.

There is no record of the conversations they had with each other, but they must have known of each other's feelings. We do know that in 1669, when Margaret joined Fox in London, the two decided it was clear they should marry. Their mutual affirmation and time together was brief, for Fox was again called away by the Yorkshire Quakers to help them establish a monthly meeting. So, Fox and Margaret parted ways, still unmarried but at least with the promise of it in their hearts.

From Yorkshire, Fox followed the immediate leading of his heart and headed for Ireland. After making a clockwise circuit around the county, Fox was thrilled at his reception in Dublin. He saluted their faithfulness to God and admonished them to treat all men fairly so that the Lord would be honored through their lives. With that successful visit, he headed home to England and his future wife.

Being reunited with Margaret, he went beyond his guidelines for marriage, taking great pains that every Quaker be involved with it. Some of this had to do with rumors that surfaced regarding their close friendship. Some felt that Margaret had been in love with Fox from the beginning. They also took great pains due to the fact that Margaret was a wealthy woman. Fox didn't want anyone to think he was marrying for money, especially since Margaret was ten years older than him and past childbearing age. He felt that their marriage should be seen, in some way, as an emblem of unity for the whole movement. Since Fox was the founder of the Quakers, he felt that he belonged to each of them. So he wrote to every Quaker community, speaking of his intentions with Margaret.

Fox cleared himself from any ministry commitments, and he and Margaret appeared before every Quaker community, just as he had outlined, as if they all were a family.

Then Fox gathered all of Margaret's children, along with their spouses, and asked their permission to marry their mother. Finally, on October 27, 1669, in the Broadmead Meeting House in Bristol, the wedding took place. As many Quakers from around the country that could attend did. Over ninety people signed the marriage certificate, approving of the union. The newlyweds stayed a week in Bristol. At this point, Fox was forty-five, and Margaret was fifty-five. After their stay in Bristol, the couple parted as Fox left for another preaching tour and Margaret returned to Swarthmoor to assist the northern Quakers.

For another twenty years, they would continue to share their work, only meeting together for short periods of time. The work of the Lord was their first priority.[67]

Setting Sail: West Indies and Jamaica

For some time, it had been on Fox's heart that he should go across the ocean and visit the Quakers in the West Indies. But Margaret had recently been imprisoned, and Fox had spent most of his free time seeing to it that she was released.

When the Lord gave clearance to go to the West Indies, Margaret was simultaneously released from prison. A few days before the ship was to sail, she was able to come to London and spend time with Fox before he departed. The couple shared a very affectionate parting, because, in those days, if one traveled overseas, the chances of seeing one's home and family again were slim.

Elizabeth Hooten, the first Quaker convert, and several others accompanied Fox on the trip. Their voyage to the West Indies would take the greater part of two months. The trip went without incident, except for one occurrence three weeks into their journey.

One afternoon, they saw a warship from another nation approaching them at a rapid speed. Realizing they would be fired upon when in close distance, the captain of the ship found Fox and asked what they should do.

Fox replied that he was no mariner; what did the captain think? There were only two choices: One, try to outrun the warship; or two, remain on course and hope all would be well. Fox replied that it would be ridiculous to try to outrun a warship. The captain was extremely nervous and growing more anxious by the minute. Fox told him that it was a trial of his faith and that the Lord was to be waited upon for counsel.

With that, Fox determined to rest in his spirit and wait for the Lord to give an answer. Not long after, the Lord showed Fox that His power was placed between them and the ship that pursued; the best thing to do was stay on course.

Fox wrote in his journal,

> About the eleventh hour, the watch called and said they were just upon us. This disquieted some of the passengers, whereupon I sat in my cabin, and looking through the porthole, the moon not being quite down, I saw them very near us. I was getting up to go out of the cabin but remembering the word of the Lord, that His life and power was between us and them, I lay down again. The captain and some of the seamen came again, and asked me if they might not steer such a point. I told them they might do as they would. By this time the moon was gone down and a fresh gale arose, and the Lord hid us from them, and we sailed briskly on, and saw them no more. [68]

The First against Slavery

Every Sunday they held a public meeting on the ship, and great blessings abounded to them all. However, Fox began to suffer a great deal on this trip. It was clear to all that his health was deteriorating, mainly due to all the imprisonments he had suffered. The climate of the West Indies further complicated matters because Fox was not accustomed to such humidity and heat. But he was pleased and satisfied to see so many faithful and strong Quakers thriving in Barbados.

Here, Fox noticed that a large portion of the Quakers held slaves, and he was firmly against such behavior. He had the wisdom to realize that they couldn't set them free all at once because the slaves themselves would suffer, having no livelihood. So, he admonished the Quakers there to train the slaves up in the Lord and teach them skills so that, after a few years, they could set them free to live on their own.

Let me bring in a side note here. The American and English Quakers were very much against slavery in any form. As early as 1688, Quakers sent a formal protest against slavery to the Philadelphia Yearly Meeting in America. [69] That means that approximately 174 years before the Emancipation Proclamation was first drawn up in 1862, the Quakers had fought against slavery. That's another first we can credit to them. They were petitioning for slavery to be abolished long before the public became universally aware of it. Perhaps it was the seeds of their gentle protests that caused America to rethink its position on slavery in the mid-1800s!

Fox stayed in Barbados for three months. Before Fox left the West Indies, he drew up guidelines to help the Quaker movement remain strong. From there, he sailed for Jamaica where, soon after they landed, Elizabeth Hooten, now an elderly woman, died.

Staying in Jamaica a little over a month, Fox felt a leading to head for the colonies in America. Little did he realize that he was heading into a journey that would pack even more adventure into his short, dramatic life.

Rough and Rowdy America

If jolly old England had been rough to the Quakers, they had no idea how rough the New England Puritans would be! You might think, that because of their own search for religious freedom over fifty years earlier, they would welcome the Quakers. Wrong!

The New England tragedies have always been a black page in the history of America. The original Puritans had firmly held to the belief that any disagreement from their doctrines was heresy, and therefore, should be treated with severity. That severity increased even further with their successors. They had evolved into such narrow-minded, religious taskmasters that they were more willing to kill someone than be challenged on an issue. The Puritans of the very late seventeenth century had created a religious monster that was raging out of control.

Here, we again see the deceptive spirit of religion at work. People who care more about their religion than the Holy Spirit are the most evil and malicious group of people you'll ever meet. Don't let their surface holiness fool you.

It was this Inquisition-like atmosphere that the Quakers found as they arrived in the free land. Distorted rumors of the British Quakers had reached the New Englanders, and they went to great extremes to keep them from their shores.

Many times, if the religious fathers heard that a Quaker was on board a ship in the harbor, that Quaker was commanded to stay on the ship and be returned to England at the captain's expense. Eventually, they made a law forbidding any captain to bring a Quaker to their shores. They were so afraid that if they didn't nip the Quaker heresy in the bud, it would blossom throughout the colonies as it had England!

A fellow New Englander had once been kind to a Quaker woman. As a result, he was fined a large sum of money and, in the middle of an intense winter, was banished from the borders of Massachusetts to survive on his own.

Finding his way to Rhode Island, he met up with a kind Native American who took him into his home for warmth and food. When asked why the New Englander was out on his own in such weather, the man told the story. Amazed, the Indian said, "What a God have the English, who deal so with one another about their God!"[70] Only those like this Indian, a heathen, could see the hypocritical irony of it all.

But the Puritans weren't as ready for the Quakers as they thought. Persecution and threats had never stopped the Quakers, and New England was no different. The Quakers kept coming, until the region was soon overrun with them. Many died by hanging, and many were imprisoned and starved to death. A proclamation was issued that anyone directly or indirectly causing a Quaker to come to Massachusetts could be fined and jailed, have his tongue bored through with a hot iron, have his ears cut off, or be severely whipped.

Still, the Quakers flourished; and many fearless New Englanders, in spite of the rigorously carried-out threats, dared to stand with the Quakers and align themselves with the growing group.

Their perseverance is a great and honored chapter in American history.

His Favorite Audience: Indians

Fox's journey to America was a perilous one, taking seven weeks. The ship had run out of food, and the passengers were almost starved.

By the time he reached the shores of Maryland, Fox was thrilled to see land, though he was weak from the journey. As soon as he landed, he was met by a Quaker minister named John Burnyeat who promptly informed Fox that he was just in time for a meeting. Forgetting his physical weakness, Fox joyfully entered the meeting, which was a very large and heavenly meeting lasting four days!

At the close of the four-day meeting, the Quakers in Maryland met with Fox to receive further guidelines and instruction, gleaning from his wisdom and insight. When the meeting with leaders ended, they all went their separate ways on various preaching tours.

Fox loved the Native Americans and was intrigued with their common sense and genuine hearts. Perhaps this is why Fox enjoyed traveling the backwoods and isolated areas of young America. He paid more attention to this ethnic group of people than any other, and they

Fox preaching in Maryland.
North Wind Picture Archives

attended his meetings that were held near their territory. Many of the Puritans looked upon the Indians as their enemies, trading with them but not treating them as friends. Many in that day even questioned whether Native Americans had souls!

Fox had no sympathy for this theology, so he made it a point to visit every Indian village he could find. He and Burnyeat traveled through the backwoods toward New York, always finding friendly Indians who were eager to share their food and lodging. While he was in America, Fox so implored the Quakers to follow their duties with the "red man" that an 1812 historian wrote that "the best defense against the Indians was the dress of a Quaker."[71]

"The Great Spirit Will Burn You!"

Fox spent two years traveling on horseback throughout Maryland and portions of New England. He wrote in his journal that two Indian guides led them through the dense wilderness. Then he told a story.

Once, a straggling Native American came to him and, after awhile, began to grope at him and touch him, saying that Fox was good blood. Knowing that some of the tribes were rumored to be cannibals, Fox wasn't sure of the the man's intentions with him, although he felt the peace of God. Finally, after the man continued to probe Fox as though he was looking for something to eat, Fox lifted his hand up to heaven, then back down to earth. Getting the immediate attention of the Native American, Fox then told him that, if he touched Fox, the Great Spirit would burn him. With that, the probing Native American went away![72]

Fox's journal is filled with detailed writings concerning the Native Americans, complimenting them on how receptive they were to his message. He commented how some of the Native Americans told him that the Quaker religion was the best they had heard. Fox noticed that some of the tribes already acted like the Friends, so his message only confirmed what they knew to be truth.[73]

He found Rhode Island to be a "heretic's haven."[74] It did him good, however, to discover that many high officials, and some that had left office, were all Quakers. The magistrates there were so impressed with Fox that they discussed among themselves if they had enough money to hire him as their minister or not. When Fox heard of it, he said, "It is time for me to be gone; for if their eye is so much on me, or any of us, they will not come to their own Teacher." [75]

After a brief stay in Rhode Island, he turned and headed south again, omitting a visit to Massachusetts; however, he did send another representative to tour the region on his behalf. He sent a letter to the governor of Connecticut in hopes that he would not further persecute the Quakers there.

Boarding an open boat for Long Island, Fox was met by the refugee Quakers in the area and a large host of Indians. After holding the large meeting, some Native Americans approached Fox, telling him that some of their race had adopted the religion of the New Englanders but, in doing so, were worse off than before. They believed that Quakerism was a true way, but they feared to convert, afraid that the other professors would hang them. [76]

The Broken Neck Miracle

One of the greatest miracles performed through Fox took place as he headed for New Jersey. A Quaker by the name of John Jay had been riding with them from Rhode Island when he was violently thrown from a running horse. Fox was in a different place when the news of his accidental death reached him. Getting to the scene as quickly as he could, Fox found that Jay had broken his neck and was dead.

Being moved with pity for the man's large family, Fox grabbed Jay by the hair. He placed Jay's dangling head between his knees, put one hand under his chin, the other behind his head, and raised it up and down two or three times with all his strength, popping it into place. Fox perceived that Jay's neck "began to grow stiff again," and a rattling sound came from his throat. Then Jay began to breathe, opening his eyes. [77]

To the amazement of the onlookers, Fox admonished them to take heart and carry Jay into the house. He was given something warm to drink and put to bed. The next day, John Jay made the sixteen-mile trip by horseback, through bogs, woods, and a river, along with the others!

Time to Go Home

Fox traveled down to Carolina and portions of Virginia, where he continued his meetings. The early American theory that Indians didn't have a soul continued to whet Fox's spiritual appetite. He attacked that vicious lie by pulling a Native American to the front and asking him questions. The man's answers proved to the unbelieving that he indeed had a very active soul.

Only once in America did Fox encounter authorities who tried to put him in jail. It happened a day or so after he returned to Maryland, but Fox soon won the sheriff over and was released without incident. It was now after Christmas in 1672, and the winter was hard. Fox and his party found themselves trudging through snow, drenched by freezing rain, sleeping outside, and finding their water frozen solid sitting by the fire.

In 1673, the house he stayed in as a guest burned down. Fox lost all of his possessions, along with his clothes and books. He continued to travel and itinerate through young America for most of the year. Finally, his heart was settled that he had visited most of the nation. Satisfied at the overall spiritual condition of the Quakers there, he felt led to return to England.

As soon as his ship docked in Bristol, he sent a letter to Margaret at Swarthmoor, announcing his return and the faithfulness of God. As soon as she read the letter, Margaret was quickly on her way to Bristol to be reunited, after more than two years, with her incredible husband.

The Last Prison Battle

Fox and Margaret stayed only a little while in Bristol before heading to London. While there, Fox sensed he would soon be in prison again. Telling his wife to return to Swarthmoor, she reluctantly agreed.

Sure enough, Fox was arrested a few days later and put into prison. He seemed to have been sure that prison was as much God's will for him as liberty was for others. He accepted it willingly and never flinched from his stand. As soon as he was released, the authorities found yet another charge against him and put him in prison again for refusing to take an oath at the hearing.

Fox's health was in very bad condition, causing Margaret to take immediate action. She appealed to the chancellor who told her the only hope was a pardon from the king. This infuriated Fox. He was also angered at the chancellor's response. He replied, "I am not free to accept a pardon, knowing that I have done no evil. I would rather lie in prison all my days than come out in any way dishonorable to the truth."[78]

Penn's Influence: The Birth of Pennsylvania

William Penn, the famous Quaker leader who founded Pennsylvania, was now also in the picture, and he did all in his political power to get Fox released.

Penn was a strong supporter of Fox. He was the son of Admiral Sir William Penn and had moved to Ireland to manage his father's estate when he came in contact with the Quakers there and was converted. His admiral father had great plans for Penn, and, when he chose to be a Quaker, it broke his father's heart. All the dreams he had for his son were lost. The admiral had no idea that God had other plans for William and that his son would go down in history a greater man than even his father had dreamed. He carved his way into history when he persuaded Charles II (who owed his father money) to allow them to set up a colony in America solely for the use and freedom of Quakers. The king granted his request, instead of giving him the money, and the colony became known as Pennsylvania.[79]

Penn's strong influence, coupled with countless letters from Quakers around the region, finally persuaded the magistrates to allow Fox to appear before the courts, convincing them that he had no sinister purpose against the government in all his itinerant travels. But after refusing to take an oath or to swear, he was put back in prison.

By now, Margaret was desperate. Fox's bad health was constantly plaguing him, and she feared she would never see him again. Finally, pulling the strings of high authorities, a judge ruled there were numerous errors in Fox's indictment, and he was freed.

Weak in Body, Strong in Spirit

Returning to Swarthmoor to recover, Fox's health was so weak that he did not attend the yearly meeting that shortly followed his release. Instead, he wrote admonishments to those who attended. While recuperating, Fox remained at Swarthmoor for nearly two years and, instead of traveling, wrote various tracts and pamphlets.

Although he never acknowledged it, Fox's wandering itinerant lifestyle was rapidly coming to a close. Now when he traveled, he had to go slowly, being content to rest himself in an attempt to restore his failing strength.

But his traveling days were not entirely over as he was still able to visit Holland and found much Quaker business to attend to. After three months there, he returned to England. He found the Quaker movement growing so rapidly in London that he decided to make the city his home base.

Near the end of his life, Fox witnessed another change in government. Charles II died and James II replaced him. The new king was very sympathetic to the Protestants and ordered the liberty of all Quakers and Nonconformists from the prisons. Approximately sixteen hundred Quakers were released from jail at his order.[80] It was a day that Fox was overjoyed to witness, and he used the occasion to admonish Quakers to make it one of increased holiness and gratitude to God.

By now, Fox's health had so declined that he was unable to sit through an entire meeting. Quakers would help the ailing Fox to someone's home after a service, where he would have to rest in order to make the trip back home.

"I Am Fully Clear. All Is Well."

The last year of Fox's life was a quiet one. In 1690, Fox saw the passing of the Toleration Act, which brought government-backed freedom for the Quakers. No longer could they be thrust into vile dungeons to die of disease or confinement. Never again were they to be whipped in the streets or personally mistreated. It had to be immensely satisfying for Fox to see this act pass before he died. Now it seemed all he had stood for, all he had suffered through, would bear fruit worldwide. The future now looked bright for the Quakers, but it didn't come without a tremendous price.

In 1690, his strong voice was feeble, his hair thin and white, and his eyesight dim. Though it seemed he had to crawl the half mile from his home to the meeting, his intelligence was unimpaired, and his mind was as keen as ever. Though his body was wasting away, it seemed his spirit was renewed as a young man's, ready to fly as an eagle with wings.

In the latter part of the year, Fox settled down in London and met almost daily with other Quakers. On January 10, 1691, he wrote a letter to the followers in Ireland, and then in his journal to update it.

The next morning was very cold, but Fox insisted on attending a meeting where he preached and prayed. He assured the crowd that he felt well, better than he had for some time. But as soon as the meeting was over, Fox complained of a pain near his heart. After the meeting, he went to the house of a Quaker, Henry Gouldney, to rest. It was a very cold day, and, as the cold hit his chest, he shivered. Still, he quickly told the group, "I am glad I was here; now I am clear, I am fully clear."[81]

After resting, Fox attempted to get up but found that he needed to lay back down. Trying to get up once more, he groaned and fell back into the bed. Within a couple of hours, his strength failed.

Realizing that his time was short, he asked to see some of his associates. William Penn was among them, and Fox requested that they continue to spread books and the truth in every place. "All is well," he assured them, "the seed of God reigns over all and over death itself."[82]

"He Died as He Lived, a Lamb"

By Tuesday, January 13, Fox's illness had stretched out over three days. Early in the evening, he grasped the hand of an associate, asking him to give his love to all those he had met through his travels. Late in the evening of that day, Fox simply shut his eyes, closed his mouth, and took his last breath. He never fought it; in fact, he looked as though he had just fallen asleep. One of his associates wrote, "One would have thought he had smiled."[83] He was sixty-six years old.

History never recorded what Fox died from. He suffered from no disease. It seemed that his physical body just gave out, and all his strength was depleted.

Penn was the one to write Margaret, telling her of the news. "He died as he lived, a lamb," wrote Penn, "minding the things of God and His church to the last in an universal spirit."[84]

✯✯✯✯✯

For the next three days, Quakers found easy admission to view the body of Fox, lying in state. His leaders from around the nation gathered together for the painful task of arranging his funeral. The service was constantly interrupted by tears and groans from men of stature, such as Penn—men who usually kept their emotions hidden. One elderly man stated that he had buried all of his family without shedding a tear, but, now, he was overcome and would "never forget this day's work."[85]

The funeral lasted for two hours, and over four thousand people crowded to hear the voices of the twelve men who spoke at it. The great man was confined into a simple wooden casket, and it took over two hours for the massive group to walk to the cemetery.

Fox was buried in Bonehill (Bunhill) Fields, an ancient burial ground for the Quakers. At first, no marker was placed identifying his grave. Later, a simple headstone with his initials was secured at his grave, denoting the place where one of God's mightiest generals lay sleeping, in sure and certain hope of the glorious resurrection promised to him.

Margaret lived another eleven years, all the while exhorting the young and strengthening the work, before she finished her course. She went home to be with the Lord at eighty-eight years of age. Before she died, she called her youngest grandson to her side, admonishing him to stand for God. She died in the arms of her daughter, whispering, "I am in peace!"[86]

An older Fox.
Friends Historical Library, Swarthmore College

☆☆☆☆☆

Where Are the Quakers Today?

As I finish writing this chapter, I am almost left speechless at the unrelenting commitment and undying spiritual strength of such a great man.

Of course, my thoughts turn to the Quakers and what they represent today. The majority of the sacrifice was made generations before they were born, through the blood of those who went before. Now, the Quakers' course is to remain true to the roots and the spirit that paid that incredible price.

Much of the direction of this chapter was inspired by a delightful brother in the Lord, Cooper Beaty. Where the theological history that I read was unkind, he helped to shed more light on the path, enabling us to have a deeper understanding of George Fox and the Quakers.

The Reverend Beaty is the director of his personal ministry, Light for Living Ministries in Broken Arrow, Oklahoma. Now in his mid-eighties, he spent thirty years of his life as a Quaker pastor, seven years as a Quaker itinerant minister, and the last twenty years as a full-time instructor at a nondenominational Bible School. He teaches several courses at the Bible school, and church history is one of them. He regards some of his out-of-print books on George Fox as his most prized possessions.

Today, there are several small branches of Quakers, but the group as a whole has splintered into three main categories: Liberites (rationalists), Whilberites (traditionalists), and Gurneyites (evangelicals). Beaty commented that the Evangelical Quakers today are the closest to the old-time Methodists (John Wesley), and he believes they cleared the path one hundred years before the Methodist movement.

The Evangelicals have remained true to the teachings of Fox. Their honesty and integrity are still untarnished. They still believe in the new birth, holiness through the sanctification of the Spirit, and their services are filled with lively music and praise. Through the years, the only fault with this particular sect of Quakers is that they turned inward instead of outward. They are evangelical yet not evangelistic, mainly due to the lifestyle of severe persecution that has seeped through their heritage. However, to my satisfaction and hope, the Rev. Beaty stated that today the Evangelical Quakers are once again returning to their original, evangelistic roots, reaching out to the youth and to the lost in major cities throughout the United States. After all, it was a promise their forefathers had made to George Fox.

Although he is now involved with an international, nondenominational ministry, Rev. Beaty speaks with great admiration for and fondness of his Quaker roots. It produced a spiritual strength and stability within him that can never be shaken. He stated that his change from being a Quaker to becoming a member of a nondenominational group was very easy because the beliefs were so similar. [87]

What Does God Think of Our Generation?

Not long ago, I preached a sermon entitled, "Is God Ashamed of Being Your God?" I believe God is grieved and ashamed when our generation becomes lethargic or passive concerning His truths. When someone or a group of people go against the grain, daring to speak the truth in spite of the cost, I believe it is a stench in the nostrils of God when others counsel them to settle down or to be normal.

Our societies and nations are crying and begging for reform. The generals of the past have passed their torch to us—it's our turn to take a stand.

We cry for God to move, and, then, when He does, we try to quench it because it pulls back the veils around our hearts and shows us what is really there. You can always tell when people don't want their veils to be removed. They fight, scratch, and persecute those who dare to live boldly for God. They twist the Scriptures, attempting to water them down or teach that they really mean something different than what they say. They yell at the government to make the changes needed within the nation, when, in reality, they are asking for something that the pastor himself wouldn't do. You need to look to the white throne—not the White House. You need to look to the Gospel—not your government. Look to the Person of the Holy Spirit—not your Parliament. The change our society desperately needs is a reformation, and that can only come from the people who know God and are willing to lay down their lives for Him.

★★★★★

I have written this book not only for you to have a working knowledge of God's greatest generals, but also for you to look deeply within your own soul and your own lifestyle. Many of you are saying "all is well"—but all is not well. Some of you have opened the gates of your eyes, your ears, and your heart to other voices that have reasoned you out of your call and out of your purpose in life. Other noises have grown so loud in your life that you can no longer hear the calling voice of God to come out of lethargy and out of darkness. You've become drugged by the sounds of the times, so numbed that you can't hear the voice of God calling to this generation. Do you hear what He's saying?

Let me say again, very strongly, that our societies and our nations are crying and begging for reform. The stand that was taken by so many past generations isn't enough for the troubles that are surfacing in our day. They've shown us how to live, but now they have passed the torch; we have the baton.

We must shake ourselves and stop feeding on the wrong source of spiritual nourishment, the wrong type of false hope, and the wrong pursuit of material things. The road that is great before God has the most resistance upon it. You'll never find greatness in the things of God without a battle, you'll never find change without confrontation, and you'll never find a new generation unless you learn to preach it, to shout it, and to live like it's already here.

As I write this book, there is no single nation that is leading the world in a reformation move of God. We've all had outpourings. We were visited by God, but no one carries a habitation from heaven. What our nations need is reformation. This kind of reformation occurs when we each agree to live with Him here on this earth, continually paying the price to keep Him first.

When we live with God, there is a continual confrontation, or examination that goes on in our lives. Our hearts and minds are continually being x-rayed; our families, our churches, our work, our ministries are constantly under the microscope of God as we ask if everything is right. That is good to do, but it could be done better. This personal confrontation happens because God wants to be the Lord of our lives, and there is no greater peace than to have that.

When you live with God, your earthly priorities become dim; you are set on heavenly things, ever mindful of eternity. You don't want to be something you're not. You don't give up or fall back if you're not a Benny Hinn or a Billy Graham—you don't sit around hearing teachers and merely comment, "Good point." In order to have the reformation that our age requires, you have to move from the passive comment of "good point" into a true, decisive heart action. God won't give you a new anointing if there's not a new vessel to put it in. Besides, the true anointing has more than "oohs" and "aahs." It has a backlash that follows it, a labeling from veil-covered people, or a deserting of friends and fellowships—and most aren't willing to pay the price for it. You can only become the battle-ax of God in a nation based on who you are privately and how vulnerable you are to the hand of God.

Live for heaven. Strive to be branded with Jesus and the Holy Spirit and to have the hand of God upon you, whether people applaud you or not.

I am glad that you have read this chapter and this book; I believe you want to address the religion that holds us back so that a true, divine hunger for God can draw us and consume us. I believe you want the real thing instead of a cheap imitation. Reformation can never be born without that kind of hunger. The day you are satisfied is the day your religious life begins. The day you are satisfied with your Christian walk is the day your religious resistance begins. I refuse to be called merely an American—I live for heaven. I crave the spirit of reform. I'm not worrying about a label, or a camp, or a group. I want to be branded with Jesus and the Holy Spirit and have the hand of the Father upon me, whether the people applaud or not.

That's exactly what George Fox did. He stood for the truths of the Word, and it caused a backlash from his family, his ministers, his friends, his relatives, and everyone who knew him. He was willing to be alone if it meant being with God. He willingly endured the persecutions that many of us will never know, all because he knew the touch of God and what it meant to live with Him while on the earth. He was ever mindful of an eternal goal, knowing that his life here was but a vapor. And from his continual face-to-face relationship with the living

God, he became a Reformer, touching every area of his generation. Over three hundred years later, his voice still speaks.

So, I close his chapter and this book with his words, praying it will burn as a continual fire in your soul, birthing a true revolution that will transform your heart and your nation. May the spirit of reformation come again to the earth. And may it come through you.

> This generation we know, and the generation of the faithful we know: here is a separation between the precious and the vile, between the holy and the profane; so all people weigh and consider in what generation you are. [88]

Notes

[1] George Fox, *The Journal of George Fox* (London, England: Temple Press/J. M. Dent and Sons, Ltd., 1948): 12.
[2] Major Douglas, *George Fox—The Red Hot Quaker* (Cincinnati, Ohio: Revivalist Press, n.d.): 39.
[3] H. Larry Ingle, *First among Friends, George Fox and the Creation of Quakerism* (New York, N.Y.; Oxford University Press, Inc., 1994): 3. Excerpts from *First among Friends, George Fox and the Creation of Quakerism* by H. Larry Ingle, © 1996 by Oxford University Press, Inc. Used by permission of Oxford University Press, Inc.
[4] Ibid., 12, 19.
[5] Cecil W. Sharman, *George Fox and the Quakers* (Philadelphia: Friends General Conference; London: Quaker Home Service, 1991): 31.
[6] Elfrida Vipont, *George Fox and the Valiant Sixty* (Northumberland Press Limited, Gateshead, 1975): 4.
[7] Sharman, 34–35.
[8] Douglas, 6.
[9] Ingle, 24–25.
[10] Ibid., 25.
[11] Douglas, 8.
[12] Sharman, 42.
[13] Fox, 5.
[14] Ingle, 41.
[15] Ibid., 42.
[16] Cooper Beaty, Telephone Interview (2 February 2001).
[17] Ingle, 43.
[18] Douglas, 13.
[19] Ibid., 17.
[20] Ibid.
[21] Ingle., 54.
[22] Sharman, 67–70
[23] Ingle, 113.
[24] Ibid., 61.
[25] Beaty.
[26] Ingle, 59.
[27] Ibid., 60.
[28] Ibid., 113–114.
[29] Douglas, 42.

★★★★★

[30] Ibid., 22.
[31] Fox, 11–12.
[32] Ibid., 13.
[33] Ibid.
[34] Ibid., 17–18.
[35] Ibid., 38.
[36] Ibid., 17–20.
[37] David Hodges, *George Fox and the Healing Ministry* (Surrey, England: Friends Fellowship of Healing, 1995): 28–29.
[38] Ibid., 26.
[39] Ibid., 38.
[40] Fox, 92–93.
[41] Ibid., 92.
[42] Henry J. Cadbury, ed., *George Fox's "Book of Miracles"* (Philadelphia: Friends General Conference; London: Quaker Home Service, 2000): 42–43.
[43] "Cromwell, Oliver," *The World Book Encyclopedia* 4, (Chicago, Ill: Field Enterprises, Inc., 2003): 1151–1152.
[44] Douglas, 38.
[45] Ibid., 38–39.
[46] Christopher Hill, *God's Englishman: Oliver Cromwell and the English Revolution,* (New York: Weidenfeld and Nicholson, 1970), 155.
[47] Ibid., 9.
[48] Douglas, 38.
[49] Sharman, 75.
[50] Ibid., 79–80.
[51] Ibid., 92.
[52] Vipont, 41.
[53] Ibid., 42.
[54] Ibid., 43.
[55] Ingle, 93.
[56] Ibid.
[57] Ibid., 103–106.
[58] Ibid., 107, 110.
[59] Ibid., 114.
[60] Beaty.
[61] Sharman, 133–138.
[62] Ibid., 155.
[63] Ibid., 167.

[64] "London," *World Book Encyclopedia* 12, 441.
[65] Douglas, 59.
[66] Ibid., 79.
[67] Sharman, 174–175.
[68] Douglas, 89–90.
[69] Ibid., 91.
[70] Ibid., 67.
[71] Ibid., 92–93.
[72] Fox, 285.
[73] Ibid., 291.
[74] Ingle, 238.
[75] Fox, 290.
[76] Ingle, 239.
[77] Fox, 293.
[78] Douglas, 97.
[79] "Penn, William," *World Book Encyclopedia* 15, 241–242.
[80] Douglas, 100.
[81] Ingle, 283.
[82] Ibid., 284.
[83] Fox, 347.
[84] Ibid.
[85] Ingle, 285.
[86] Vipont, 126–127.
[87] Beaty.
[88] Ingle, 78.

About the Author

ROBERTS LIARDON

From a young age, Roberts Liardon was destined to become one of the most well-known Christian authors and orators of the twentieth century. He has, to date, sold over 15 million books worldwide that have been translated into more than 60 languages. Having ministered in over 125 countries to members of the public and world leaders, Liardon is recognized internationally and has experienced great success as an author, public speaker, spiritual leader, church historian, and humanitarian.

Roberts Liardon was born in Tulsa, Oklahoma, the first male child born at Oral Roberts University. His career in the ministry began at the young age of thirteen, when he gave his initial public address. At seventeen, Liardon published the book, *I Saw Heaven*, which catapulted him into the public eye. The book sold over 1.5 million copies and by the following year, he had become one of the leading public speakers in the Christian community all over the world. This established him as a leading Protestant church historian, a role he carries with honor to this day. God spoke to Liardon and inspired him to write and produce a book series and DVD series entitled *God's Generals*. Its mission is to chronicle the lives of the leading Pentecostal and charismatic leaders. It was an immediate success and became one of the bestselling Christian DVD series in history. In 1990, Roberts Liardon moved to Southern California and founded his worldwide headquarters in Orange County. Here he started one of the largest Christian churches and Bible colleges in the region.

Roberts Liardon Ministries helps millions of lives through the power of the Holy Spirit. Liardon is a significant contributor towards building God's kingdom, with the belief that relationships is the key element that bonds the staff at Roberts Liardon Ministries to people around the world. Each year, millions are touched through this worldwide ministry, a genuine resource of victory for the entire body of Christ.

Roberts Liardon continues to speak to this generation of believers, and reaches out to those who are eager to read and learn relevant messages that draw the heart closer to God. For over thirty years, he has continued to complete a demanding speaking schedule along with writing books and mentoring a new generation of world leaders to effect change for the church and society.

From his ministry, Liardon established, financed, and sent almost five hundred men and women to various nations on the globe to help those less fortunate and spread God's Word across the world. Through his ministry's Home2Home project, he has expanded his services to people in various countries, where he provides ways for people to bring positive change to the world. Liardon does everything he can to assist local communities lead better and more fulfilling lives. He has spent time in Namibia, Africa, where he received permission to go into the schools and educate people on the effects of HIV/AIDS and its prevention and protection through abstinence and medication.

Liardon continues to manage and expand his international headquarters in Orlando, Florida, and his office in London, England. Find him on:

www.facebook.com/RobertsLiardon
www.twitter.com/RobertsLiardon
www.instagram.com/robertsliardonofficial

Welcome to Our House!

We Have a Special Gift for You

It is our privilege and pleasure to share in your love of Christian books. We are committed to bringing you authors and books that feed, challenge, and enrich your faith.

To show our appreciation, we invite you to sign up to receive a specially selected **Reader Appreciation Gift**, with our compliments. Just go to the Web address at the bottom of this page.

God bless you as you seek a deeper walk with Him!

WE HAVE A GIFT FOR YOU. VISIT:

whpub.me/nonfictionthx

About the Author

ROBERTS LIARDON

From a young age, Roberts Liardon was destined to become one of the most well-known Christian authors and orators of the twentieth and twenty-first centuries. He has, to date, sold over 15 million books worldwide that have been translated into more than 60 languages. Having ministered in over 125 countries to members of the public and world leaders, Liardon is recognized internationally and has experienced great success as an author, public speaker, spiritual leader, church historian, and humanitarian.

Roberts Liardon was born in Tulsa, Oklahoma, the first male child born at Oral Roberts University. His career in the ministry began at the young age of thirteen, when he gave his initial public address. At seventeen, Liardon published the book, *I Saw Heaven*, which catapulted him into the public eye. The book sold over 1.5 million copies and by the following year, he had become one of the leading public speakers in the Christian community all over the world. This established him as a leading Protestant church historian, a role he carries with honor to this day. God spoke to Liardon and inspired him to write and produce a book series and DVD series entitled *God's Generals*. Its mission is to chronicle the lives of the leading Pentecostal and charismatic leaders. It was an immediate success and became one of the bestselling Christian DVD series in history. In 1990, Roberts Liardon moved to Southern

California and founded his worldwide headquarters in Orange County. Here he started one of the largest Christian churches and Bible colleges in the region.

Roberts Liardon Ministries helps millions of lives through the power of the Holy Spirit. Liardon is a significant contributor towards building God's kingdom, with the belief that relationships is the key element that bonds the staff at Roberts Liardon Ministries to people around the world. Each year, millions are touched through this worldwide ministry, a genuine resource of victory for the entire body of Christ.

Roberts Liardon continues to speak to this generation of believers, and reaches out to those who are eager to read and learn relevant messages that draw the heart closer to God. For over thirty years, he has continued to complete a demanding speaking schedule along with writing books and mentoring a new generation of world leaders to effect change for the church and society.

From his ministry, Liardon established, financed, and sent almost five hundred men and women to various nations on the globe to help those less fortunate and spread God's Word across the world. Through his ministry's Home2Home project, he has expanded his services to people in various countries, where he provides ways for people to bring positive change to the world. Liardon does everything he can to assist local communities lead better and more fulfilling lives. He has spent time in Namibia, Africa, where he received permission to go into the schools and educate people on the effects of HIV/AIDS and its prevention and protection through abstinence and medication.

Liardon continues to manage and expand his international headquarters in Orlando, Florida, and his office in London, England. Find him on:

www.facebook.com/RobertsLiardon

www.twitter.com/RobertsLiardon

www.instagram.com/robertsliardonofficial